Oracle SOA Governance 11*g* Implementation

Successfully implement SOA governance using Oracle SOA Governance Suite 11*g* with the help of practical examples and real-world use cases

Luis Augusto Weir

Andrew Bell

[PACKT] PUBLISHING enterprise
professional expertise distilled

BIRMINGHAM - MUMBAI

Oracle SOA Governance 11*g* Implementation

First published: September 2013

Production Reference: 2031013

Published by Packt Publishing Ltd.
Livery Place
35 Livery Street
Birmingham B3 2PB, UK.

ISBN 978-1-84968-908-3

`www.packtpub.com`

Cover Image by Sandeep Babu (`sandyjb@gmail.com`)

Credits

Authors
Luis Augusto Weir
Andrew Bell

Reviewers
Ivan Dimovic
Peter Obert
Phani Krishna Pemmaraju

Acquisition Editors
Edward Gordon
Akram Hussain

Lead Technical Editor
Sweny M. Sukumaran

Technical Editors
Pooja Arondekar
Sampreshita Maheshwari
Menza Mathew
Amit Shetty

Project Coordinators
Arshad Sopariwala
Priyanka Goel

Proofreaders
Stephen Copestake
Ameesha Green

Indexers
Rekha Nair
Hemangini Bari

Graphics
Sheetal Aute
Ronak Dhruv
Disha Haria
Yuvraj Mannari
Abhinash Sahu

Production Coordinator
Adonia Jones

Cover Work
Adonia Jones

Foreword

In the early years of web services and service-oriented architecture, it felt as if people working for Microsoft, IBM, and a handful of startups were the only ones who really understood the power of what was being defined and created. At that time, I had the bittersweet opportunity of working for Talking Blocks with Mark Potts, Mark Perreira, and Dave Stanton. We focused heavily on web services management and it frequently felt as if we were Don Quixote chasing the IT windmills. When Talking Blocks was acquired by Hewlett-Packard (and then HP subsequently acquired Mercury Interactive which had acquired Systinet), it felt as if I had the opportunity to work with another group of like-minded people who truly understood the power we held in our hands and had experienced many of the same trials and tribulations that I had in those early days of SOAP, WSDL, and UDDI. It was both rewarding and invigorating. Looking back, many of those startups and the ideas that were created were so far ahead of the market.

Today, we are seeing the power of those innovative, architectural concepts manifesting themselves as everything becomes a service; from infrastructure, to application construction and integration platforms, to applications. But, perhaps more subtle are the changes driven out from the adoption of service-orientation, such as the shift from waterfall methodologies to more iterative approaches, automated build systems enabling continuous integration of these loosely-coupled systems, and now API Management to engage and enable the latest generation of developers to tap that valuable content and those integrated systems traditionally locked up behind the corporate firewall delivering truly innovative applications on mobile devices. The results of these changes have led to an explosion in the interconnected nature of devices everywhere, now called the Internet of Things; the resulting data these devices are capable of constantly churning out is driving the notion of Big Data.

What becomes very clear is that the principles of SOA Governance are more important than ever. Industry wide, we must remain focused on how to effectively engage and communicate with a community of developers. How can organizations define and guide communities of developers in the most effective and efficient way possible to maximize the value of their work, both within the typical enterprise and now beyond the firewall with the explosion of mobile applications? More than 10 years on and with millions of web services created, the value of SOA Governance is now easier to explain and understand than it was in those early days.

SOA Governance remains focused on people and processes; where the adoption of anything new is nearly always met with resistance. In the pages that follow, the complex interconnections between people, processes, and technology that make up SOA Governance are explored using easy to understand examples extracted from real experiences. As you follow the journey of Weir & Bell Telecom, I hope you can better understand the relationship between the people and the processes involved in achieving robust and effective SOA Governance and are able to begin to apply these principles and technologies within your organization. But, most importantly, the success of your SOA Governance initiative will be based on your ability to apply pragmatism both in terms of the speed of change that your organization can support and effectively engaging the community of stakeholders who will ultimately drive the processes and achieve the desired goals and objectives.

Tim E. Hall

Vice President of Product Management,
Integration & Business Process Management,
Oracle Corporation.

About the Authors

Luis Augusto Weir is HCL's Director for Oracle Fusion Middleware solutions in the EMEA, ASIA Pacific regions. With more than 11 years of experience in implementing IT solutions across the globe, Luis has successfully delivered several large and complex Service Oriented Architecture (SOA) solutions for Fortune 500 companies. He has led SOA and middleware capabilities for different renowned SIs such as CSC, Cognizant, and Capgemini. Luis is focused on assisting customers leverage the full range of Fusion Middleware offerings to resolve integration problems, improve their businesses, and establish effective technology roadmaps. Key to this success has always been Luis's special focus around governance (people, processes, and tools) and also in always having a structured and agile delivery.

Luis is an expert in SOA and also is a thought leader in this field. Having always had a natural talent for software, computers, and engineering in general, Luis's career in software started from an early age. Even before starting university, Luis's entrepreneurial spirit led him to start several ventures including the very first social media website in his country of origin (Venezuela) as well as a small software development firm. Although none of these ventures turned into a multi-million corporation, the experience and knowledge gained during this period led him to develop the passion for distributed software computing which inevitably led to SOA.

Luis is widely considered as a leader in the SOA/BPM field. In an effort to share his real-life experiences when implementing complex SOA solutions, Luis has written his first book, *Oracle SOA Governance 11g Implementation*, published by *Packt Publishing*.

Acknowledgments

First of all I would like to thank my co-author Andy Bell for his help in writing this book. Without his support this book would not have been possible.

Secondly I would like to thank my employer, HCL, especially Richard Turner, for giving the support required to commit to such a task.

I would also like to thank my reviewers, specially my editors, and project managers at Packt Publishing for their valuable feedback; and also Oracle, especially Juerguen Kress, Tim Hall, and Kevin Li for all the assistance provided throughout this journey.

Last but by no means least, I would like to thank my beautiful family (Mom, Dad, siblings), my daughter Helena for being my sunshine, but most importantly to my partner Elena who provided the much needed support over the past several months. Her love inspired me and her support gave me the confidence to carry on.

Andrew Bell has more than 26 years of experience in the IT industry covering a wide range of software products and industry verticals. He has more than 21 years of experience working with Oracle products including 6 years of solid experience with Oracle SOA Suite and Oracle BPM. Andrew first started working in the SOA space 10 years ago and has successfully delivered many Oracle Middleware projects for large and blue chip clients. He currently works at CSC, where he is employed as a BPM/SOA Solution Architect for the Oracle Global Practice.

Andrew is well respected for his in-depth SOA and BPM knowledge. He has a strong team lead and communication skills, and a deep technical knowledge covering both Oracle and Java.

I would like to thank my boys, James, Christopher, and George, for their patience while Dad was busy writing this book. I would also like to thank Luis for giving me the opportunity to write this book with him and Stephen Pitchfork for his valued technical assistance. Much appreciated.

About the Reviewers

Ivan Dimovic is the Senior Technical and Management Consultant specializing in Oracle Fusion Middleware with focus on Oracle SOA Suite and SOA Governance engaged on more than 40 end-client sites with more than 15 years of consulting.

Since 2004, Ivan has led Experts Network for Success (eNet4S) Group (`www.enet4s.com`), an Oracle partner, consulting, and technical resources augmentation company with comprehensive expertise in SOA Suite, OSB, OWC Suite, OIM Suite, OER, OSR, OEM, and so on, that provides a consulting service in the areas of SOA & SCA Architecture and Implementation, IT & SOA Governance, System & Application Integration, Troubleshooting, Performance Tuning, and Optimization. eNet4S is a partnership of Oracle trained and certified consultants, satisfying high standards of expertise, professionalism, and work ethics, growing based on client shifting skill needs, talent gaps, expertise, and staffing requirements to meet aggressive project timelines and successful deliveries.

We have continuous expertise in improvement practice, productivity, and adoption of bleeding edge technologies, and we keep redefining our skills in this shifting continuum where SOA Governance is a mandatory enabler for continues business transformation resulting in improved ROI and time to market. This is a must-have book for anyone who is in charge of SOA Governance.

Peter Obert was born in 1969 in Bojnice, Slovakia and had a childhood filled with sports and exploration. In eighth grade, he ranked 4th in the Slovak, in the 1979 Pythagoras Competition in Math and Logic. At the grammar school, he attended a special class with extended study of Math, Programming, and Algorithms.

This mathematical and physics fascination prepared him for the following study at the Slovak Technical University (STU). He entered the Electro-technical faculty of STU in 1988. Later, he was attracted by Special Architectures of VLSI. He graduated in 1993 and wrote and programed his graduation work on the subject of "Compilation of Configuration and Programming Language OCCAM".

He worked for Softec Bratislava spol. s r.o. from 1993 till 2007. During these 15 years of consulting practice, he went through programming, UML analysis, team leading, and project managing. His last position within Softec was J2EE Architect.

Peter Obert became a part of Oracle International Cloud Competence Center ECEMEA in 2008. He started as the J2EE and SOA Technical Architect. Currently he appears as the Design Authority for Oracle Fusion Middleware, SOA, and Integration. He delivers FMW product family training for Oracle University and Oracle Partner Academy. In critical solutions, he provides design for the FMW disaster recovery implementation and SOA/BPM performance tuning strategies.

His outcomes are typically fitting into the Enterprise Architecture Process (EAP). One of his specialties is Enterprise Governance Process as a part of EAP, and SOA Governance as the part of Enterprise Governance.

I want to thank Packt Publishing and Oracle Consulting Organization for giving me the opportunity to participate in an outcome outside nonpublic projects and product-specific deliverables.

Phani Krishna Pemmaraju has more than 8 years of IT experience with expertise in JEE/Spring technologies and Oracle Fusion Middleware products. He completed his master's degree in Computer Applications as a topper from Osmania University, Hyderabad in India. He has rich implementation expertise in EAI/SOA integrations, and worked on some challenging projects across different verticals. He has extensive experience in architecting, designing, developing, and testing solutions using various SOA technology (SCA/JBI) products such as Oracle Fusion, Java Caps, and Glassfish ESB. Phani has worked for highly respected IT consulting companies for various prestigious clients and played a key role in architecting and designing solutions. He is currently working as a JEE/SOA consultant for a respected retail company in UK.

www.PacktPub.com

Support files, eBooks, discount offers, and more

You might want to visit www.PacktPub.com for support files and downloads related to your book.

Did you know that Packt offers eBook versions of every book published, with PDF and ePub files available? You can upgrade to the eBook version at www.PacktPub.com and as a print book customer, you are entitled to a discount on the eBook copy. Get in touch with us at service@packtpub.com for more details.

At www.PacktPub.com, you can also read a collection of free technical articles, sign up for a range of free newsletters and receive exclusive discounts and offers on Packt books and eBooks.

PACKTLIB

http://PacktLib.PacktPub.com

Do you need instant solutions to your IT questions? PacktLib is Packt's online digital book library. Here, you can access, read and search across Packt's entire library of books.

Why Subscribe?

- Fully searchable across every book published by Packt
- Copy-and-paste, print and bookmark content
- On-demand and accessible via web browsers

Free Access for Packt account holders

If you have an account with Packt at www.PacktPub.com, you can use this to access PacktLib today and view nine entirely free books. Simply use your login credentials for immediate access.

Instant Updates on New Packt Books

Get notified! Find out when new books are published by following @PacktEnterprise on Twitter, or the *Packt Enterprise* Facebook page.

Table of Contents

Preface

Service Oriented Architecture (SOA) is an architectural style for distributed computing that promotes the use of discrete software modules, known as services, which interoperate to deliver larger software solutions. The main goal of SOA is to deliver value to the business by bridging the gap between business and IT to maximize business benefits. To do so, SOA architectures adhere to a series of guiding principles such as the ones described in the SOA Manifesto (`www.soa-manifesto.org`).

Although the potential behind SOA has never been questioned, costly lessons learnt have indicated that, without rigorous governance upfront, the chances of SOA delivering value are remote. Moreover, many concluded that the challenge of implementing SOA does not reside in the intrinsic complexity of its underlying technology platform. It was recognized that the real complexity of SOA lies in aligning people and processes from different lines of business in order to deliver enterprise-wide solutions.

What is **Governance** in relation to SOA? Although this is a very common question among practitioners, you are likely to be presented with several different answers depending on who you ask. However, the real question is not really what it is, but what it means to an organization and what benefits it can bring to a business. How can it be successfully implemented, and what tools and processes are required to achieve it?

SOA Governance is a commonly misunderstood term and is often confused with other disciplines such as **Software Development Lifecycle** (**SDLC**), configuration management, and naming standards. In practice, although SOA Governance covers all of these concepts, its scope is broader and covers everything from planning, analysis, service discovery, design, build, and testing stages of a SOA Solution (Design-time Governance), to live operations and monitoring (Run-Time Governance).

This book defines SOA Governance as the interaction between policies (what), decision makers (who) and processes (how) (*SOA Governance: Framework and Best Practices – An Oracle Whitepaper*: `http://www.oracle.com/us/technologies/soa/oracle-soa-governance-best-practice-066427.pdf`).

A SOA Governance implementation can only be successful if it can realize measurable benefits for the business and Return on Investment (ROI). Failing to do so basically means that SOA will be seen as a complex and expensive technology, and not as an architectural style aimed at delivering business benefits.

In reading this book, SOA practitioners will embark on the journey of implementing SOA Governance (what-how-who) using the Oracle SOA Governance Solution. This will be achieved by walking through the common problems that different organizations face when implementing SOA, and how these can be solved by implementing best practice processes, standards, and other techniques, along with using the Oracle Governance Solution toolset.

The components that build up the Oracle SOA Governance Solution infrastructure are depicted in the following diagram:

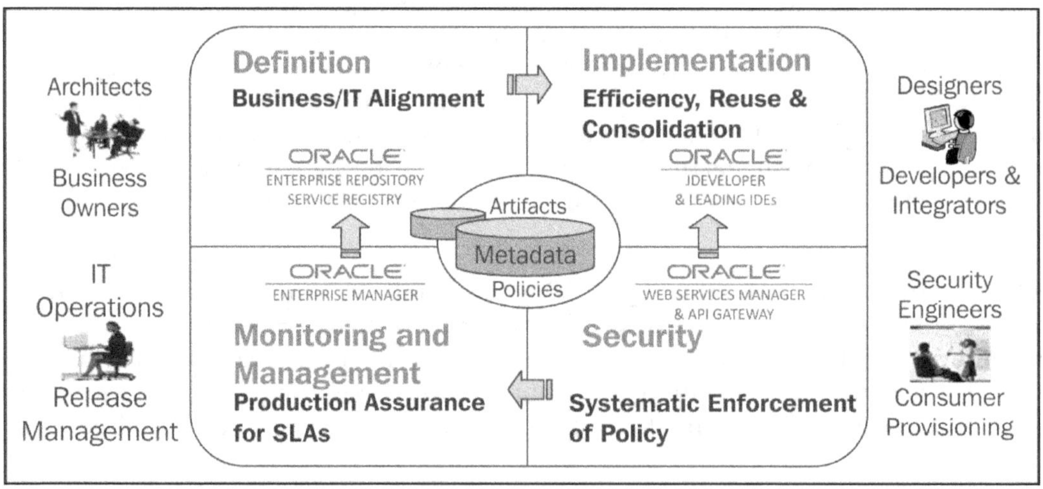

The components are as follows:

- **Oracle Enterprise Repository (OER)**: Oracle Enterprise Repository implements a design-time Governance toolset used to support service lifecycle and other key stages of a solution, such as service discovery, and to provide a framework to promote service re-use.
- **Oracle Service Registry (OSR)**: Oracle Service Registry is a UDDI Version 3-compliant registry used to support runtime governance. It provides a runtime interface to the Enterprise Repository, allowing service consumers to dynamically lookup service locations at runtime.
- **JDeveloper**: It is Oracle's preferred integrated development environment (IDE) for the development of software solutions using Java, SOA Suite, and other technologies such as SQL, PLSQL, XML, PHP, among others. JDeveloper offers a wide variety of plugins to integrate with other products such as OER and OSR.
- **Web Service Manager (WSM)**: This is a security policy manager that allows administrators to centrally define and manage security policies in a non-intrusive manner. Policies can be attached to services in order to enforce security and to enforce compliance to enterprise security policies. Policies can be attached during the design phases as well as at runtime.
- **Oracle API Gateway (OAG)**: Former Oracle Enterprise Gateway, OAG is a standalone for implementing robust security polices into services. OAG is typically deployed as a policy enforcement point (PeP) in demilitarized zones (DMZ) where services are consumed or exposed by applications located in untrusted networks.
- **Oracle Enterprise Manager (OEM)**: This is a web based application for managing and monitoring the Oracle-based infrastructures on which services execute. The OEM SOA Management Pack is an add-on for Oracle Enterprise Manager that delivers a complete toolset for configuration management and monitoring of SOA infrastructures.

While there appears to be many different definitions and perceptions of SOA Governance in the SOA community at large, leading to much confusion around the subject matter as a whole, there is one common denominator shared by all SOA practitioners. All Service Orientated Architecture implementations are doomed to failure without implementing at least some level of governance.

This book presents the concepts, guidelines, and tips required for the successful implementation of design-time and runtime SOA governance using the Oracle SOA Governance Solution.

What this book covers

The main objective of this book is to deliver key concepts along with practical guidelines on how to implement service governance using the Oracle SOA Governance Solution. The initial chapters of the book are focused on implementing design-time Governance while subsequent chapters deal with runtime governance and focus on more advanced features of the toolset.

Chapter 1, SOA Governance, describes in detail the key concepts around SOA Governance and the Oracle SOA Governance Solution infrastructure.

Chapter 2, Implementation Case Study, highlights the typical problems and requirements addressed by a typical SOA Governance implementation and highlights the key critical success factors for the implementation.

Chapter 3, Introduction to Oracle Enterprise Repository, describes the core concepts, management consoles, and capabilities supported by OER.

Chapter 4, Initial Configuration, describes the prerequisites and illustrates the steps to be considered when configuring OER for the first time.

Chapter 5, Harvesting, describes the prerequisites and steps for bootstrapping and harvesting assets into OER.

Chapter 6, Asset Lifecycle and Workflow, describes how to implement policies, compliance templates, and workflows in OER in support of the different asset lifecycle stages.

Chapter 7, Oracle Service Registry, describes the core concepts, management consoles, and capabilities supported by OSR. It also provides a practical insight into how to architect an OSR solution.

Chapter 8, Design-time Service Promotion and Discovery, describes how service designers and developers can discover and consume existing services and the complex process of promoting assets to different environments.

Chapter 9, Implementing Basic Runtime Governance, describes how to use the out-of-the-box Oracle Enterprise Manager (OEM) and Web Services Manager (WSM) components to implement runtime governance.

Chapter 10, Extending Runtime Governance, describes the business case for implementing Oracle Enterprise Manager (OEM) and Business Transaction Manager (BTM) in an organization and illustrates how to configure Oracle Enterprise Repository (OER) to monitor SOA Suite infrastructures.

Chapter 11, Extending Governance with AIA Foundation Pack 11g, describes the business case for implementing Oracle Application Integration Architecture (AIA) Foundation Pack to accelerate and de-risk the implementation of a Master Data Management (MDM) and illustrates how to integrate Oracle Enterprise Repository (OER) with the AIA Foundation Pack.

Appendix, Installation Tips and Tricks, delivers a summary, tips, and techniques for installing Oracle Enterprise Repository (OER), Oracle Service Registry (OSR), and Business Intelligence Publisher (BI Publisher).

What you need for this book

This book makes use of the following software:

- JDeveloper 11*g* PS6 (11.1.1.7)
- Oracle Enterprise Repository 11*g* PS6 (11.1.1.7.0)
- Oracle Service Registry 11*g* PS5 (11.1.1.6.0)
- Oracle BPM Enterprise 10*g* (10.3.2)
- OBI Publisher Enterprise 11*g* PS6 (11.1.1.7.0)
- Oracle Application Integration Architecture Foundation Pack 11*g* PS6 (11.1.1.7)
- Oracle Enterprise Repository Cloud Control 12*c* Release 3
- Oracle Business Transaction Manager 12*c* Release 3
- Oracle SOA Suite 11*g* PS6 (11.1.1.7.0)
- Oracle BPM Suite 11*g* PS6 (11.1.1.7.0)
- Oracle Service Bus 11*g* PS6 (11.1.1.7.0)

Who this book is for

This book is mainly intended for Enterprise Architects, Solution Architects, Technical Architects, and SOA consultants (in general) that have, or wish to implement, SOA Governance using the Oracle SOA Governance Solution.

It is essential that the reader has previous experience or knowledge on the following subjects:

- JDeveloper 11*g*
- Oracle SOA Suite 11*g*
- Oracle Service Bus 11*g*
- XML technologies in general

Conventions

In this book, you will find a number of styles of text that distinguish between different kinds of information. Here are some examples of these styles, and an explanation of their meaning.

Code words in text, database table names, folder names, filenames, file extensions, pathnames, dummy URLs, user input, and Twitter handles are shown as follows: "The standard convention used by default is <major version>.<minor version>, for example, 1.0."

A block of code will be set as follows:

```
./harvest -url http://localhost:7101/oer -user
admin -password <password> -file ./test/samples
```

When we wish to draw your attention to a particular part of a code block, the relevant lines or items will be made bold:

```
./harvest -url http://localhost:7101/oer -user
admin -password <password> -file ./test/samples
```

Any command-line input or output is written as follows:

```
./osb11g-harvest.sh -preview true
```

New terms and **important words** are shown in bold. Words that you see on the screen, in menus or dialog boxes for example, appear in the text like this: "The **Configure Categorizations** window allows for the creation and modification of Categorizations. Click on **Add** to create a new Categorization".

> Warnings or important notes appear in a box like this.

> Tips and tricks appear like this.

Reader feedback

Feedback from our readers is always welcome. Let us know what you think about this book—what you liked or may have disliked. Reader feedback is important for us to develop titles that you really get the most out of.

To send us general feedback, simply send an e-mail to `feedback@packtpub.com`, and mention the book title via the subject of your message.

If there is a topic that you have expertise in and you are interested in either writing or contributing to a book, see our author guide on `www.packtpub.com/authors`.

Customer support

Now that you are the proud owner of a Packt book, we have a number of things to help you to get the most from your purchase.

Downloading the example code

You can download the example code files for all Packt books you have purchased from your account at `http://www.packtpub.com`. If you purchased this book elsewhere, you can visit `http://www.packtpub.com/support` and register to have the files e-mailed directly to you.

Errata

Although we have taken every care to ensure the accuracy of our content, mistakes do happen. If you find a mistake in one of our books—maybe a mistake in the text or the code—we would be grateful if you would report this to us. By doing so, you can save other readers from frustration and help us improve subsequent versions of this book. If you find any errata, please report them by visiting `http://www.packtpub.com/submit-errata`, selecting your book, clicking on the **errata submission form** link, and entering the details of your errata. Once your errata are verified, your submission will be accepted and the errata will be uploaded on our website, or added to any list of existing errata, under the Errata section of that title. Any existing errata can be viewed by selecting your title from `http://www.packtpub.com/support`.

Piracy

Piracy of copyright material on the Internet is an ongoing problem across all media. At Packt, we take the protection of our copyright and licenses very seriously. If you come across any illegal copies of our works, in any form, on the Internet, please provide us with the location address or website name immediately so that we can pursue a remedy.

Please contact us at `copyright@packtpub.com` with a link to the suspected pirated material.

We appreciate your help in protecting our authors, and our ability to bring you valuable content.

Questions

You can contact us at `questions@packtpub.com` if you are having a problem with any aspect of the book, and we will do our best to address it.

1
SOA Governance

This chapter will introduce the main concepts surrounding **SOA Governance** and set out the goals and aspirations for the governance effort. We will focus on the key objectives and benefits of an SOA Governance framework and discuss the steps necessary to introduce and enforce such a framework.

SOA Governance overview

Service Oriented Architecture (**SOA**) is a strategy for constructing business-focused software systems from loosely coupled, interoperable building blocks (called services) that can be combined and re-used quickly, within and between enterprises, to meet business needs.

Oracle defines SOA Governance as an agile and efficient decision and accountability framework, to effectively direct and assist in realizing the benefits of SOA, while encouraging a cultural evolution in how an organization delivers SOA to the enterprise.

SOA Governance defines the interaction between policies (what), decision makers (who), and processes (how).

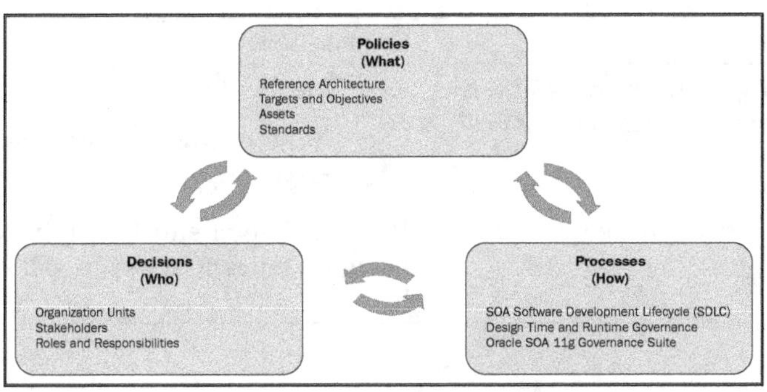

In order to implement a successful SOA Governance, organizations need to understand how to align processes, people, and tools in order to maximize business benefits.

But what does it mean to deliver business benefits? In simplistic terms, it means creating reusable assets and eliminating liabilities.

In SOA terms, **Assets** are electronic artifacts such as APIs, XML documents (XSDs, WSDLs, or XSLTs), documents (requirements, designs, and so on), systems, and services that add measurable value to the business. For example, a service that supports multi-channel submission of sales orders delivers value in the form of cost savings by way of re-use. Should a new channel be introduced at a later date, let's say mobile apps, the existing service can potentially be re-used thus avoiding the costs of defining, designing, building, and testing a service specific to the new channel.

Assets are usually electronically stored in a repository and can be associated with other Assets. Throughout the chapters of this book, Assets will be elaborated further and concepts such as asset types and asset taxonomies will be described.

Liabilities on the other hand are duplicated, deprecated, redundant, or unused Assets that no longer deliver business benefits and potentially introduce additional cost. For example, having several services delivering identical functionality represents a liability since the total cost of supporting and running each service exceeds the cost of having a single-consolidated service.

> It is not common to use the term liability when talking about SOA Governance. However, we felt that, if there is a description to describe what adds value to the business, there should be another one to define what takes the value away from it.

Challenges that prevent organizations from realizing the benefits of SOA can also be considered as a liability. The following table lists some of the most common challenges and their consequence to the business:

Challenge	Consequence
Lack of visibility of the existing assets and their performance characteristics.	• No asset re-use • More duplication (increased liabilities) • Higher costs
Tactical projects over strategic solutions.	Projects deliver **short-term** benefits, but bring no **enterprise-wide** value or long-term benefits.

Challenge	Consequence
Poor decision making and lack of accountability.	No sense of ownership makes decision making, policy enforcement, and accountability almost impossible.
Low quality Assets that become difficult to maintain and change.	Assets are difficult to change and their cost is high. Changing an asset is considered risky and costly, which prevents new and innovative solutions from being introduced.
Poor estimation techniques and inaccurate planning.	Projects overrun, ending up costing more than originally budgeted.

Understanding the goal of SOA Governance is an important step forward; however, it is not a guarantee for success. A successful governance implementation must tick several boxes and answer several questions, such as:

- **What artifacts are required to deliver governance?** It is vital for the success of a governance implementation to have a clear understanding of the artifacts to be delivered, what their purpose is, and what value they add to the overall governance implementation. The main artifacts are:
    - **SOA strategy**: It defines the goals and objectives for adopting SOA in the enterprise. Moreover, it defines the success criteria needed to ensure that the business benefits are realized by the adoption of SOA.
    - **SOA reference architecture**: It defines the core building blocks for an SOA solution.
    - **SOA policies and standards**: Guidelines such as patterns, anti-patterns, conventions, and best practices to be considered or adopted when designing solutions.

> Policies define principles and assertions to be evaluated when making decisions. Standards define clear guidelines on what is or isn't allowed. Policies are usually but not exclusively created to enforce standards.

-
    - **SOA Assets and taxonomies**: It defines all the SOA Assets available in the enterprise, their description, and type.

- **How can it be delivered?** The necessary tools, processes, and procedures required to deliver governance and its objectives. The key artifacts that should be created or influenced are:
    - **SOA Roadmap**: It defines the activities required to deliver an SOA strategy and milestones for implementation. This topic will be covered in more detail later in the chapter.

> A roadmap must set realistic targets, ones that are achievable based on the organization's current maturity state. Not doing so means that wrong expectations will be set for the business, inevitably leading to failure.

    - **Design-time and Runtime governance**: These two fundamental concepts will be described in detail later in the chapter.
- **Who is responsible for delivering it?** A description of all the participants required to deliver the artifacts previously listed, including their roles and responsibilities.

SOA Governance framework

The answers to these questions, together with the concepts and tooling outlined in this book, provide the foundation for implementing a robust **SOA Governance framework** that underpins an end-to-end SOA ecosystem.

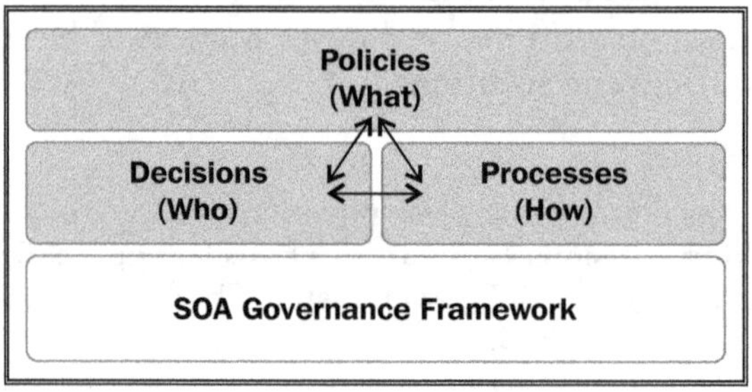

An SOA Governance framework defines the approach, artifacts, processes, tools, and people required to implement governance.

Having an effective and strong SOA Governance framework in place is extremely important as it delivers a common and consistent language for the enterprise to define and manage semantics, processes and standards, and accountability for an entire SOA **lifecycle**.

Indeed, without a well-defined SOA Governance framework, it is highly likely that the members of an organization, or its partners, will have their own understanding of what SOA represents and how it is best implemented, leading to misalignment and duplication of effort across departments and between the collaborating organizations. In large and complex SOA implementations, this situation leads to poor implementations and, almost inevitably, failure to deliver meaningful SOA.

Without implementing a strong and well-defined SOA Governance, underpinned by a robust SOA Governance framework, an enterprise-wide SOA implementation will almost certainly fail to achieve the true promise of SOA and the subsequent benefits that ensue.

SOA Governance framework scope

An SOA Governance framework defines the roles, responsibilities, processes, and procedures (what-how-who) that are needed to enforce the governance of all aspects of the service lifecycle (what-how-who). An SOA Governance framework is imperative for the success of an SOA implementation.

This book sets out to discuss the tooling and concepts provided by Oracle Corporation to achieve successful SOA governance. The following diagram depicts in more detail what an SOA Governance framework would look when put into context of the Oracle SOA Governance solution. We will explore the concepts illustrated in the following diagram throughout this chapter, showing how each contributes to the overall framework:

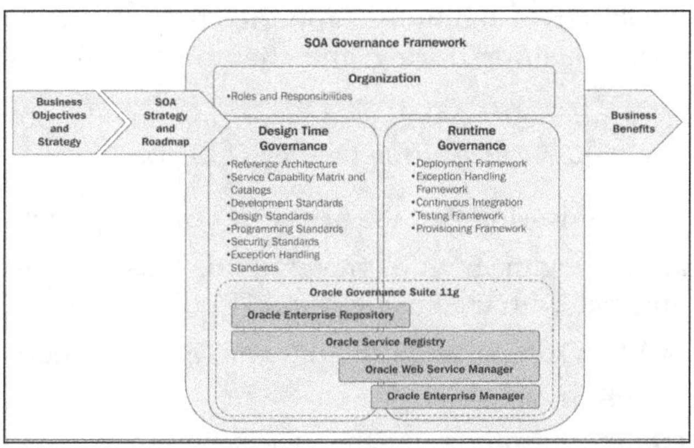

The preceding diagram shows how the business objectives and strategy are the fundamental drivers of an SOA Governance implementation. Without a clear focus on the business drivers and on how SOA can help achieve these business goals, an SOA implementation will most likely fail to deliver and end up being perceived by the management as yet another expensive technology that adds little value.

SOA Governance, on the other hand, helps to define metrics that can be used to demonstrate how SOA is being effectively utilized and to measure the tangible benefits to the business.

Prior to the introduction of SOA Governance into an organization, an **SOA Strategy** and a clearly defined **SOA Roadmap** should be defined as illustrated in the following diagram:

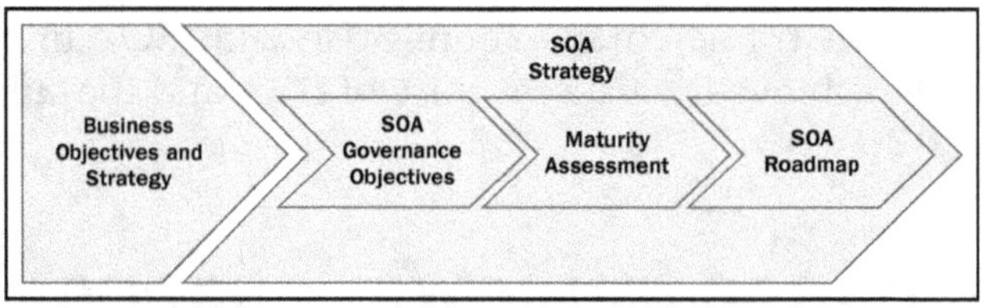

SOA Governance objectives

In order to ensure that SOA Governance is achieving real business benefits, it is imperative to understand the objectives of an SOA Governance implementation.

Understanding the business goals and business strategy will dramatically improve the chances of success for an SOA implementation. Equally, and as said earlier, without clear objectives an SOA implementation can be perceived as failing to deliver measureable benefits to the business.

When defining the objectives for an SOA Governance implementation, one should bear in mind that all objectives should be supported by clear success factors that are achievable and measurable prior, during, and after the implementation.

The following principles should be followed when defining the objectives of an SOA Governance implementation (*Introducing Oracle SOA Governance, Oracle Corp. 2008*):

- **Business value**: Ensuring that the project investments yield business value
- **Alignment**: Keeping the SOA aligned with the business and its architecture, and in compliance with the business and IT policies
- **Business agility**: Gaining visibility into your SOA for more rapid decision making
- **Risk reduction**: Controlling dependencies, managing the impact of change, and enforcing policies
- **Cost savings**: Promoting consolidation, standardization, and reuse

Once the objectives have been defined, these should be well-documented and presented to the key stakeholders within the business and IT departments to obtain the desired level of sponsorship. This sponsorship is critical to achieve the required level of assistance from different departments in order to elaborate the maturity assessment and roadmap, and to secure any extra funding if needed.

Oracle maturity assessment and roadmap

A maturity assessment allows the key decision makers to evaluate the current state of SOA maturity within their organization. A maturity assessment consists of evaluating the as-is and the to-be levels of the SOA implementation within the enterprise, and then quantifying the gap between the two. There are many ways by which this can be achieved, and there are several maturity models in the market that can be used for this purpose. However, this book recommends that a maturity assessment is conducted using the **Oracle SOA Maturity Model** along with the Oracle SOA Maturity Model calculation tool that has been provided in conjunction with this book.

The Oracle SOA Maturity Model

The Oracle SOA Maturity Model was designed by Oracle to help the customers to achieve SOA Maturity. Customers evaluate their current state of maturity within their organization and define a roadmap to achieve the target level of maturity. The model consists of five levels. Each level represents a particular state of maturity for an SOA implementation, ranging from ad hoc use of services to a very mature business-focused implementation. In addition, Oracle makes use of eight different capability domains that must be evaluated within each level when defining the maturity of an SOA implementation.

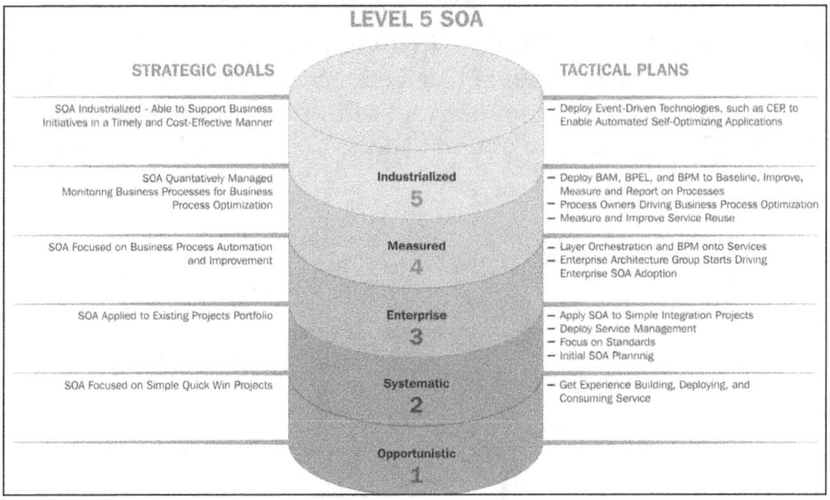

The five levels of the Oracle SOA maturity model defined as follows:

1. **Opportunistic**: SOA implementation focuses on quick win projects and service enabling some applications. At this level, it is expected that the IT department starts to get familiar with the service orientation by consuming and exposing services. At this level, business benefits are measured from small wins such as the reusability of some business logic that is embedded in a legacy system. This reuse saves on the acquisition or development of a new application.
2. **Systematic**: Service orientation is considered as a fundamental building block of the solution architecture for projects. SOA standards are introduced and there is more focus on the governance and service lifecycle. Reuse of assets becomes a fundamental aspect of the SOA implementation. With the increased number of SOA projects being commissioned, reuse of the SOA Assets can bring considerable benefits to the business in the form of cost savings in the development effort.
3. **Enterprise**: SOA strategy is now fully aligned to the business and is focused on enabling the business processes layer. Business process implementers can benefit from a broad catalogue of SOA services. SOA implementation is governed by the enterprise architecture, meaning that SOA spreads across the entire organization; it is no longer perceived as an IT department tool. SOA Governance implementation is central and a priority in implementing an IT strategy.
4. **Measured**: Process optimization and reporting become central to the SOA strategy. SOA can be measured in terms of key process indicators (KPI) and business intelligence (BI) reports that are able to drive the business process improvement. Furthermore, asset reuse (not only services but also processes) delivers considerable measurable benefits to the business.
5. **Industrialized**: SOA and BPM initiatives can deliver rapid and cost-effective solutions to the business. **Event-driven** technologies such as complex **event processing** are used to automate and self-optimize applications. Business relies on SOA and BPM to operate and to continuously improve.

SOA Capability Domains

SOA Capability Domains identify the different areas of an Enterprise that have a potential impact on the readiness of the SOA initiatives. The following diagram depicts the eight capability domains covered in the approach:

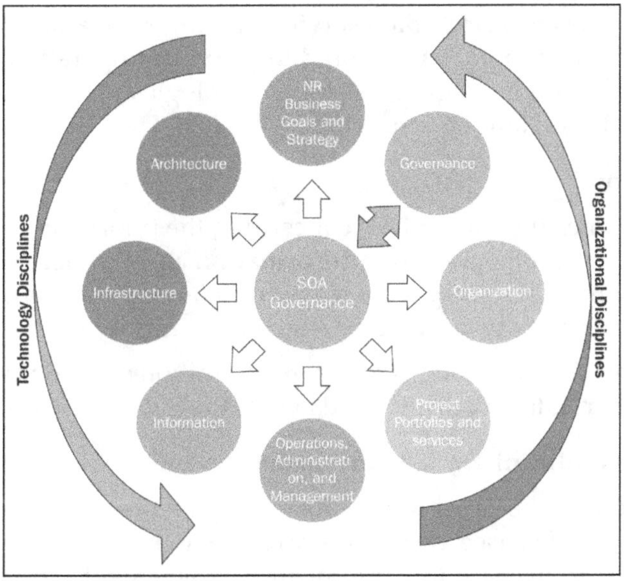

Capability domains are described as follows:

- **Business goals and strategy**:
    - Defines the capabilities that provide the high-level constructs that allow the SOA initiative to proceed. This includes things such as business motivation, expected benefits, guiding principles, expected costs, funding model, and so on.
    - A key aspect of this domain is the identification of success drivers that can be used as metrics to measure success.
- **Architecture**:
    - Defines the capabilities concerning the definitions of the overall architecture and guidelines for various practitioners to ensure adherence to the architecture.
    - This domain is where the target reference architecture is defined.

- **Infrastructure**:
    - Defines the capabilities concerning the service infrastructure and tools that provide the technical foundation for the SOA initiative.
    - This domain defines the platform required to enable different views of the defined architecture (for example, integration, business services, data services, monitoring, among others) and also the topologies required to guarantee operation continuity (for example, high-availability topologies, disaster recovery, and grid, among others).
- **Information**:
    - Defines the capabilities concerning the information aspects of SOA, for example, providing **Information as a Service (IaaS)**. This includes shared data models, message formats and schemas, master data management, content management, and so on.
    - This domain also provides the definitions of canonical models and other data structures used across the SOA initiative.
- **Operations, administration, and management**:
    - Defines the capabilities concerning the post-deployment aspects of solutions based on service-oriented architectures. For example, the operations, administration, and management aspects of SOA.
- **Project portfolios and services**:
    - Defines the capabilities concerning the planning and building of services, and the service usage guidelines of the service consumers.
    - This domain defines the methodologies and processes in place to deliver SOA projects; ideally in an agile-like approach.
- **Organization**:
    - Defines the capabilities concerning the development of corporate competency around SOA, including the organizational structure and skills development.
    - SOA is still seen in many organizations as a new technology and many users lack proper understanding and training around the SOA principles.
    - This domain should focus on providing the means to allow the relevant staff to embrace the technology by understanding its potential and the ability to utilize SOA proactively.

- **Governance**:
    - Defines the capabilities concerning the governance structures and processes that support and guide the SOA effort. Maturity and adoption of an adequate amount of governance are a leading indicator of the overall SOA success.
    - Governance enables the enterprise to enforce the policies that will allow the SOA initiative to mature in each of the eight domains.

Creating the roadmap

The SOA Maturity Model calculation tool provided along with this book delivers a robust model with more than 300 capabilities for all capability domains. The tool can be used to quantify the as-is and to-be levels of SOA implementation and to identify the gap between the two. Once all the individual capabilities have been evaluated, the tool will produce a diagram similar to the following:

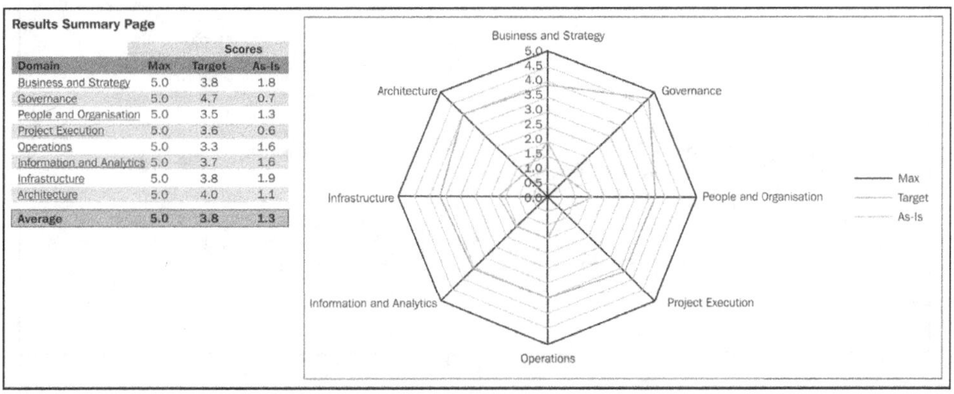

Results Summary Page

Domain	Max	Target	As-Is
Business and Strategy	5.0	3.8	1.8
Governance	5.0	4.7	0.7
People and Organisation	5.0	3.5	1.3
Project Execution	5.0	3.6	0.6
Operations	5.0	3.3	1.6
Information and Analytics	5.0	3.7	1.6
Infrastructure	5.0	3.8	1.9
Architecture	5.0	4.0	1.1
Average	5.0	3.8	1.3

The outcome of the maturity assessment should be carefully evaluated in order to identify what actions are needed to reduce the gap between the as-is and the to-be (target) SOA implementations. Once all actions and their dependencies have been identified, these should be used as the foundation to formulate and elaborate an SOA Roadmap.

When elaborating an SOA Roadmap one must ensure that it is comprehensive and easy to interpret. This is because the target audience of the roadmap will be not only IT but most importantly the business. If the business fails to understand that roadmap, it is possible that they will raise impediments when or if more funding is needed.

It is also worth highlighting that an SOA Roadmap is not a project plan. The aim of a roadmap is to be broadly right and not accurately wrong. Details are not needed in a roadmap as a project plan can (and probably will) be defined to manage the execution of the different projects.

The following diagram depicts the different aspects that define a comprehensive SOA Roadmap:

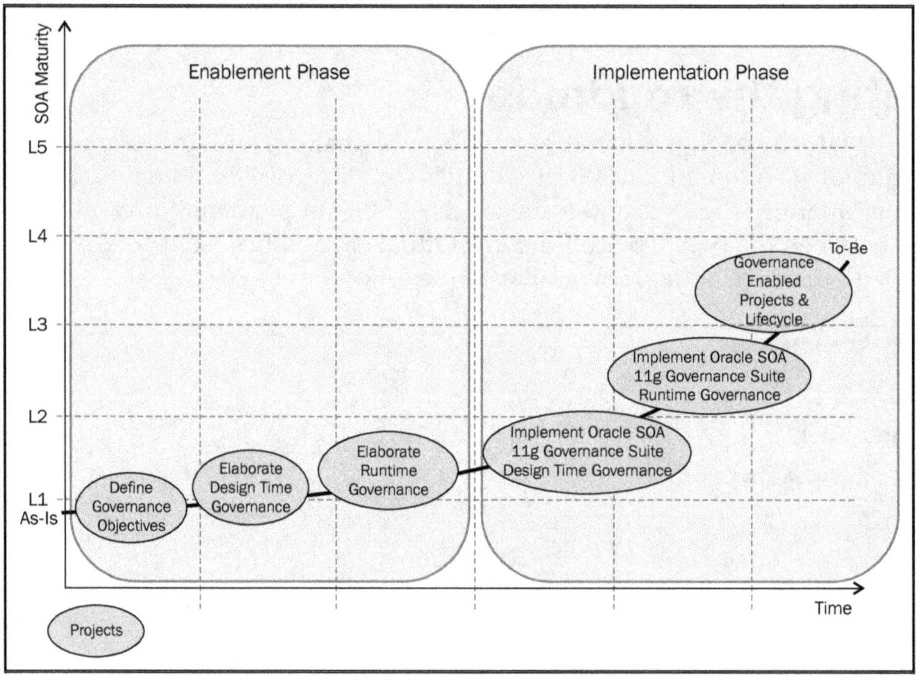

Enablement phase

This phase underpins the entire governance implementation as it is responsible for elaborating the governance objectives and the Design-time and Runtime Governance assets that are required to implement the Oracle SOA Governance solution.

The following sections enumerates the minimum set of assets that should be delivered as a part of the elaboration of the SOA Governance framework.

Design-time Governance framework artifacts

These artifacts are created to support the implementation of **Design-time Governance**. The artifacts are:

- **SOA architecture principles**: Lists the underlying tenets, restrictions that must be observed, and preconceived views that will guide the service approach, selection, design, governance, and ultimately the operations.
- **SOA reference architecture**: It defines the different components or building blocks that shape the SOA landscape of an enterprise. Reference architectures can be defined to address one or multiple areas of IT (for example, SOA, business architecture, security architecture, and others). Usually reference architectures are defined in 3 levels of abstraction: Conceptual, Logical, and Physical.

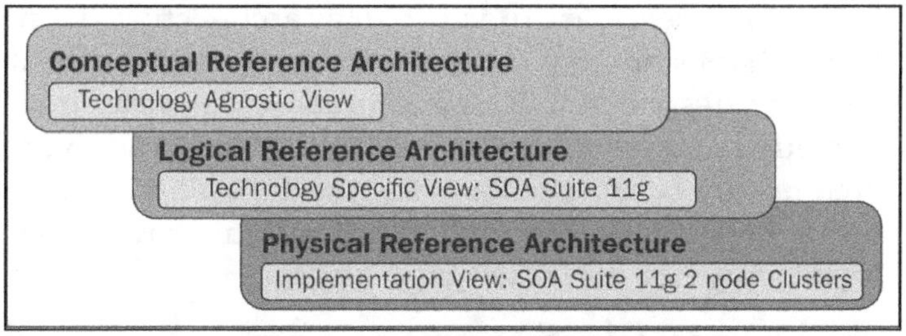

  - **Conceptual reference architecture**: Describes the concepts and components that build up an architecture at the highest level of abstraction. A conceptual reference architecture does not specify what technology is used or how it is implemented. Instead its purpose is to structurally identify what concerns should be addressed by IT and what the relationship between these concerns is.

    The following diagram depicts a conceptual reference architecture as defined in Oracle's reference architecture for SOA (*Document ID E15827-03*). As can be appreciated from the diagram, the main concerns addressed are enterprise development, interactions, information management, infrastructure, security, and management. There is no mention of what technology should be used.

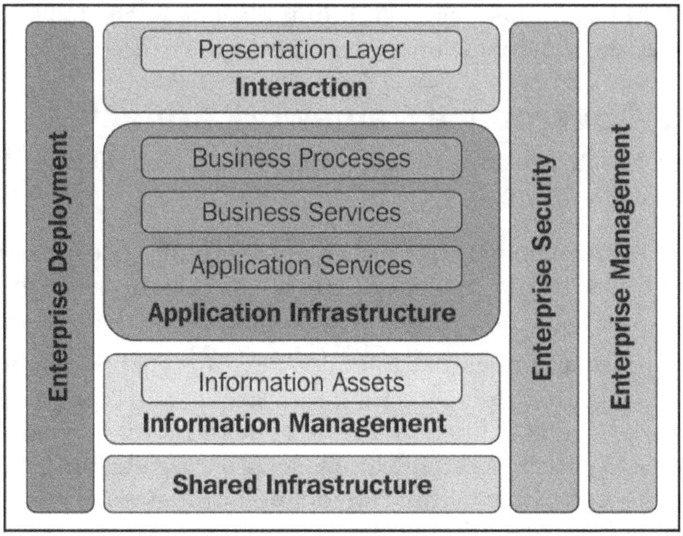

- **Logical reference architecture**: This architecture defines at a high level what technology is used in order to address the different concerns described in the conceptual reference architecture. Sometimes this architecture is also referred to as a vendor-specific architecture because it starts to introduce vendor preferred technology stacks. The following diagram provides a sample logical architecture for the Oracle SOA stack:

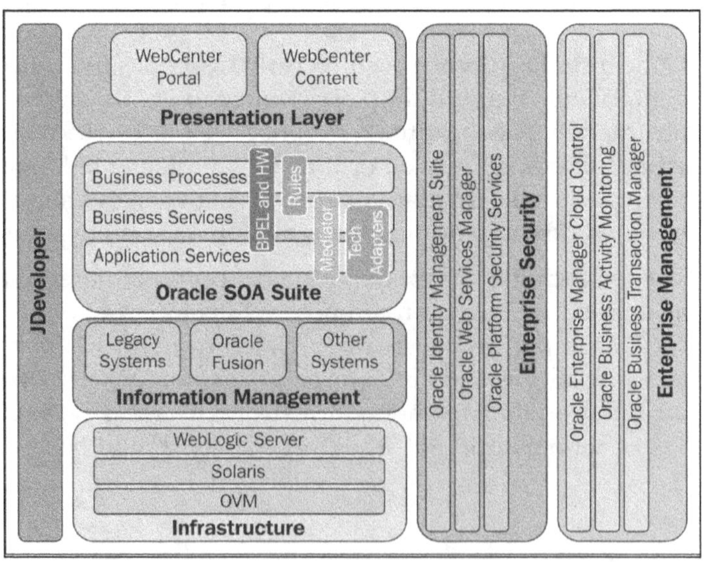

This sample logical reference architecture specifies among other things that Oracle SOA Suite will be utilized as the main application stack and that **Oracle BPEL Process Manager, Oracle Business Rules, Mediator and Technology adapter** components within a composite will be used to provide the business processes, business services and application services layers. Furthermore, this architecture implies that **Oracle Virtual Machine Server (OVM)** will be the core virtualization platform on which Solaris OS instances and **WebLogic Servers** will be deployed.

- **Physical reference architecture**: This architecture is a detailed architecture that represents how the different applications within the logical architecture are to be implemented. Because each application can have a very complex implementation view, it is recommended that different physical reference architectures are delivered for each application stack. For examples of a reference architecture for the SOA Suite 11*g* please refer to the Oracle Enterprise Deployment Guide: `http://docs.oracle.com/cd/E23943_01/core.1111/e12036/intro.htm`.

- **SOA development standards**: It defines the end-to-end software development lifecycle for the delivery of SOA Assets. Development standards should cover in some detail the end-to-end software development lifecycle including all the different assets that should be produced throughout the different phases of the lifecycle. These standards should cover key development issues such as source code management (for example, the use of tools such as subversion) and configuration management (for example, the use of trunk, tags, and branches folders, and all the guidelines to commit code and manage the line of development).
- **SOA design standards**: This document describes the service taxonomy and a pattern language that the designers should adhere to when producing designs for SOA Services. For example, **Oracle Application Integration Architecture (AIA)** defines five types of services: **Application Business Connector Services requestors** (**ABCSreq**), providers (**ABCSprov**), Enterprise Business Services, Enterprise Business Flows, and Composite Business Services. Furthermore, AIA defines certain design patterns that must be followed when implementing the AIA services. The most common pattern used by AIA is known as **VETORO (Validate, Enrich, Transform, Operate, Route, and Operate**). This pattern describes how to combine ABCSreq-EBS-EBF or CBP-ABCSprov in order to deliver end-to-end business processes and also defines which design patterns are to be used within each service type. AIA serves as an excellent example as to what should be addressed by the design standards.

- **SOA programming standards**: It defines conventions and rules that the developers should adhere to when constructing an SOA Asset. For example, naming conventions for JDeveloper would include conventions for applications and projects, composites, mediators, and BPEL components. These standards also cover programming guidelines and best practices.
- **SOA metadata standards**: It provides the standards and constraints that a designer and developer must adhere to when creating schemas and other XML artifacts. For example, namespaces, element naming standards, and schema data models should be covered in the metadata standards.
- **SOA templates**: All the SOA deliverables defined in the governance framework should have a corresponding document template. Document templates are very important because they define the content and scope that is expected of an SOA deliverable. Having document templates available means that the project can focus on delivering content and not defining it.
- **SOA deployment standards**: It defines guidelines that that should be followed when releasing/deploying SOA-related artifacts into any environment. Note that these standards will be dependent on how the runtime deployment framework is implemented.
- **SOA error and exception handling standards**: It defines guidelines that should be followed when implementing error and exception handling into the SOA services. Note that these standards will be dependent on how the runtime exception handling framework is implemented.
- **Security standards**: It defines guidelines that should be considered when defining and applying security policies into the SOA services. Note that these standards will be dependent on how the runtime security framework is implemented.
- **Monitoring and SLA standards**: It defines guidelines on the implementation of sensors and business activity, monitoring dashboards into composites and proxy services. These standards become particularly important at runtime as they enhance the search and monitoring capabilities of SOA instances once a service becomes operational.

Runtime Governance framework artifacts

These artifacts are created to support the implementation of Runtime Governance. The artifacts are:

- **Deployment framework**: Creating a framework of components that standardize the way code is promoted to different environments is extremely important, not only from a configuration management perspective but also from a project point of view. Applications such as Oracle SOA Suite 11*g* or OSB 11*g* usually consume services exposed by the external systems within a BPEL or a pipeline flow. These external systems are expressed in the form of URLs that will change from environment to environment and should therefore not be hardcoded into applications.

> Promoting code using tools such as JDeveloper or Eclipse is highly unreliable and not recommended as this approach requires a high degree of manual intervention that can introduce human error.
>
> A runtime deployment framework should standardize and centralize the way code is promoted between all environments. SOA Suite as well as OSB comes with utilities (for example, the ANT utilities or the WSLT scripts) that can be used and extended in order to create a robust deployment solution.

- **Exception handling framework**: One of the key success factors of an SOA implementation is the ability of the business as usual team (BAU) or the operations team to be able to support the solution once it has gone into production. Although this depends on many factors (for example, infrastructure, networks, storage, external systems, and so on), it is essential that errors are reported to the appropriate teams quickly and efficiently in order to minimize the risk of disruption to a business. The team running productions systems must be able to conduct root cause analysis and search for errors and logs in order to rapidly diagnose errors.

  An exception handling framework is a set of runtime component that are built with the sole purpose of standardizing the way exceptions of all types (for example, business faults, systems faults, remote faults, binding faults, composite and BPEL faults, among others) within the SOA Suite 11*g* or OSB 11*g* stack are handled, reported and diagnosed. By providing a consistent way of handling exceptions in different scenarios and for different message interactions patterns (for example, synchronous request/reply, asynchronous fire and forget, asynchronous call back, and so on), the complexity of supporting an SOA production system is dramatically reduced.

- **Continuous integration framework**: Ensuring that the code stored in the code repositories is always working and testable is one of the golden rules of continuous integration. By implementing tools such as **Jenkins** (`http://jenkins-ci.org/`) or **Cruise Control** (`http://cruisecontrol.sourceforge.net/`) to support continuous integration efforts in the SOA development lifecycle, the quality of the code, and the speed of delivery can improve dramatically. Having such components in a governance framework means that projects delivering SOA will have to align to the practices and guidelines specified, resulting in better-quality solutions and a faster delivery.
- **Testing framework**: Testing SOA Suite composites, OSB proxy and business services is not an easy task. Testing teams are not necessarily subject matter experts in the Oracle stack and, therefore, it is imperative that they are able to utilize standardized solutions to test the web services. There are several tools available that can help automate the testing of SOA services. Some of the most popular ones are:
    - **SoapUI**: It is a Java functional testing tool that allows creating and executing automated functional, regression, compliance, and loading tests against web services. **SoapUI** supports several protocols and technologies. For more information refer to `http://www.soapui.org/`.
    - **Test Suite**: It provides an automated test suite framework for creating and running repeatable tests on an SOA composite application. For more information refer to `http://docs.oracle.com/cd/E28280_01/dev.1111/e10224/bp_testsuite.htm`.
- **Code Compliance Inspector (CII)**: It is a JDeveloper add-on that checks for good coding practices in SOA Suite projects. More information is available in *Chapter 3, Introduction To Oracle Enterprise Repository*.

> Using some of these tools can be complex and time-consuming if not done properly. For this reason, the framework should also provide facilities and scripts that take away most of the complexity of using the tools, allowing the tester to focus on test execution and not on the tool configuration.

- **Provisioning framework**: This often-forgotten component of a framework is, without doubt, one of the main reasons why projects fail to deliver on time and to budget. Manually installing and configuring an Oracle Fusion Middleware application such as Oracle SOA Suite 11*g* can be very complex and can take several days. Furthermore, all installations are manually executed, increasing the chance of human error. Furthermore, ideally the installation should be easily reproducible for creating further environments with identical topologies. Human error and configuration problems can be the cause of severe delays when testing code, as it becomes extremely difficult to identify the root cause of issues. To avoid such issues and the many others that can result in a poor infrastructure configuration management, a framework should be constructed to automate software installation. The framework should make use of response files, **WebLogic Scripting Tool** (**WLST**), and scripting languages (such as ANT) to automate the installation and configuration of **Oracle Fusion Middleware** (**FM**) applications. Oracle FM provides several features and APIs that makes this task feasible, and the benefits of having such a component framework in a governance framework can be considerable.

The Implementation phase

This phase consists of the implementation of the Oracle SOA Governance solution in combination with the defined design-time and runtime Governance processes and standards. The result of this phase should allow projects to make full use of the SOA Governance framework in order to successfully implement the SOA solutions.

The next section will focus on providing more details on design-time and runtime governance.

Implementing SOA Design-time Governance

Design-time Governance can be defined as the combination of processes, tools, and people needed to support the analysis, design, and build phases of an SOA implementation.

Design-time SOA Governance should support the following project phases and SOA Asset lifecycle activities:

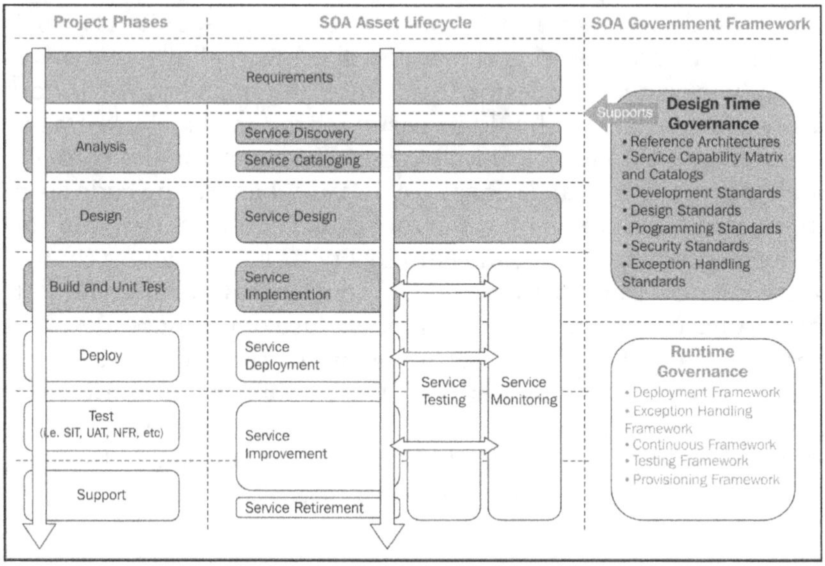

Identifying system requirements

During this phase, as the name suggests, the requirements for the project or project iteration are elaborated. For an SOA project, requirements are usually captured in the form of use cases, requirement backlogs (if following the Agile/Scrum methodology), user stories, and process models (for example, Level 1 to 3 BPMN models).

Requirements are meant to capture, in plain English, what the business expects from a particular solution (a system, a business process or even a single SOA service). Clearly, without properly documented requirements one should never proceed to other phases of the project. Unfortunately, as obvious as this may sound, many projects end up doing exactly this.

System analysis

Once all the functional and non-functional requirements have been identified, they must be validated, clearly documented, made unambiguous, actionable, measurable, testable, and traceable. Once this has been completed, the process of identifying candidate services to support the required functionality can commence.

For an SOA Asset, this means two things:

- **Service discovery**: This crucial phase of an SOA Asset lifecycle consists of identifying the SOA capabilities that are required in order to deliver a particular requirement, or set of requirements.
- **Service cataloging**: During service discovery all defined capabilities should be classified and mapped to the existing SOA Assets where possible. This process is defined as service cataloging. For example, if a new capability is needed and there isn't an existing asset that could be used or extended, then a new potential service is identified and should classified as a proposed service. This process is repeated many times during this phase, meaning that the list of services will grow. A normalization exercise should then take place in order to avoid duplication of services and inconsistencies.

  The SOA Governance framework should provide templates for service catalog and capability analysis to capture the outcome of this phase. The use of templates can dramatically improve the outcome and quality of this phase as the scope and expectations in terms of content and detail are known upfront.

System design

The output of the analysis phase will include a list of candidate services that will deliver a particular and traceable set of business requirements. The design phase translates these proposed services into actual service designs that are suitable and fit-for-purpose and that deliver the desired business functionality.

When designing a service the following assets are usually delivered:

- **Functional contract**: A functional contract is a document asset that defines the functionality that the service should deliver and the desired non-functional requirements such as service ownership, service-level agreements (SLAs), and service operational requirements (such as service availability).
- **Technical contract**: The technical contract defines signature (data elements that are needed in order to consume the service), protocols (for example, what binding will be used such as SOAP binding over HTTP) and policies (for example, message security or MTOM for sending attachments). A technical contract is usually defined during detail design and is reflected in the design document as well as in the WSDL and schema of the service.

- **Service detail design**: Contains a component and sequence diagram that describes the static and dynamic views of the service. A static view defines the SOA composites and SCA components required for a particular service. The dynamic view shows how the information flows between the composites, what manipulation takes place to the data (for example, transformation) and what orchestration is required (for example, in BPEL). A detail design should also cover the definition of the technical contract that encompasses definition of data mappings, WSDL and schemas definition, and unit test scripts.
- **Service versioning**: Versioning is a critical and fundamental activity required when designing services. Having the correct versioning strategy in place is critical for the success of an SOA implementation. All existing and/or identified assets should be subject to versioning.

> Service versioning is not to be confused with version control. The latter, also referred to as revision control or source control, is a discipline for managing code throughout the asset lifecycle. For example, a service at Version 1.0 may undergo to several code revisions before it even reaches production. Whereas the service version has a direct impact on the consumers of the service, consumers are unaware of the several code revisions the asset went through.

The following diagram illustrates the different Assets within a service that can be versioned:

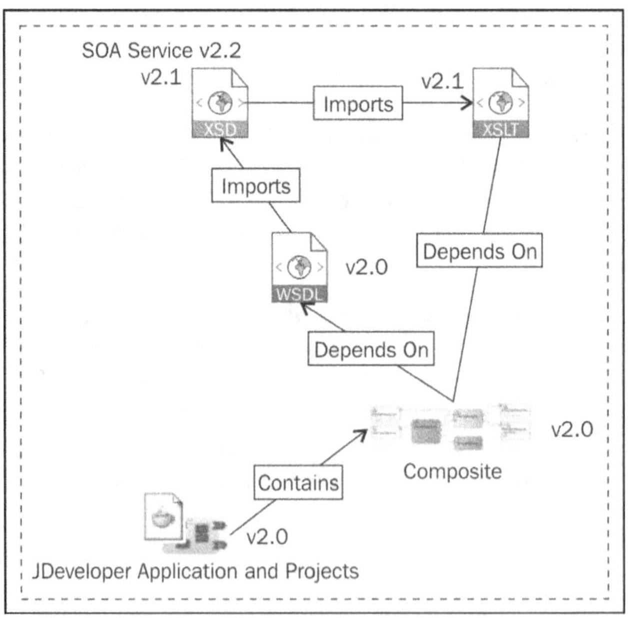

Regardless of what asset is being versioned it is fundamental to consider the following principles:

- **Minor versions**: A minor version usually represents a change to a service that is backward-and-forward compatible. Minor versions are usually represented with decimals. For example, in an XSD of Version 2.1, the decimal (1) represents the minor version.

> **Backward compatibility** means that newer clients must be able to consume older services without change. **Forward-compatibility** means that older clients must be able to consume newer services.

- **Major versions**: A major version of an asset represents a change to a service that breaks backward and/or forward compatibility. Major versions are usually represented with digits. For example, in an XSD of Version 2.1, the digit (2) represents the major version.
- **Terms of service**: A contract that formalizes the terms and conditions under which a service is provided and consumed. This will convey how clients and service providers deal with versions. For example, a term of service that communicates only three versions of a service that will be available—preview, current, and prior—and that clients are expected to move from prior to either current or preview within 1 year of the current service becoming prior.

SOA Governance framework artifacts such as architectural principles, reference architectures, and most notably design standards are critical to enforcing the quality of the design phase. Usually design standards deliver rich service taxonomy and a pattern language that can be leveraged to deliver rich functional/technical contracts and service detail designs.

System build

During this phase, services are constructed and unit-tested as per the service design. It is during this phase that the main assets of a service are created (for example, JDeveloper and Eclipse projects, test suites, XSLT or XQUERY transformations, BPEL processes, among others).

Following are some of the assets that are created while implementing a service:

- JDeveloper and/or Eclipse Projects (for OSB).
- Composites.

- Business Services and Proxy Services (for OSB).
- XSD Schemas.
- WSDLs.
- XSLT's transformations.
- Test Suites (for SOA Suite only) or SoapUI projects.

Ensuring that standards such as programming standards, exception handling frameworks, deployment frameworks, and continuous integration frameworks are adopted during the build and unit test phase are crucial to obtain the expected quality of code and to streamline the build and unit test phase.

Implementing SOA runtime governance

Runtime governance can be defined as the combination of processes, tools, and people needed to support the deployment, testing, and production support phases of an SOA implementation project.

Runtime SOA Governance should support the following project phases and activities of the SOA Asset lifecycle:

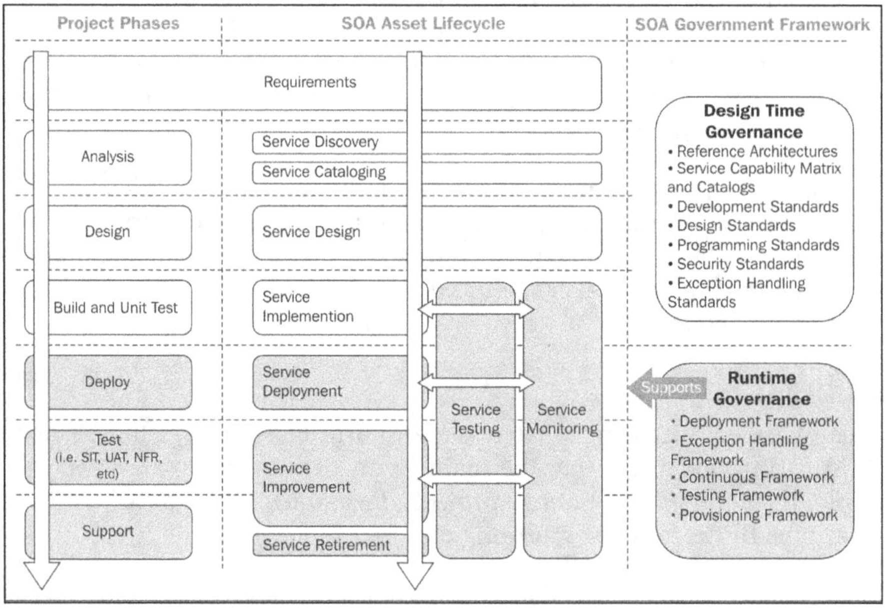

Deployment

This phase covers the promotion of code between the different environments of the project (for example, development, system integration test, user acceptance test, and so on).

Service deployment is achieved by executing the predefined processes and techniques that are required for deployment SOA Assets between environments. A deployment framework should ideally be employed during this stage, to automatically compile and promote services between environments without having to worry about manually changing the settings, such as environment specific endpoints or internal service dependencies.

Testing

The testing phase can be divided into different stages depending on the objectives of the tests being executed. In a typical project the testing phase consists of:

- **System test**: Targeted at testing the integrity of the system in isolation
- **System integration test**: Focused on testing that all of the systems in context can in fact interoperate with each other to deliver the required functionality
- **User acceptance test**: Business-driven test for business users to assert that the system delivers the desired business functionality
- **Performance testing**: The non-functional requirements to ensure that the system can handle the amount of usage that is expected once the system goes live

In the SOA Asset lifecycle, the three main activities that take place during each testing stage are:

- **Service monitoring**: This stage of the lifecycle spans across different stages of the project and its purpose is to ensure that all the services and core infrastructure components are fully operational and performing satisfactorily. This stage is also responsible for identifying any errors or issues that may arise as part of the monitoring process.
- **Service testing**: Utilizes available testing tools in order to ensure that the developed services are deployed into the SOA infrastructure, and that they fully address the business and technical requirements.

- **Service improvement**: Sourced from the outcomes of the service monitoring and service testing activities, this stage is responsible for implementing the changes that are required in order to ensure that the SOA infrastructure and/or the SOA services deliver the expected functional and non-functional requirements. Although this phase is really an extension of the service implementation phase, it is separated from it as the required tasks are executed by separate teams whose main responsibility is to apply bug fixes to the code and optimize system configuration settings.

It is during the test phase of an SOA project that the effectiveness, quality, and robustness of the SOA Governance framework become obvious. Should all the design-time and runtime components of an SOA Governance framework be successfully delivered, and the design-time standards properly enforced during development phases, then the tasks of monitoring and testing the services should be fairly straightforward and the complexity of this stage should be kept to a minimum. This is because the complexity of such tasks should have been hidden by the framework, and the project should be following a script and not trying to reinvent the wheel. For example, a robust testing framework should allow a project to test different types of services (request/reply, fire and forget, call backs, publish/subscribe, and split/join) with the minimum amount of effort. Furthermore, monitoring and troubleshooting tasks should be fairly straightforward, if features such as composite sensors and e-mail notifications were taken into consideration during design-time.

System support

Once a service is promoted into a production environment, it officially enters the support phase. The support phase is most definitely not the end of the service lifecycle, however; in fact, far from it. SOA Governance should also include monitoring of the SOA infrastructure to feedback critical information that can be used to optimize SOA Assets (services and automated processes). For example, BAM dashboards should be employed where it is appropriate to monitor the efficiency of processes. Activities such as service testing, service monitoring, and service improvement should remain active during the operational lifetime of service.

Once a service has served its purpose and has been deprecated or is no longer needed, then the following activity should take place:

- **Service retirement**: Service retirement encompasses more than just disabling and undeploying a service. It also covers the process of managing dependencies to ensure that no other systems, applications, processes, or services are negatively affected by the retirement of the service. This task can become quite complex, especially if for whatever reason it is not clear who the service consumers are, or what functionality is exposed. All of these dependencies should be properly managed in order to ensure that the business is unaffected during a retirement exercise.

Roles and responsibilities

As described earlier in the chapter, it is only when the processes and tools are combined with people and appropriate decision making, that the governance is fully realized. Having an accountability and responsibility framework is crucial for people to acknowledge the scope of their duties, and their participation on an SOA implementation.

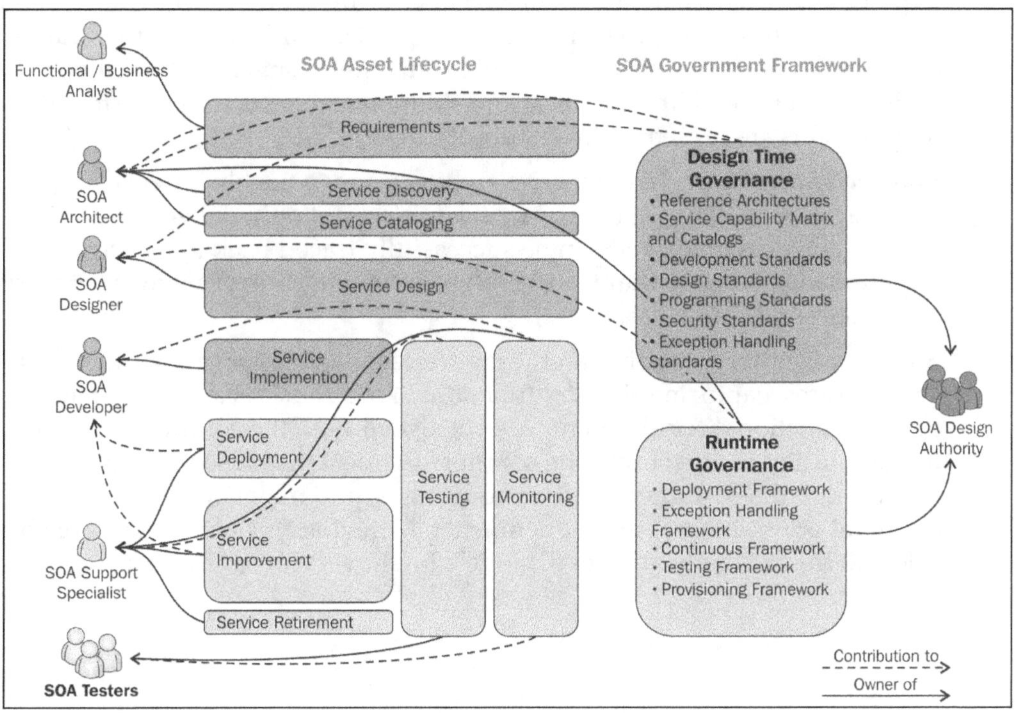

The diagram describes an accountability framework that mainly consists of two categories of roles:

- **Owner**: Responsible for the execution of a task (the creation and maintenance of an asset, or the execution of a task) and accountable for its proper execution
- **Contributor**: Collaborates towards the execution of a task (the creation and maintenance of an asset or the execution of a task); however, does not share accountability for the results realized from it

The accountability framework suggests that the following people and roles are required in order to implement end-to-end design-time and runtime governance:

- **C-Level executive sponsors**: Although not depicted in the diagram, C-Level sponsorship is imperative in any SOA implementation. Having the right level of sponsorship will ensure that the organizational, behavioral, and cultural changes needed to implement the governance processes and procedures are embraced by the enterprise and not ignored.
- **Functional/Business analyst**: Responsible for producing suitable functional requirements such as functional design document, future process model, and/or business rules catalog. The functional analyst should, among other things, engage with the business to ensure that all the functional requirements are well understood and with the technical and solution architects to ensure that the requirements are presented in an appropriate format.
- **Enterprise architect**: An enterprise architect is responsible for ensuring that the solution being delivered by the project not only delivers to the desired business goals and can be successfully traced back to its original requirements, but also that the overall solution aligns to the wider enterprise strategies and standards.
- **Solution architect**: Solution architects are responsible for producing Solution architectures, capturing the non-functional requirements and also ensuring that the functional requirements are consistent with the solution as defined in the solution architecture. The solution architect may also participate and/or influence the definition of detailed designs, and may take part in the approval or rejection of these documents. Note that this is a well established role and this text only aims to provide a brief overview of the role.

- **SOA architect**: The SOA architect is a subject matter expert (SME) in the technologies in context (for example Oracle SOA Suite 11*g*) but also understands and practices general architecture principles. The role of the SOA architect is to:
    1. Analyze all of the requirements and ensure that these conform to the expected level of quality.
    2. Discover and catalog the SOA Assets and ensure that these can be backward or forward traceable.
    3. Provide technical leadership and guidance to the design and development teams.
- **SOA designer**: Responsible for providing suitable detailed designs that successfully deliver all of the desire business and technical functionally. The designer is also responsible for providing further clarification and guidance to the development teams. An SOA designer will also the create XML assets such as WSDLs and schemas, and define the unit test scripts that should be executed by the developer.
- **SOA developer**: Responsible for building and unit testing SOA services. The developer is also responsible for packaging the code ready for release, and for producing any relevant documentation that is required to support the deployment of the code (such as release notes). The SOA developer may partially contribute to the deployment and monitoring of services.
- **SOA testers**: Test teams are responsible for defining and executing the test scripts to support different testing stages (for example, system test, system integration test, user acceptance test, performance test, among others).
- **SOA support specialist**: Responsible for the deployment of SOA services between different environments and also monitoring of the SOA infrastructure. Once a service has gone live, the support specialist is also responsible for performing bug fixes and regression testing on the code.
- **Configuration manager**: Owner and gatekeeper of code packs and releases. This role, among other things, coordinates and decides which releases can be promoted between environments.
- **SOA design authority**: Not a single role, but instead a collection of different roles and people that together have delegated authority and shared accountability for creation of design-time and runtime governance frameworks, and the enforcement of these into different phases of a project.

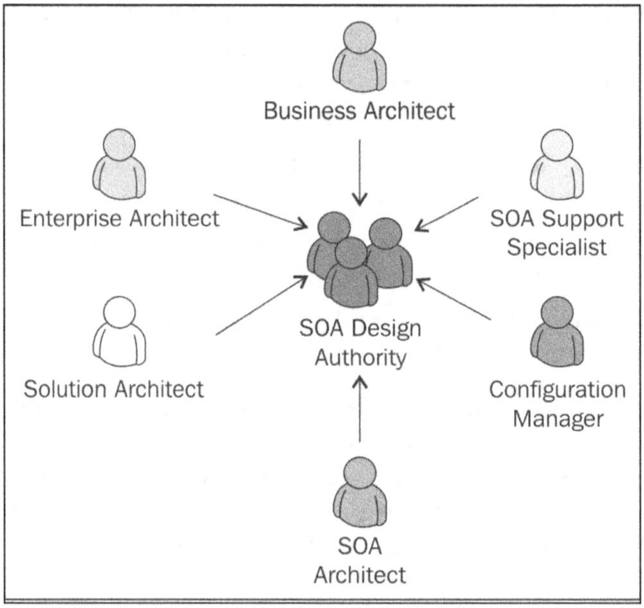

As can be seen in the preceding diagram, the SOA design authority should encompass all of the capability domains. An SOA design authority group should have well-defined **terms of reference** and should meet at least biweekly with the objective to cover topics such as SOA pipeline, project issues and status, review and approval of the designs, and definition of roadmaps.

Summary

Through the different sections of this chapter, we have introduced the fundamental concepts that facilitate the SOA Governance. We have discussed the absolute requirements for proper governance to fully realize the business benefits that can be attained through the successful implementation of service-orientated architectures. Topics such as business stakeholder buy-in, SOA maturity assessment, and SOA Roadmaps have been discussed and elaborated in detail together with the essential processes and procedures that constitute the full SOA Governance. We have explored the full service lifecycle from requirements gathering to service deployment and monitoring, and how frameworks can be employed to expedite service implementation and enforce quality. Finally, we introduced the organizational changes necessary to oversee the successful SOA implementations.

The following chapters of this book will make use of these concepts but will delve deeper into the steps needed to implement the SOA Governance using Oracle SOA Governance solution.

2
Implementation Case Study

This chapter introduces a case study that will be further developed throughout this book. It will introduce a fictitious company that is looking to implement SOA Governance following a maturity assessment and a SOA Roadmap elaboration. The case study will help you to understand the concepts being presented in this book, as well as how to apply them to implement Oracle SOA Governance in an easily digestible form by illustrating the typical problems faced by organizations introducing governance, and how the benefits derived from its inception must be measurable and tangible.

The case study is based on actual scenarios experienced by the authors and therefore should provide a realistic view of the key challenges faced when implementing SOA Governance, and how they can be overcome.

Case study description

Weir & Bell Telecom is a manufacturer and retailer of mobile phones and devices that has experienced rapid growth, following a number of highly successful marketing campaigns, and aggressive growth on the high street and internet. It has a very strong line up of products that are considered niche products and that result in high profit margins.

With competitors poised to release similar products, the company realizes that, in order to achieve its business objectives and thus maintain its leadership position, it needs to vastly improve and exploit its IT processes and infrastructure. Having grown rapidly, the IT department has not developed in line with the business strategy and the board has recently appointed a new **Chief Information Officer (CIO)** to oversee the IT department, and to develop an IT strategy that is closely aligned with the business strategy. The aim is to allow the organization to increase the efficiency and responsiveness of its supply chain processes by making effective use of digitized processes.

Weir & Bell Telecom has been quite progressive in its IT development to date, and has been using SOA for a number of years. However, SOA has been employed tactically rather than strategically. Furthermore, the company had made some initial investment in Oracle Fusion Middleware products such as Oracle SOA Suite 11*g*, WebCenter, and Oracle Database. The new CIO has identified SOA as a key enabler to allow the IT department to respond in an agile manner to business and regulatory changes.

The assessment

The new CIO immediately commissioned a review of the existing SOA infrastructure and an assessment of the maturity of service delivery. The assessment was executed in three primary phases as depicted in the following diagram:

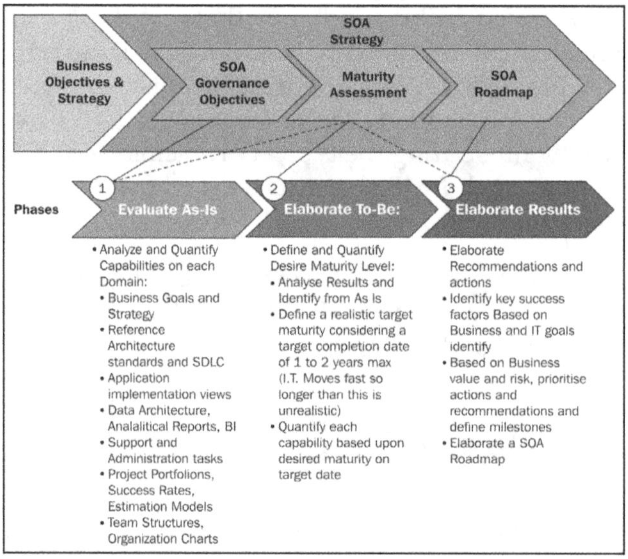

In order to gather all the information in a structured way and to subsequently quantify the results in a meaningful fashion, the Oracle Maturity Model was employed. The model was used to quantify each capability domain using a tool created by the company (similar to the tool distributed along with the book). This allowed the CIO to obtain an accurate view of the "As-Is" situation and to develop and quantify a realistic "To-Be" model.

The CIO set aside a period of three weeks (one week per phase) for the execution of the assessment, the elaboration of recommendations and the resulting SOA Roadmap. As the timeframe was very aggressive, it was agreed that the organization should commission the consultancy services of a niche player with a background in SOA and SOA Governance.

The phases of the assessment consisted of the following:

- **Evaluate the As-Is**: This phase consisted of gathering current information from each capability domain and quantifying it as accurately as possible. The main deliverable of this phase was the assessment model populated with the As-Is data.
- **Evaluate the To-Be**: In this phase, a target maturity level was defined for each capability based upon realistic and viable assumptions. For example, a period of one year was assumed as the target period to achieve the desired maturity. It was considered that a longer period might prove too long in a rapidly evolving market and would result in W&B losing its competitive edge in the retail space.
- **Elaborate the results**: In this phase, the outcome of the maturity assessment was mapped to a SOA Roadmap by specifying how the gap between the As-Is and the To-Be could be addressed.

The results

The results of the SOA Maturity Assessment mentioned in the previous section were as shown in the following diagram:

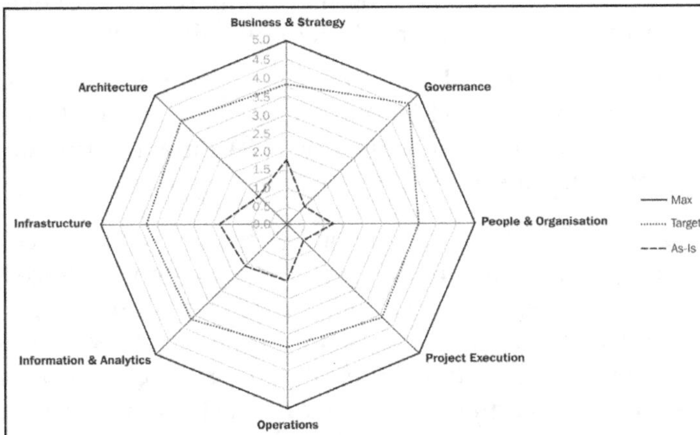

Domain	Max	Target	As-In
	Scores		
Business & Strategy	5.0	3.8	1.8
Governance	5.0	4.7	0.7
People & Organisation	5.0	3.5	1.3
Project Execution	5.0	3.6	0.6
Operations	5.0	3.3	1.6
Information & Analytics	5.0	3.7	1.6
Infrastructure	5.0	3.8	1.9
Architecture	5.0	4.0	1.1
Average	**5.0**	**3.8**	**1.3**

The consultancy conducting the maturity assessment identified a number of key challenges as follows:

- The IT department has grown immaturely while trying to constantly react to the demands placed on it by strong retail sales. Consequently, there has been a lack of overall architecture and governance, with IT developments being very tactical in nature. Each business unit within Weir & Bell Telecom has commissioned and developed its own IT systems with little regard for what had already been developed previously.
- Partly due to the lack of architecture and visibility over existing assets, many IT projects have been delivered late and there has been little reuse of existing assets. This has resulted in a poor perception of IT by key business stakeholders.
- Development teams have had little guidance; immature processes and an ill-defined software development lifecycle have resulted in estimates for development being at best optimistic and at worst poorly thought through. This has caused severe problems to the business as IT systems are continually developed late despite best intentions and lots of overtime. Poor estimation models and lack of architecture were identified as key contributors to poor planning, execution, and dependency management.
- SOA has not lived up to expectations with duplicate services being developed on a per-project basis with virtually no reuse of existing assets. This was attributed to the distinct lack of overall governance.
- In occasions, services were being overused, meaning used above the maximum throughput for which the service was designed to support. This resulted in performance penalties in the SOA infrastructure and therefore damaging the user experience.

The assessment concluded that, in order to bring the current maturity level of 1.3 to the required level of 3.8, strong architecture and a new governance framework were required. This would result in other dependent disciplines being intrinsically matured (such as project management and support). The following diagram illustrates the identified health status of the different areas of Governance when compared to a Reference Governance Framework (such as the one described in *Chapter 1, SOA Governance*):

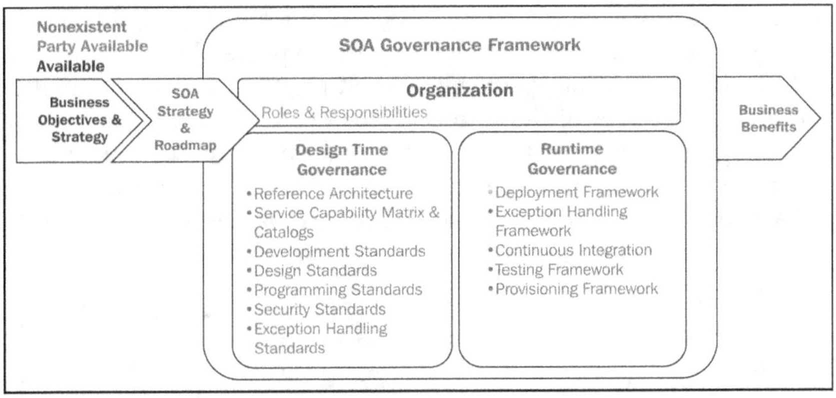

Furthermore, the outcome of the assessment suggested that, because of a lack of overall strategy and almost nonexistent design-time and runtime governance, SOA initiatives had failed to deliver any measurable business benefits.

The objectives

The CIO responded to the results of the SOA Maturity Assessment by creating an enterprise architect team whose responsibility was to ensure that business needs were clearly reflected in all future IT development efforts, and that the underlying infrastructure was able to scale to meet business demands. The team was also responsible for rationalizing existing systems and services and for reducing or removing redundancy.

One of the first actions for the architecture team was to create a reference architecture that specified a blueprint for all IT systems within Weir & Bell Telecom. The reference architecture supported IT agility by putting SOA at the heart of system development. This would allow the IT department to keep pace with the demands of the business moving forward and facilitate the introduction of new sales channels as identified in the business strategy for growth.

The enterprise architecture team also set out clear objectives for SOA Governance. Moreover, it was concluded that, in order to achieve these objectives, appropriate tooling would be required to support the desired processes and responsibilities. While the targeted objectives of the framework were known (as it can be appreciated from the following diagram), the tools needed to support these objectives was yet to be determined. Invitations to tender were consequently sent out to the main software vendors and a selection process was undertaken to determine which could provide the infrastructure required to underpin the governance effort.

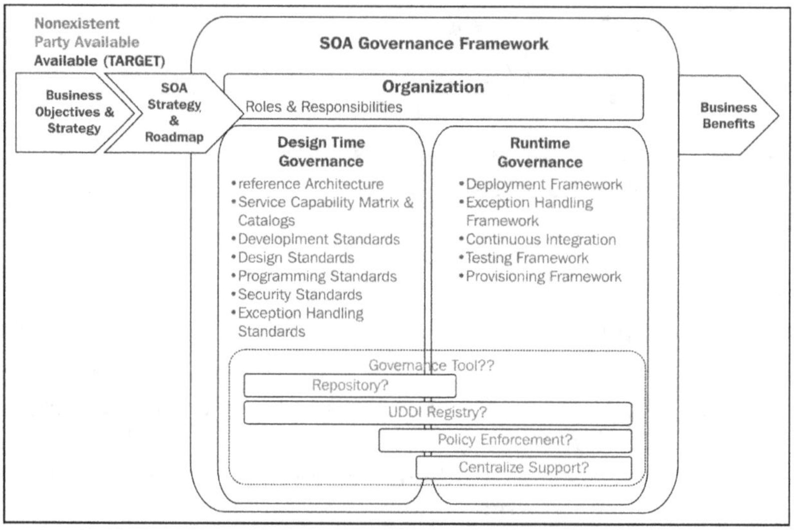

A key driver for product selection was support for design-time governance, encompassing service discovery, and cataloging for reuse, dependency management, service lifecycle, and support for the enforcement of policies and standards. The product was also required to support effective runtime governance with support for a common UDDI registry, runtime policy enforcement (including security), exception handling, service deployment, and system monitoring.

After an exhaustive product selection exercise, the Oracle SOA Governance Solution was chosen as the preferred software toolset to support the implementation of SOA Governance at Weir & Bell Telecom.

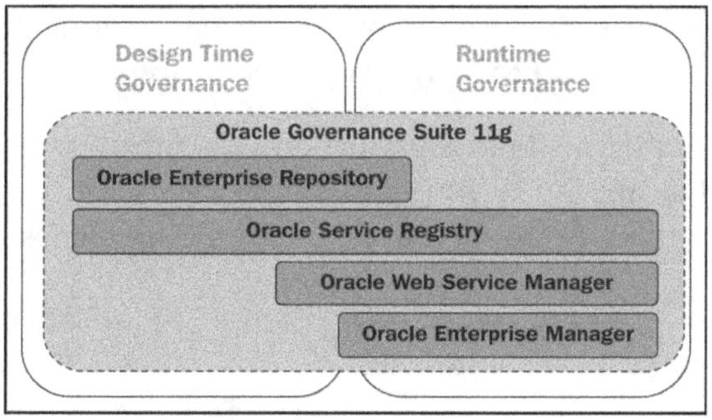

As the preceding diagram suggests, the decision was made mainly for two reasons. Firstly, the product offering from Oracle was extremely strong at supporting design-time and runtime Governance, and therefore was highly aligned with the team's objectives for its governance effort. Secondly, as Oracle already had a considerable footprint in the technology landscape at Weir & Bell telecom, it was concluded that implementing the Oracle SOA Governance Solution would have considerable benefits as these products were certified to integrate with other Oracle Fusion Middleware products already implemented in the company, such as the Oracle SOA Suite 11*g*.

The business case

The enterprise architecture team, under the guidance of the new CIO, created a compelling business case that was presented in the board of directors at Weir & Bell Telecom. The outcome of this presentation was pivotal to transforming the image of the IT department, which was perceived as being inefficient and slow to react to business changes, and also to secure any needed funding.

SOA was at the heart of the business case. The CIO recognized SOA to be the primary vehicle for introducing the agility required to meet the aggressive demands placed on the IT function by the retail arm of Weir & Bell Telecom. The maturity assessment was an essential part of the business case and it gave the CIO a real understanding of the strengths and weaknesses of his department and allowed him to focus on areas that needed to be addressed immediately. The alignment of IT strategy to business strategy was fundamental to realizing maximum **return on investment** (**ROI**) in terms of services and infrastructure.

The business case, together with supporting evidence gathered during the SOA Maturity Assessment, highlighted how real synergy between IT and the business could result in automation and improvement of vital processes in the supply chain. Rationalization of the underlying infrastructure and a move to virtualization, together with the elimination of redundancy in terms of software applications and services across business units, could lead to significant cost savings across the organization.

The following diagram depicts how a governed SOA implementation could significantly reduce the number of integration points and hand-offs between business units, paving the way to increased process efficiencies and cost savings:

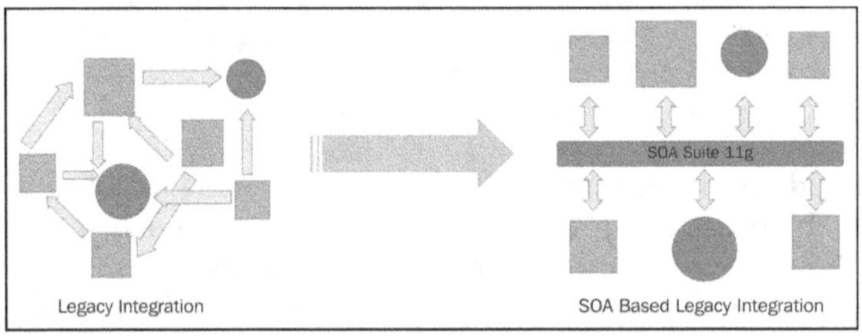

The business case discussed how the introduction of Oracle Enterprise Repository to support design-time Governance was essential to ensuring that services were rationalized across the enterprise. Better insight into existing services together with the introduction of design patterns as part of the governance effort would give rise to services that were more granular and more consumable for new processes. This in turn would allow IT to introduce new sales channels by utilizing existing services that communicated with back end order and logistics systems. It described how the reuse of service assets led to the decreased cost of development while the introduction of a new **Software Development Lifecycle** (**SDLC**) and continuous integration would lead to better quality software being produced by developers. This in turn would have a huge impact on the test department who were traditionally viewed in a bad light by management. Previously, quality was almost invariably introduced at the testing stage as testers battled with poor quality code leading to a huge testing cycle that in turn led to late delivery of software and increased costs.

The Oracle Enterprise Repository combined with the Oracle Service Registry to enhance runtime Governance allowed Weir & Bell Telecom to share its services with third parties and preferred suppliers, leading to further efficiency savings in the supply chain processes. It illustrated how a large number of requisitions could be automatically raised when supplies fell below a threshold value; depending on business rules, some could even be automatically approved and sent to suppliers without human intervention. This would lead to much smoother delivery of important components and reduced component lead time while allowing the manufacturing department to have a far better control of inventory; all key factors in allowing the business to react to successful marketing and sales campaigns.

Subsequent sections of the business case focused on justifying the cost of implementing governance and illustrated how the benefits would outweigh any spending in a relatively short period of time. This provided the board with key metrics for return on investment. It documented how savings could be realized in different areas. For example, on the current SOA implementation there was little or no reuse of existing services. Huge savings could be realized in the software development costs (CAPEX), by promoting code reuse by strict design-time Governance and by enforcing policies using Oracle Enterprise Repository.

The business case also showed how reuse and policy enforcement would have a positive impact on operating support costs (OPEX), since with proper governance the number of services would increase gradually and not exponentially. Therefore, fewer people are required to support the services and also tasks that are usually complex, such as troubleshooting, would become more predictable since all services would implement known patterns and utilize a common exception handling framework. It is further explained that, by employing **Oracle Web Services Manager** (**OWSM**) to secure services in the production environment, the code itself could be separated from the security implementation, bringing with it the ability to declaratively define security for all service implementations, and delegate definition of security policies to the security department. OWSM also provided the ability to monitor whether SLAs were being met.

Another key justification presented in the business case centered around how critical business logic embedded in old and extremely complex legacy systems could be extracted and presented as web services, and could be utilized in key value chain processes. The SOA layer would be used to provide an abstraction layer between legacy systems and the business processes themselves. This would allow the legacy applications to be replaced at a later date without having to change the process itself. The impact of change would be absorbed by the service implementation and transformation logic, the process being unaffected as the service interface would not change. This would, in turn, facilitate legacy modernization that was attractive to the board of directors and it served to illustrate how SOA could be used in different ways to deliver business benefits.

Moving forward, all service implementations would be written to exacting standards to ease their consumption in the future processes and Oracle Enterprise Repository would act as a single source of truth for the SOA portfolio. Architects and analysts would be able to use the repository for version control, dependency tracking, impact analysis, and service discovery and cataloging. In short, the entire service lifecycle would be properly governed both at design-time and at runtime.

The business case concluded by explaining how SOA Governance would lead to better management of the heterogeneous SOA landscape and would deliver greater visibility of end-to-end service networks and better tracking of usage, allowing the IT department to report on return on investment for SOA assets across the enterprise. All of this would ultimately transform into benefits to the business in the form of costs savings and greater flexibility. In short, a win-win situation for the business.

The business case was presented to the board of directors and the feedback was very positive. The budget to begin the roadmap activities was approved. However, the board demanded that all benefits, as documented on the business case, should be supported with critical success factors that could be measured at different checkpoints throughout the SOA program.

Critical success factors

Based on the feedback from the board of directors, the new CIO of Weir & Bell Telecom placed the monitoring and measurement of critical success factors and business metrics at the heart of the architectural effort. By aligning the IT strategy with the business strategy and being able to report back to the board on the return on investment for IT-related projects, he would be able to demonstrate the effectiveness of IT across the enterprise. The key here was to prove that the use of SOA would result in significant cost savings while also increasing development productivity and reducing software maintenance costs. The resulting performance improvements were expected to have a significant impact on business agility and enable the organization to respond quickly to competitive challenges.

The critical success factors for the architectural effort were heavily reliant on the fact that development and support costs would be reduced by enforcing governance, most notably in the reuse of existing SOA assets. The reasoning behind this proposition is explained in the following paragraphs.

A SOA asset's estimated value is based on the development costs avoided by reusing rather than recreating. By reusing existing assets, an organization avoids both the costs of repeatedly developing the same functionality and the cost of maintaining different implementations of the same functionality. Thus, re-use consolidates functionality and reduces redundancy. The more that re-use occurs, the greater the savings as the diagram suggests.

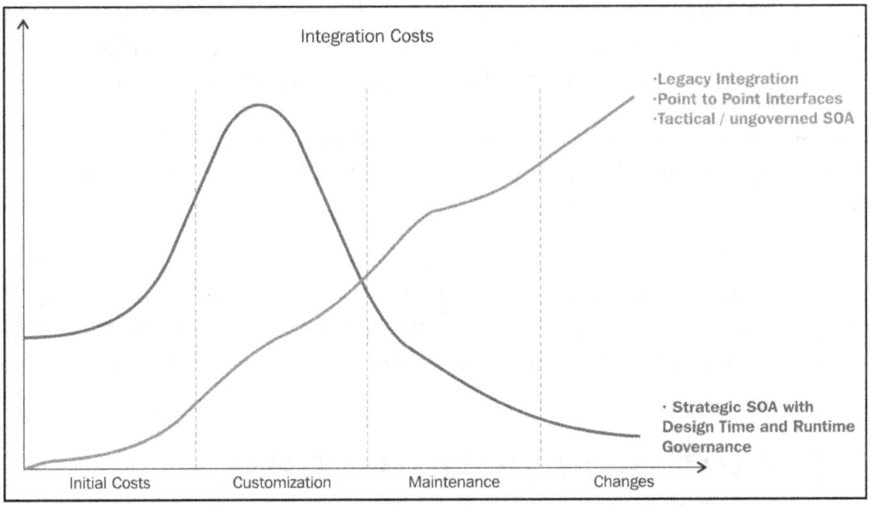

The difference between the time a developer would spend building an asset for single use and the time needed to use a reusable version of that asset is referred to as Predicted Net Hours Saved. This represents the development cost avoided through re-use of the asset. The following formula was used to make these calculations:

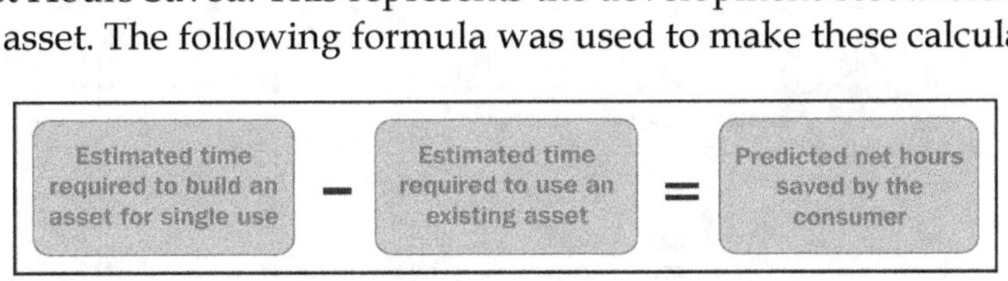

Establishing the expected ROI of assets within the portfolio requires consideration of the annual usage of each asset, and the conversion of the total Predicted Net Hours Saved to a monetary value.

An enterprise registry/repository with the appropriate capabilities is essential in tracking progress towards organizational SOA and re-use goals. It should be utilized to track each Asset's value, state (defined, designed, implemented, upgraded, and retired); then, as Assets are used, the registry/repository should gather the necessary data to generate reports that details an Asset's value. This provides a way for organizations to compare the estimated ROI to the actual returns in an SOA initiative.

While reusable assets may vary in their size, scope, and purpose, their estimated valuation and the accurate reporting of their actual value are essential in guiding SOA Governance efforts to ensure sustainable alignment with business goals.

SOA Governance is essential for increasing the value of assets by insuring their alignment with and support of policies and standards as established at the architectural, IT, and corporate levels.

An asset's value is determined not solely by its reusability or re-use, but also by the contribution it makes in moving the organization toward its business goals. To that end, the importance of effective SOA lifecycle governance in guiding the design, development, support, and retirement of assets cannot be overstated.

A new reference architecture

The enterprise architecture team began by creating a new reference architecture that would be strongly aligned to the business strategy. This is presented in the following diagram:

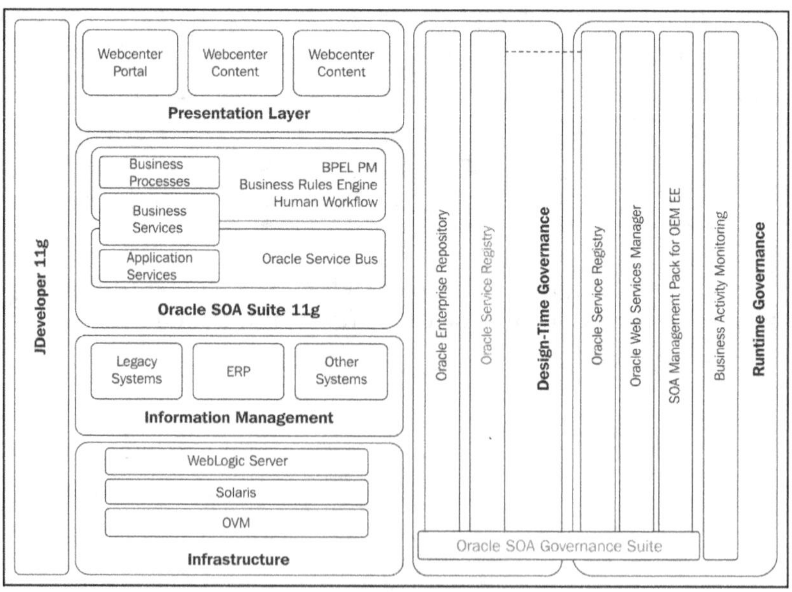

The IT strategy was developed with the target operating model in mind including the requirement for new sales channels. The underlying infrastructure was ported to a private cloud-based model to allow for the rapid growth predicted by the business and also in light of expected acquisitions that were due to be made over the coming years. SOA was endorsed as the preferred architectural style for software development with existing and new commercially available and off-the-shelf (COTS) products having little or no customizations moving forward.

Proposed IT developments were assessed and aligned to the IT strategy with a number of projects scrapped and new initiatives introduced.

The new governance process

A new governance process was introduced across the enterprise to reduce redundancy of all software development efforts between business units. A clearly defined SOA Roadmap was created indicating how the current state of the IT organization could move as efficiently as possible to the new To-Be model.

A whole suite of governance standards was created, documented, and distributed to the development teams. These standards clearly specified the development, programming, and deployment standards that were to be adopted for all SOA initiatives enterprise wide.

Design-time governance was introduced, covering all aspects of service discovery, design, versioning, and decommissioning. The Oracle Enterprise Repository was introduced to support design-time Governance by ensuring that all service metadata and XML artifacts were accessible across the enterprise in an effort to promote re-use, and therefore to ensure that key benefits were realized from existing investment in services.

Oracle Enterprise Repository was also used to harvest assets enterprise-wide, ensuring that existing investment was not lost as part of the governance initiative.

Oracle JDeveloper was already used by the development teams for creating services. Integration of the JDeveloper SOA development environment with the Repository and Service Registry was seen as a key requirement to enable developers to access and synchronize between the repository and the development environment to automatically harvest assets and enhance productivity.

Runtime governance standards were defined and documented. A new deployment framework was created to standardize system set up and service deployment. This would enable IT infrastructure to grow efficiently as the business demands increased. Oracle Service Registry was introduced to facilitate rapid discovery and consumption of existing services.

Improved visibility

Another key recommendation highlighted as part of the SOA Maturity Assessment was the requirement to improve runtime visibility of SOA assets. As a result, the runtime engines (such as the Oracle Service Registry and Oracle Enterprise Manager) were integrated with Oracle Enterprise Repository to ensure that key metrics around service utilization and service re-use were feedback into the asset's details page. Having design-time and runtime systems integrated, empowered project managers, SOA architects, and designers to enforce policies around service re-use, which ultimately accounted in savings to the company.

Standardized error reporting and system monitoring was introduced with **Oracle Enterprise Manager (OEM)** being adopted across the enterprise. **Business Activity Monitoring (BAM)** was also introduced on selected business processes, following a review of business metrics and key performance indicators with the business. Oracle BAM and OEM gave the support team increased visibility into application performance and availability, allowing them to more proactively monitor problems and suggest improvements to a number of key business processes. In some cases, process lifecycles were decreased by as much as 60 percent and cost savings in one area ran into thousands of pounds. This exercise rapidly improved the availability of essential services and processes, which in turn provided a genuine real good factor to the business. The latter was important as the board started to fund further process improvement projects.

Furthermore, continuous integration was implemented so that software was tested regularly ensuring that the quality of software was much higher than had previously been the case.

The SOA Roadmap highlighted further areas of business automation and senior business executives were able to understand and digest how IT could now work hand in hand with the business to introduce real cost savings and to streamline the supply chain further.

The exercise conducted for identifying key business metrics and KPIs also helped the business to focus on important processes that were key to the success of Weir & Bell Telecom. Understanding the business metrics helped the stakeholders to stop and realize a number of business improvements particularly in areas where previously hand-offs between business units were creating unnecessary delays and inefficiencies. Very importantly, IT and the business now had the ability to measure, qualitatively and quantitatively, key business areas, allowing the board for the first time to have a real understanding of the impact of IT investment moving forward. This could range from bottom line costs savings to simply improving the lives of some of its staff by freeing them from tasks that could otherwise be automated, thus freeing them up for more value-added activities.

Summary

In this chapter we described a case study based on a real live SOA Governance implementation as experienced by the authors. The chapter illustrated how the governance concepts described in *Chapter 1, SOA Governance* such as maturity assessments, reference architectures, SOA assets, and design-time and runtime Governance, were put into practice in order to successfully implement SOA Governance into an organization.

This chapter emphasized the importance of having the right level of sponsorship and buy-in from the business before embarking on a governance implementation. This was achieved up front, since without business sponsorship the benefits that SOA can bring to the table would have not been visible or achievable. Additionally, the chapter described how by presenting a business case with clear business benefits and objectives it was possible to qualitatively and quantitatively measure success. This in turn allowed the board of directors to understand the positive impact that IT and SOA can bring to business.

The chapter concluded by describing how the Oracle SOA Governance toolset was implemented alongside the company's existing Oracle SOA and technological landscape in order to deliver design-time and runtime Governance.

The chapters that follow will elaborate, in detail, how Oracle Enterprise Repository, Oracle Service Registry, Web Service Manager, and the SOA Management Pack are implemented in order to realize the benefits described previously.

3

Introduction to Oracle Enterprise Repository

This chapter will cover a high-level architecture of the product, the different software components that are part of the product architecture, and the core concepts and capabilities available in Oracle Enterprise Repository. The chapter also describes concepts such as managed **Asset** visibility using Oracle Enterprise Repository Solution Packs, such as the Harvester Solution Pack and the Base Data Pack.

An overview of Oracle Enterprise Repository

Oracle Enterprise Repository (**OER**) is Oracle's flagship product for supporting the **design-time Governance** aspects of the **Oracle SOA Governance** solution. The runtime components of the solution integrate with OER to provide data for metrics such as service usability and service re-use, providing important information to assist with the design-time decisions.

OER delivers critical information to architects, SOA designers, and developers at design time to empower them to make more informed decisions when designing services. For example, determining if there are opportunities for service re-use rather than create new ones when updating a service catalogue, or determining if there is a risk of a service being overused.

The repository also provides vital information to business analysis and business architects about the available capabilities. This can be extremely useful when, for example, elaborating a process model that can benefit from existing capabilities, such as to submit a purchase order, search a customer database, or address validation.

OER is feature-rich with access to features configured, based on the roles. This allows organizations to implement existing **Role Based Access Control** (**RBAC**) models and therefore limit access to Assets based on user role.

In OER an Asset is any document, piece of code (XML, Java, or any other programming language or notation), or any other electronic document that can be considered to add value to an SOA implementation. For example, the following Asset relationship model describes the different types of Assets that are usually related to an SOA service. OER is capable of harvesting different sources and subsequently building up an Asset relationship view similar to the diagram:

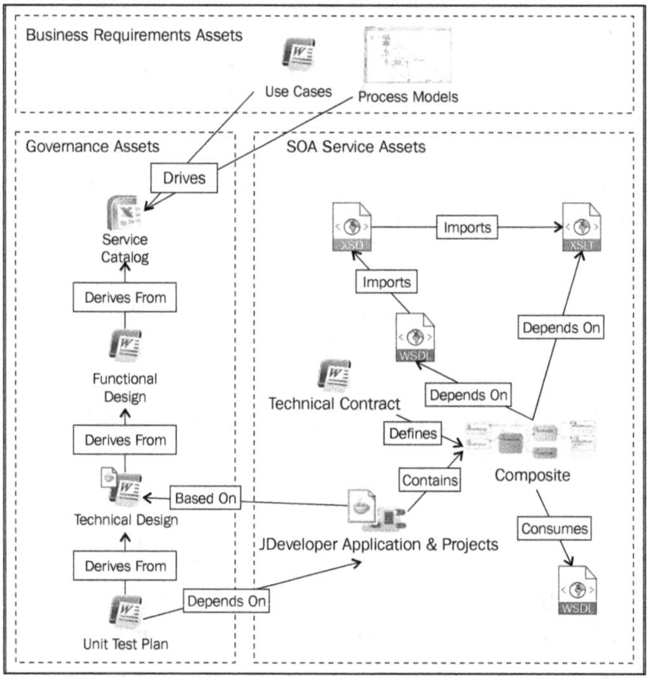

OER allows for Assets that have been harvested to undergo an approval workflow using an in-built Asset workflow module. During this approval process, design-time policies can be enforced. For example, Assets that comply with existing policies can be accepted while those that do not can be rejected. Approvers in the lifecycle process can upload documents to provide evidence in support of their decisions. Furthermore, consumers of the Assets can reference information to assist in the decision to use a particular service.

Some of the features that are available within OER to support the service lifecycle are:

- Direct integration with IDEs (such as JDeveloper and Eclipse) allowing the prescription of Assets for new projects and the easy browsing and consumption of existing Assets
- An Asset Harvester that automatically populates OER with SOA Assets and tracks updates to artifacts automatically
- A built-in process engine with a set of standard processes that can be modified to meet organizations' governance process workflows
- Built-in automated notification on a selection of lifecycle events, plus discretionary notification of Asset subscribers
- An event engine that can publish repository events to any process service endpoint
- A bi-directional registry exchange feature that keeps information synchronized between the enterprise repository and the service registry
- A rich SOAP-based API that allows organizations to programmatically update the repository, keeping it in sync with the IT and business environment that it describes
- Summary of runtime performance metrics from runtime environments
- Rich Analytics features such as the amount of re-use of services in the entire lifecycle, compliance scorecards, and runtime performance metrics

> Source: `http://docs.oracle.com/cd/E28280_01/doc.1111/e16581/install.htm`.

In summary, OER enhances Design Time Governance and allows for policies to enforce on services from the moment of conception, through design, development, and rollout stages of a project. Furthermore the ability to feed OER with runtime metrics (such as service utilization and degree of re-use) together with the rich reporting features helps architects to provide tangible evidence of the ROI for all services.

Understanding OER architecture

The OER product architecture is complex and often difficult to understand since there does not exist a single architecture diagram available that describes it. Oracle does not provide an Enterprise Deployment Guide as they do for other products such as the SOA Suite. For this reason, in order to assist readers with their understanding of the product architecture, we have created a hybrid architecture view of the core components that make up the OER system. This is shown as follows.

As the diagram suggests, the OER architecture does not rely on a single set of binaries deployed into a single WebLogic instance; instead, the product itself depends on other binaries and applications, such as Oracle Business Process Manager 10*g* and Java Web Start, to deliver its functionality:

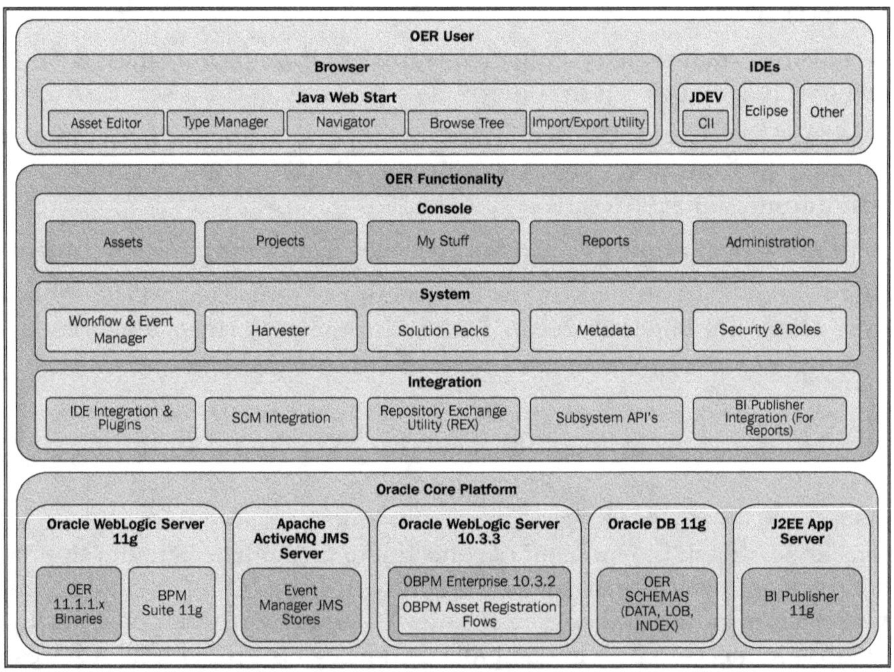

As we can see in the preceding diagram, we have divided the components that build up the architecture into three main groups: **OER Core Platform, OER Functionality**, and **OER Users**.

OER Core Platform

The components of the OER Core Platform are the building blocks of the OER ecosystem. If any of the components depicted on the diagram are unavailable, installed, or configured incorrectly, the system will probably malfunction or misbehave. It is therefore critical that the architect responsible for the delivery of the logical and physical architectures for an OER implementation clearly understands these components and their responsibilities within the system.

> This section does *not* provide a step-by-step guide on the installation of the product or its systems pre requisites. Please refer to *Appendix, Installation Tips and Techniques* for a summary of the installation steps required to install the components depicted in the OER Core Platform component of the diagram.

Oracle WebLogic Server 11*g* and 10.3.3

As the OER product resulted from the acquisition of BEA, most of the OER functionality sits on top of the **Oracle WebLogic Application Server**. Furthermore OER 11*g* makes use of **Oracle Business Process Manager (OPBM) 10.3.2 Enterprise Edition** for the implementation of the pre-built **Asset Registration Flows** (the exact versions are required as this means that the registration flows are certified against this specific version).

> Note that, as of OER patch set 6 (11.1.1.7), Oracle supports the use of **Oracle BPM Suite 11*g*** for custom process flows and Oracle encourages customers to do so. The use of BPM 11*g* in the context of OER will be described in more detail in *Chapter 6, Asset Lifecycle and Workflow*.

Oracle provides a useful URL (`http://www.oracle.com/technetwork/middleware/bpm/obpm-config-matrix-085247.html`) that provides important information on supported configurations for the OBPM 10.3.2 product. We recommend installing OBPM 10*g* on a WebLogic infrastructure (as specified in the section **Oracle BPM Enterprise for WebLogic 10.3.2** of the same URL) rather than installing the standalone version of the product as the OER 11*g* installation guide would suggest. The reason being, we think that having a single and consistent WebLogic stack (even if versions do differ) will make installation, configuration, and support tasks a lot easier. Installing the standalone version of OBPM 10*g* introduces a **Tomcat Application Server** and pre-configured topology that might not be suitable to address some of the governance requirements.

> The implementation of the OBPM 10*g* product set is outside the scope of this book so we refer the reader to the following URL's for further information:
>
> OBPM 10*g* topologies: `http://www.oracle.com/technetwork/articles/bpm-environment-explained-097155.html`.
>
> OBPM 10*g* interoperability guidelines: `http://www.oracle.com/technetwork/middleware/bpm/obpm-config-matrix-085247.html`.
>
> OBPM 10*g* documentation: `http://docs.oracle.com/cd/E13154_01/bpm/docs65/index.html`.

The OER binaries themselves can be deployed into a WebLogic 11*g* instance. OER has been written to support **High Availability** and therefore it can be deployed into a **WebLogic Cluster**.

When architecting an OER implementation, one of the key decision points surrounds specifying the versions of the various Oracle products to utilize and how these fit into the overall product stack. This is very important as there might be slight but meaningful architectural changes incorporated into the latest patch sets for each product. For example, according to the supported **Oracle Supported Systems Configurations** documentation, OER version 11.1.1.6.3 is certified against WebLogic Server 10.3.5 and 10.3.6 (URL `http://www.oracle.com/technetwork/middleware/ias/downloads/fusion-certification-100350.html`). Although in most cases it is often desirable to go for the latest certified patch set (in this particular example it would be WebLogic 10.3.6) the decision as to which version to use should also take into account other required products in the architecture. Based on the author's previous experiences, it can be tricky to get the combination correctly specified. OER will invariably be just one product amongst many other Oracle products being implemented in the overall architecture. It is possible that some of the other Oracle products are only supported on previous WebLogic platforms (in this case 10.3.5) and therefore to keep the stack consistent the architect may opt to go with an older patch set in order to achieve a consistent product stack.

The JMS server

A less obvious and yet extremely important component of the architecture is the WebLogic JMS server. This component is required by the Event Manager. The **Event Manager** is the component of OER that is responsible for managing events, such as subscriptions and deliveries. Asset Registration Flows rely on event managers and therefore they are an integral building block of the product architecture.

OER uses a standalone version of **Apache ActiveMQ JMS Server**, which is configured out-of-the-box for the implementation of Event Manager queues. This configuration, however, can be modified and an external JMS provider, such as the WebLogic JMS provider, can be used instead. We would recommend setting up the environment in this way for similar reasons as outlined above with regard to stand alone OBPM 10.3.2. That is to ensure that the architect does not introduce additional components that need to be supported in to the software stack. Furthermore these components will introduce unnecessary complexity when delivering highly available and disaster recovery solutions with complex clustered topologies.

Database

All of the Oracle products required to implement OER require a backend database. While OER 11*g* is certified against databases from different vendors, Oracle recommends the use of an Oracle database. If the topology chosen is a highly available one then OER 11*g* also supports **Real Application Cluster** (**RAC**).

> Please refer to the **Oracle Supported Systems Configurations** documentation for further information on exact versions supported. `http://www.oracle.com/technetwork/middleware/ias/downloads/fusion-certification-100350.html`

Java Application Server

The reporting functionality of OER relies on an instance of BI Publisher version 11*g* being available for its use. Although the configuration of BI Publisher is described in the OER Configuration Guide (`http://docs.oracle.com/cd/E28280_01/admin.1111/e16580/bipub.htm#sthref868`), the installation of this product is not covered in any of the OER guides.

Please refer to *Appendix, Installation Tips and Techniques* for practical step on how to install and configure this component.

> Alternatively refer to the **Oracle Business Intelligence Documentation Library** for instructions on how to install BI Publisher. `http://docs.oracle.com/cd/E28280_01/bi.htm`.

OER Functionality

Having covered the product architecture for OER, let us now turn our attention to the rich functionality that it provides to support overall SOA Governance.

This book has *purposely* segmented the functionality from the core platform and user desktop components to reflect the relative priority of different readers. After all, many readers of this book are less concerned with the product architecture and more interested in how the product supports Return on Investment for services, Service Catalog creation, and maintenance and the degree of service re-use. This section summarizes the key functionality delivered by the OER product so the same can be conveyed to a broad and diverse audience.

OER Console

The **OER Console** is the main and only frontend for the OER application. The entry point into OER is through the logon screen. It is worth nothing that, as OER is a J2EE-based application and is fully compliant with the **Java Authentication and Authorization Service** (**JAAS**), almost any LDAP compliant directory (for example Oracle Internet Directory or MS Active Directory) can be used as the repository for user identities and passwords:

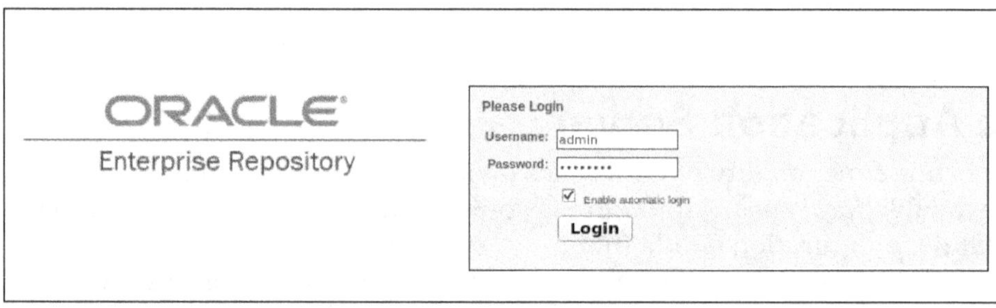

Once a user has successfully authenticated, they will be redirected into the OER home page. Within the home page itself, the user can access the different menus available as well as conduct various searches on Assets using the search pane (located on the left-hand side of the home screen):

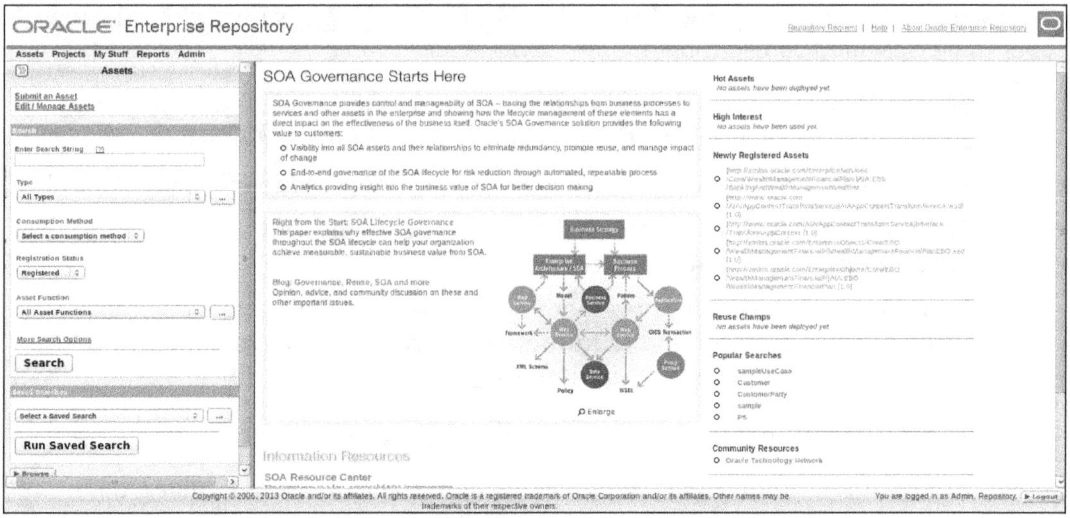

The main menu bar runs across the console, allowing user navigation across the different product capabilities. The entire console is role-based, allowing administrators to configure menu access and content based on user roles:

The home page can be customized to reflect corporate identity and standards. This page includes embedded features that display information about new additions to the repository, the most frequently used Assets, and a list of users who have achieved the highest levels of Asset re-use. It can even be customized to provide different roles with different home pages that in turn deliver different content.

The following sections describe each of the different menu items available from the Home Page.

Assets page

As described earlier in the book, an Asset is basically anything that is stored in OER repository. Services, technical and functional contracts, standards, business processes, and even test plans are some examples of what can be defined as an Asset. In short, an OER Asset is more than just a piece of code and extends to cover other tangible electronic documents such as best practice and reference architectures.

As Assets can be, and often are, different in nature, OER allows for different Asset types to be classified as listed below:

- Service Assets are basically web services and associated Assets (for example technical specifications, test plans, functional design, and others)
- Process Assets (business processes such as BPMN 2.0 models or BPA models)
- Governance and Policy Assets (standards such as development and programming standards and policies)
- Requirements Assets (requirement documents such as system use cases, functional specifications, a requirement traceability matrix, and any other document classified as a requirement)

The Asset page can be used to execute the following actions:

- Create Assets: Although Assets can be automatically created using the Harvester or using the IDE integration, it is also possible to manually submit Assets using the Asset Editor applet
- Edit Assets: All Assets can be modified using the Asset Editor applet
- Search Assets (note that this functionality is also available through the home page via the search pane)
- View the Asset Registration Status
- Access the Type Manager applet: This tool allows for all different Asset types to be managed
- Access the Asset Navigator applet: It delivers a comprehensive tree-like view of the Assets and its relationship
- Access the Import/Export Asset applet: A utility to import and export Assets from different file formats

One of OER's strongest features is its flexibility to model any Asset type. Asset types can be created or modified using the Type Manager applet. An Asset itself can be managed using the Asset Editor. Both tools will be described in further detail in a subsequent section.

Note that *Chapter 4, Initial Configuration,* of this book will focus on the use of the Asset page to support the entire lifecycle.

Projects page

As stated earlier, in OER all users are assigned roles that define the OER functionality that can be exercised by that user. In order for a user to access any files associated with Assets in OER, the user must be assigned to a project. Projects are the primary means of gathering metrics in OER. OER tracks Assets produced by projects, as well as Assets consumed by projects. Projects are hierarchical, which enables organizations to, for example, establish a program that can spawn many projects. Projects are also a channel for governance practices. OER Compliance Templates (usually taking the form of Architecture Blueprints or Project Profiles) can be applied to projects.

OER users are assigned to projects; when a user submits a new Asset, they are prompted to enter a project code. Similarly, when a user wants to re-use an Asset, they are prompted for the project on which the Asset is to be re-used.

Both Users and Projects are assigned to Departments. This is convenient from a reporting standpoint, as organizations can then track the production and consumption of reusable Assets down to a specific department.

Reports can be generated to show things such as the degree of service re-use savings per project. It also enables OER to report on the savings generated by Asset production teams. The Projects page is the entry point for creating and managing projects and is as shown below:

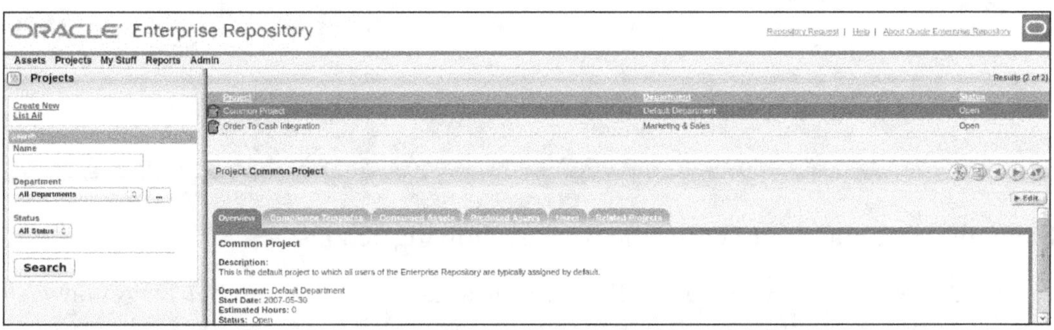

Projects can be located from this page and it is possible to drill down further to elicit more details. Project information such as description, department, start date, hours and status is displayed in a series of tabs as described below:

- **Compliance Templates**: Shows compliance templates that have been assigned to the project.
- **Consumed Assets**: Any Asset that has been associated to the project. Note that these could be used Assets or Assets being considered for use.

- **Reported Asset Value**: Represents the effort in hours saved by reusing an Asset in the project. Note that only the role of Project Leaders has visibility of the information displayed on this tab.
- **Produced Assets**: List of all Assets produced by the project.
- **Users**: Users (including their roles) that have been associated with the project.
- **Related Projects**: Defines the relationship to other projects. Note that this feature needs to be enabled.

My Stuff page

This page, as the name suggests, delivers a personalized home page for all OER users:

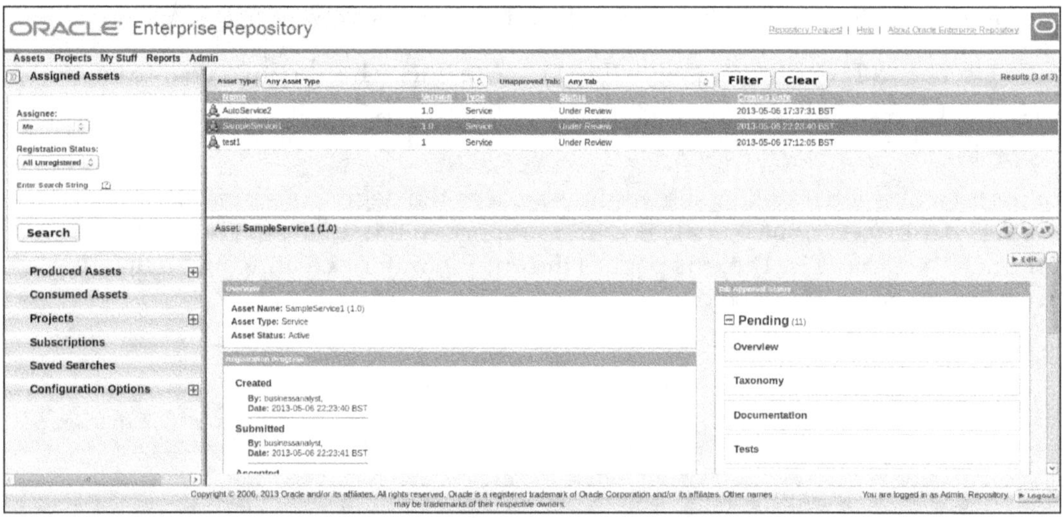

From this page a user will be able to do the following actions:

- **Assigned Assets**: Lists of all Assets assigned to the user either for review or processing (during the registration process). Assets assigned to users can be searched based on assignation (for example, unassigned, any assignee or assigned to me) or status (registered, unregistered).
- **Produced Assets**: List of all of the Assets (of any type) submitted by the user.
- **Consumed Assets**: Lists of Assets being used (or In-Process Assets).
- **Projects**: List of projects (open or Closed) to which the user has been assigned.
- **Subscriptions**: Users can subscribe to receive updates on Asset updates. This feature lists all subscriptions of the user.

- **Saved Searches**: A feature that allows for searches to be saved for future use. A list of all saved searches is provided.
- **Configuration Options**: Self-Service functionality such as password change and email notifications.

Reports page

OER provides rich reporting capabilities offering more than 20 pre-configured reports that can be used to track and report on important metrics such as Asset usage, amount of re-use, and others.

As described earlier, OER leverages BI Publisher for the generation of reports however, the reports page is the entry point of the generation of these. The reports available in this page can be grouped in to five main categories:

1. The **Project Portfolio Productivity** reports: Shows the overall productivity of project teams, including their level of compliance with prescribed Asset usage requirements, and the value they have realized by leveraging the existing Asset portfolio. The reports also spotlight each project team's contribution to the Asset portfolio.
2. The **Asset Portfolio Management** reports: Used primarily by architects and registrars, these reports show the quality, status, and value of the Asset portfolio. These reports also monitor the Asset supply and demand, as well as assisting with Asset portfolio taxonomy refinements.
3. The **Asset Release Management** reports: Used primarily by Asset producers and maintainers, these reports inform these users about Asset refinements and enhancements, and determine the effect of an Asset change to the consumer community and consuming projects. In addition, these reports identify stakeholders who need to be notified about changes.
4. The **Performance** reports: These reports allow individual users to quantify the value of their contributions to the organization. They also inform department heads about the performance of the producers, consumers, and project leads in their organizations.
5. The **Program Management** reports: Used primarily by various managers, these reports expose the value that the program brings to the organization (ROI) and indicates whether the program successfully meets goals, demonstrates program growth and progress and serves as the basis for incentives and governance.

[Source: `http://docs.oracle.com/cd/E28280_01/user.1111/e15747/intro.htm#BHCGDDGJ`.]

Reports can be generated from the Reports page in formats such as HTML and/or PDF. For large reports PDF is recommended; however, either can be used.

Administration page

As described earlier in the Projects section, all Assets are associated with a Project. Projects in turn belong to a Department that has Users assigned to it. Assets are used by Projects. Users can have different Roles assigned to them. The **Administration** page provides a facility to maintain this complex relationship of entities and enforces referential integrity when performing the configuration.

The following model describes in detail the relationship between Projects, Departments, Assets, Users, and Roles:

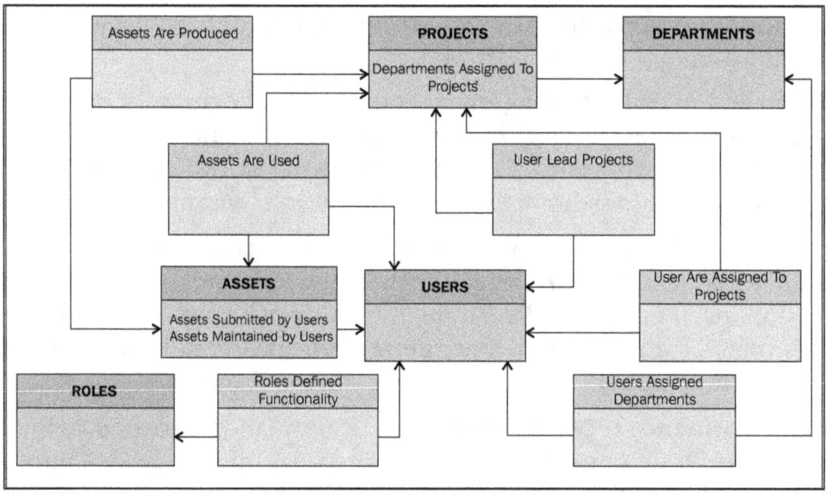

The main activities that can be executed on the **Administration** page are:

- **Departments**: List, create, and modify Departments.
- **Users**: List, create, and modify Users as well as assigned Users to different Departments and even cloning User's details.
- **Projects**: List, create, and modify Projects as well as assign Users to Projects, Close Projects, and establish relationship between projects.

- **Roles**: List, create, and modify User Roles. Note that access details are based on User Roles therefore it is important that this is done carefully and properly. Note that users assigned with the Admin role will have unlimited access to all OER functions. Also a user account named as admin will be assigned the admin role by default.
- **Access Settings**: In this page the administrator can assign permissions to each individual role. Access settings define the functions that a particular role is allowed to execute. There are 2 levels of access settings: Basic Access Settings (BAS) is a simpler access control model to model pages. This configuration is recommended for implementations that have a small number of projects. And Custom Access Settings (CAS) supports a full Role-Based Access Control (RBAC) that enforces authorization not only at page level but also at specific Assets or Asset Groups. This configuration is more complex and only recommended when the implementation requirements cannot be address by a standard BAS configuration.
- **Sessions**: Provides administrations with visibility and control over which users are logged into OER.

> It is very important that, when configuring OER for the first time, Departments, Projects, Users, and User Roles are created properly using the **Administration** page. Oracle recommends a specific order on doing this.
>
> Please refer to section **Basic Configuration** of the **OER Configuration Guide** for further details on this. `http://docs.oracle.com/cd/E28280_01/admin.1111/e16580/basic.htm`.
>
> Note, that as this book aims to cover the broader aspects of implementing Governance, these details will not be covered in detail in subsequent sections.

OER System

This boundary represents the core components of the application that work under the cover to enable the functionality available in OER. In an N-Tier architecture model this would be the business logic layer where all of the complex processes and rules are executed. This layer presents the functionality to the console layer and consumes the integration components when needed to make use of functionality that is externally available (for example to consume the Asset Registration flows or to connect to the queues implemented by the JMS server).

Workflow

The Workflow engine is at the heart of the **Asset Registration** process as it is responsible for implementing the human workflows elements of the product. OER relies on Oracle Business Process Manager 10*g* for the implementation of the **Asset Registration Flows** and on the **Event Manager** for events integration into the flows.

The Asset Registration Flows are a fundamental component of the OER architecture for the following reasons:

- Policies can be enforced so Assets are created and consumed according to corporate standards and procedures
- For the automation of the Approval human workflows
- It ensure that events are fired on the different stages of the lifecycle and also the Asset Registration process
- It allows for customization of flows in accordance with the corporate requirements (one solution does not always fit all)

The following diagram describes a high-level view of the different interactions between the OER components during the Asset Registration Flow:

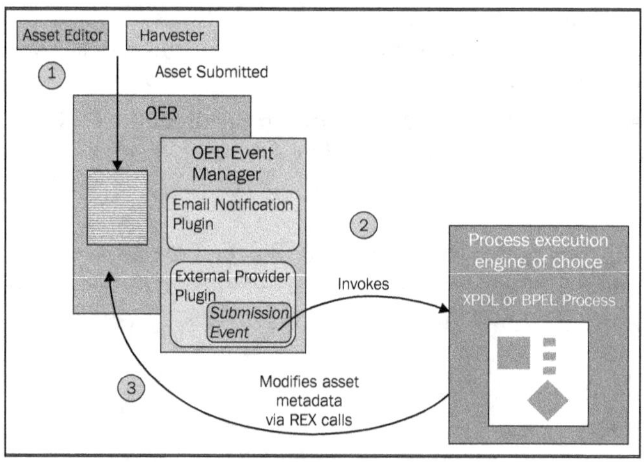

As depicted, the key activities are as follows:

1. An Asset is either harvested using the Harvester (this will be covered in a later section) or directly using the Asset Editor.
2. Once the Asset has been submitted an event is triggered, which in turn invokes a process in the OBPM 10*g*. Note that the Asset Registration flow will depend on the type of event Asset.

3. The process implements the business logic and conducts actions such as determining whether or not to act on this Asset, based on a set of parameters such as, for example, which user submitted the Asset, the metadata content, and others.

The flows implemented in OBPM 10*g* can be modified following the standard OBPM Software Development Lifecycle. Note that this will not be covered in this book; however, further information is available in the OBPM 10*g* documentation for developers (`http://docs.oracle.com/cd/E13154_01/bpm/docs65/index.html`).

Event Manager

The **Event Manager** is the component of OER that is responsible for managing events such as subscriptions and deliveries. The **Asset Registration Flows** fully rely on the **Event Manager** as this is the channel from which processes are further triggered.

The following Oracle diagram (extracted from the OER Configuration Guide – URL `http://docs.oracle.com/cd/E28280_01/admin.1111/e16580/oerwf.htm#CJHHBAII`) depicts the Event Manager architecture:

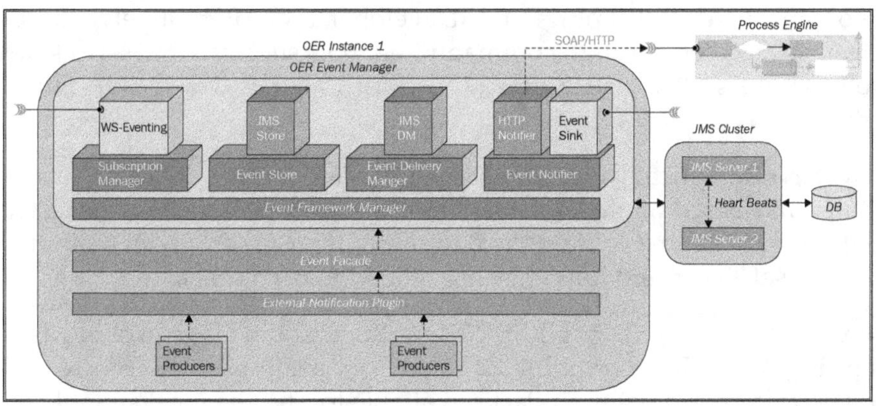

Some of the key features of the **Event Manager** are:

- The Event Model is based on XML Schemas.
- **Stores Events** to a persistence JMS provider for reliability. JMS providers can be Active MQ (installed out of the box) or externalized to use another provider such as the WebLogic JMS provider.
- Exposes a **Subscription Service** that can be consumed to subscribe to OER events.

- Subscribes to interested events and registration of Web service endpoints where matched events are delivered.
- Matches the incoming events to each subscribed Endpoint and delivers the filtered events to an internal Notification Service.
- Notification Service.
- Notifies the registered Endpoint using SOAP/HTTP with pluggable extensions to additional transport protocols.
- The External Notification Plug-in allows integration with events triggered by external system.

Harvester

Harvesting is the process of gathering information from different design time and runtime sources and then submitting the harvested Assets into OER. Harvesters are tools that enable OER to discover and register Assets that reside in different design time and runtime sources.

OER offers several ways of harvesting Assets. Assets can be harvested during **design time** by configuring the OER plugin for JDeveloper 11*g*. Alternatively Harvester utilities can be executed through command line tools such as ANT scripts or WSLT scripts to harvest Assets from runtime repositories such as Oracle SOA Suite, Oracle Service Bus.

The Harvester automatically creates Assets, populates Asset metadata, and generates relationship links based on the information in the artifact files. The Harvester relies on the **Solution Packs** that contain the definition of an Asset Model that ultimately dictates the Asset Types and how they are related to each other.

The process of harvesting Assets into OER for the first time is referred to as **Bootstrapping**. When Bootstrapping OER, an organization can make use of the different Harvesters and Solution Packs available to find the most suitable ways to load the Assets and their relationship into OER.

There are some considerations to make when using the Harvester. *Chapter 5, Harvesting* will elaborate on the process of harvesting in greater detail.

Some of the key features of the Harvester are:

- Publish standard SOA artifacts such as SCA Composites, BPEL, WSDL, XSD and XSLT, BPMN 2.0, and WS-Policy (from Oracle and other vendors) to OER.
- Capture dependencies between the artifacts for impact analysis
- Handle nested WSDL and XSD files

- Create abstract Interface Assets and concrete deployment / Endpoints
- Capture BPEL partner link dependencies and relating them to Interfaces
- Capture BPEL PM dependencies to Transformations
- Store or reference artifact content in OER for reusability
- Calculate Software File IDs (SFIDs) for artifacts for duplicate detection
- Publish artifacts from nested directories, remote servers, ZIP files, JAR files, SOA composites, or Oracle BPEL suitcases
- Publish artifacts in a transactional fashion
- Publish artifacts from a command line, and from an automated Ant build process using the Harvester Ant task
- Publish Oracle Service Bus project artifacts such as Proxy Service, Business Service, XQuery, MFL, XSLT, and WS-Policy
- Integrate the harvesting process as part of WLST deployment scripts
- Harvest into SSL enabled SOA server

> Please refer to *Chapter 5, Harvesting* for a practical elaboration on harvesting and the bootstrapping process.

Solution Packs

OER **Solution Packs** are bundles that contain pre-configured metadata and content that can be imported into OER. Solution Packs are essential as they define fundamental Assets, Asset Types and their relationships, and other metadata required by OER to:

- Deliver a vanilla configuration that implements best practices
- Successfully interpret and load the information retrieved during the harvesting process
- Support Integration with other applications and systems such as Oracle Application Integration Architecture, Oracle Service Registry, Oracle Enterprise Manager, and many others

The following Solution Packs are required by OER:

- **Base Pack**: This pack is automatically installed during the installation process and it delivers the base definition of Asset Types required by OER. The metadata delivered as part of this pack is based on well-documented best practices and provides templates that can be leveraged when customizing OER to support a bespoke implementation. The metadata delivered as part of this pack should not be deleted or modified directly. Instead, metadata should be cloned when an extension to the base is needed.
- **Harvester Solution Pack**: This pack is bundled with the Oracle Enterprise Repository 11*g* installation in a file named **11.1.1.x.x-OER-Harvester-Solution-Pack.zip**. The Asset Types and other metadata available in this pack are needed when harvesting Assets from Oracle products such as SOA Suite, Service Bus, Enterprise Manager, BPEL PM, Service Registry, and others.
- **AIA Solution Pack**: This pack is optional and is available with the purchase of the **AIA 11*g* Foundation Pack**. This pack is required to harvest Assets from a SOA Suite implementation that makes use of the AIA Foundation Pack. Refer to *Chapter 11, Extending Governance with AIA Foundation Pack 11g*, for further details on the implementation of this pack.
- **Contract Management Solution Pack**: This optional pack imports the metadata required in OER to support the negotiation of contracts between service providers and consumers. The pack allows the creation of **Terms of Use** that define the conditions (policies) under which a service is provided or consumed. The pack also includes Boilerplate contract compliance templates, sample artifacts, and documentation.

> Refer to section **15 Configuring Contract Management** of the OER Configuration Guide for more information on this pack.
> `http://docs.oracle.com/cd/E28280_01/admin.1111/e16580/contract.htm`

Chapter 5, Harvesting of this book covers in detail the harvesting process and implementation of Solution Packs.

Asset metadata

In OER, all data that is associated with an Asset is referred to as **metadata**. Understanding this simple and yet important concept is critical. Attributes are used to store metadata for all Assets, such as OER reference models, Asset metrics, usage histories, performance SLAs, asset documentation, and many more.

Security and roles

As previously described in the Administration page section, OER can be configured using either role-based access or the more advanced RBAC access. Unlike most of the Oracle Fusion Middleware products, OER does not rely on WebLogic and the **Oracle Platform Security Services** (**OPSS**) for integration with external LDAP directories such as **Oracle Internet Directory** (**OID**) or MS Active Directory. Instead, a component called the **OER LDAP/Active Directory Connector** is utilized to connect to an LDAP directory that can act as the single source of truth for users, credentials and roles. The configuration of the OER LDAP/ Active Directory Connector is made through the **Systems Settings** pane of the **Administration** page.

> For further details refer to the section **Configuring Oracle Enterprise Repository to use External Authentication Tooling** of the **OER Configuration Guide** for further details `http://docs.oracle.com/cd/E28280_01/admin.1111/e16580/extauth.htm`.
>
> This document describes the steps that must be taken into consideration when using an external directory for the definition of users and roles or when other complex configurations, such as single sign-on, are required.

Integration

One of the most pertinent features of OER is its ability to interrogate many external systems and repositories to mine all available Assets throughout an enterprise. Using a rich set of integration tools, OER can connect to existing systems and repositories to harvest currently deployed Assets and their relationships. Centralization of all enterprise Assets into a single repository (OER) is essential when governing a large SOA implementation. Once details have been collected and stored, OER provides a single source of truth providing the ability to maximize the re-use of all existing artifacts.

This section provides an introduction to the main components that make up OER's rich integration capabilities.

IDE integration and plugins

Repository access using a development IDE is possible via an OER plugin through the implementation of the Harvester Solution Pack. Plugins are available for a number of IDE environments including JDeveloper. This provides developers with design time access to the repository, allowing them to search for relevant Assets, evaluate Asset metadata, and select Assets for re-use. Developers can also harvest their completed work into OER, which automatically generates Assets and relationships based on the harvested artifacts.

> Please refer to the **Oracle Fusion Middleware Supported System Configurations** page for a list of supported IDE's in OER version 11.1.1.6.3 (`http://www.oracle.com/technetwork/middleware/downloads/fmw-11gr1certmatrix.xls`).

The section entitled Harvesting Existing Assets from IDE's in *Chapter 5, Harvesting,* will elaborate more on this topic including the IDEs that are supported and the features and capabilities available via the plugins.

Code Compliance Inspectors (CCI)

CCI is a JDeveloper add-on that checks for good coding practices in SOA Suite projects. Using a set of predefined assertions based on industry best practices, CCI checks for design consistencies and good coding and documentation practices. The outcome of CCI is a report concluding if the code evaluated is compliant, conformant, or fully conformant.

> For more information on CCI please refer to section **5 Integration with Code Compliance Inspector** of the **OER Integration Guide**. `http://docs.oracle.com/cd/E28280_01/doc.1111/e15754/codecomplianceinsp.htm`.

SCM integration

Integration with **Software Configuration Management** (**SCM**) systems is possible by creating **Artifact Stores** using the Asset Editor. An Artifact Store is basically a holding location where files relevant to an Asset are stored. Configuration of the store depends on the type of Artifact Store created.

Out of the box, OER allows Artifact Stores to be created and configured to support integration with standard file systems, Clear Case, Clear Quest, Harvest-HTTP repository, and Serena PVCS Dimensions.

Moreover, several types of Artifact Stores are supported. For example using the type **Raw SCM** it is possible to create Artifact Stores for popular version control systems such as CVS and Subversion. The default types supported are:

- FTP: Accesses files on an FTP server.
- HTTP: Accesses files on a Web server.
- HTTPS: Accesses files on a secure Web server.
- UNC: Accesses files using a Windows or Samba share.

- Raw URI: Access files via a raw URI.
- Raw SCM: Access files via a raw SCM. The selected SCM type automatically populates the Download Path URI Suffix field, but the field can be modified however necessary.

> Please refer to **Part I Oracle Enterprise Repository Connectors** of the **OER Integration Guide** for instructions on creating and configuring Artifact Stores. `http://docs.oracle.com/cd/E28280_01/doc.1111/e15754/partpage.htm#sthref8`.

Repository Exchange Framework (REX)

The **Repository Extensibility Framework** (REX) is a web service-based API that can be used for standards-based integration with OER. The RPC-style web services available as part of the REX API, allow third-party applications and systems to interoperate with OER and therefore to hook into the Asset Lifecycle. The REX API is a rich interface, exposing many of the operations that are available within the OER subsystem internal API's.

The following diagram shows the architecture of the REX:

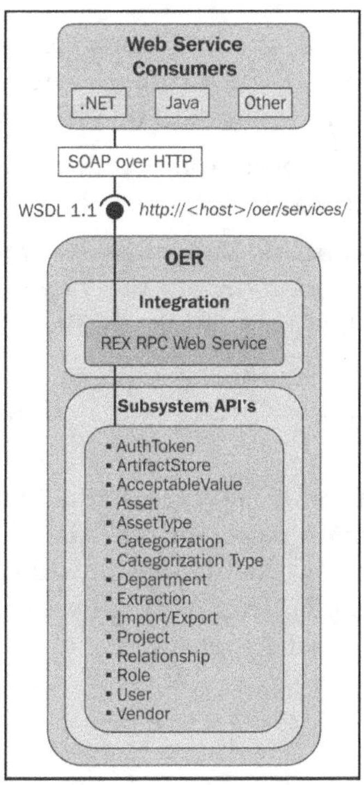

The web service API is defined using the standard **Web Service Description Language (WSDL)** Version 1.1 and implemented as RPC-Encoded SOAP bindings through HTTP. The API exposes CRUD-Q-like operations (create-read-update-delete-query) against the subsystems listed in the preceding diagram.

Note that, when designing solutions that make use of the REX OER interface, as with any web service based API, system performance must be taken into account during the design phase. Overuse of this API may result in poor performance due to marshalling and un-marshalling of SOAP messages.

> For further reading on the REX API and its utilization, please refer to section **12 Repository Extensibility Framework** of the **OER Integration Guide** `http://docs.oracle.com/cd/E28280_01/doc.1111/e15754/overview.htm#CHDEIAGB`

Subsystem APIs

The Subsystem APIs are internal APIs that can be consumed by any service consumer when creating a custom integration with OER. They are the same APIs exposed by REX web services. As depicted in the preceding REX architecture diagram, the list of Subsystem APIs available are:

- **AuthToken**: This authentication API exposes the operations needed to create and maintain an **Authentication Session Token**. Note that this token is required in every invocation of a REX API.
- **ArtifactStore**: This API exposes query and create operations that can be use to maintain OER Artifact Stores.
- **AcceptableValue**: Acceptable Value Lists are metadata elements used in single and multiple-selection drop-down boxes when creating Asset Types. This API exposes CRUD-Q operations on these lists.
- **Asset**: Assets are the core entities in OER as described in earlier sections of this book. This API exposes CRUD-Q operations that can be use to manage OER Assets.
- **AssetType**: The structure of Assets is defined by the definition of Types. Types consist of two main parts: **Editor** (basically the metadata that is stored for the Asset) and **Viewer** (that defines how the metadata is displayed in the Asset detail pages of OER). This API exposes CRUD-Q operations that can be used to manage OER Asset Types.

- **CatergorizationType**: Categorization Types provide the means to define custom taxonomies. Categorizations are not directly assigned to Assets. This API exposes CRUD-Q operations that can be use to manage OER Categorizations.
- **Categorization**: Categorizations are subsets of Categorization Types, and, unlike Categorization Type, these are assigned directly to Assets. This API exposes CRUD-Q operations that can be used to manage OER Categorizations.
- **Department**: This API exposes CRU-Q (excluding Delete) operations that can be use to manage OER Departments.
- **Extraction**: Extraction API is used to access the Asset payload otherwise referred to as the **Use-Download** process. This API exposes CRU-Q (excluding Delete) operations that can be use to manage OER Extractions.
- **Import/Export**: This API allows to import and/or export metadata into or out of OER.
- **Projects**: This API exposes CRU-Q plus Validate (excluding Delete) operations that can be used to manage OER Projects.
- **Relationship**: Relationship Types defines the relationships between two Assets. This API exposes CRU-Q (excluding Delete) operations for establishing OER Relationship Types on Assets.
- **Role**: This API exposes CRUD-Q operations that can be used to manage Roles in OER.
- **User**: This API exposes CRU-Q operations (excluding Delete) that can be used to manage Users in OER.
- **Vendor**: Vendors in OER are a single unique string used to specify the original source of an Asset. A Vendor in OER is also responsible for supporting the Assets assigned to them. This API exposes CRUD-Q operations that can be use to manage Vendors in OER.

> For further reading on the OER APIs and their utilization please refer to **Part IV Developing Custom Integrations** of the **OER Integration Guide.** `http://docs.oracle.com/cd/E28280_01/doc.1111/e15754/partpage3.htm#BHAGDECA`

BI Publisher Integration

Even though the OER console is the entry point for generating all the reports, the actual host of these must be **Business Intelligence** (**BI**) Publisher. OER comes with a collection of pre-configured BI Publisher content (including a BI Publisher repository especially for OER) that can be loaded into a BI Publisher instance for the exclusive use of the OER. Note that, when acquiring an OER license, Oracle also provides a limited license for using BI Publisher. This restricted license allows for the reporting features of OER to be used.

> The integration of BI Publisher and OER requires the execution of several steps, all of which are available in the section **15 Configuring BI Publisher Enterprise Server** of the **OER Configuration Guide.** `http://docs.oracle.com/cd/E28280_01/admin.1111/e16580/bipub.htms`

OER Users

An OER User is anyone that needs access to OER in order to perform an action as part of the SOA Asset Lifecycle.

> Refer to *Chapter 1, SOA Governance,* section *Roles and responsibilities* for a list of the different actors and their responsibilities within Governance Design-time.

From an OER User perspective, a web browser is used as the main user interface for accessing most of the OER functionality. The OER Console can be accessed using a standard browser such as Firefox 3.5+ or IE 7+.

> For a list of supported browsers please refer to the **Oracle Fusion Middleware Supported System Configurations** page (`http://www.oracle.com/technetwork/middleware/downloads/fmw-11gr1certmatrix.xls`).
>
> In addition to the supported browser, it is a prerequisite that Java Web Start is available on the user desktop. Java Web Start is a browser plugin that runs files with JNLP extensions. The reason this is required is because the Asset Editor, Type Manager, Navigator Applet, Browse Tree Applet, and the Import/Export utility have been developed using this technology. For details on the installation of Java Web Start please refer to section **3.2 Install Java Web Start** in the **OER Installation Guide** (`http://docs.oracle.com/cd/E14571_01/doc.1111/e15745/post.htm#CIHCBHDG`).

Asset Editor

Whereas the OER Console provides the means to browse and view Asset Details, the **Asset Editor** is used to manage OER Assets and their related metadata.

The **Asset Editor** can be accessed through the Assets Page. The following screenshot provides a sample look and feel of the **Asset Editor**:

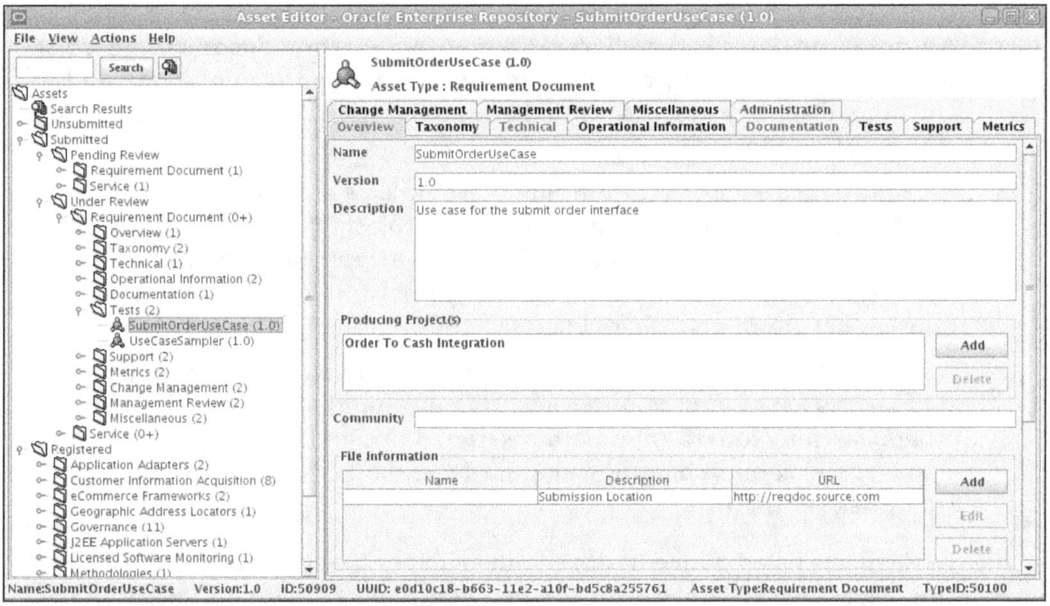

Through this screen the user is able to perform a series of actions against an Asset. Actions include:

- Browse or search Assets.
- Visualize Asset Details.
- Configure Acceptable Value Lists, Categories, Asset Relationships, Artifact Stores, and Vendors.
- Assign Users to Assets.

[*Chapter 4, Initial Configuration,* will elaborate the use of the **Asset Editor** in further detail.]

Type Manager

As described earlier in the *Solutions Pack* section, many Asset Types are loaded into OER at configuration time. The Type Manager is a comprehensive tool that allows for Asset Types to be managed. The Type Manager defines the look and feel of OER artifacts as they appear in the **Asset Editor** and the Asset Detail screens.

In OER an artifact can be:

- An **Asset**: As described earlier, in OER an Asset is any document, piece of code (XML, Java, or any other programming language or notation), and/or any other electronic document that are can be considered to add value to a SOA implementation.
- A **Compliance Template**: Compliance Templates are used to communicate Asset requirements to internal or external project teams. Compliance Templates are typically generated by the teams responsible for the Asset and Project Portfolios. Architecture Blueprints and Project Profiles are both samples of Compliance Templates.
- A **Policy**: Policies are applied to assets in order to enforce corporate standards such as governance (development standards, quality gates, and others), architecture (design patterns, detail design templates, programming standards, exception handling standards, and others), and any other enterprise standards.

Each of the artifacts listed above has predefined Types that are loaded into OER by the Solution Packs. **Asset Types**, **Compliance Template Types**, and **Policy Types** can all be managed and maintained using the Type Manager.

The **Type Manager** is a Java Web Start application that can be launched from the **Asset Editor** itself:

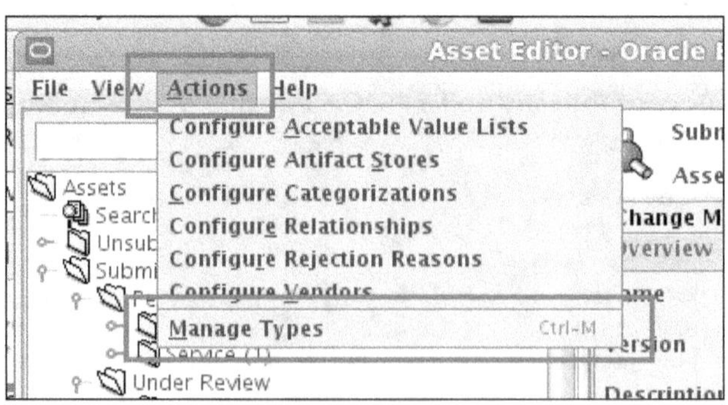

Once the **Type Manager** has been launched, the look and feel of the different Types can be viewed or modified as the following screenshot demonstrates:

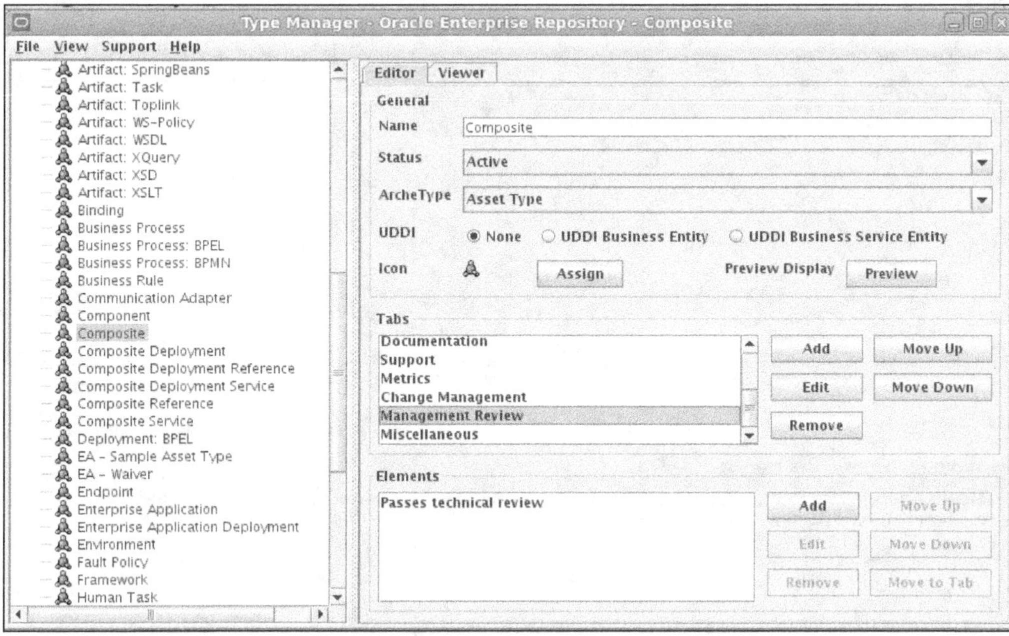

> *Chapter 4, Initial Configuration,* will elaborate further the use of the **Type Manager**.

Navigator applet

The **Navigator** applet is a very useful feature of OER that allows for a graphical and 3D view of an Asset, Projects, and all of its relationships. The **Navigator** applet is launched by clicking on the **Navigation Icon** on any Asset Detail or Project page.

The Navigation icon looks as follows:

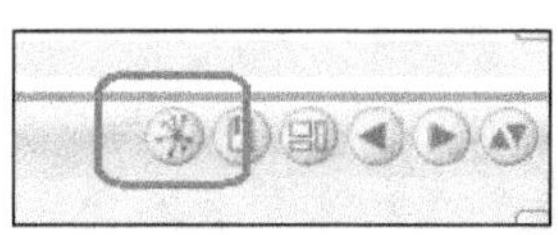

Once the **Navigator** applet has been launched the **Navigator** page is displayed:

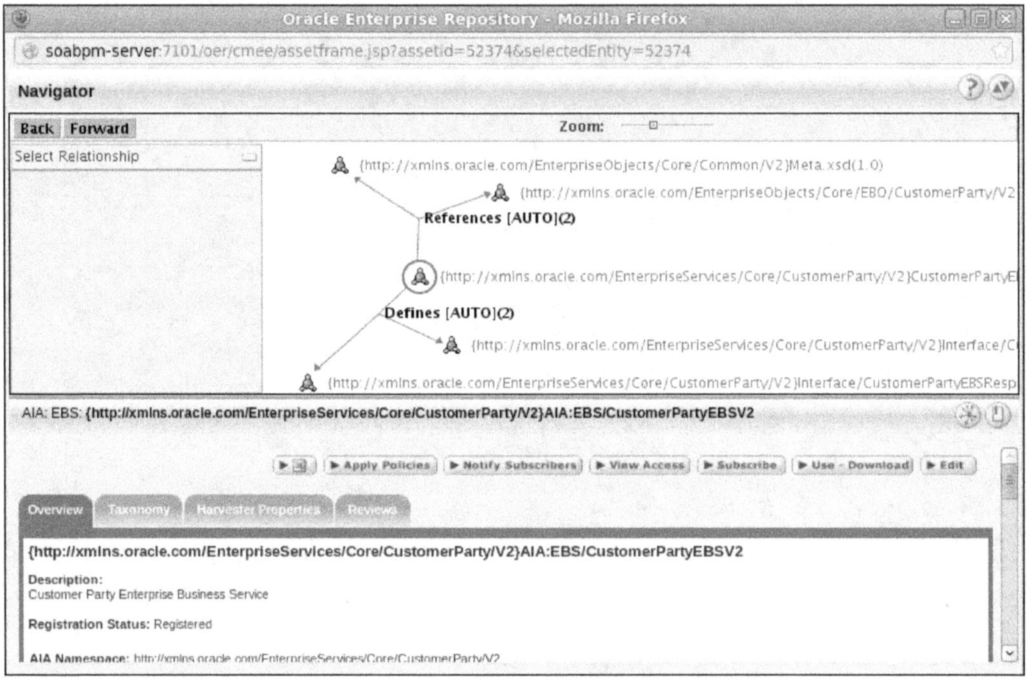

The page is divided in two distinct areas. The upper section displays a 3D view of the selected Asset or Project and all of its relationships to other artifacts. This page can be very useful to understand the impact that modifying an Asset or Project would have on its related artifacts. The lower section of the page shows the Asset's detail.

The Browse Tree applet

The Browse Tree applet is used to browse through the existing Assets using a hierarchical menu. This applet is available from the Assets Page by clicking on the Browse button in the Assets sidebar:

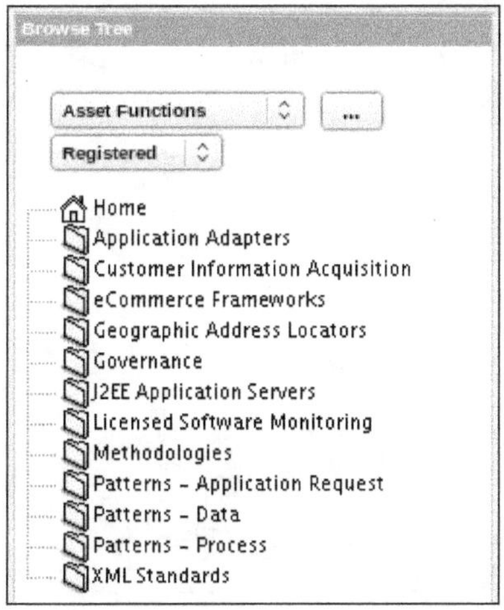

Applet Assets can be filtered by their **Type** and/or **Asset Function** by using the drop-downs as necessary to filter the results.

Import/Export utility

The OER Import/Export Tool allows for the interchange of assets and related metadata between different Oracle Enterprise Repository instances. In implementations where there is more than one OER instance, this tool can be used to export and import configuration changes made to the repository metadata and/or Assets. It can also be used as a backup utility.

As with the **Asset Editor** and **Type Manager**, the **Import/Export Utility** is a Java Web Start application. The utility can be accessed through the Administration page. Note that only users with the Admin role assigned to them can access this utility:

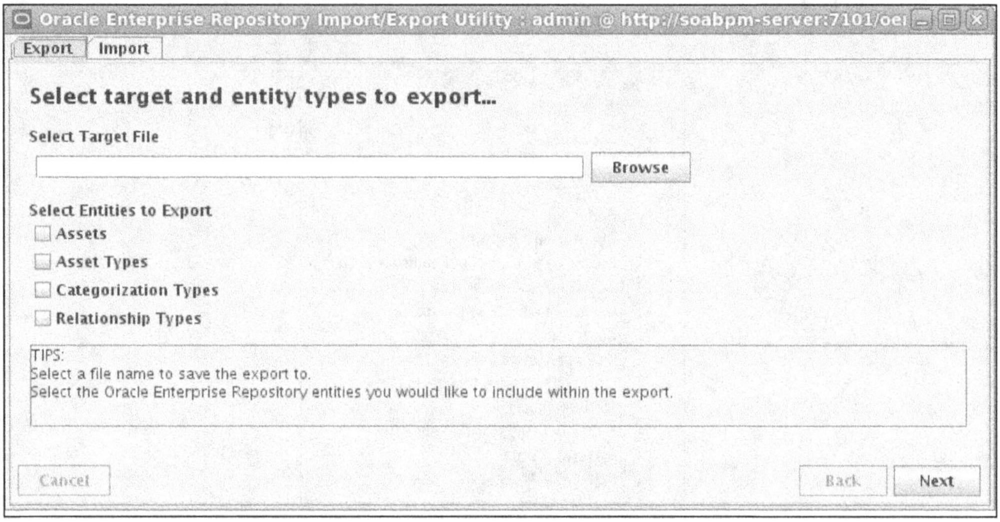

There are a number of considerations that must be made when importing and exporting metadata using this utility. It is necessary for the administrator to clearly understand the interdependency between Artifacts and Artifacts Types so that data can be exchanged in a consistent fashion. The most basic considerations to bear in mind are to understand that:

- **Assets**, **Compliance Templates**, and **Policies** rely on **Types**
- **Asset Types**, **Compliance Template Types**, and **Policy Types** rely on **Categorization Types** and **Relationship Types**.

Not paying attention to the above dependencies may results in issues resulting in importing metadata back into OER.

> Please refer to the **Section 4 Import Export Tool** of the **OER User Guide** for further instructions on how to use the tool `http://docs.oracle.com/cd/E28280_01/user.1111/e15747/impexp.htm`

Summary

In this chapter we have covered the most important architectural components of the OER application as well as key concepts, core functionality, and external dependencies that have to be in place in order to successfully implement OER.

All of the information provided in this chapter will be necessary for the understanding of the subsequent chapters.

The next chapter describes how to configure OER for the first time and the implications of doing so.

4

Initial Configuration

In this chapter the implementation of use case will be elaborated further. We will highlight additional implementation requirements and the changes required to the Asset Lifecycle in order to gain maximum benefits from the introduction of Governance. Furthermore, the chapter will deliver a how-to guide into performing an initial configuration of OER.

While this chapter assumes that the Harvester Solution Pack and the AIA Pack have been installed, we will defer the implementation of these components until the later chapters.

Use case

As described earlier in *Chapter 2, Implementation Use Case*, **Weir & Bell Telecoms** faced several challenges with their initial SOA implementation. A fundamental challenge identified by the **SOA Assessment** exercise was around the lack of visibility of existing SOA Assets at design time resulting in the duplication of Assets. The reason is simple, if an Architect or an **SOA Designer** is unable to view existing services when producing a design, chances are that the functionality will be duplicated across the enterprise leading to unnecessary effort and redundancy. Other challenges such as lack of team collaboration and lack of methodology contributed to the issue of visibility.

This exact situation occurred at **Weir & Bell Telecoms**. The company had around 60 existing SOA Composites at the time of the SOA Assessment. The capabilities delivered by these services were mainly around the **supply chain** and **order-to-cash**. For example, purchase order creation, credit checks, invoicing, inventory management, fulfillments, and others. The SOA Assessment also discovered plans to create around 80 new services across the enterprise to address new business requirements for the same supply chain and order-to-cash processes.

Taking a step back after the SOA Assessment, the Architects started to analyze existing services against new requirements to see if the existing services could be enhanced or augmented to satisfy the new requirements. The results were startling!

The SOA Assessment had concluded that the cost of delivering a new SOA service from the moment of its conception to the production rollout was around $32K.

Applying some simple math to these numbers, the Architects calculated the cost of the new development effort as follows:

$32K (cost of delivering a service end-to-end) X 80 (new services) = $2.5 million Dollars

Thus it was clear that it would cost **Weir & Bell Telecoms** around 2.5 million Dollars to deliver the new functionality. The problem was no one could easily determine how much of that functionality already existed in the current estate since visibility of existing services across departmental boundaries was hazy to say the least! It was clear from the assessment that apart from an outdated Excel document, the functionality supported in the existing SOA services was not captured anywhere and the Architects had not referred to this document when specifying new services.

After undertaking a quick analysis of the new service requirements versus what was known of the existing services, the Architects were able to conclude that there was an opportunity to address around 40 percent of the new requirements by the re-use of existing Assets. However, this is not an exact science and it is recommended that one has to aim at being broadly right and not accurately wrong.

From this quick analysis, the Architects were able to calculate the potential savings of re-use as follows:

$2.5 million Dollars (approximate calculated cost of new services) X 40% (of potential savings if re-use is enforced) = $1.02 million Dollars

The case for enforcing services re-use was clear and the results were alarming.

When the numbers were presented and described to the business stake holders, there was a new appetite to implement a robust **SOA Governance** (*Chapter 2, Implementation Use Case*, describes this in more detail). It was clear that the first and most immediate priority was to resolve the issue of service visibility to substantially reduce the development costs. In addition, when the Architects analyzed the total cost of ownership of all the services through the maintenance, enhancement, and bug correction of duplicated functionality, the figures were even worse! It was important to act quickly as many projects were already in flight and if this problem was not solved quickly, the window of opportunity would be lost.

The first remedial step undertaken was to analyze the existing **SOA Design-time Governance**. The following diagram depicts a summary of the **SOA Software Development Lifecycle** (**SDLC**) followed by **Weir & Bell Telecoms**:

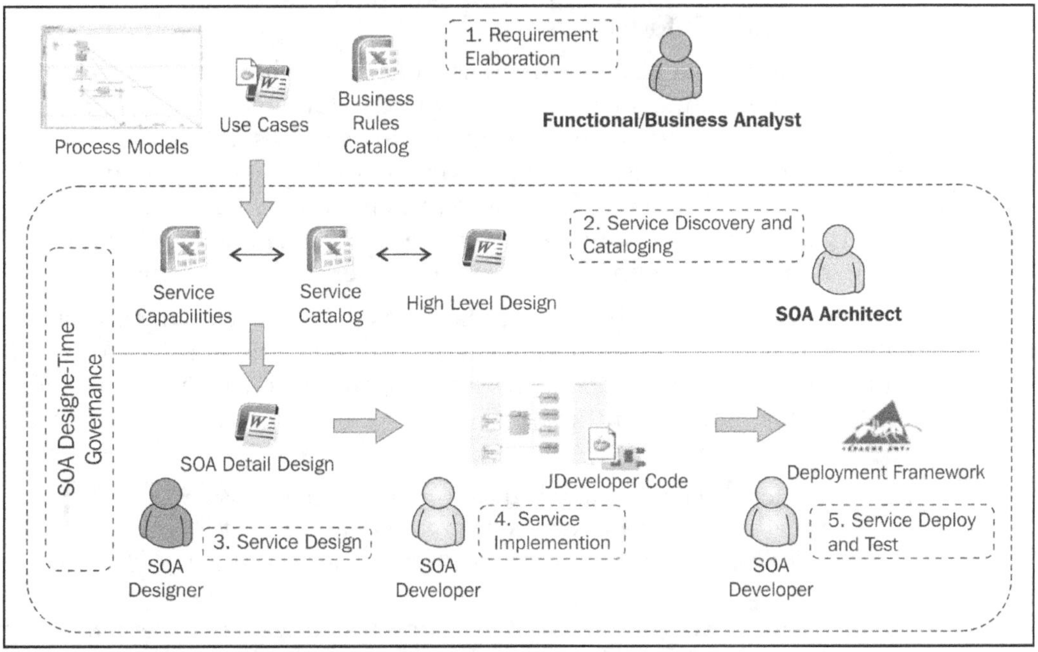

The top five problems identified with this approach after careful analysis were:

- When the **Service Discovery and Cataloging** activities took place in initial projects, the outcomes were captured in Excel documents. Although this approach started off being acceptable, it wasn't enforced rigorously enough by a governing body. As the number of projects increased and the time pressures ensued, the Excel document quickly became outdated and eventually was no longer in use.
- Since the **Architect** and/or **Designer** did not have full visibility of the available Assets, (as the Excel was outdated) new Services were routinely designed every time a new functionality was identified. This was despite the fact that existing services might already be available with similar capabilities.
- Generally, documentation was all over the place and not version controlled or stored in a content server. Invariably, it was not possible to deduce which version of a document was the latest one or which one actually corresponded to a particular version of a service.

- Access control to the documentation and source code was not controlled and it was not possible to audit accessibility or access restrictions. This imposed a huge security risk as external consultants (or even internal consultants) without the appropriate clearance had the potential to find and utilize Assets containing sensitive information.
- Asset dependency was also identified as a big issue. The impact of changing a service on its consumers was not clearly understood or visible. For this reason, when changes were required to existing services, rather than changing the service, a new version was created which would run in parallel to its older sibling. There was no service retirement policy in place, mainly because IT did not want to remove a service without understanding the impact of doing this. In short, services were never decommissioned.
- Poor quality data can also be an issue. Services did a great job in exposing data that was previously inaccessible; however, the quality of the data itself was questionable. Duplicates, inconsistencies, and irrelevances in data were some of the data issues identified.

> The topic of data quality and issues that this caused **Weir & Bell Telecoms** are covered in greater detail in *Chapter 11, Extending Design-time Governance with AIA Foundation Pack 11g.*

To solve these problems, it was clear that the existing processes needed enhancement and governance. It was concluded that OER would be used as the single and centralized tool for:

- Architects and Designers to search existing Assets and their status.
- Architects and Designers to catalogue and prioritize candidate services.
- Designers and Developers to search and use existing Assets using their IDE.
- Designers and Developers to catalogue new built Assets using their IDE.
- Architects to classify all Assets depending on their type.
- Architects to specify architecture blueprints and other architectural relevant templates.
- Establishing the relationship between Assets, Asset types, and consumers.
- Managing Asset versions and their status.

All of the preceding should be possible despite the fact that projects might be running in parallel.

Furthermore, it was decided that all the document deliverables would be version controlled. For this reason, new additional requirements were identified as follows:

- All the document deliverables such as **Use Cases**, **High Level Designs**, **Detail Designs**, and **Unit Test Plans**, should be associated in OER to their relevant Assets.
- More rigorous **Access Control Restrictions** should be enforced so that it would be possible to restrict the visibility of sensitive information when necessary.

Based on the preceding requirements, an updated view of the process was created in which the individual and outdated Excel documents were superseded by the use of OER for the discovering and cataloguing services. In addition, OER would also be used by Designers and Developers to further discover and harvest services throughout the design and build stages of the lifecycle. The new process looked as follows:

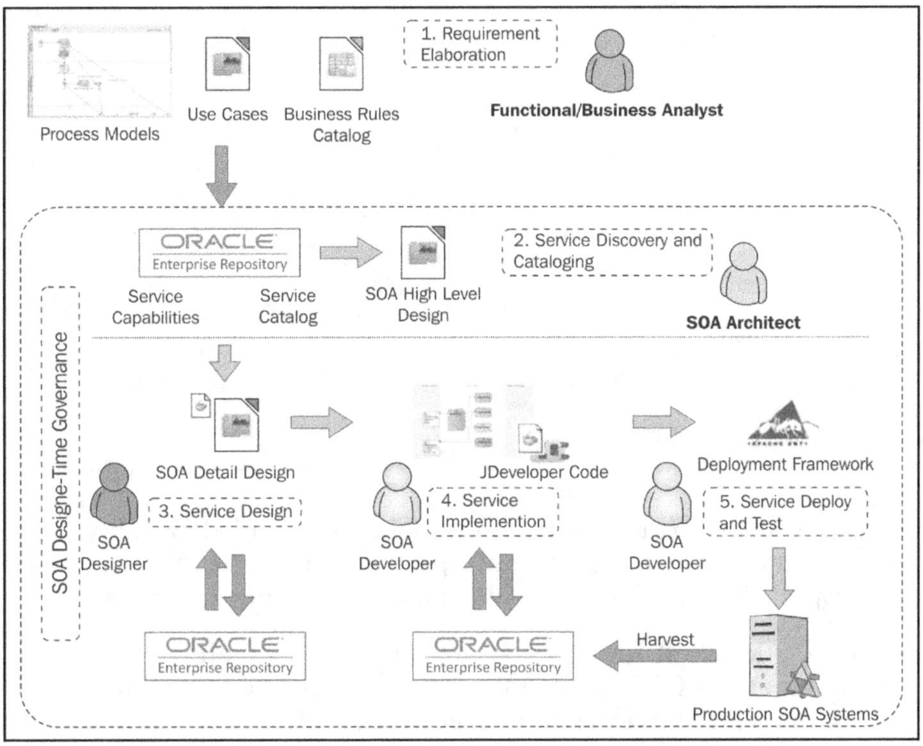

These simple yet effective changes allowed **Weir & Bell Telecoms** to realize substantial cost savings through service re-use. Also, by allowing Architects, Designers, and Developers to discover and catalogue new services in OER, it was possible to identify opportunities for re-use earlier in the lifecycle.

Furthermore, because all the documentation was now version controlled in a content server, it was possible to harvest these as Assets into OER and then associate them with the relevant services. The following **Asset Relationship View** was modeled in OER:

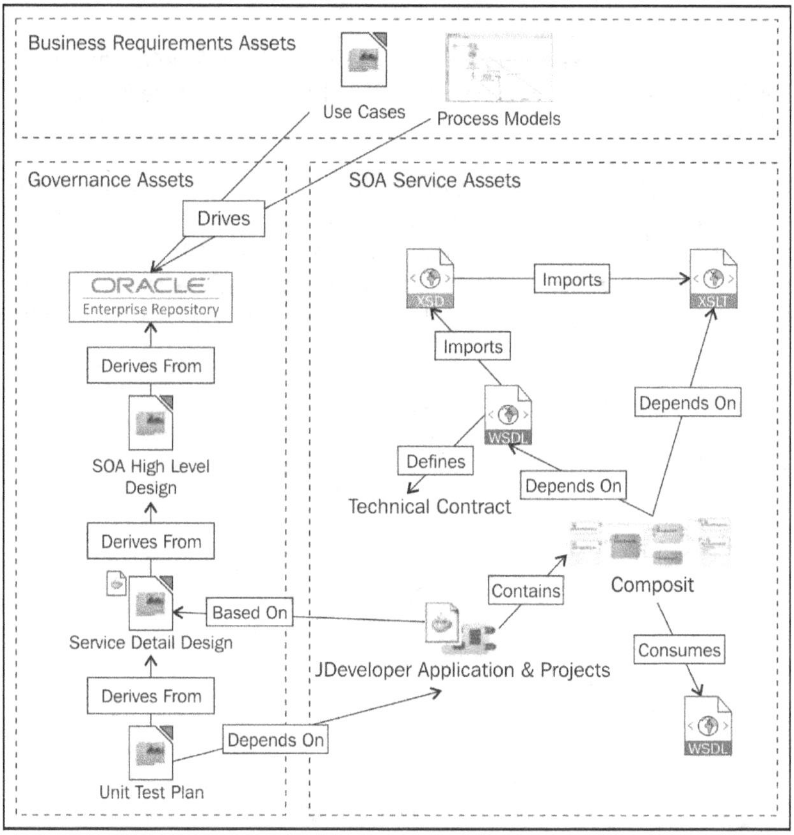

Having a full relationship view of the Assets not only provided visibility of existing Assets but also, importantly, the relationship between the Assets. This proved to be invaluable, especially when it came to understanding the impact of change.

The following sections will deliver a comprehensive guide on how to perform an initial configuration of OER so that the requirements listed previously can be addressed by using the **Harvester** and **Asset Lifecycle** features of the product. The latter features will be covered in *Chapter 5, Harvesting*.

Preparing the browser

The first step that must be completed before logging into the OER console is to install Java Web Start 1.4.2 or greater. Java Web Start is needed in order to use the **Asset Editor**, **Type Manager**, Navigator, Browser Tree, and the Import/Export Utility.

> Note that Java Web Start is included in the Java Runtime Environment (JRE) as a part of Java SE 6 which can be downloaded from the URL `http://www.oracle.com/technetwork/java/javase/tech/index-jsp-136112.html`.

It is possible that the JRE is already installed on your desktop. To find out if this is the case, open a command prompt and run the command:

```
java -version
```

If JRE is installed, the result should be similar to the following screenshot:

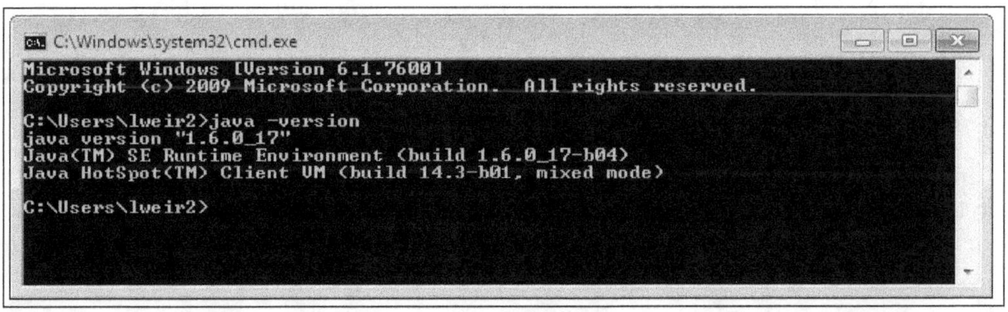

Once JRE is installed, you can enable Java Web Start by clicking on the **Java** icon available in the **Windows Control Panel**:

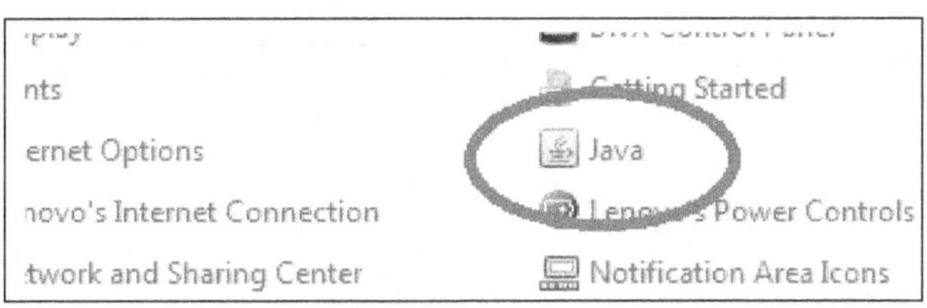

When the **Java Control Panel** window opens, go to the **Advanced** tab and ensure that all the relevant browsers are selected in the **Default Java for browsers** option, and that the **JNLP File/MIME Association** is **Always allowed**:

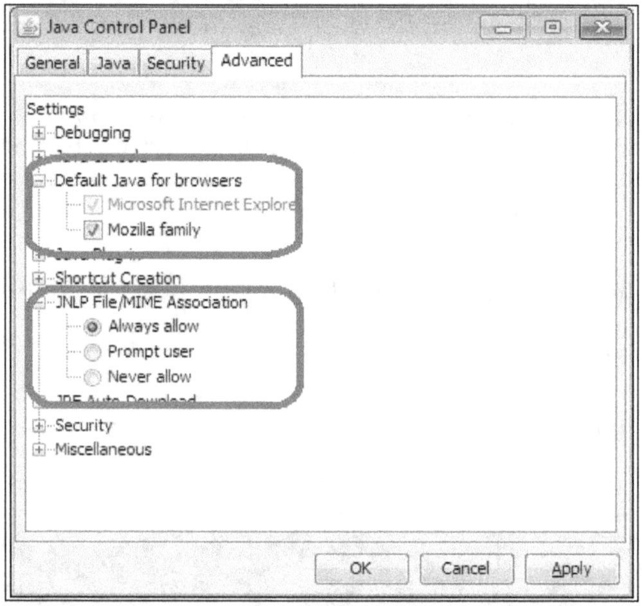

To verify that Java Web Start was correctly installed and configured, you should log on to the OER console by opening the OER URL `http://<server name>:<port>/oer` using a supported browser.

> Note that Firefox and Internet Explorer are both supported browsers but some features such as printing search results are only available in the latter.

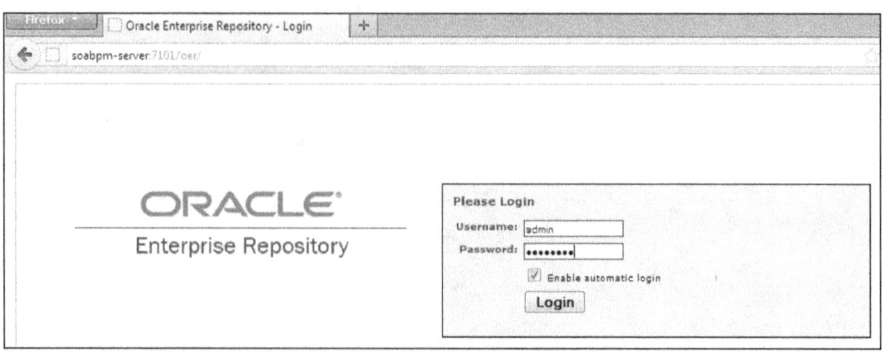

> You can log on using the admin account which was set up during the initial installation of OER.

Once you are logged into OER, click on the **Edit / Manage Assets** link located on the upper right-hand side of the page to open the **Asset Editor** window:

The browser should be able to associate the JNLP extension to Java Web Start and it should be possible to tell the browser to always open the JNLP extensions with this application:

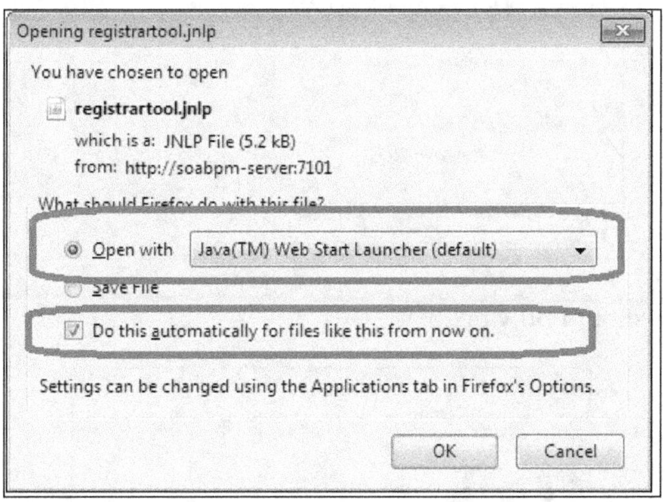

If all worked successfully, the Java Web Start application should start downloading the **Asset Editor** applet:

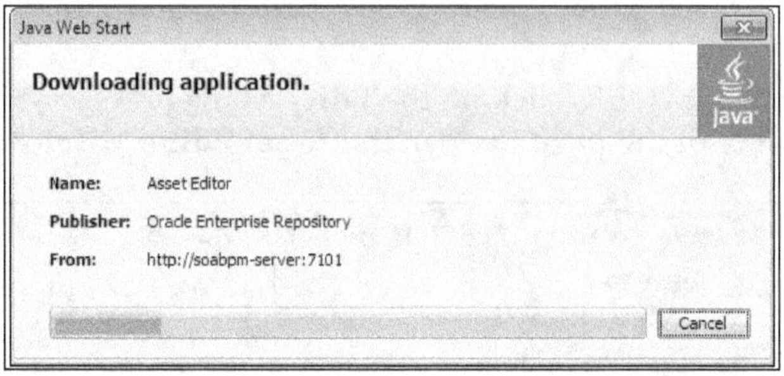

Once the application has been downloaded, if you are using Windows, it is likely that a **Security Warning** window will appear. If this is the case, just tick the box **to Always trust content from this publisher** and then click on **Run**:

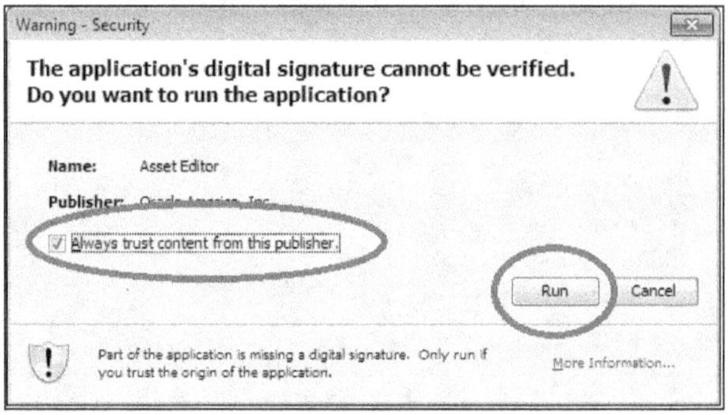

The **Asset Editor** should now open:

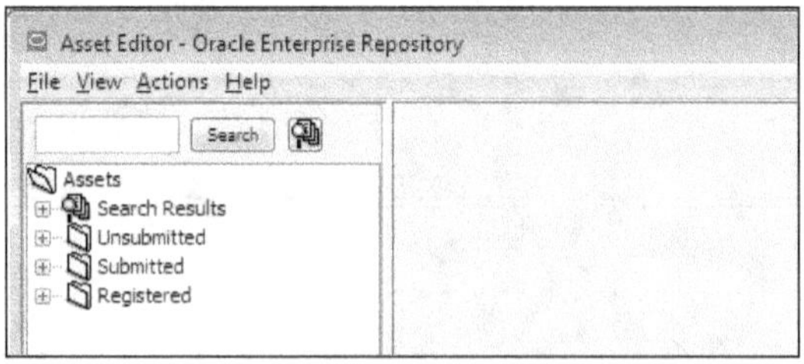

> In case of issues installing or configuring Java Web Start, we recommend reading section *3.2.2 Troubleshooting Java Web Start* of the *OER Installation Guide* available at the URL `http://docs.huihoo.com/oracle/middleware/fusion/11g/doc.1111/e15745/post.htm#CIHCBHDG`.

Creating departments, projects, users, and roles

As described in *Chapter 3, Introduction to Oracle Enterprise Repository*, all the users in OER must belong to a project and a department. It is therefore very important before doing the OER initial configuration to have good understanding of your company's organizational structure. In the case of Weir & Bell Telecoms' Governance implementation, it was decided to simplify the departmental structures to simplify OER setup. Therefore, only two main departments were created as follows:

- **Business**: Basically, any member of the business such as Business Analysts, Department Managers, and other members of the business community.
- **IT**: IT Managers as well as Architects, Developers, and other members of the Support staff belonging to the IT department.

Furthermore, as OER supports role-based authorization, the following roles were defined:

> Note that the roles highlighted with the * character are roles available when installing the product.

- ***User**: It is the default OER role and provides limited access to OER including viewing and submitting Assets, viewing projects, and the generation of reports.
- ***Business Analyst**: Members of the business analysis community responsible for defining requirements such as functional specifications and use cases.
- ***Advance Submitter**: This role is usually assigned to system users created for the Asset Builder or the different Harvester.
- ***Registrar**: The role assigned to the users who are responsible for accepting or rejecting Asset submissions.
- ***Access Administrator**: This role allows the creation of users and the assignation of different access permissions to them.
- ***Registrar Administrator**: Similar to the Registrar role, however, this role allows Types to be managed using the Type Manager.
- ***Project Administrator**: This role allows users to manage projects including assigning users to projects and generating reports.
- ***System Administrator**: This role allows system settings to be modified.

> Note that the user admin belongs to all the administration groups.

- **Third-Party Consultant**: A read-only account that allows third-party consultants to discover and submit Assets for specific projects only.

In the case of the Weir & Bell Telecoms' Governance implementation, most of the user roles required were available out-of-the-box. Do note that as described in *Chapter 3, Introduction to Oracle Enterprise Repository*, OER access settings are highly configurable and more complex RBAC configurations are supported.

> *Section 4, Configuring Advanced Role-based Access Control* of the *OER Configuration Guide* provides a detailed description on how to configure OER to support more complex use cases: `http://docs.oracle.com/cd/E14571_01/doc.1111/e16580/rbac.htm`

Note that OER supports the use of external identity sources such as the LDAP directories, for example, MS Active Directory or OID as the master repository for users and roles. In the case of **Weir & Bell Telecoms**, it was decided not to integrate with the corporate LDAP (which was an AD domain) because of the size of this system and the fact that it would take around five working days for a change to be made in this directory. Instead, as the number of OER users was limited (a maximum of 20 users initially), it was decided to use a local identity store. Note that the decision as to whether or not to use an external identity source depends on each individual implementation. In some cases it might make sense but in others, such as the example used in this book, it might not be required.

> For further information on how to configure OER to authenticate from external sources, please refer to *Section 3, Configuring Oracle Enterprise Repository to use External Authentication tooling* of the *OER Configuration Guide*: `http://docs.oracle.com/cd/E14571_01/doc.1111/e16580/extauth.htm`

Creating departments

Once the organization and access requirements have been identified, the next step is to create the departments as follows:

1. Log into OER as admin and click on the **Admin** menu, which is located on the upper right-hand side of the home page:

2. Once in the administration page, click on the **Departments** menu located on the left panel. This will expand the departments menu and will display some of the actions available:

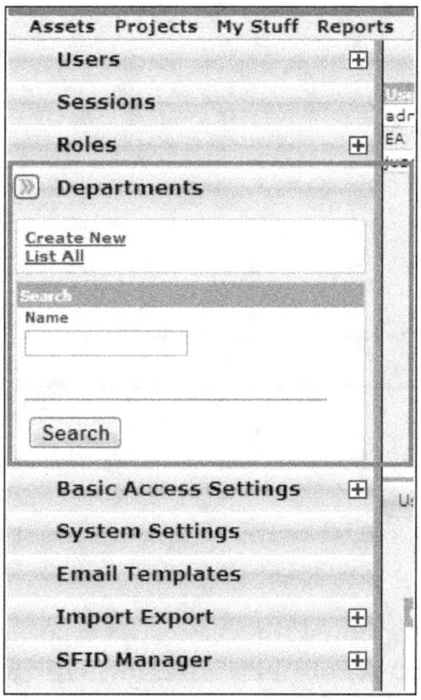

3. Once you are on this page, click on the **List All** link to list all the available departments:

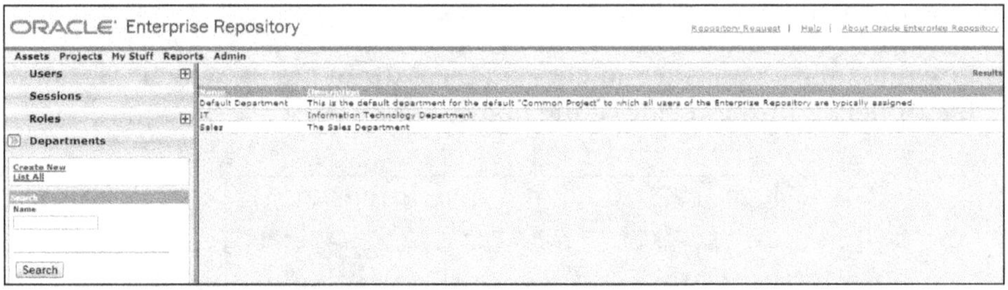

4. In this particular example, the department **IT** already exists, however the **Business** department has to be created. To create a new department, click on the **Create New** link located on the left panel under the **Departments** menu. This link will open up a popup window in which the details of the new department can be added and saved:

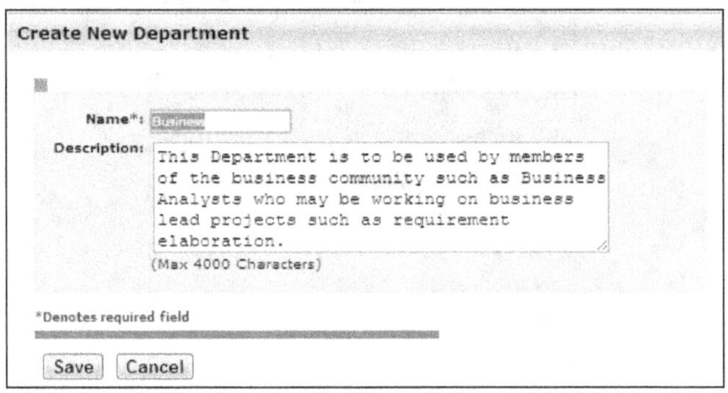

Creating roles

Now that all the departments exist within OER, we must ensure that all the roles identified are also available.

As discussed earlier in this section, OER comes with some pre-defined user roles. However, the **Business Analyst** role as well as the **Third-Party Consultant** role are not available by default and therefore have to be created.

1. Roles are managed within the same administration page under the **Roles** menu located on the left panel:

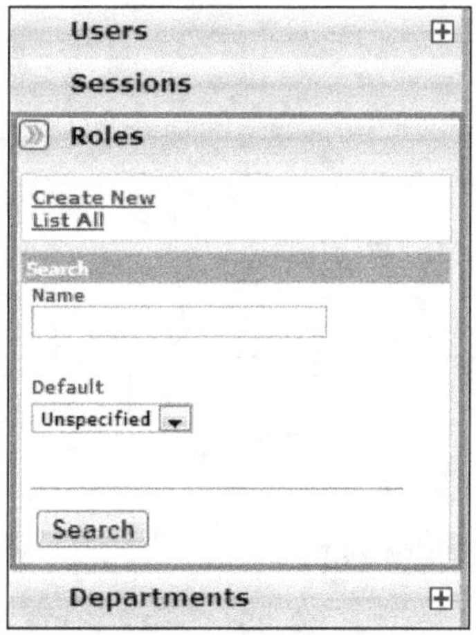

2. New roles can be created by clicking on the **Create New** link under the **Roles** menu. Once clicked, a popup window will open and details of the new role can be added and saved:

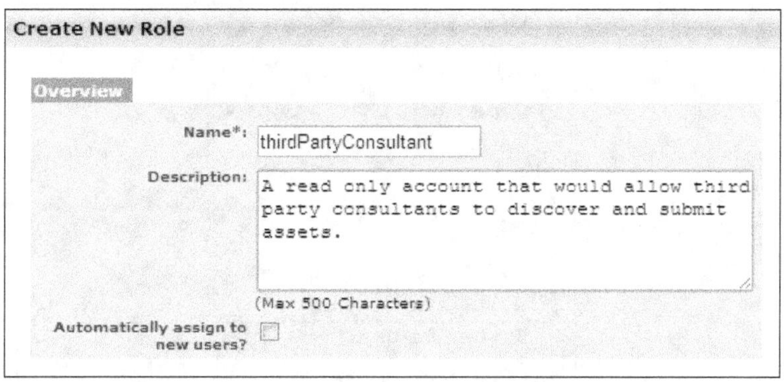

For this particular example, you can see that we followed a different convention with the name. This is a recommended practice to avoid conflicts with external identity stores if these are ever used.

3. Once all roles have been created they can be listed by clicking on the **List All** link under the **Roles** menu. All roles created should appear on the list:

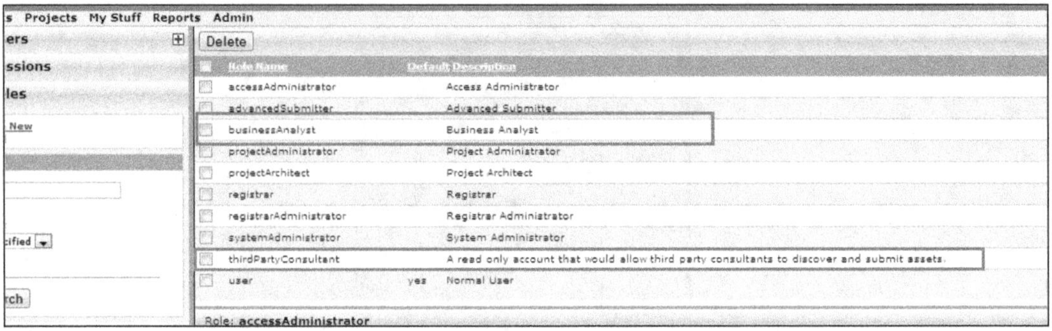

Basic access settings

Once all the missing roles are created, access restrictions to the roles must be assigned.

Access restrictions are assigned to roles within the same administration page under the **Basic Access Settings** menu located on the left panel:

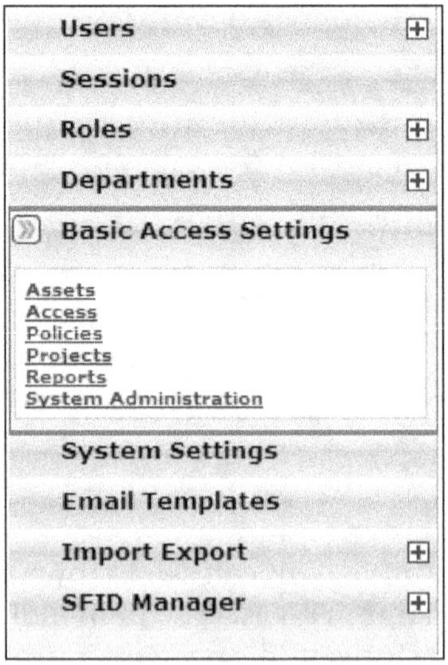

Through this menu, a user who is a member of the `accessAdministration` role can set the basic access settings for the OER roles. In this menu, there are five links that provide different access restrictions to OER:

- **Assets**: This defines the different access restriction for asset-related tasks and functionalities such as the **Asset** page, **Asset Editor**, **Asset Stores**, and **Type Manager**, amongst other asset-related functionality. For example, to allow a user to view, edit, and submit Assets, the user must belong to a role which has been granted the **View**, **Edit**, and **Create/Submit** permissions through this link. The following is a sample snapshot of a basic access configuration made on the **Assets** link:

Set Permissions

	View	Use	Download	Review	Notify	Edit	Accept	Approve Tabs	Register	Create / Submit	Launch Asset Editor	Edit Artifact Stores	Edit Type
advancedSubmitter	✓	✓	✓	✓	✓	✓				✓	✓		
registrar	✓	✓	✓	✓	✓	✓	✓	✓	✓	✓	✓		
registrarAdministrator	✓	✓	✓	✓	✓	✓	✓	✓	✓	✓	✓	✓	✓
user	✓	✓	✓	✓						✓			

- Not Granted ✓ - Granted ✗ -Denied

Note - All Permissions are **Most** Restrictive

- **Access**: This defines the different access restriction for the administration page excluding the **System Settings** and **Email templates** menus. Usually, only the administration roles are granted access-related permissions. The following is a sample snapshot of a basic access configuration made on the **Access** link:

	View	Edit	Create	Delete
accessAdministrator	✓	✓	✓	

- Not Granted ✓ - Granted ✗ -Denied

- **Policies**: This defines whether a user is allowed to apply a policy to other Assets. Policy permissions are usually granted to Architects so that they can configure standard policies that should be applied. By default, no role has been granted with policy access permissions. However, this can easily be achieved as follows:
    1. Click on the **Edit** button located on the upper right-hand side:

    2. When the popup window opens, select the option **Show all available Roles**. This will allow all the available roles to be displayed in the window. Then tick the box on the role that will be granted with **Apply Policy** permissions. In our example, it is the **Project Architect** role that is given such permissions:

    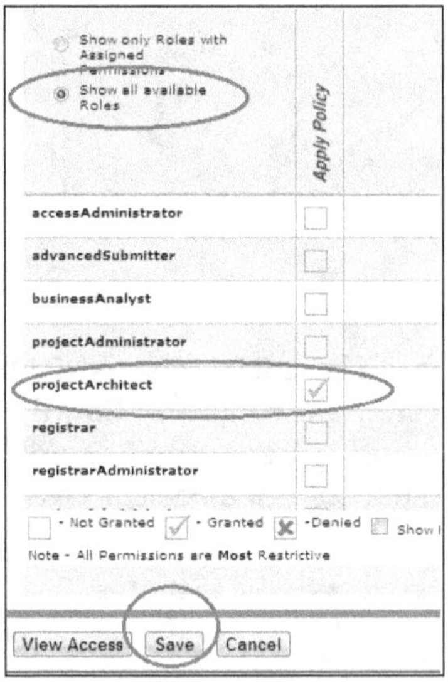

- **Projects**: This defines the different access restriction for the **Projects** page and applying templates to projects. The following is a sample snapshot of a basic access configuration made on the **Projects** link:

	View	Edit	Create	Apply Template
accessAdministrator	✓			
advancedSubmitter	✓			
businessAnalyst	✓			✓
projectAdministrator	✓	✓	✓	✓
projectArchitect	✓			✓
registrar	✓			
registrarAdministrator	✓			
systemAdministrator	✓			
user	✓			

- Not Granted ✓ - Granted ✗ -Denied

- **Reports**: This defines the view access restriction for the **Reports** page. The following is a sample snapshot of a basic access configuration for Assets. In our example, all the users have been granted with the **View** reports permission.

	View
accessAdministrator	✓
advancedSubmitter	✓
businessAnalyst	✓
projectAdministrator	✓
projectArchitect	✓
registrar	✓
registrarAdministrator	✓
systemAdministrator	✓
user	✓

- Not Granted ✓ - Granted ✗ -Denied

- **System Administrators**: This defines the view access restriction for the System Administration and Email Template menus within the administration page. The following is a sample snapshot of a basic access configuration for **systemAdministrator**:

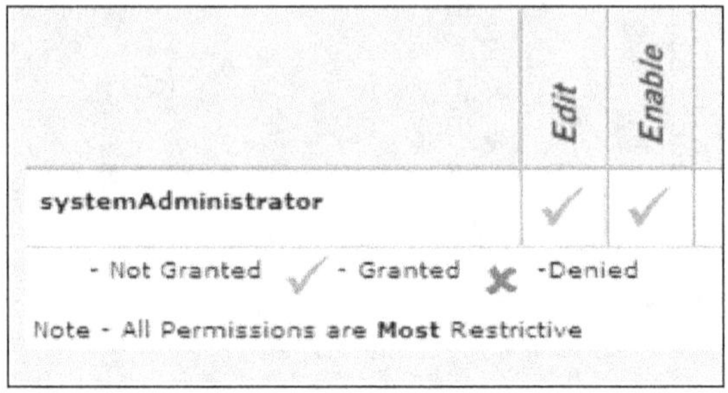

> For a detailed description of the Basic Access Control option, refer to *Section 4, Configuring Advanced Role-based Access Control* of the *OER Configuration Guide* at `http://docs.oracle.com/cd/E14571_01/doc.1111/e16580/rbac.html`.

Custom access settings

The Third-Party Consultants role has to be configured such that the users belonging to this role can only see and action Assets for specific projects. There are many examples for which these complex access configuration requirements are needed. An obvious one is the case of external consultancies being tasked with the delivery of specific projects. In this case, the external consultancy will have its own Architects, Designers, and Developers and therefore will require access to OER. In this scenario, **Weir & Bell Telecoms** was concerned that external consultants would have visibility of all its internal Assets registered in the repository. The solution offered was to limit the external consultant's visibility of Assets exclusively to those available for the project they are working on. Furthermore, any submission or creation of new Assets by external consultants should undergo approval of the Project Architect.

Basic access settings do not support the implementation of access restrictions to individual Assets and therefore, complex access settings are required in order to restrict external consultants from having access to Assets other than the ones they require for a specific project. The following is an example of how to perform the configuration of roles to enforce such restrictions.

Firstly, a basic **Submit/Create** role which could be assigned to the external consultants should be created. This will extend the default user role and allow creation/submission of Assets into OER.

1. As described in the preceding lines, this can be done in the administration page by clicking on the **Create New** link of the **Roles** menu that is located in the left pane:

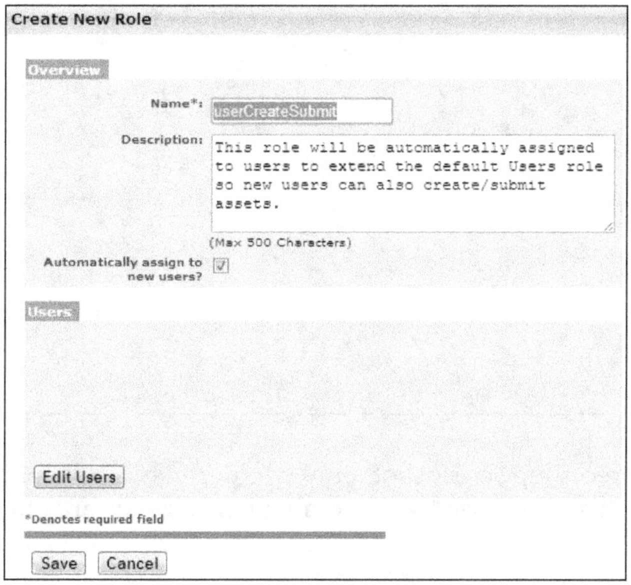

To be consistent with the naming convention used, the role was named `userCreateSubmit`.

> Note that the tick box **Automatically assign to new users?** was set so that any new user created is automatically assigned to this role by default.

2. Now the following **Basic Access Settings** need to be applied to the role. This can be done by clicking on the **Assets** link available within the **Basic Access Settings** menu. Click on the **Edit** button within this page and a popup window will open that will allow the modification of asset restrictions:

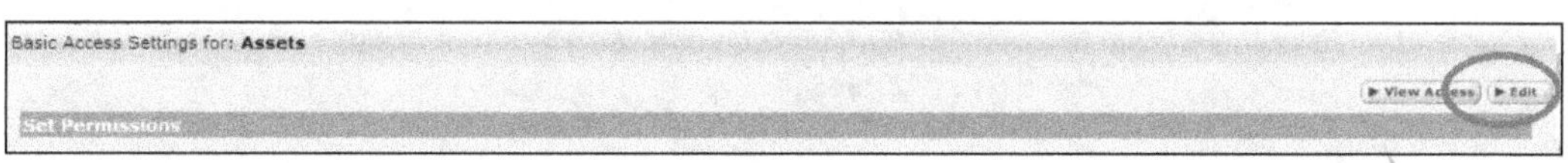

3. On the popup window, select the option **Show all available Roles** so that all the roles are displayed. Then on the newly created role, `userCreateSubmit`, assign permissions as shown:

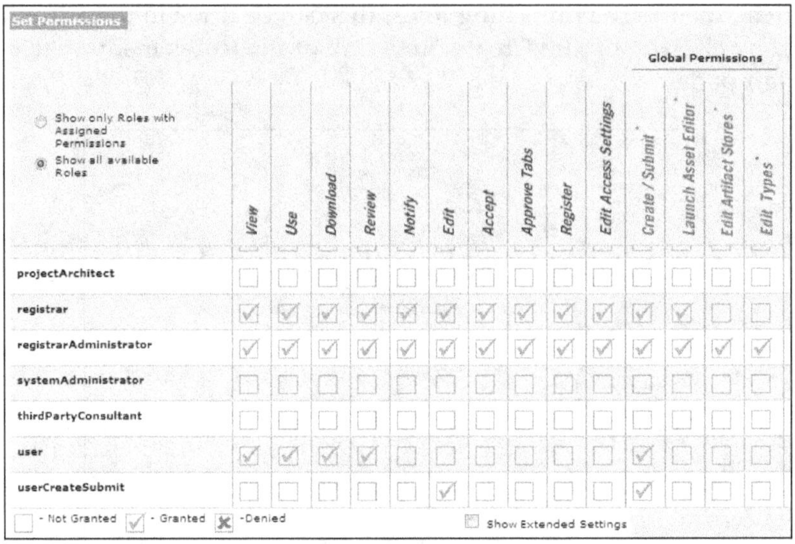

As shown in the preceding screenshot, only two permissions were granted: **Edit** and **Create / Submit**. This is because the remaining permissions are already available in the default role **User**.

The second step is to enable **Complex Access Settings** in OER. This feature is not enabled by default when installing OER.

1. Log into OER with an admin account and go to the administration page. Once you are on this page click on the **System Settings** menu:

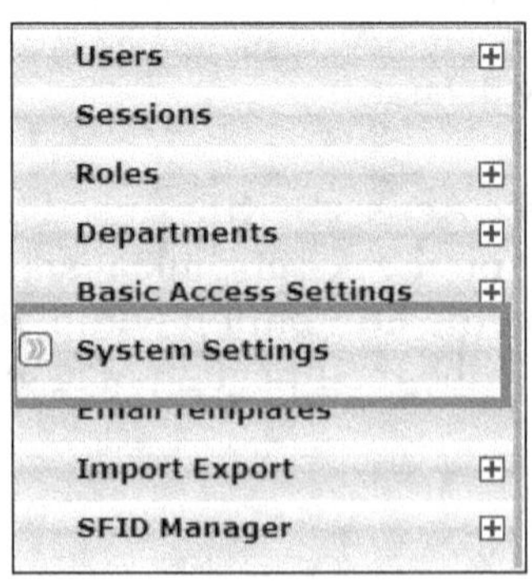

2. Once the **System Settings Page** loads, scroll down to the **Access Control** option and set the **Custom Access Settings** setting to **True**:

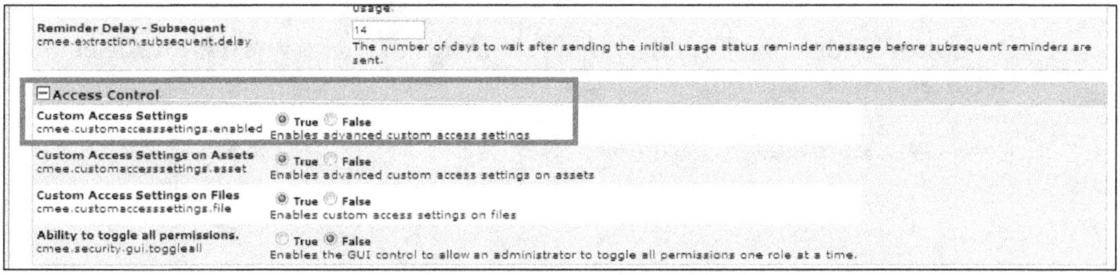

3. Click on **Save** located at the bottom of the screen to save the changes:

4. Once done, the **Custom Access Settings** menu should appear on the left pane on refreshing the administration page:

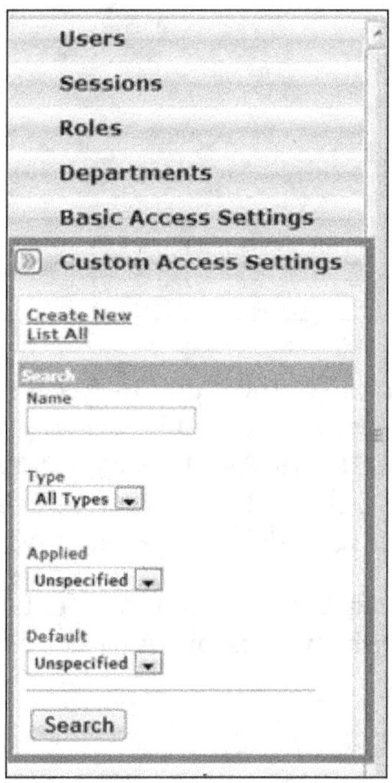

5. By default, no **Custom Access Settings** are available in OER. To create a new custom access, click on the **Create New** link as shown in the preceding screenshot.

   A popup window will open so that the details of the new **Custom Asset Settings** can be entered:

   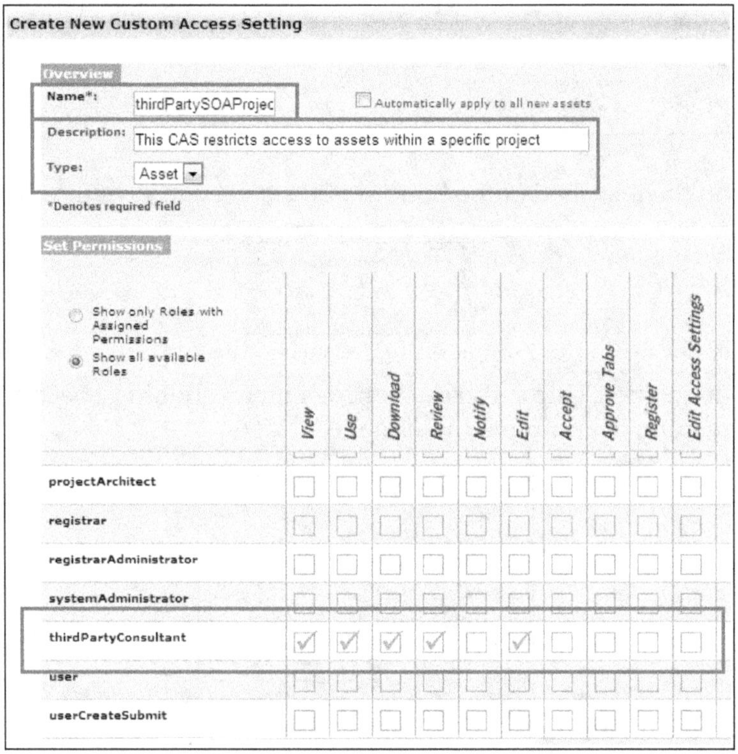

   In this example, the name of the **Custom Access Setting** is set to `thirdPartySOAProjectAssets` and has been granted with **View**, **Use**, **Download**, **Review**, and **Edit** Assets permissions. The naming convention employed reflects the fact that this custom access restriction is used to limit third-party company's SOA Project Assets only.

Now that the custom setting has been created, the next step is to create a project and assign a project profile to it with the **Custom Access Settings** applied to it.

A project profile in OER is a type of compliance template. As described in *Chapter 3, Introduction to Oracle Enterprise Repository*, compliance templates are used to communicate the Asset requirements to internal or external project teams. For our scenario, a project profile will be used to enforce the complex access setting `thirdPartySOAProjectAssets` so that the users of this project can only access Assets from within the project.

Creating the project

In OER, projects can be created from the **Projects Page** as follows:

1. Click on the **Create New** link:

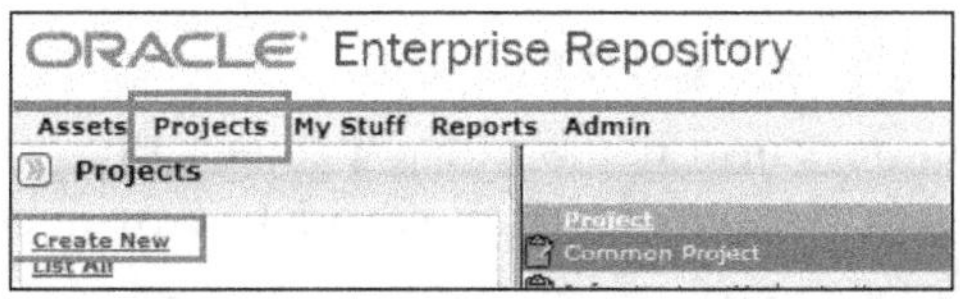

2. A popup window will open and the project details can be entered as follows. Once all the details have been entered, submit the project by clicking on the **Save** button:

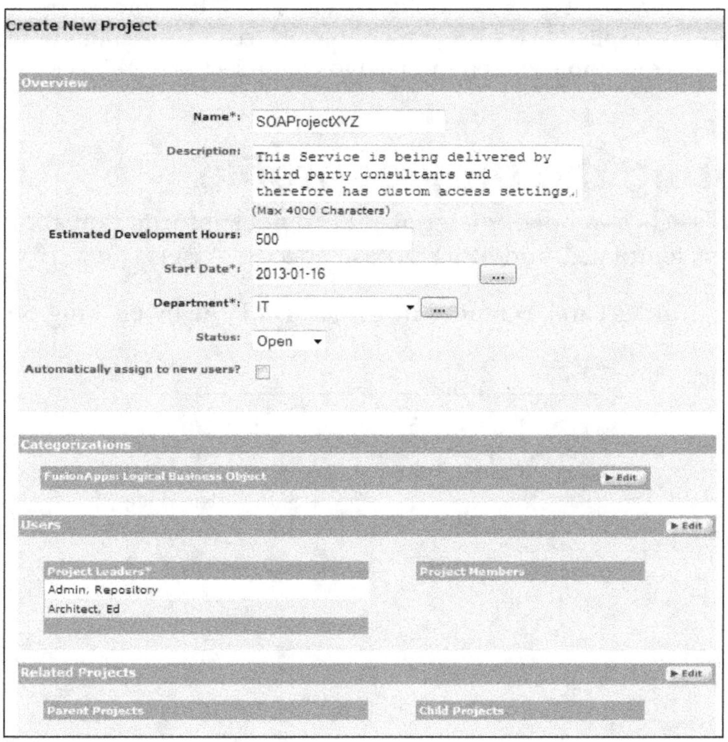

The screen properties are as follows:

- **Name**: The name of the Project. In this example, we called it as the project `SOAProjectXYZ`.
- **Description**: A brief description of the project.
- **Estimated Development Hours**: The total estimated hours. This is the field which is particularly important as it will be used by the reporting features of OER in order to calculate costs and other factors.
- **Start Date**: The date when the project starts.
- **Department**: The department that owns the project.
- **Status**: Open or closed.
- **Categorizations**: Default categorization.
- **Users**: Project Leaders and users of the project. Project Leaders differ from users in that they will have elevated rights to a project.
- **Related Projects**: Any relationship with other projects. For example, this could be a child project within a large program of work or it could be a standalone project as in this example.

> Note that until a compliance template of type project profile is applied to the project, no custom access restrictions or other constraints will be enforced to the project.

Configuring the project profile

A project profile acts as a bill of materials. It provides information about services to be used, process templates, and other project specific Assets.

1. Project profiles can be created in the **Assets Page** by clicking on the **Submit an Asset** link:

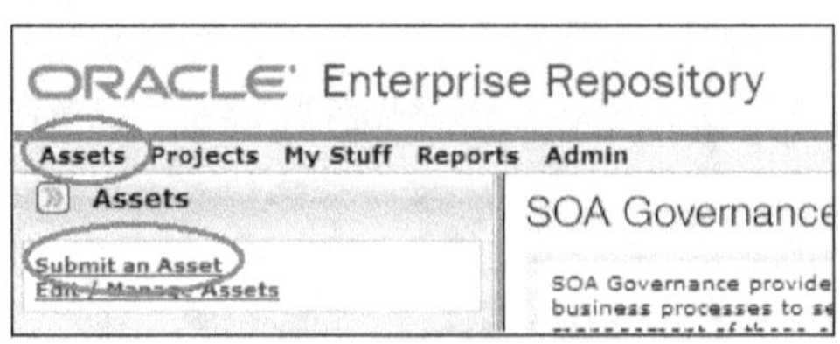

2. A pop-up window will open and the Asset details can be entered:

> Note that a project profile is an Asset of type project profile as the following snapshot suggests:

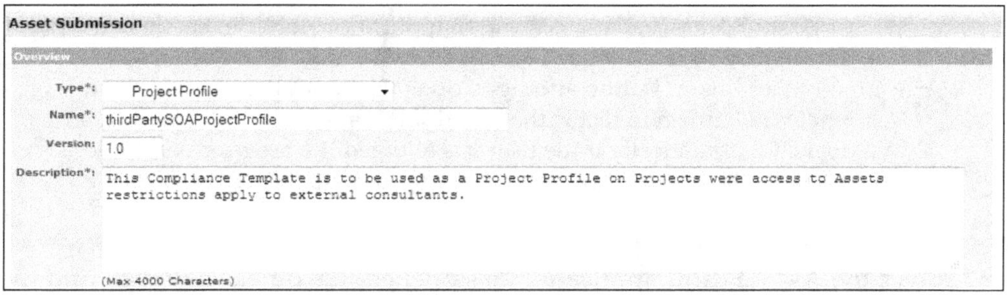

> Note that a **File Location URL** field is mandatory, however if a project profile file is not available text such as `N/A` can be entered instead.

3. Once all the details have been entered, submit the project profile by clicking on the **Save** button:

The project profile will then be submitted and a workflow process initiated. The Asset will have to be accepted and registered by a user that belongs to the role Registrar.

As we are logged on as admin, we can directly review and register this Asset. This can be done as follows:

1. Go to the **My Stuff** page. On the **Assignee** dropdown, select **Unassigned** and click on **Search**. Once the results are displayed on the main page, select **Project Profile** from the **Asset Type** dropdown, and click on the **Filter** button:

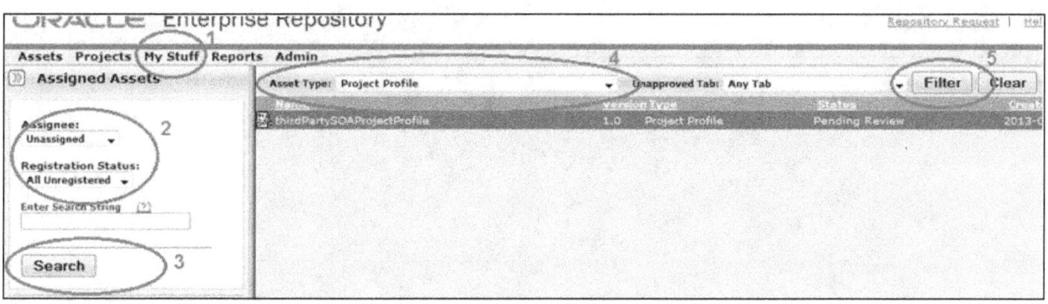

2. All the Assets of the type **Project Profile** will be listed. Click on **thirdPartySOAProjectProfile** so that the Asset details are displayed on the button page.
3. In the Asset details section, click on the **Edit** button to open the **Asset Editor** window.

> As **Asset Editor** is a Java Web Start application, it has to be opened through a `registrartool.jnlp` file. When the **Edit** button (or any other link or button aiming to open the **Asset Editor**) is clicked, what will happen in fact is that the JNLP file will be downloaded and opened automatically if the user has allowed the browser permissions to do so. Otherwise, it will be necessary to double-click on the JNLP file once it has been downloaded.

4. Once the **Asset Editor** application has opened, the quickest way to find the project profile is by doing an **Advanced Search**. Click on the **Advanced Search** button (located next to the **Search** button) and then, from the **Asset Editor Advanced Search** window, select **Project Profile** from the **Type** dropdown and click on **OK**:

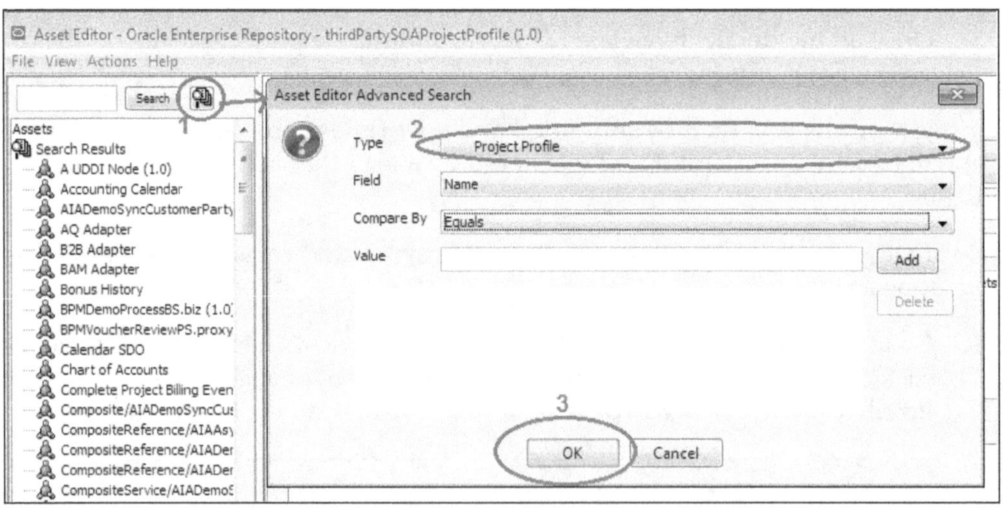

When all the Assets of type project profile show up on the left menu, select the relevant project profile and all the details of the Asset will appear on the right-hand side:

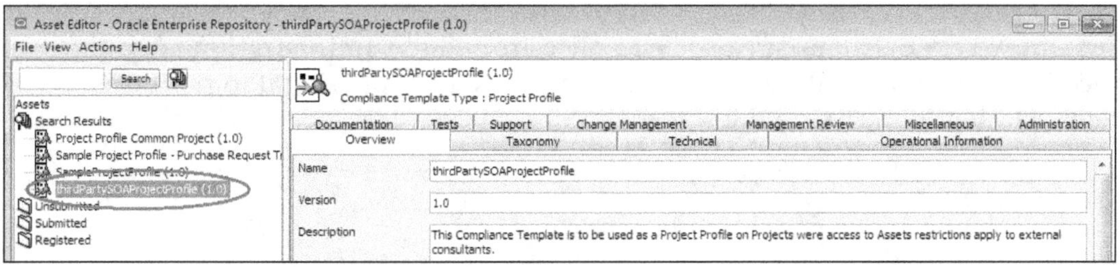

5. Assets can be accepted and registered from the **Administration** tab. Select this tab and click on the **Accept** and **Register** buttons **Project Profile**:

[From this screen, a number of administration functions can be done such as **Accept/Unaccept**, **Register/Unregister**, **Assign Users**, **Change Status**, assign **Complex Access Settings**, and so on.]

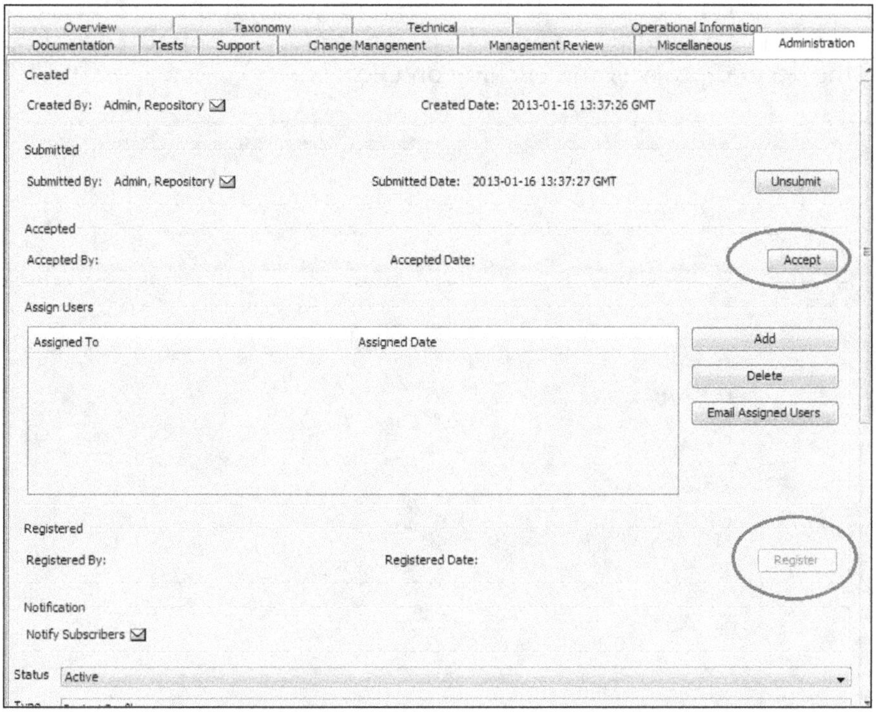

> Note that the **Approval/Registration Workflows** will be covered in greater detail in *Chapter 6, Asset Lifecycle and Workflow*.

Custom Access Settings can also be applied from the **Administration** tab by selecting an item from the **Available** settings box and applying it to profile as demonstrated in the following screenshot:

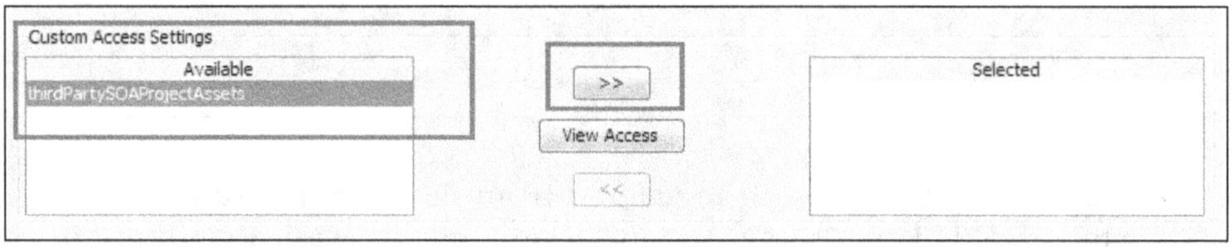

> By applying a custom access setting to a project profile, all the projects to which this profile has been applied will be enforced with the access settings.

The project profile can be applied to the desired project(s) from the **Overview** tab by clicking on the **Add** button within the section **Projects Applied To** and then by selecting the desired projects and clicking on **Ok**:

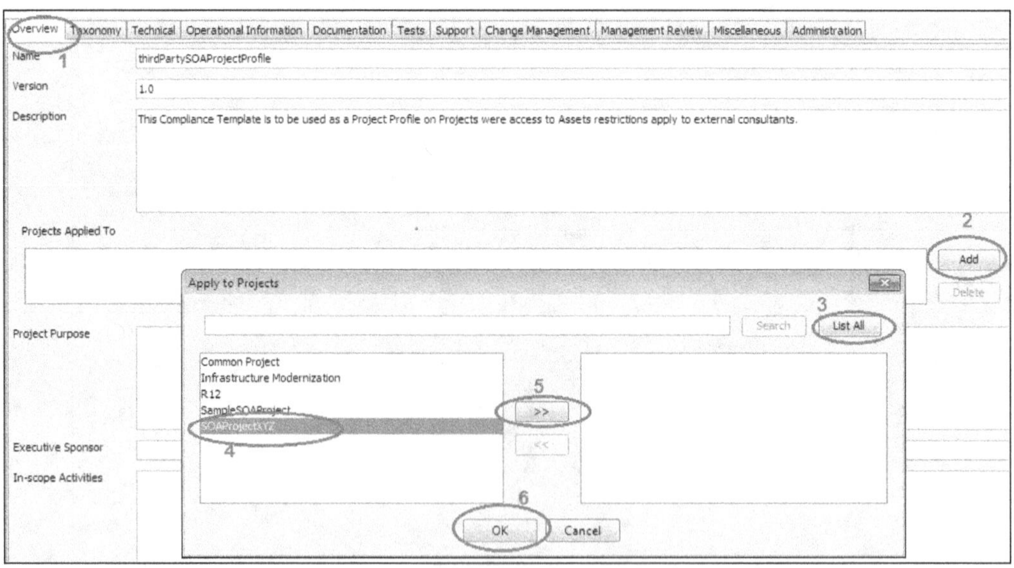

Once all the desired changes have been made to the Asset, save all the changes by selecting the **Save** option from the **File** menu:

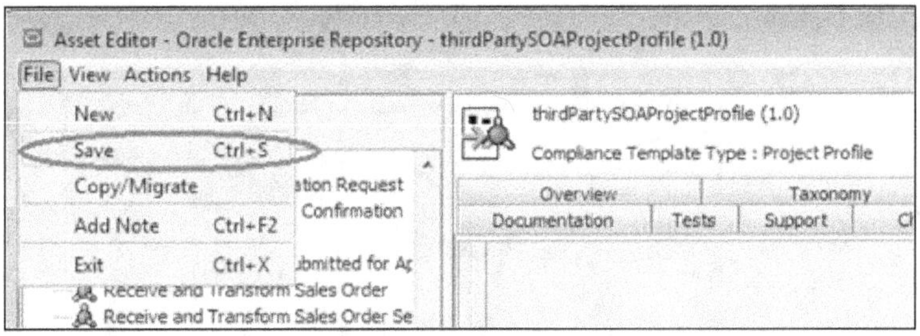

Adding users

Once the departments, roles, access settings, project profiles, and projects have been configured, we can start adding user accounts into OER.

> Note that it is possible to add users before the initial configuration is done, however it is not desirable and not recommended. Some of the main reasons are because users might be given the wrong role and/or access restrictions, as these might have not yet been defined if users are added before the configuration analysis is done.

Users are managed in the **Administration** page from the **Users** menu located on the left pane. From this page, users can be created, listed/searched, and modified (including the assigning of roles) by an Access Administrator.

As described earlier, **Weir & Bell Telecoms** had a requirement to restrict the visibility of Assets to third-party consultants Assets to the project to which they are assigned.

In the previous section, we described how to create a role named `thirdPartyConsultant` to which the custom access settings `thirdPartySOAProjectAssets` were applied. Furthermore, we created a default role named `userCreateSubmit` that extends the User role by granting **Edit** and **Create/Submit** permissions. Lastly, we showed how to assign the `thirdPartySOAProjectAssets` custom access setting to project profile which could be assigned to any project that requires third-party consultants.

The relevant roles must then be assigned to the users for which restrictions apply. This is done as follows:

1. From the **Users** menu, click on the **Create New** link:

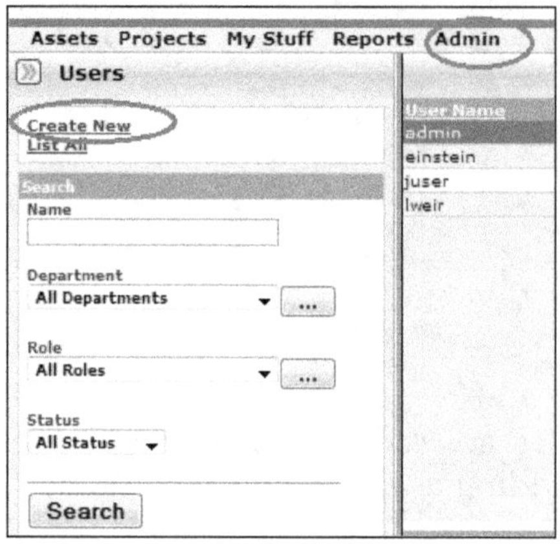

2. On the popup window, enter the user details in the **Overview** section:

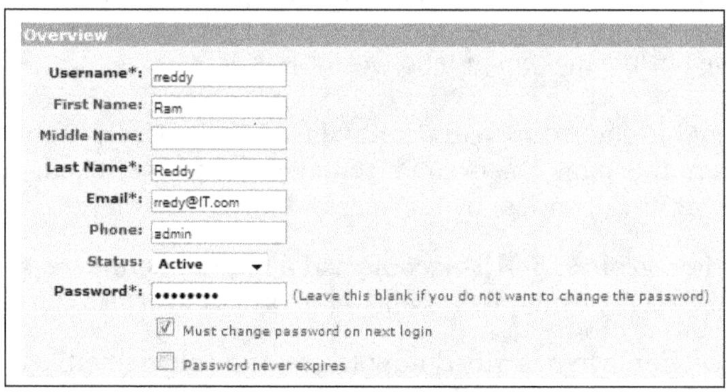

Note that since the checkbox **Must change password on next login** was selected, the first time this user logs on, a change password page will show up.

3. Assign the roles `thirdPartyConsultant` and `userCreateSubmit` to the user as shown in the following screenshot:

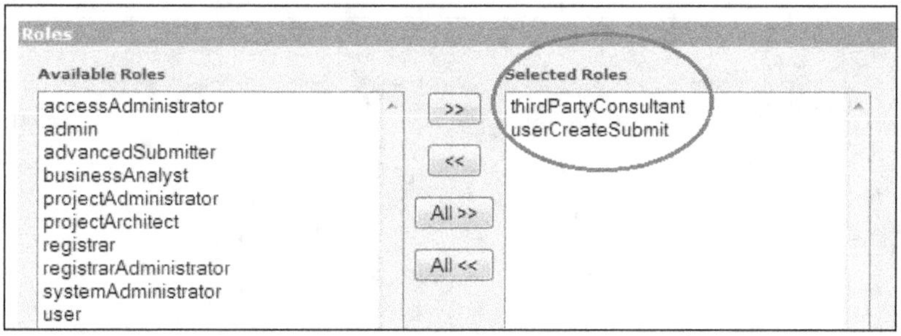

> Note that the default role User must be deselected otherwise the new user will be granted with all the default User access. In our example, as this is a third-party consultant, the intention is restrict visibility to all information except for the project to which the consultants are assigned.

4. Assign the relevant **Departments** and click on **Save**:

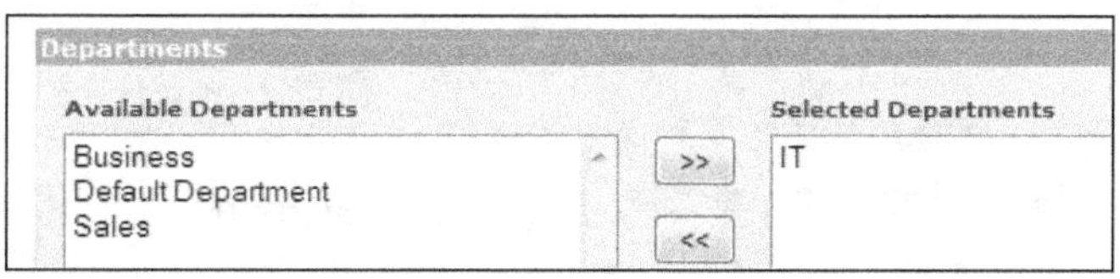

Verify that the user has been set up properly as follows:

1. Create a similar user following the same steps previously described (however with dummy details). Take a note of the username and password used.
2. Log into OER using the user's credentials.

3. The first thing that should appear after login is the **Change Password** page. Enter the new password and click on **Change Password**:

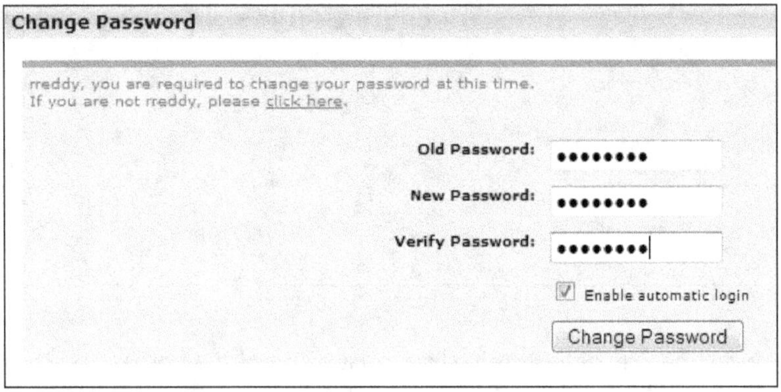

4. After changing the password, the user should be redirected to a very limited home page that has only two items in the main menu: **Assets** and **My Stuff**:

5. Do a search and check that only the Assets associated with the project appear in the search results:

Follow similar steps to create all the users needed for your OER implementation. Ensure that all the users have been assigned the correct roles and restrictions by creating sample users when required and accessing OER to check that access settings were properly configured.

Summary

This chapter explained the thought process and considerations that must be undertaken prior to the initial configuration of OER. It described in some detail the main configuration tasks and how these are performed.

We have demonstrated how departments, roles, projects, project profiles, basic access settings, and complex access settings are created and configured. The chapter has also explained how to use the **Asset Editor** window to modify the project profile and to show how more complex RBAC configurations are supported.

The chapter also elaborated on the project profile compliance templates and described how these can be created and applied to projects.

In the next chapter, we will cover how to use the Harvester and other Asset-specific features to support asset-related requirements as described in the use case section.

5 Harvesting

This chapter describes the typical steps that should be fulfilled when defining the Bootstrap Strategy and the subsequent actions required to successfully execute the **Harvester**.

The chapter walks through the process of:

- Cataloging and classifying the existing Assets.
- Importing **Solution Packs**.
- Creating new Categorizations and Asset Types.
- Configuring and executing the Harvester.
- Submitting new Assets using the Asset Editor.
- Searching Assets.

Use case

When Oracle Enterprise Repository (OER) is being implemented for the first time, one of the first questions asked by an organization is how can they bootstrap hundreds of existing Assets in a clean, organized, and exploitable way. There is little point in implementing OER, if hundreds (or even thousands) of Assets have to be manually entered into the tool. An even worse case scenario occurs when Assets are automatically loaded (harvested) but uncategorized, meaning that it is impossible to make sense of the information. That said, OER relies heavily on the Harvester and the Solution Packs to perform such tasks.

> Bootstrap or bootstrapping is referred to as the process of Harvesting Assets into OER for the very first time.

As described in *Chapter 3, Introduction To Oracle Enterprise Repository*, Harvesting is the process of gathering information from different design-time and runtime sources, and loading these into OER. Harvesters are tools that enable the OER to discover and register Assets from design-time sources such as JDeveloper, for example, or runtime repositories such as an SOA production instance.

Harvesting is a continuous process and can be done in a variety of ways. For example, by the command line, using ANT, WSLT, JDeveloper plugins, and even custom scripts employing the REX API.

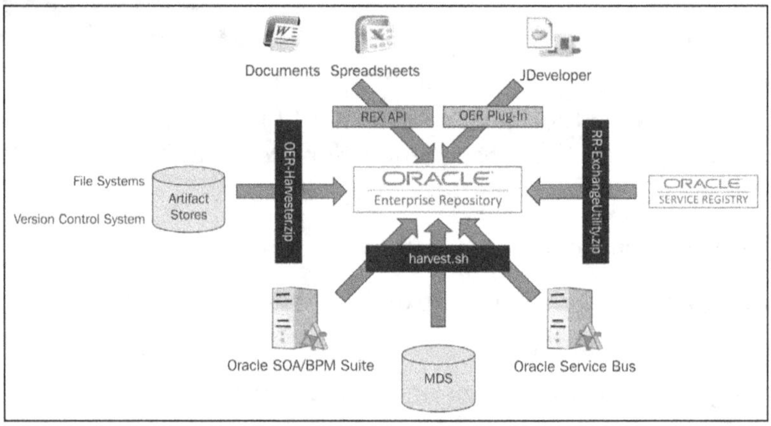

> *Section 6: Configuring and Using Automated Harvesting in Design-time and Runtime Environments* of the *OER Configuration Guide* elaborates exhaustively on the Harvesting features and techniques. Please refer to this guide for more advance details on the use of the Harvester: `http://docs.oracle.com/cd/E23943_01/admin.1111/e16580/harvest.htm#CEGHBGIJ`

Before bootstrapping the repository, it is imperative to have a good understanding of the as-is Asset state and document the same. By having an accurate view of what the Assets are, where they reside, and what their current state is, it will be possible to define the best Bootstrapping Strategy and thereby to employ the right Harvester and Harvesting technique.

In the case of Weir & Bell Telecom, the main Assets and Asset Types were well known and this can be seen in the *Asset Relationship View* available in *Chapter 4, Initial Configuration*. Furthermore, during the maturity assessment exercise of the Project Enablement phase, information about Assets such as type, location, and status was gathered, quantified, qualified, and mapped against the corresponding OER Asset Type, if available. This information was later used to define the right Harvesting and Bootstrapping Strategy. The following table provides a summary of the information gathered:

Asset Name	Document Type	Category	OER Asset Type	Amount	Location(s)	Qualification
SOA Strategy and Roadmap	Word Document	Governance Framework à Strategy	N/A	1	Content management system (accessible via browser)	Up-to-date
Service Catalogue	Excel Spreadsheet	N/A	N/A = Strategy	1		Outdated. Unreliable.
SOA Reference Architecture	Word Document	Governance Framework à Reference Architecture	N/A = Governance Document	3		Up-to-date.
Development Standards	Word Document	Governance Frameworkà Standards	N/A = Governance Document	1		Up-to-date.
Design Standards	Word Document		N/A = Governance Document	1		Up-to-date.
Programming Standards	Word Document		N/A = Governance Document	1		Up-to-date.
Runtime Framework Detail Designs	Word Document	Governance Frameworkà Framework Component Detail Design	N/A = Design Document	4	Subversion	Up-to-date.

Asset Name	Document Type	Category	OER Asset Type	Amount	Location(s)	Qualification
System Use Case	Word Document	Project Deliverables à Requirements	N/A = Requirement Document	20~	Subversion	• Mix (some outdated, some up-to-date). • Several versions are available. • In many locations. • In SVN project /tags folder latest versions (which correspond to Production Version).
Functional Design	Word Document		N/A =Design Document	20~		
SOA High Level Designs	Word Document	Project Deliverables à High Level Design	N/A = Design Document	5~		
Service Detail Design	Word Document	Project Deliverables à Detail Design	N/A = Design Document	60~		
Data Mapping Document	Spreadsheet	Project Deliverables à Detail Design	N/A = Design Document	60~		
Unit Test Plans	Word Document	Project Deliverables à Test Plan	N/A = Design Document	60~		
JDeveloper SOA 11*g* Application & Projects	Folders and XML Documents	Project Deliverables à Code	N/A	150+		
Eclipse OSB 11*g* Projects	Folders and XML Documents		N/A	150+		
WSDLs	XML Documents		Artifact : WSDL	Unknown (Many)	Subversion MDS SOA Suite OSB	• Several versions available. • In many locations. • Latest versions in the production system (SOA Suite and OSB).
Schemas (XSD)			Artifact : XSD			
XSLTs			Artifact : XSLT			
SCA Composites			Composite			
Fault Policies			Fault Policy			
Other XML Documents	Adapters, Mplans, Rules, JCA, and others.		Many available in Solution Pack			

Having elaborated an as-is view of the Assets state and their status, it was possible to elicit the most reliable Harvesting Strategy.

> Information about which Asset Types and Repositories are supported by OER is available in the following sections of the OER Configuration Guide:
>
> *6.1.3 Artifacts/Products Version Matrix*
>
> `http://docs.oracle.com/cd/E23943_01/admin.1111/e16580/harvest.htm#BABGCDID`
>
> *6.2.1 Obtaining the Harvester*
>
> `http://docs.oracle.com/cd/E23943_01/admin.1111/e16580/harvest.htm#CIHDJGJF`
>
> *A.8 Asset Type Inventory*
>
> `http://docs.oracle.com/cd/E23943_01/admin.1111/e16580/appx.htm#CEGEDEJA`
>
> Additionally you may refer to the *OER Asset Type Catalog* for a full list of the Asset Types available in the solution and base packs: `http://www.oracle.com/technetwork/middleware/repository/overview/asset.xls`

Based on the qualification made, the Harvesting Strategy was as follows:

1. Bootstrap Assets by Harvesting the Oracle SOA Suite 11*g*, **Oracle Metadata Services Repository** (**MDS**), and **Oracle Service Bus** (**OSB**) using the command line utility. The decision was made because it was generally agreed that the production systems contained the latest working versions of all SOA Services implemented deployed to it.

   Alternatives such as Harvesting from Subversion or Artifact Stores were considered, but ultimately discarded as these repositories contained several versions of the same Assets in different folders, for example, trunk, tags, and branches, and it was concluded that identifying the latest version for each Asset would have been more difficult than getting the latest version from production.

2. As documents such as Governance Standards, Framework Components, High Level Designs, Detail Designs, and Test Plans (among others) were not available in the production systems, these were added manually using the OER console. It would have been possible to develop a custom script using the REX API. However, given the limited number of this type of Asset, the cost involved in developing the script would have been greater than the cost of manual entry (in the end it only took around three days to add these manually into OER). Furthermore, during the project stages, business analysts, architects, and designers could continue to use the OER console to register Project Assets such as Use Cases, Functional Specifications, Design Specifications, and Test Plans.
3. Once the Repository was fully bootstrapped, designers and developers would use the JDeveloper OER plugin to consume and register Assets during the development stages of the lifecycle.

> When it comes to defining the right Harvesting/Bootstrapping Strategy **one size does not fit all**. Therefore, it is highly recommended that proper analysis is done and a decision is based on a qualification similar to the one described earlier.

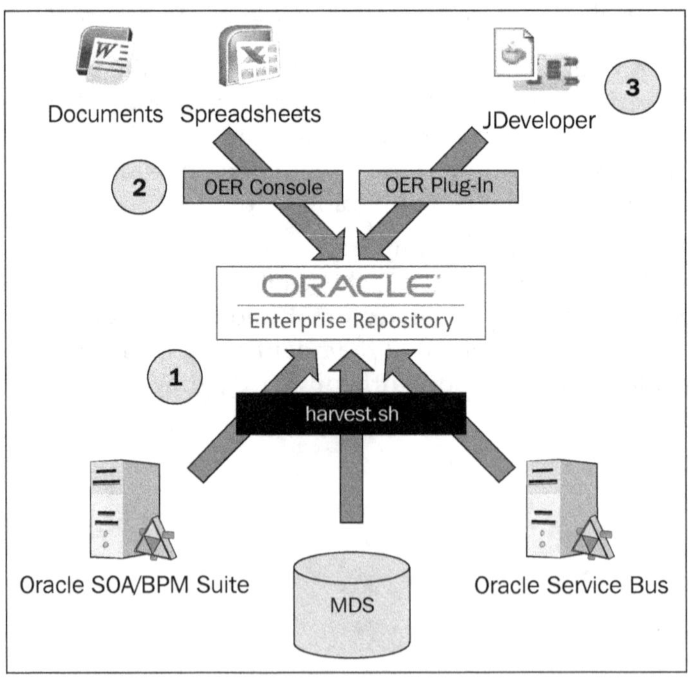

Further to the Strategy, it was identified that the following **Categorizations** and **Asset Types** were not available in the Base Pack or Solution Pack and therefore had to be created in OER:

Categorizations:

- Governance Framework.
    - Strategy.
    - Reference Architecture.
    - Standards.
    - Framework Components Detail Design.
- Project Deliverables.
    - Requirements.
    - High Level Design.
    - Detail Design.
    - Test Plan.
    - Code.

Asset Types:

- Requirement Document.
- Governance Document.
- Design Document.

> Most OER Asset Types allow for Asset-related Documentation to be added as metadata, but Weir & Bell Telecom preferred to define explicit Asset Types for key Document/Electronic Assets, and then define the relationship of these Document Assets to the actual Code. This would allow relationships to be graphically visualized using the Navigator applet (for example, a composite application relationship to its corresponding detail design, and so on) instead of these being hidden as a content of the tab.

The following sections will provide a comprehensive guide on how the Repository was Harvested and configured based upon Weir & Telecom's defined Harvesting Strategy.

Prerequisites

Before going ahead and bootstrapping the registry, the following prerequisites should be completed:

1. Installation of Solution Packs.
2. Creation of new Categorizations.
3. Creation of new Asset Types.

> This section assumes that an OER Instance and its dependencies have been successfully installed and post-configured. For further information on installation instructions please refer to *Appendix, Installation Tips and Techniques* and *Chapter 4, Initial Configuration*.

Installing Solution Packs

As described in *Chapter 3, Introduction To Oracle Enterprise Repository*, there are different types of Packs available for OER. The **Base Pack** is installed by default during the product installation and requires no further configuration. However, the following Solution Packs need to be manually installed:

- **Policy Management Solution Pack**: This pack is required while using the Policy Management features
- **Harvester Solution Pack**: This pack is required for the use of Workflows, Harvester, and the Oracle Registry Repository Exchange Utility (which will be covered in a later chapter)
- **Enterprise Architecture Solution Pack**: This pack is required when using the Architecture Blueprints Compliance Templates

All Solution Packs can be found on the OER server, under the following path:

```
<MIDDLEWARE_HOME>\repository111\core\tools\solutions
```

> A **Middleware Home** consists of the directory where the binaries for **Oracle WebLogic Server** home and other WebLogic based products reside. `http://docs.oracle.com/cd/E12839_01/core.1111/e10105/concepts.htm#CHDGBFCJ`

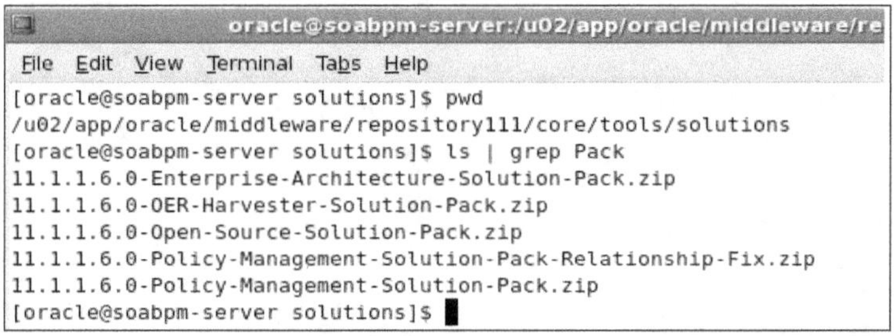

The installation of Solution Packs is achieved through the use of the **Import/Export** tool. Additionally, the Policy Management Solution Pack requires that the **Policy Management System Settings** are enabled. This is done from the **System Settings** menu of the **Admin Page** under the **Policy Management** section. In this section, the options **Enable Compliance Templates**, **Enable Asset Policies**, and **Collapse Policy Assertions** must be set to **True**, and the **Asset Policy Relationship** drop-down must be set to **Policy Applies To**. Once applied, the changes should be saved.

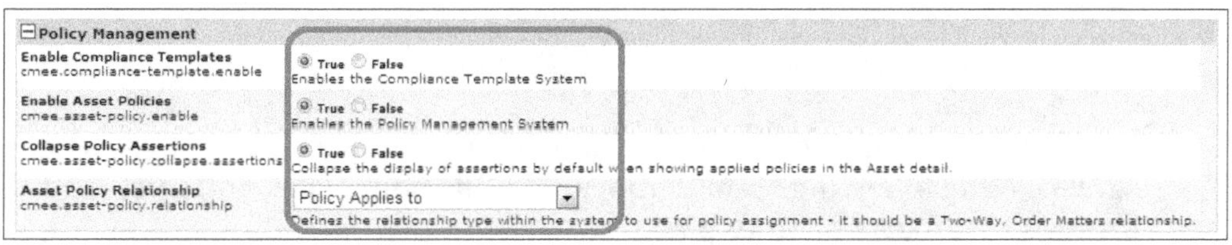

> Performing the preceding actions as well as using the **Import/Export** Utility requires the use of an account that belongs to the System Administration Role.

The **Import/Export** tool is accessed from the Admin page under the **Import/Export** menu on the left panel. The tool is launched by clicking on the **Import/Export Client** link. To import a pack, perform the following steps.

> This is also a Java Web Start application and therefore the Java Web Start Client must be installed in the user desktop in order to open JNLP extensions.

1. Once the **Import/Export** tool opens, click on the **Import** tab.

2. Click on **Browse**, select the pack to **Import**, and then click on **Next**.

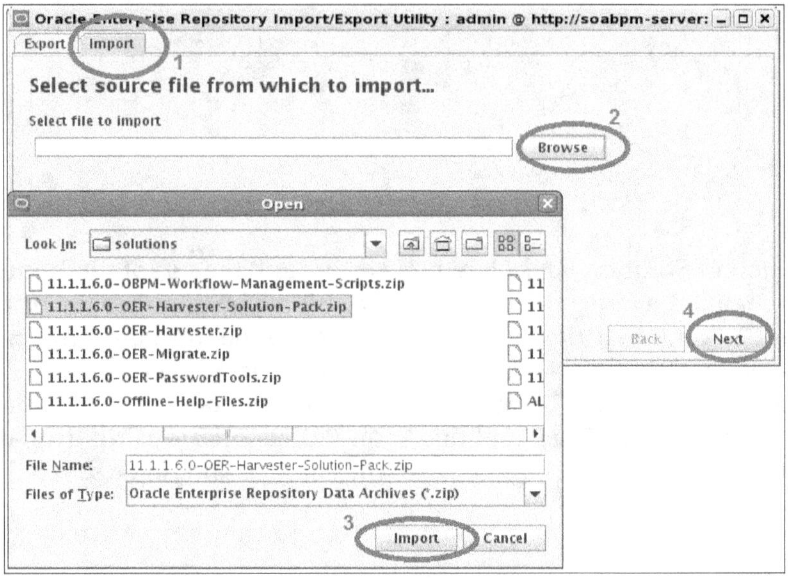

3. On the next screen, click on **Next** again and if all goes successfully, a screen similar to the following should appear. At this point, click on **Finish** and proceed to import the other packs.

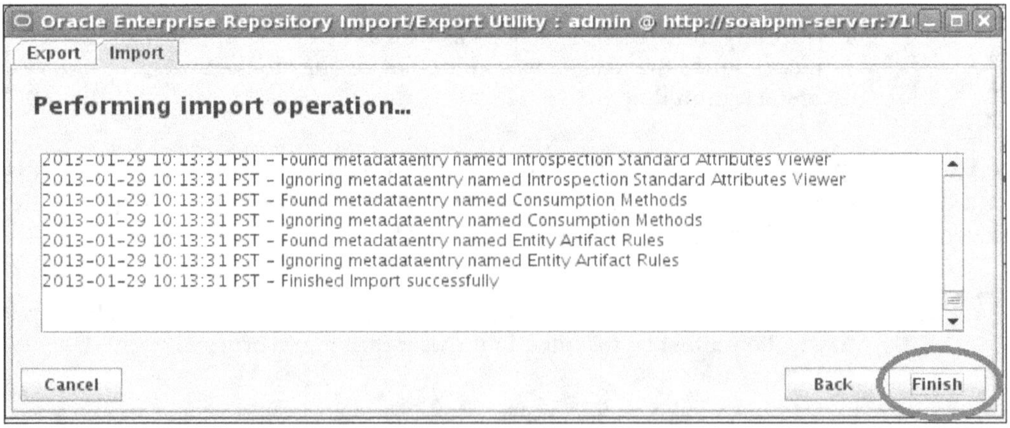

4. Repeat the same steps to import `11.1.1.x-Enterprise-Architecture-Solution-Pack.zip`, `11.1.1.x-Policy-Management-Solution-Pack.zip`, and `11.1.1.x-Policy-Management-Solution-Pack-Relationship-Fix.zip`.

Creating Categorizations

Categorizations are created or edited using the **Asset Editor**. Note that the user must belong to the **registrarAdministrator** role to create or modify Categorizations. Categorizations are created as follows:

1. Open **Asset Editor** by clicking on the **Edit/Manage Assets** link available in the **Assets** page.
2. On the top menu **Actions**, select the **Configure Categorizations** option.

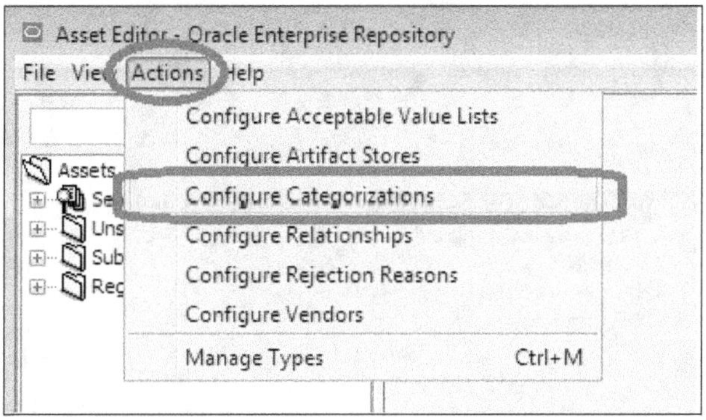

3. The **Configure Categorizations** window allows for the creation and modification of Categorizations. Click on **Add** to create a new Categorization.

4. Once the **Add Categorization** window opens, you must enter the **Element Name** which is how this Categorization will be referred to later on when assigned to a type.

> The **Element Name** must not contain white spaces, otherwise an error will be thrown by the **Asset Editor**.

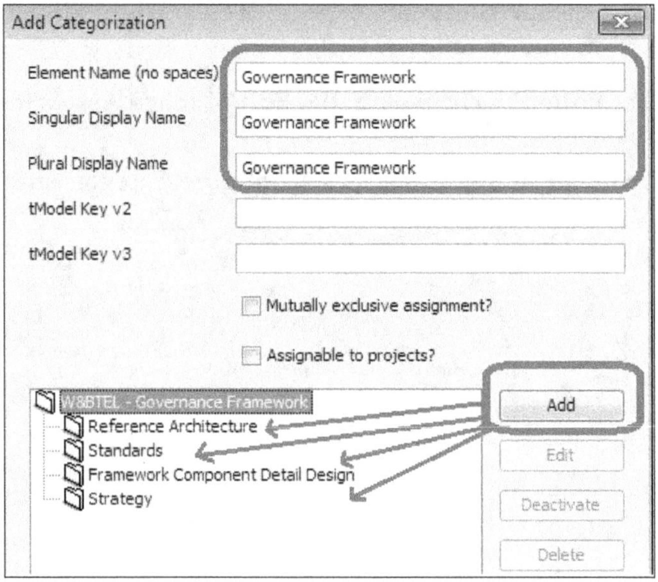

> It is recommended that the **Element Name** is the same (although without white spaces) as the **Singular Display Name**. Also note that there is no need for **Plural Display Name** in this particular example, and therefore it was kept similar to the **Singular Display Name**.

5. Once all the Categorizations are added, click on **OK** to save the Categorization.

6. These steps can be repeated for the creation of any Categorization such as the **Project Deliverables** as shown in the following screenshot:

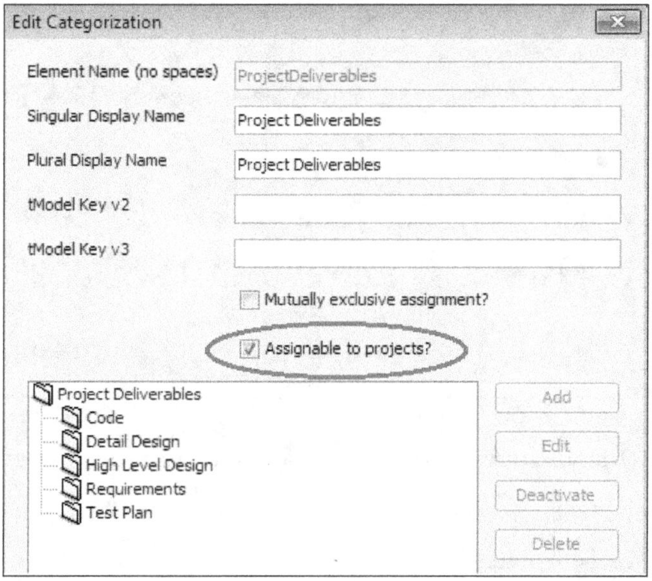

For the Project Deliverables Categorization we ticked the option **Assignable to projects?**. This is because we recognize that the Solution Packs already provide types for most of the SOA Suite 11*g* and OSB 11*g* artifacts. However, this Categorization was intended to be used to better classify the projects depending on what the nature of the expected outcomes were. With this option enabled, it will be possible to assign any of the created Categorizations to a new or existing project.

Creating Asset Types

Categorizations are created or edited using the **Type Manager**. Note that a user must belong to the **registrarAdministrator** role to create or modify Asset Types. Asset Types are created as follows:

1. To open **Type Manager**, first launch the **Asset Editor** by clicking on the **Edit/ Manage Assets** link available in the **Assets** page.

2. Then from the top menu **Actions**, click on the **Manage Types** option.

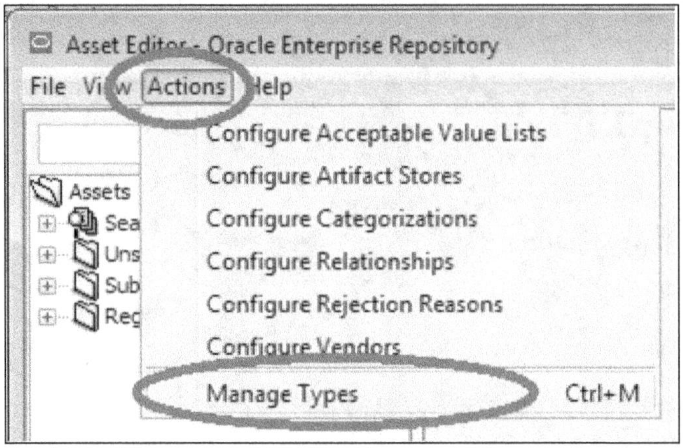

There are three Artifacts Types that can be managed from the **Type Manager**:

- Asset Types.
- Compliance Templates Types.
- Policy Types.

> Refer to the *Type Manager* section of *Chapter 3, Introduction To Oracle Enterprise Repository*, for the description of these artifacts.

> When creating a new Type you must select an existing one as the **Type for Default**. The newly created Type will be identical to the selected **Type for Default**. The recommendation is therefore to evaluate Types using the **Type Manager** and then select an existing Type with similar properties to the desired New Type and select this as Default.

The following **Types for Default** were identified as suitable for the required Asset Types:

New Type Name	Artifact Type	Type for Default	Customization Needed
Governance Document	Asset Type	EA - Sample Asset Type	• **Tests** tab not needed. Remove from both **Editor** and **Viewer**. • Rename the **Documentation** tab and Element to **External Documentation**. • Replace Categorization **Enterprise Architecture Model** with **Governance Framework** in the **Taxonomy** tab.
Requirement Document	Asset Type	Governance Document	• Replace Categorization **Governance Framework** with **Project Deliverable** in the **Taxonomy** tab.
Design Document	Asset Type	Requirement Document	None required.

In the following steps, we will demonstrate how to create the **Governance Document** Asset Type as defined in the table. Similar steps can be followed to create the remaining types.

1. To create a new Type, select **New** from the **File** menu.

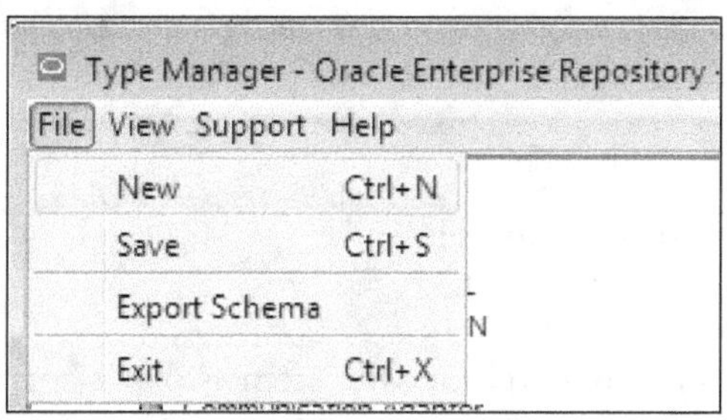

2. In the **Create New Type** window, enter the **Type Name** and select the **Type for Defaults**.

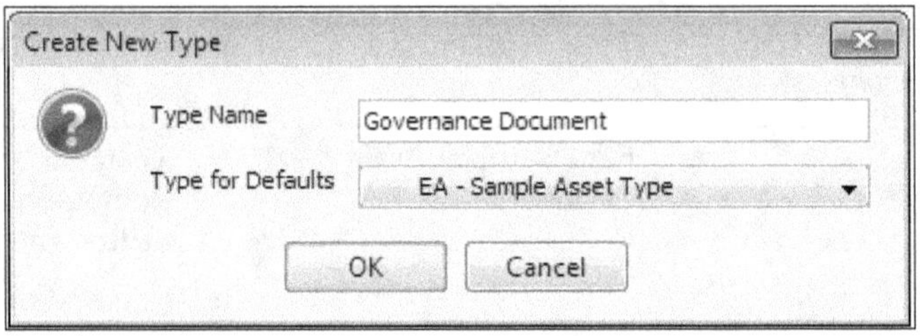

3. The new Type should now appear in **Type Manager** under the **Asset Type** in the left pane. Select it to modify the Type. The **Editor** tab should be displayed by default.

Removing the Tests tab

The first customization is done as follows:

1. Select the **Tests** item in the **Tabs** box and then click on **Remove**.

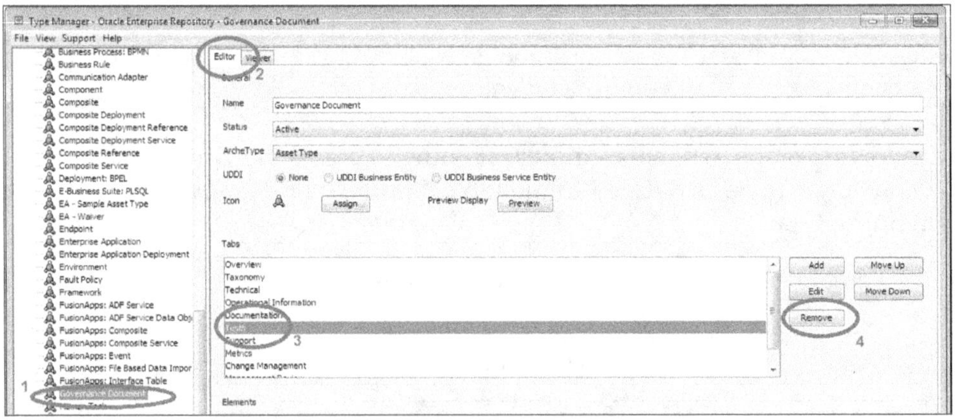

2. Click on **Yes** to confirm the deletion.

> In this case it is safe to remove this Item as this is a new Type. If a change is being done to a Type for which Assets already exist, either ensure that no information will be lost or simply do not perform the change.

Now similar steps must be completed for the **Viewer** tab (otherwise the item will be displayed when viewing the Assets from the console).

1. Click on the **Viewer** tab, then under the **Groups** section from the **Column Two** box select the item **Tests** and click on **Remove**.

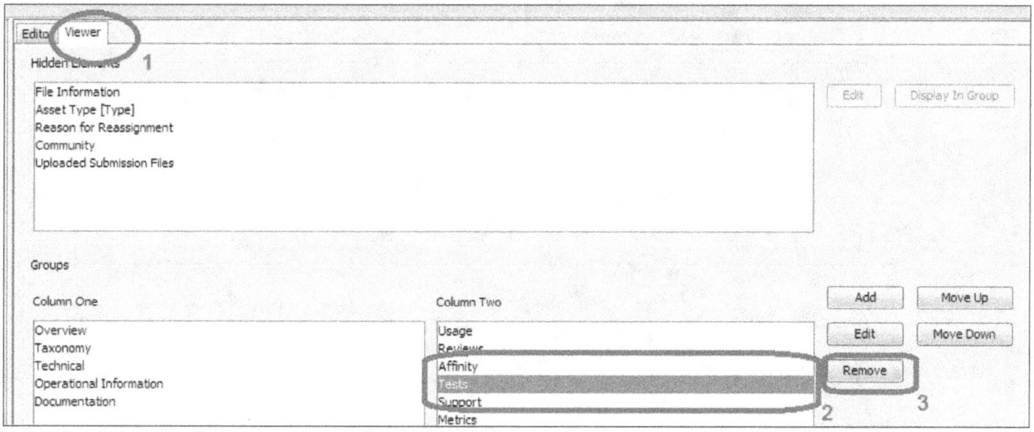

2. Click on **Yes** to confirm the deletion.

Renaming the Document tab

The next customization is to rename **Documentation** to `External Documentation` in the **Editor** and **Viewer** tabs.

1. In the **Editor** tab, in the **Tabs** box, select the **Documentation** item. Then click on **Edit** and once the **Tab Information** window opens, enter the new name in the **Tab Name** field and click on **OK**.

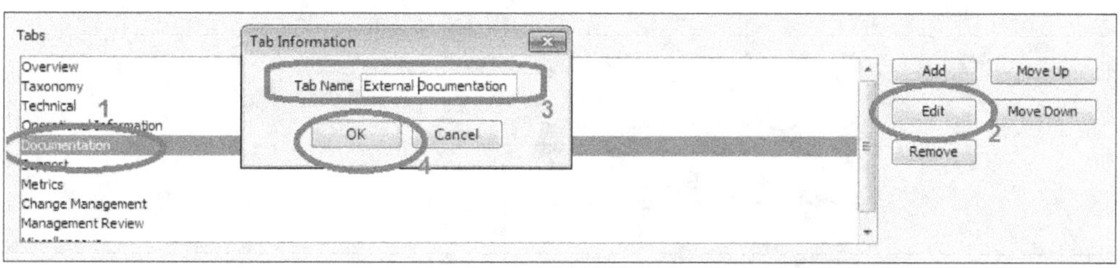

2. To rename the **Documentation** element, select the item **Documentation** in the **Elements** box and click on **Edit**. Once the **Edit Associated Files** window opens, enter the new name in the **Display Name** field and click on **OK**.

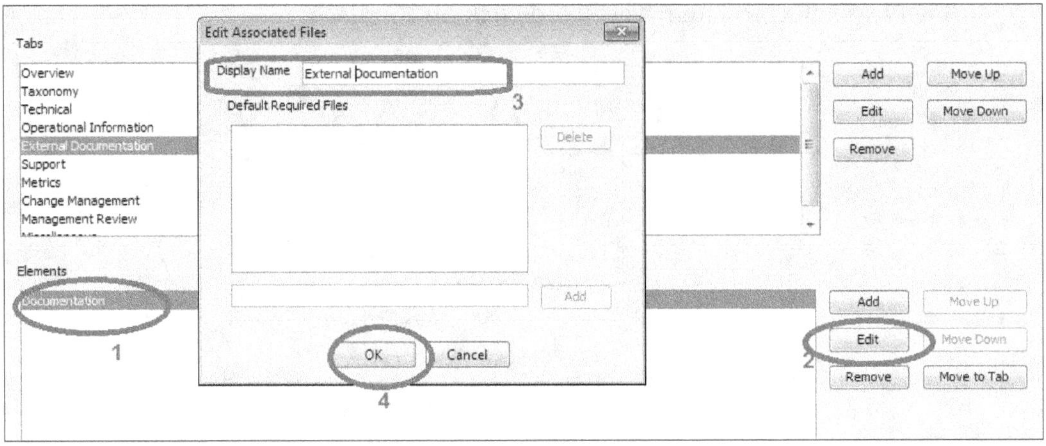

Now a similar procedure must be completed for the **Viewer** tab.

1. Click on the **Viewer** tab, then under the **Groups** section in the **Column One** box, select the item **Documentation** and then click on **Edit**. Once the **Group Information** window opens, enter the new name in the **Group Name** field and click on **OK**.

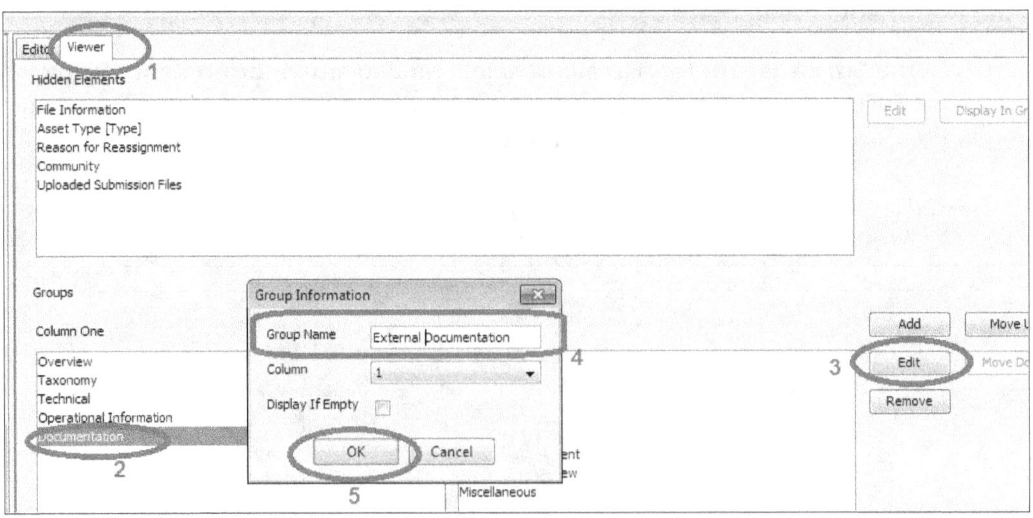

2. To rename the **Documentation** Element, select the item **Documentation [External Documentation]** in the **Elements** box and click on **Edit**. Once the **Edit Associated Files Element: External Documentation** window opens, enter the new name in the **Display Name** field and click on **OK**.

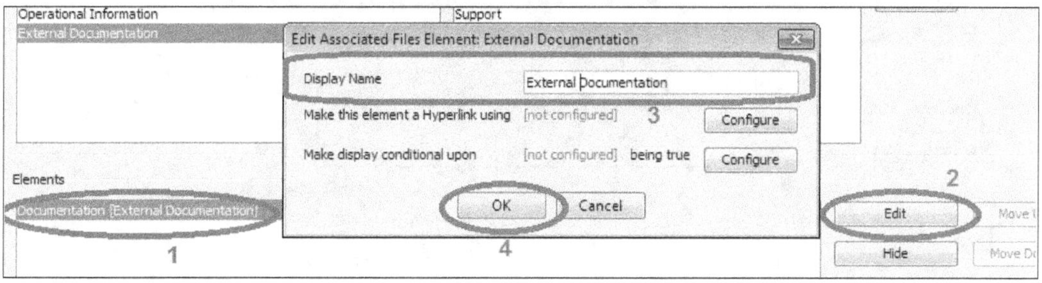

Replacing Categorization in the Taxonomy tab

The third customization required is to replace the **Enterprise Architecture Model** categorization in the **Governance Framework** categorization in the **Taxonomy** tab both for Editor and Viewer.

1. In the **Editor** tab, in the **Tabs** box, select the **Taxonomy** item and click on **Remove**. Then click on **Yes** to confirm the removal.

> It is not possible to directly replace an **Element**, therefore the alternative is to **Remove** and then **Add** a new **Element**.

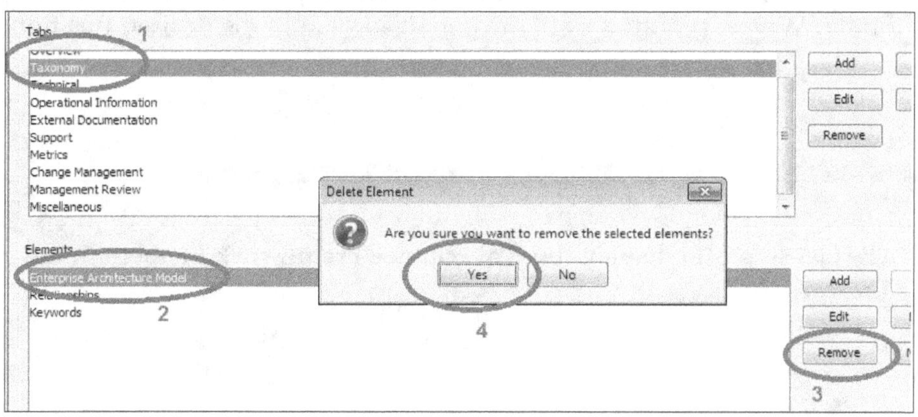

2. To add the new **Categorization**, in the **Elements** section click on the **Add** button. Once the **Select an Element Type to Add** window opens, select **Categorization: Governance Framework** and click on **OK**.

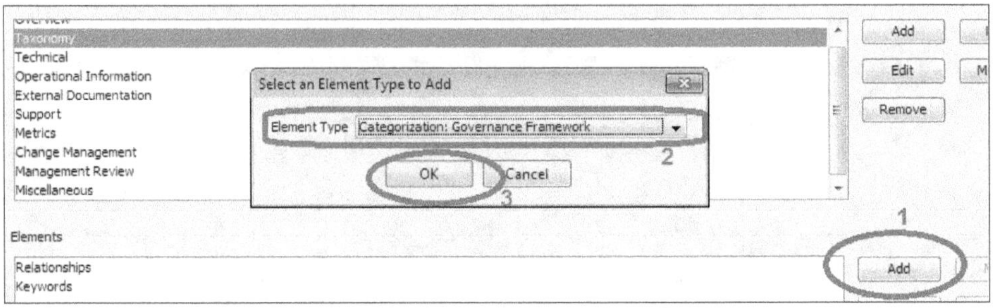

3. Modify the **Display Name** if desired. For our example we have kept it the same.

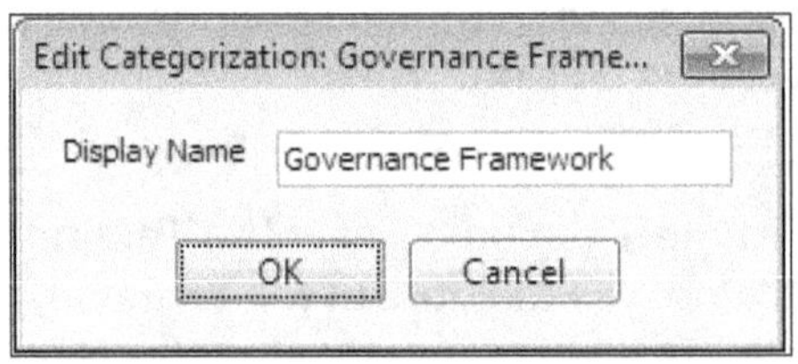

4. The new Element is added to the bottom of the box. In our case, we would like this item to show up at the top of the **Editor** (and **Viewer**) tab. To do so, in the **Elements** box, select the **Governance Framework** item and then click on the **Move Up** button until the item is located in the desired position.

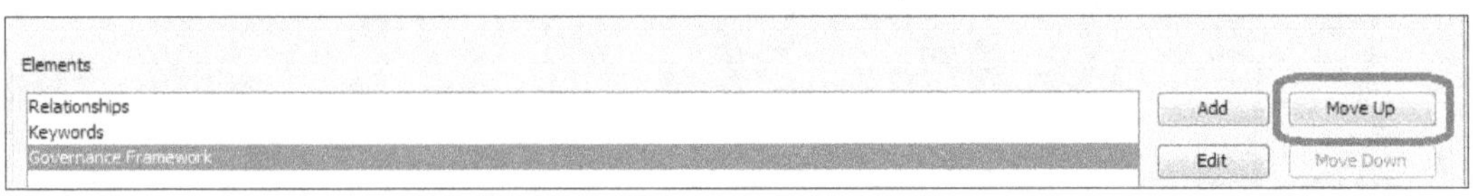

5. The last step is to display the **Governance Framework** Element in the **Viewer** tab.

6. In the **Viewer** tab, in the **Hidden Elements** box, select **Governance Framework** and then click on **Display In Group**. Once the **Move Element** window opens, select **Taxonomy** (as this is where we want to display the Element) and click on **OK**.

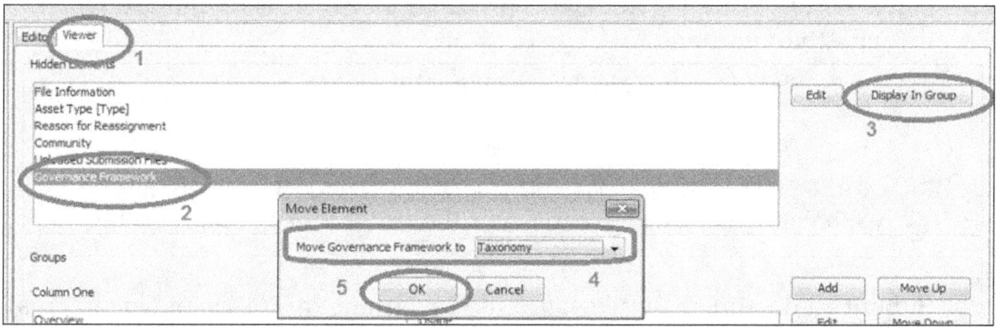

7. To display the **Governance Framework** item at the top of the group, in the **Elements** box, select the **Governance Framework** item, and click on the **Move Up** button until the item is located in the desired position.
8. Once all customizations have been done, save the changes by clicking on the **Save** option located in the **File** top menu.

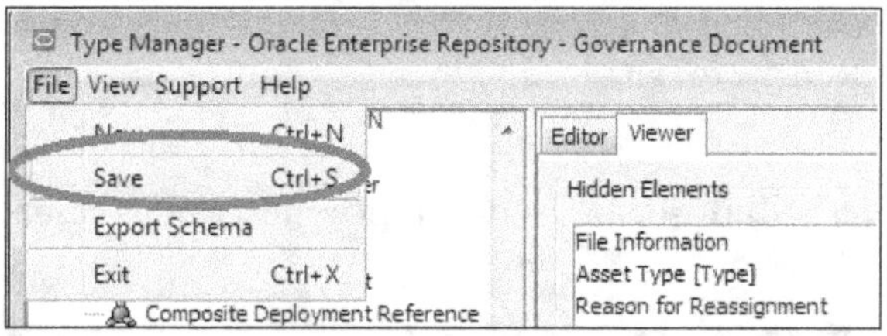

Repeat similar steps to create the **Requirement Document** Asset Type using **Governance Framework** as the **Type of Default**. In the **Requirement Document** Asset Type replace the **Governance Framework** categorization with the **Project Deliverable** Categorization and save the changes. Once this is done, create the **Design Document** Asset Type using the **Required Document** as **Type for Default**.

Bootstrapping OER

Once all the prerequisites have been fulfilled the next step is to Bootstrap OER as per the defined Strategy. There are broadly five steps required to complete this task:

1. Harvest SOA Suite 11*g* and MDS production server using the Harvester through the command line.
2. Harvest OSB using the OSB Harvester utility.

> The OSB Harvester is available from within the OSB installation binaries and not from the OER binaries as is the case with SOA Suite or MDS.

3. Submit all document Assets (such as Governance and Design Documents) using Asset Editor.
4. Configure JDeveloper with the OER plugin, so that Assets can be discovered and registered from the IDE.
5. OER may also be bootstrapped from OSR.

> *Chapter 7, Oracle Service Registry*, and *Chapter 8, Design-time Service Promotion and Discovery*, cover the integration with OSR in more detail.

The following sections will describe in detail how to complete each of these steps:

Harvesting SOA Suite 11*g* and MDS

The following steps were followed in order to harvest SOA Suite and MDS:

1. Ensure that SOA Suite, the MDS, and all SOA Composites are up and running.
2. Log on to **Enterprise Manager 11g Fusion Middleware Control** with the WebLogic user. `http://<weblogic admin server>:7001/em`

3. On the landing page, a series of dashboards should appear. In the **Fusion Middleware** section the (right-hand side of the page) and under the SOA Domain, check that **soa_server1** is up and running.

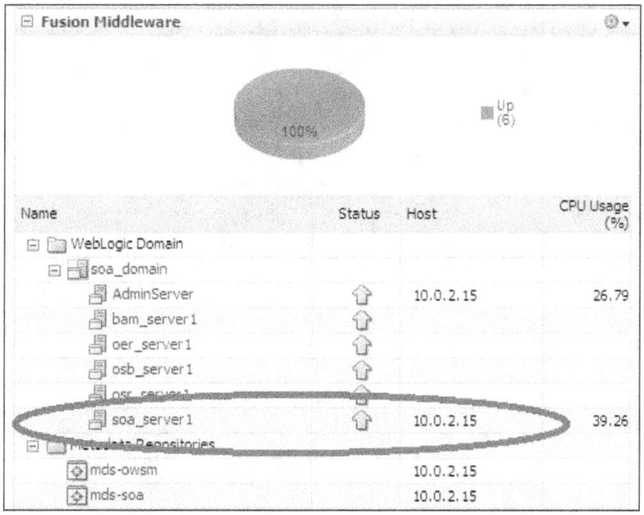

> MDS holds all of the metadata such as WSDLs, schemas, and SCA composites that are required by SOA Suite to run the deployed services. Therefore, if an SOA Suite is up and running properly it is very likely that MDS is also running properly. However, it is also possible to check the status of MDS by following the instructions described in *Section 8 Troubleshooting Oracle Metadata Repository* from the *Fusion Applications Administrator's Troubleshooting Guide*.
>
> `http://fusion.kabolly.com/~sheffiel/kabolly/fusion/doc.1111/e25450/mds_trouble.htm`

4. Within Enterprise Manage FM Control, check that the composites are up and running. This can be done by clicking on the SOA partition (for example, **default**) under the SOA infrastructure (**soa-infra**) node. All the composites will appear on the right-hand side of the page. If composites are successfully running, the **Status** should be a green arrow.

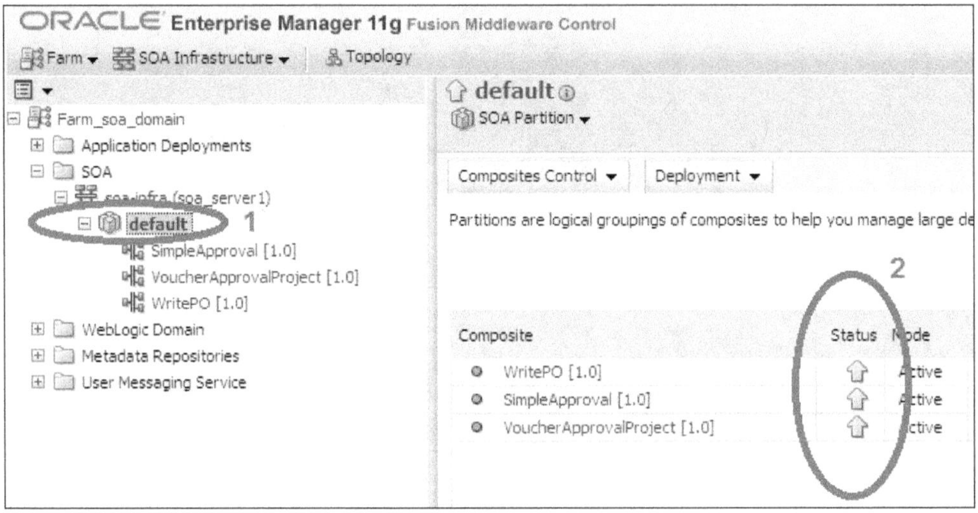

Creating a user for the Harvester tool

Create an OER user to be used for the Harvester and grant the **Basic Access Settings**: **View**, **Edit**, **Accept**, and **Register** on **Assets**. Ensure that the password for this user does not expire, and also take a note of the password as it will be required later on when configuring the connection to OER.

> Any user with these rights would suffice and a new account is not mandatory. However, we considered this to be good practice as it would provide better visibility over Assets created by the Harvester, and also more flexibility as the account details could change later on without affecting any other users.

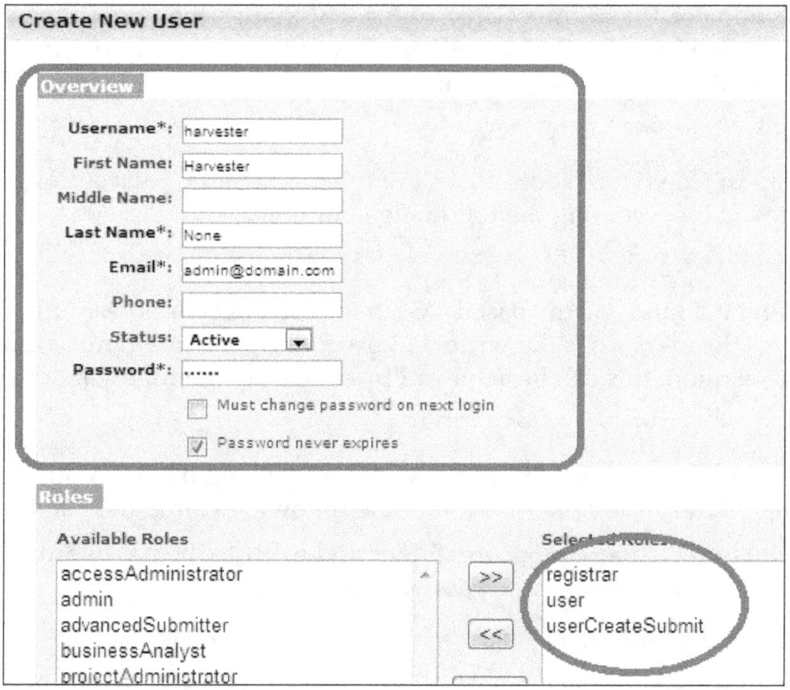

Encrypting the password

Follow these steps to extract the Harvester and password utilities, and encrypt the password for the Harvester user and for the WebLogic account.

1. With the **oracle** user (or the user used to install OER), start an **SSH** session or a **Terminal Client** session and locate on the following path:

```
<MIDDLEWARE_HOME>\repository111\core\tools\solutions
```

2. Unzip the Harvester tool. In a Linux/Unix based OS execution, this can be achieved by executing the following command:

```
unzip 11.1.1.x.x-OER-Harvester.zip -d harvester
```

> The path `<MIDDLEWARE_HOME>\repository111\core\tools\solutions\harvester` will be going forward referred to as the **Harvester Home**.

3. Additionally, on a Linux/Unix based OS, change the permissions of the Harvester Home so, the owner has the write and execute rights. This can be done with the following command:

   ```
   chmod -R u=rwx ./harvester
   ```

4. Unzip the Password tools. In a Linux /Unix based OS execution, this can be achieved by executing the following command:

   ```
   unzip 11.1.1.x.x-OER-PasswordTools.zip -d passwordtool
   ```

5. Again on a Linux/Unix based OS, change the permissions of the Password tool so the owner has the write and execute rights. In a Linux /Unix based OS execution, this can be achieved by executing the following command:

   ```
   chmod -R u=rwx ./passwordtool
   ```

6. Encrypt the password of the Harvester user using the encrypting tool. If using a Linux/Unix-based system the following command can be executed:

   Locate into the `passwordtool` folder and execute the password tool by passing the Harvester user password as input:

   ```
   ./encryptpassword.sh <Harvester user password>
   ```

   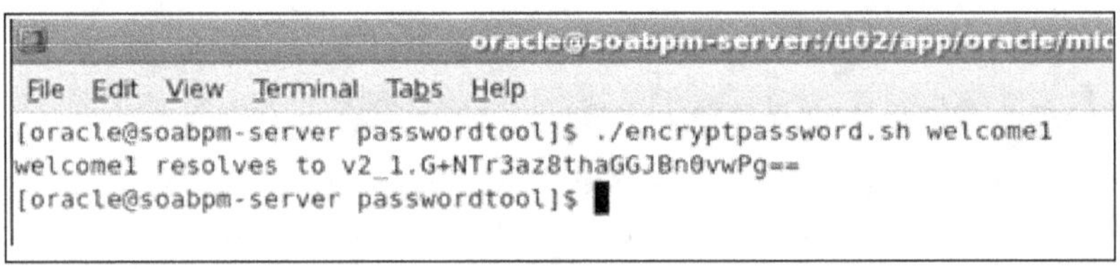

> The outcome will be the encrypted password. The user should make a note of it immediately.

7. Encrypt the password of the WebLogic user by executing the same command, but supplying the password of the WebLogic account of the SOA Suite domain. Note that an account other than WebLogic can be used provided that it has the WebLogic roles Admin, Operator, and Monitor.

Configuring the Harvester connection details

Configure the Harvester connection details to the OER and SOA Suite servers as follows:

1. Locate into `harvester` folder available inside the Harvester Home (note that this assumes that the Harvester tool was unzipped into the `harvester` folder).
2. Using a text editor open the file `HarvesterSettings.xml`.
3. Set the Registration Status of the harvested Assets by modifying the `<registrationStatus>` tag as follows:

```
<registrationStatus>Registered</registrationStatus>
```

> The valid Registration Statuses are: Unsubmitted, Submitted - Pending Review, Submitted - Under Review, and Registered. Depending on your implementation it might be desired to use a different status when bootstrapping.

4. Enter the OER connection details as follows:

```
<repository>
  <uri>http://[OER Server]:[OER Server Port]/oer</uri>
  <credentials>
    <user>[Harvester User]</user>
    <password>[Harvester user encrypted password]</password>
  </credentials>
   <timeout>30000</timeout>
</repository>
```

> Connection details can also be passed as attributes from the command line. However, these credentials will be required every time the Harvester is executed.

5. Uncomment the tag `<remoteQuery>`.
6. Enter the SOA Suite connection details as follows and comment out `<projectName>` and `<soaPartition>` so all composites from partition default are harvested.

```
<remoteQuery>
  <serverType>SOASuite</serverType>
  <!--<projectName></projectName>-->
  <uri>http://[SOA Suite Server]:[SOA Suite Server Port]</uri>
  <credentials>
    <user>weblogic<user>
```

```
      <password>[Weblogic user encrypted password]<password>
    </credentials>
    <!--<soaPartition></soaPartition>-->
  </remoteQuery>
```

> It is also possible to specify new parameters through the command line while executing the Harvester. Refer to *Table 6-4 Command Line Options for the Harvester* of the *OER Configuration Guide* for further information: `http://docs.oracle.com/cd/E23943_01/admin.1111/e16580/harvest.htm`

Executing the Harvester

Execute the Harvester using the following steps:

1. Ensure that the `JAVA_HOME` is set up properly and that it points to a JRE, that is, Version 6 or higher. A quick way to check this on a Linux/Unix-based OS is by executing the command:

   `echo $JAVA_HOME`

2. If set up properly, the outcome should be similar to the screenshot:

3. Run the Harvester in preview mode to ensure that all connection settings are correct and that all servers are up and running:

   `./harvest.sh -preview true`

> Because all the settings are included in the `HarvestSettings.xml`, there is no need to include any parameters on the command line. The Harvester tool does allow all the parameters to be provided as on the command line, if required.

4. If after executing the Harvester you get the exception **Artifact harvest failed due to: RemoteException occurred in server thread** then you must apply **Patch 13738080** as per the instructions provided in the readme file.

> For further information on this bug, please refer to the Oracle document *Harvesting All Projects From A Partition Fails With NullPointerException (ID 1475132.1)* that is available in Oracle Support.

5. Successful execution of this command should end with a summary of the Assets identified, and a message that the OER transaction was rolled back.

```
3464981 [main] INFO  com.oracle.oer.sync.plugin.writer.oer.OERWriter  - Asset of type Artifact: XSD to be created: {htt
://xmlns.oracle.com/ns/order}po.xsd (1.0)
3464983 [main] INFO  com.oracle.oer.sync.plugin.writer.oer.OERWriter  - A total of 22 new assets will be created or upd
ted

3464983 [main] INFO  com.oracle.oer.sync.plugin.writer.oer.OERWriter  - Rolling back OER transaction because harveste
s in Preview Mode
Starting OERWriter Shutdown and Clean up...
[oracle@soabpm-server harvester]$
```

6. If no errors are encountered after running the Harvester in preview mode, then proceed to execute the Harvester as following:

   `./harvest.sh`

> For further information on the usage of the Harvester tool refer to section *6.2.2.2 Selecting the Artifacts to Harvest for the Command Line* of the *OER Configuration Guide*
>
> `http://docs.oracle.com/cd/E23943_01/admin.1111/e16580/harvest.htm#BABJCIJA`

7. Check that the execution ends with a successful message.

```
[main] INFO  com.oracle.oer.sync.framework.MetadataManager  - Successfully completed the harvest
OERWriter Shutdown and Clean up...
```

8. Check that the harvested Assets appear in OER by logging into OER and searching for the SOA composites available in the production system.

Bootstrapping OSB 11*g*

Oracle highlights two main prerequisites when Harvesting OSB Assets:

- If you wish to harvest from Oracle Service Bus, install Oracle Service Bus server (Version 10.3.1.0) on the same machine as the Harvester, or on a shared file system accessible to the Harvester.

- If you wish to harvest any later versions of Oracle Service Bus 11*g*, then you have to use the corresponding Oracle Service Bus harvester version that is specifically developed for later versions of Oracle Service Bus 11*g*. This is available as part of the Oracle Service Bus 11*g* product installation.

> Further information on the Harvester is available in *Section 6.1.1 Prerequisites* of the *OER Configuration Guide*: `http://docs.oracle.com/cd/E23943_01/admin.1111/e16580/harvest.htm#BABIBEBD`

Since the version of OSB deployed in Weir & Telecom was greater than 10.3.1, we harvested using the Harvester tool bundled with the OSB binaries. This was done as follows:

1. Firstly, ensure that OSB and OSB Proxy and Business Services are up and running:
2. Log on to **Enterprise Manager 11g Fusion Middleware Control** with the WebLogic user. The URL is as follows: `http://<weblogic admin server>:7001/em`
3. On the landing page, a series of dashboards should show appear. In the **Fusion Middleware** section (the right-hand side of the page) and under the SOA Domain, check that **soa-server** is up and running.

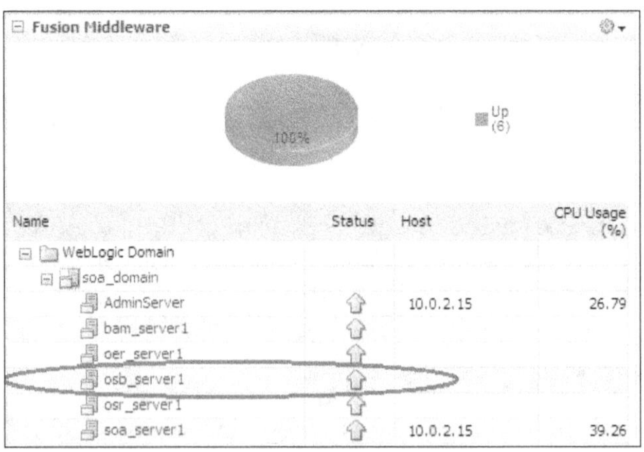

4. Open a new browser window and go to the OSB console `http://<weblogic admin server>:7001/sbconsole`

5. From the **OSB Home** page, click on the **Service Health** tab.

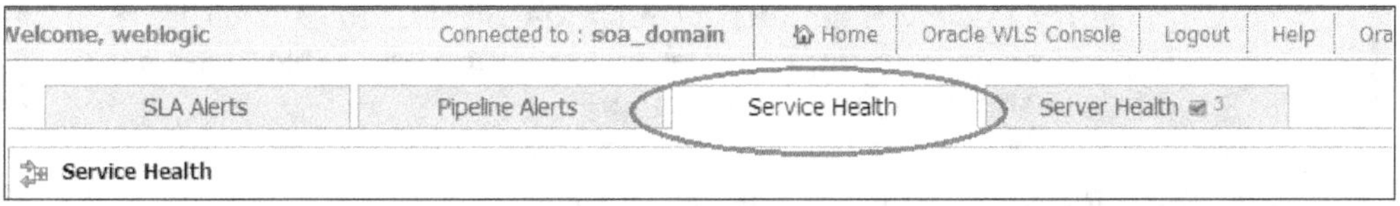

6. Check that **Endpoint URI Status** for the monitored services is **Online**.

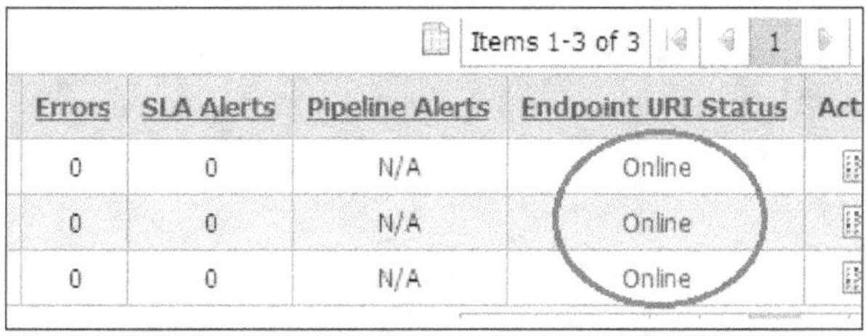

Configuring the OSB Harvester connection details

Configure the Harvester connection details for the OER and OSB servers:

1. With the **oracle** user (or the user used to install OER), start an **SSH** session or a **Terminal Client** session and locate onto the `harvester` folder available inside the OSB Home.

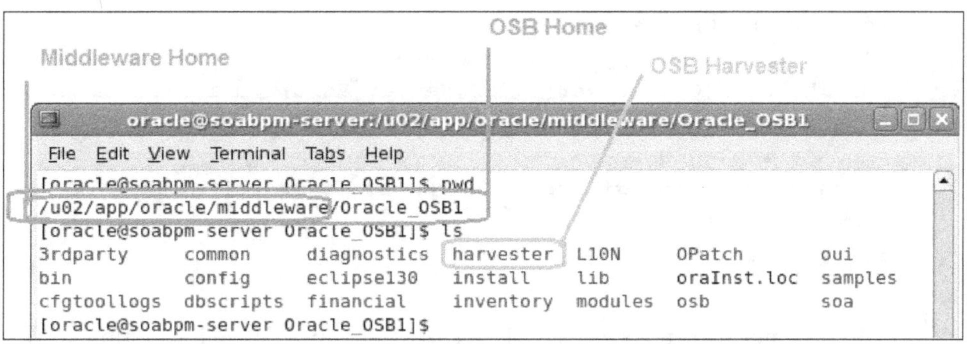

2. Using a text editor open the file `HarvesterSettings.xml`.
3. Set the status of the Harvested Assets by modifying the `<registrationStatus>` tag as follows:

```
<registrationStatus>Registered</registrationStatus>
```

> The valid Registration Status values are: Unsubmitted, Submitted - Pending Review, Submitted - Under Review, and Registered. Depending on your implementation, it might be desirable to use a different status when bootstrapping.

4. Enter the OER connection details as follows:

```
<repository>
  <uri>http://[OER Server]:[OER Server Port]/oer</uri>
  <credentials>
    <user>[Harvester User]</user>
    <password>[Harvester user encrypted password]</password>
  </credentials>
  <timeout>30000</timeout>
</repository>
```

> Connection details can also be passed as parameters from the command line. In this case, however, these details would have to be supplied each time the Harvester is executed.

5. Uncomment the tag `<remoteQuery>` (if not already uncommented).
6. Enter the OSB connection details as follows, and comment out `<projectName>` so all OSB Proxy and Business Services are harvested.

```
<remoteQuery>
  <serverType>OSB</serverType>
  <!--<projectName></projectName>-->
  <uri>http://[OSB Server]:[OSB Server Port]</uri>
  <credentials>
    <user>weblogic<user>
    <password>[Weblogic user encrypted password]<password>
  </credentials>
</remoteQuery>
```

> The same encrypted password that was generated when harvesting SOA Suite in section *Encrypting the password* can be used.

Executing the OSB Harvester

Execute the Harvester as follows:

1. Set the OSB Harvester environment variables (Middleware Home, OSB Home, and Harvester Home) by executing the command `source setenv.sh`:

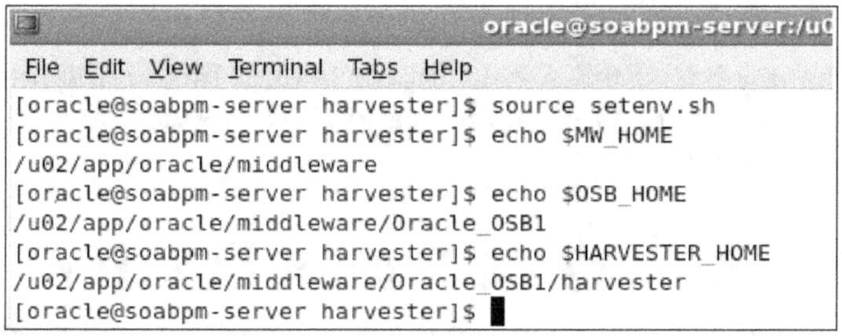

> Within this directory there is a file named `README.txt`. It is recommended that you read this file, as it provides useful information about the OSB Harvester.

2. Run the OSB Harvester in preview mode to ensure that all connection settings are correct, and that all the servers are up and running:

   `./osb11g-harvest.sh -preview true`

3. Successful execution of this command should end with a summary of the Assets identified and a message that the OER transaction was rolled back.

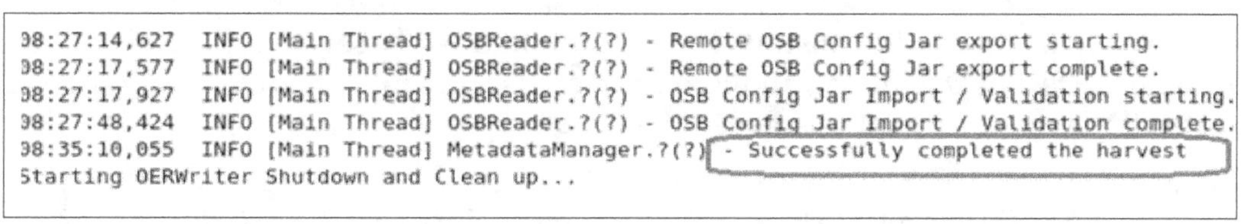

4. If no errors are displayed after running the Harvester in preview mode, proceed to fully execute the Harvester as following:

   `./osb11g-harvest.sh`

5. Check that the execution ends with a successful message.

```
08:27:14,627  INFO [Main Thread] OSBReader.?(?) - Remote OSB Config Jar export starting.
08:27:17,577  INFO [Main Thread] OSBReader.?(?) - Remote OSB Config Jar export complete.
08:27:17,927  INFO [Main Thread] OSBReader.?(?) - OSB Config Jar Import / Validation starting.
08:27:48,424  INFO [Main Thread] OSBReader.?(?) - OSB Config Jar Import / Validation complete.
08:35:10,055  INFO [Main Thread] MetadataManager.?(?) - Successfully completed the harvest
Starting OERWriter Shutdown and Clean up...
```

6. Check that the harvested Assets appear in OER by logging into OER and searching for the OSB Business and Proxy services available in the production system.

Submitting Assets with Asset Editor

At this stage all of the Assets available in the SOA Suite and OSB production systems have been harvested and are available in OER. However, important design and architecture documents that may reside in content management systems such as **WebCenter Content** are not yet available as Assets in OER. Such documents include Service Designs and Governance Documents, for example. Documents can be linked to Assets using the Asset Editor, and adding the associated document's name and URLs to the **Documentation** tab. This may be acceptable in some situations, but using this approach results in Assets that cannot be explicitly searched for or subsequently associated with other Assets such as services. This was not acceptable in the case of Weir & Bell Telecom.

In the preceding sections, we added the required Categorizations and Asset Types to support Requirement Documents, Governance Documents, and Design Documents. Now, we can proceed to add these Assets using the Asset Editor.

In this section, we will demonstrate how to submit three Assets of type: Governance Document, Design Document, and Requirement Document respectively, and how to create all the required relationships to the Assets.

> Please refer to the *Overview* section of *Chapter 3, Introduction To Oracle Enterprise Repository*, for a full picture of the Asset Relationship View used as the base for establishing the relationships between the Assets submitted.

The following steps describe how to submit an Asset, approve it, and register it through the Asset lifecycle. In this case, we will show how an SOA Detail Design document can be submitted, associated with a service and approved. We will also show how to specify applicable design standards that have been adhered to during the service implementation.

> To make this example more relevant, we have already submitted all Governance Documents and established their relationships following the steps similar to those described here.

1. Log into the OER console using an account that belongs to the Register role.
2. From the **Assets** page, launch the Asset Editor.
3. From the top menu **File** select the option **New**.

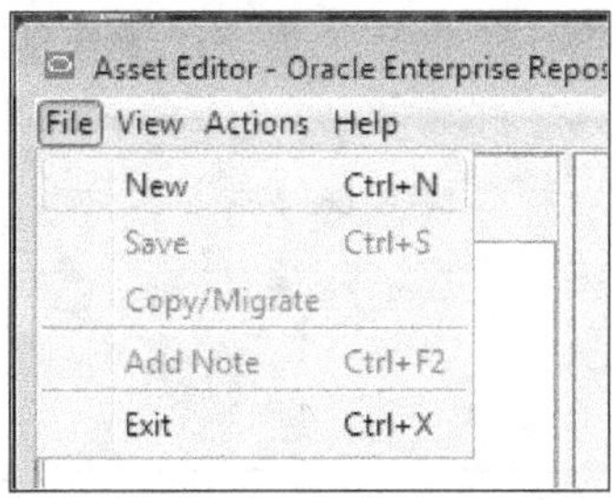

4. Enter the following details for the asset in the **Create a New Asset** window and then click on **OK**.
    - **Name**: The name of the SOA Service Design. Note that usually companies follow their own company-wide naming conventions for these types of documents. While OER itself will not enforce a particular convention, it is highly recommended that you comply with your company's convention to make it easier to search for such assets.
    - **Version**: All Assets in OER are subject to version control. The standard convention used by default is `<major version>.<minor version>`, for example, `1.0`. Versions are extremely important for many reasons, such as avoiding duplicity and change management, amongst many others.
    - **Type**: As in this sample, we are submitting a service design document, then the Asset **Type** should set to **Design Document**.

- **Initial State**: This field defines the actual **Registration Status** of the asset after submission. All Assets submitted to OER with a status of: **Unsubmitted, Submitted : Pending Review** and **Submitted : Under Review** will appear in OER as **Unregistered** assets and will undergo a governance workflow that involves a series of approvals (*Chapter 6, Asset Lifecycle and Workflow*, discusses the Asset lifecycle and workflow in more detail). If the Asset is submitted as **Registered**, no approvals are required.

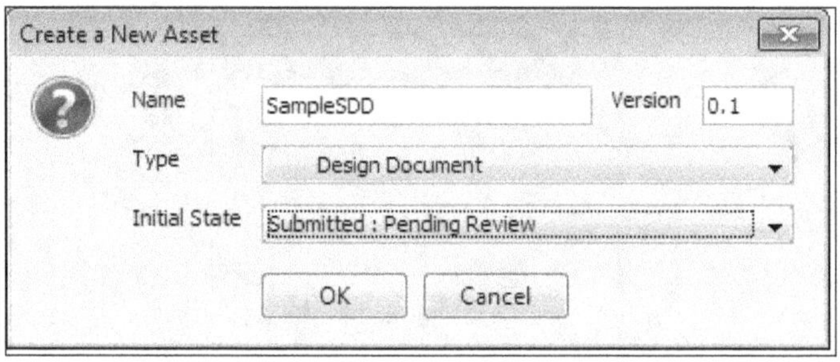

> It is possible to submit Assets via the OER console from the **Assets** page. In this case, the **Initial State** is defaulted to **Submitted : Pending Review** and the asset will then have to be accepted (and/or assigned) by a registrar.

5. From the browser tree located on the left panel, browse to **Submitted** | **Pending Review** | **Design Document(1)** and then click on **SampleSDD (1.0)** to edit the asset.

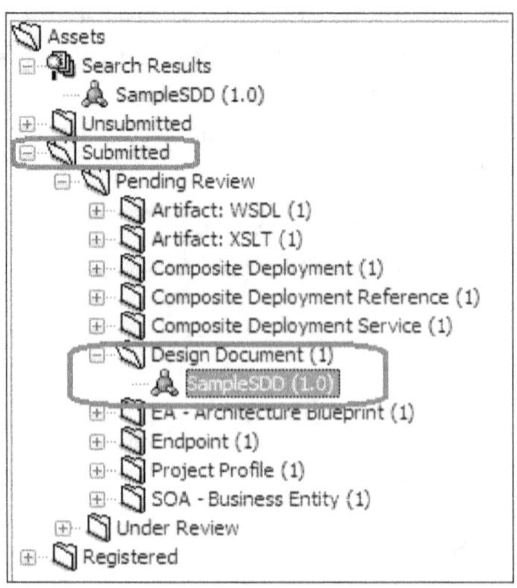

6. From the **Overview** tab, it is possible to add further details to the Asset. It is recommended that a **Description**, the **Producing Project(s)**, and the **File Information** details are added. The latter is particularly important as users will likely want to read the content of this document, so it is imperative that the **URL** is entered correctly.

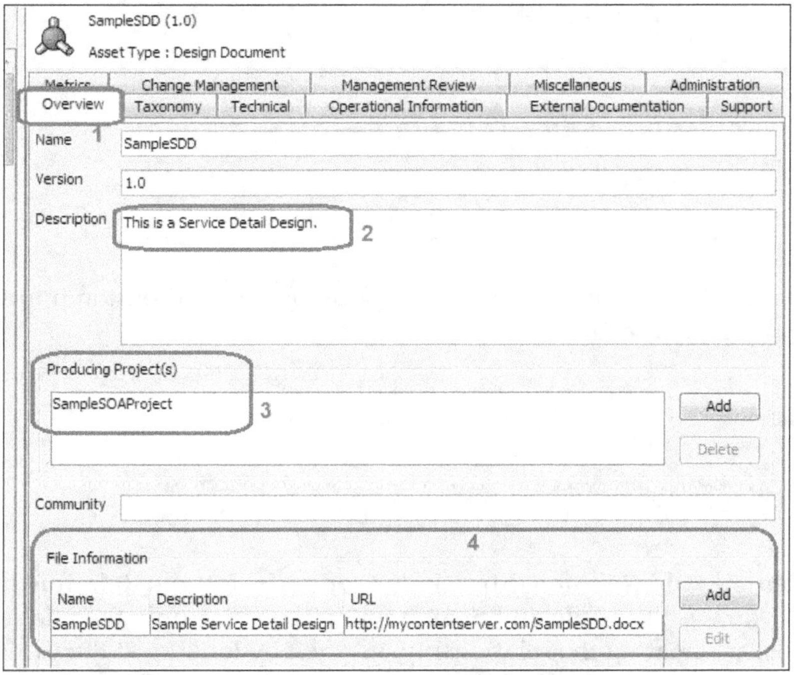

> The **URL** field can based on an artifact store path or point to a text file. In our case, we have chosen to use an external file URL, as the documents were already available in the corporate portal and it was just a matter of pointing to it.

7. Click on the **Taxonomy** tab to assign the **Project Deliverables** and **Relationships** to other Assets.

8. Under the **Assign Project Deliverables** section, click on the **Assign** button and then tick the **Detail Design** box and click on **OK**.

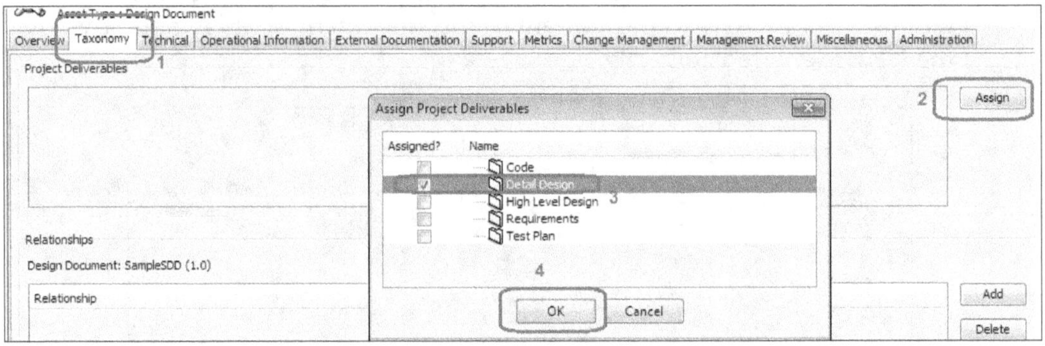

9. **Relationships** are established by clicking on the **Add** button under the **Relationships** section.

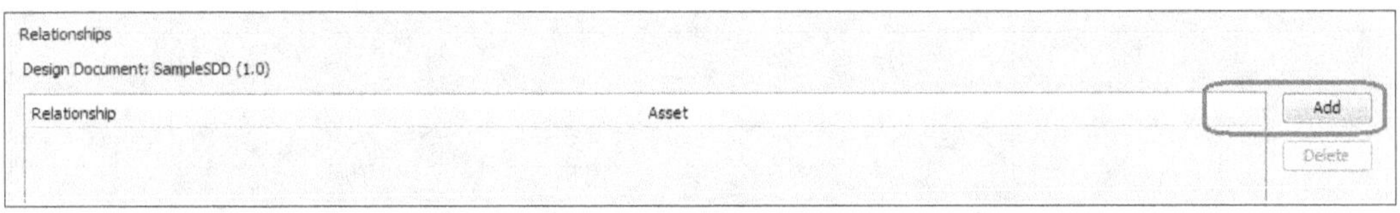

10. When the **Add Relationship** window opens, select the **Relationship Type** that you wish to apply and **Search** for an Asset to apply the relationship to. Before creating the relationship, verify it by looking at the **Confirm Relationship** section. If all looks correct then click on **OK**.

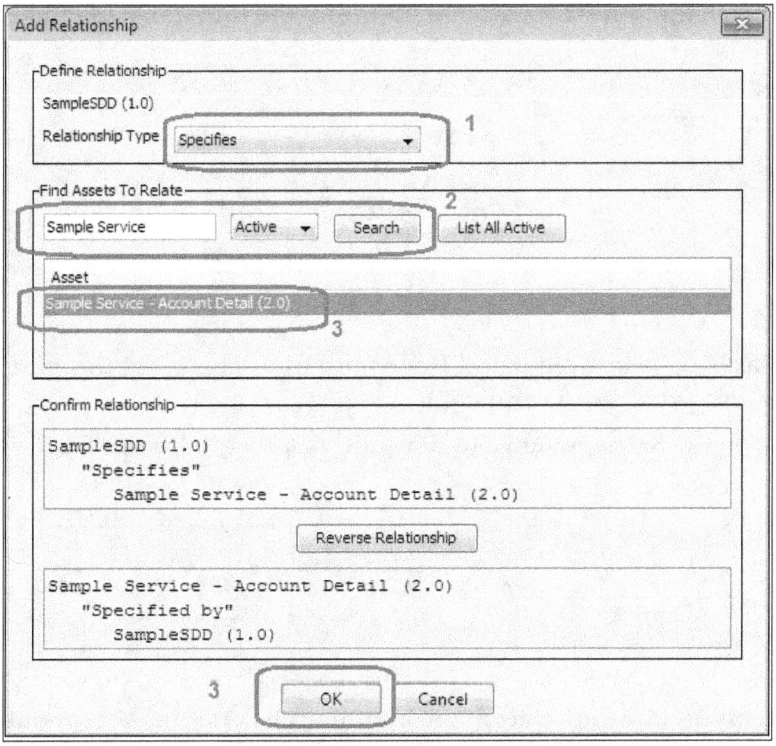

> There are several **relationship types** available in OER. These can be viewed and managed from the **Asset Editor**, **Actions** menu, the **Configure Relationships option**.

11. In our sample we create three relationships with the intention to define:
    - The **SampleSDD** is a Technical Detail Design for SOA Service: **Sample Service - Account Detail (2.0)**.
    - The **SampleSDD** content must comply with the design patterns available in the **SOA Design Standards**. The **SOA Design Standards** document is enforced by the policy **SOA Design Standards Policy (1.0)**. Therefore, **SampleSDD** is **Subject to Policies** defined in this document.

- **SampleSDD** is based on **SampleFunctionalDesign(1.0)**.

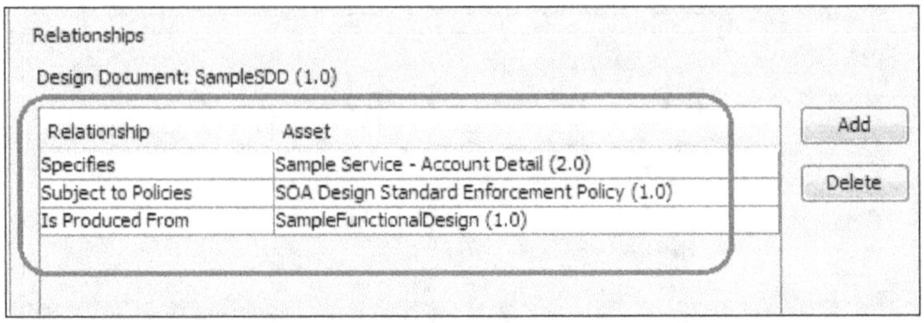

12. The last step is to **Accept** and **Register** the Asset and for this particular Asset Type also provide a **Technical Review**.
13. Click on the **Management Review** and tick on the **Passes Technical Review** box.

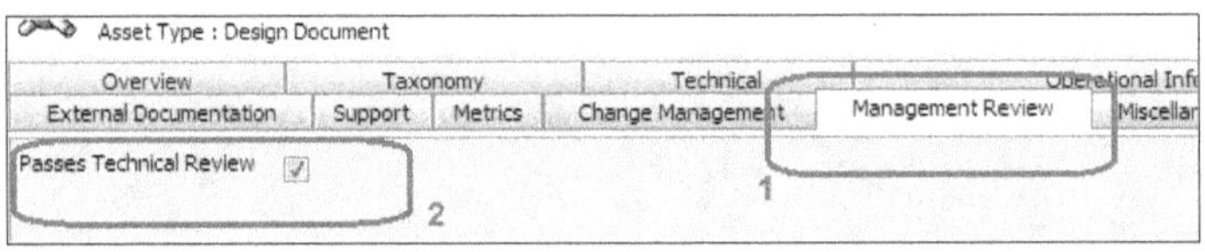

14. Click on the **Administration** tab and then click on the **Accept** button. This will change the Asset state to **Submitted : Under Review**.

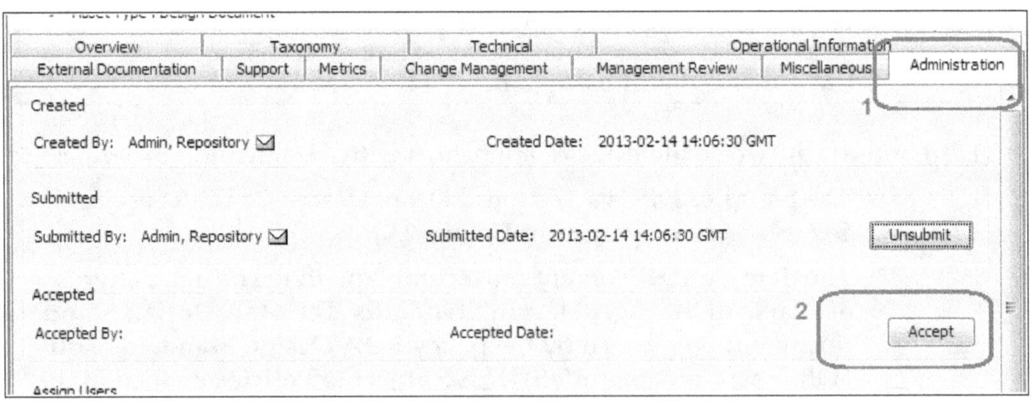

15. From the same tab, click on the **Register** button to change the Asset state to **Registered**.

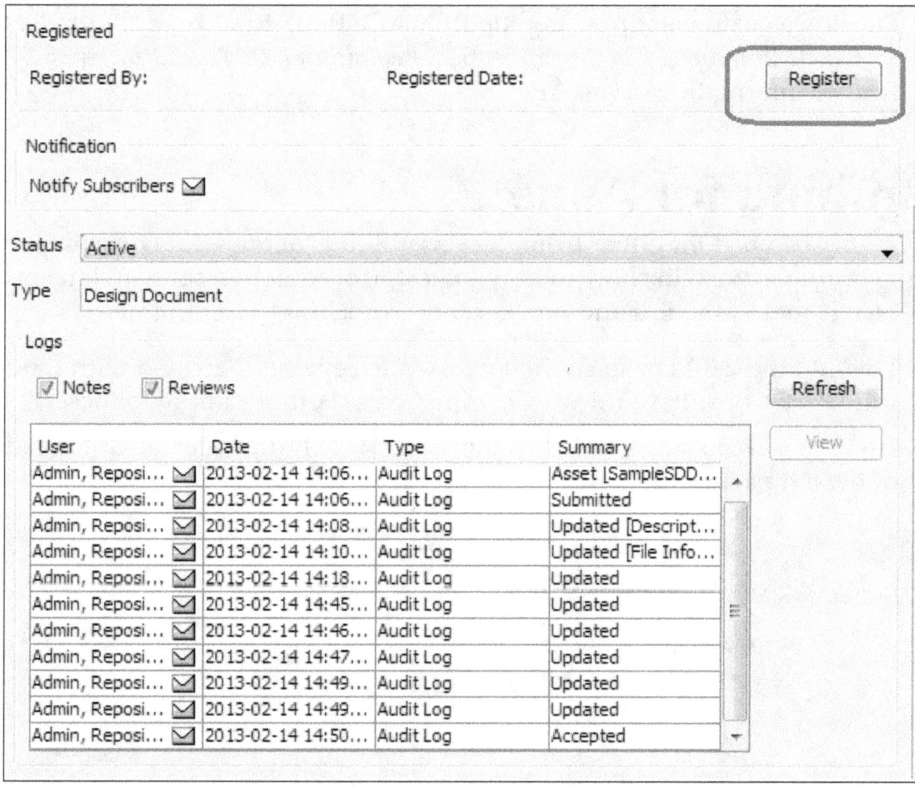

[From the **Logs** section, located at the bottom of the **Administration** tab, it is possible to visualize all the changes made to the Asset.]

16. From the **File** top menu, click on **Save** to save all changes made to the Asset.

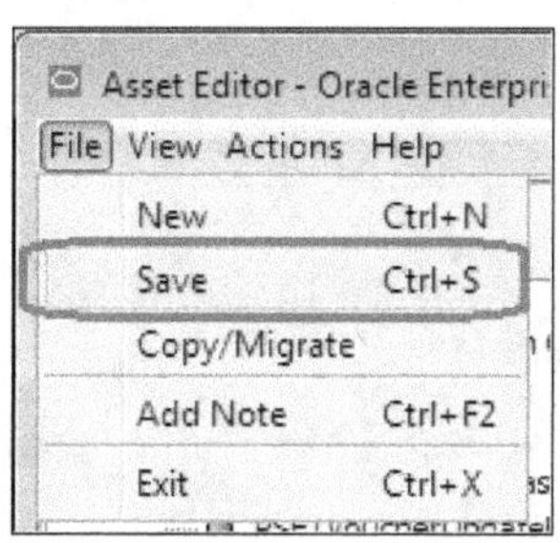

17. Following a very similar process, it is possible to manually submit all the document Assets that were not harvested automatically by the Harvester. Also note that, if this task becomes too painful and slow, it is possible to develop a custom script using the REX API. Refer to *Chapter 3, Introduction To Oracle Enterprise Repository*, section *Repository Exchange Utility (REX)* for further information of the API.

Searching for Assets

Assets can be searched for either from the Asset Editor or the OER console. In the following example, we will show to how to perform a quick Asset search from the console as it is more practical and quicker than launching Asset Editor.

1. Log into the OER console with any user, except users created with the thirdPartyConsultant role as Custom Access Settings apply to these.
2. Go to the **Assets** page and click on the **Browse** button located at the bottom of the left panel.

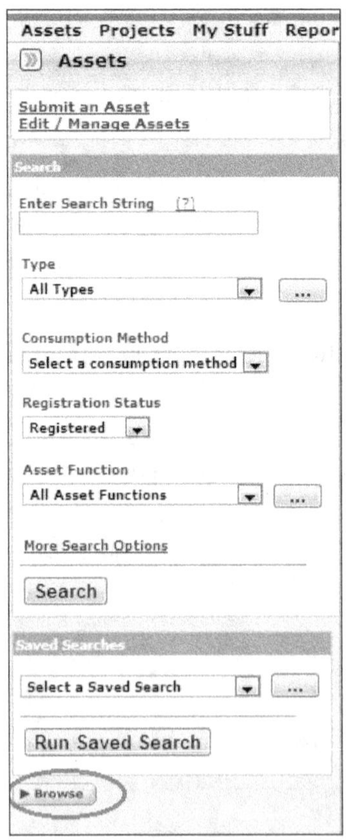

3. From the first drop-down menu, select the categorization **Project Deliverables**. From the second drop-down, select **Registered**. Finally, click on **Detail Design** to perform a search based on these filters.

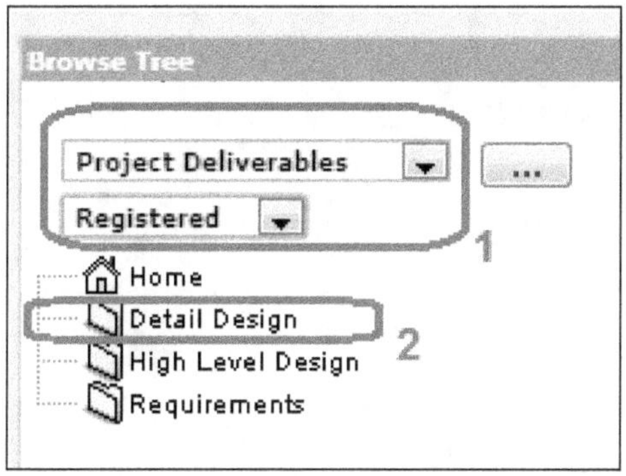

4. All Assets that match the search criteria will show up on the main page.

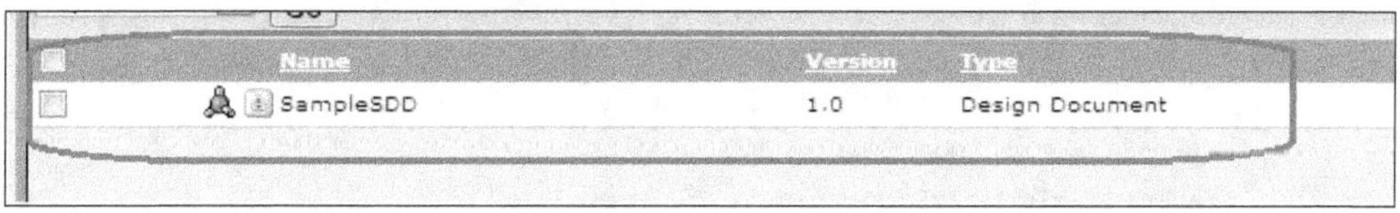

> There is a yellow exclamation mark beside the **SampleSDD** item indicating that while a policy has been applied to this Asset, the policy may not be currently supported. In *Chaper 6, Asset Lifecycle and Workflow*, we will elaborate more in the use of policies.

5. Click on an Asset to visualize more details such as relationships to other Assets.

Visualizing Asset relationships

After conducting a search on an Asset, it is possible to visualize its relationship by clicking on the **Navigator** button located in the Asset details section (lower pane of the window).

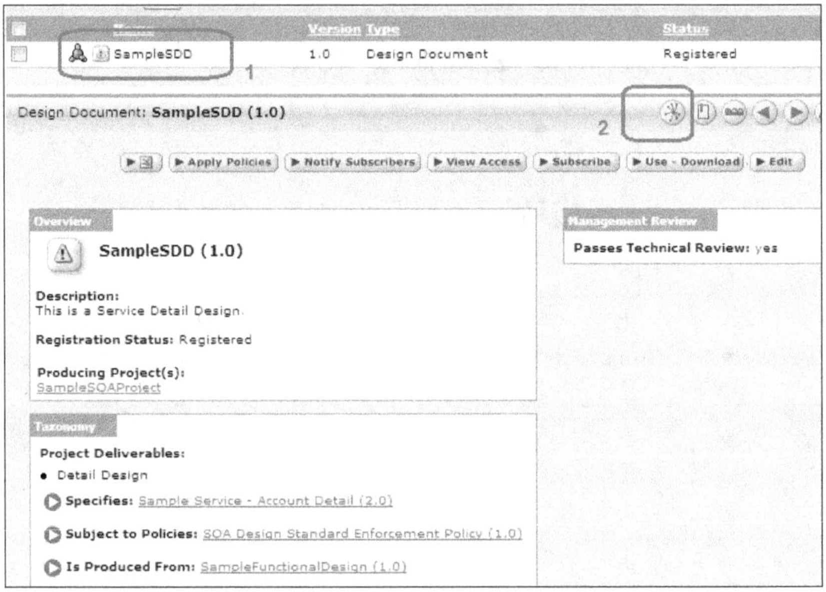

When the **Navigator** window opens, the Asset relationships will appear in the upper window section in the Navigator applet.

In the following examples, we will show the relationships between key Assets harvested and those manually submitted for the Weir & Bell Telecom implementation.

The first example shows all of the relationships established for the Asset **SampleSDD(1.0)** after following the steps described in the previous sections.

> Please note that these are only samples. While they are based on real implementations, one size does not fit all. Therefore, use these details for reference only and always base your solution on the specific needs of the companies undergoing Governance Implementation.

In this example, we show how all of the relationships for **SampleSDD(1.0)** are explicit (meaning visible and not hidden) and centered to this particular Asset. For example, it is clearly visible that this design is produced from the functional design **SampleFunctionalDesign(1.0)**, that it provides the technical specification for the SOA Service **Sample Service - Account Detail(2.0)**, that it was created or is managed by the project **SampleSOAProject** and that the design is subject to the policies specified in **SOA Design Standard Enforcement Policy(1.0)**.

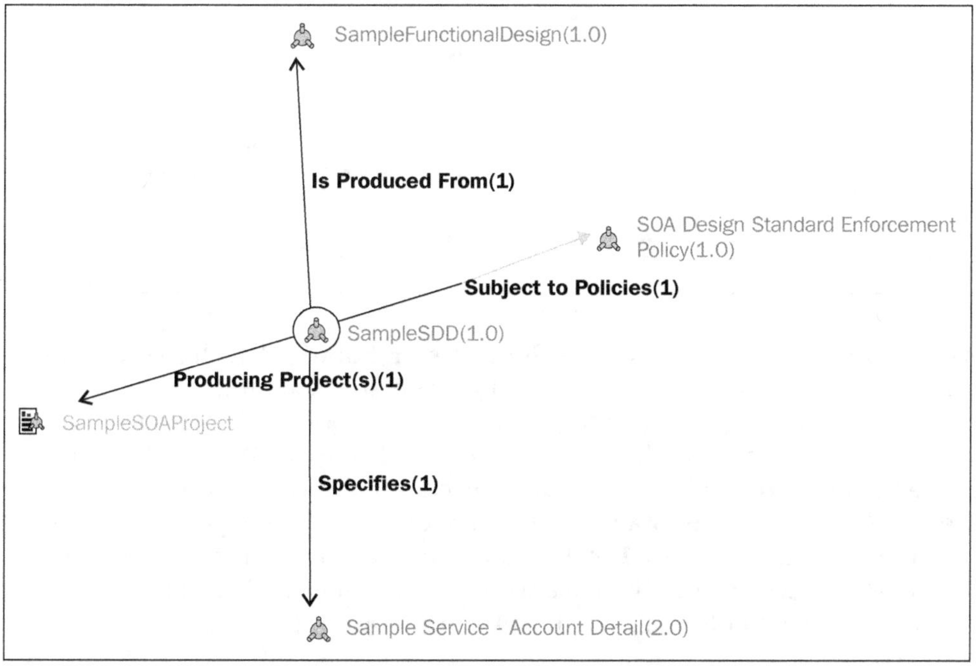

Relationships can be centered on a different Asset by clicking on any of the other Assets displayed in the applet. The second example shows a relationship view after clicking on the Asset **SampleFunctionalDesign(1.0)**.

Similarly to the previous example, this Asset is also related to other Assets. This was done purposely and based on the requirements gathered for Weir & Bell Telecom.

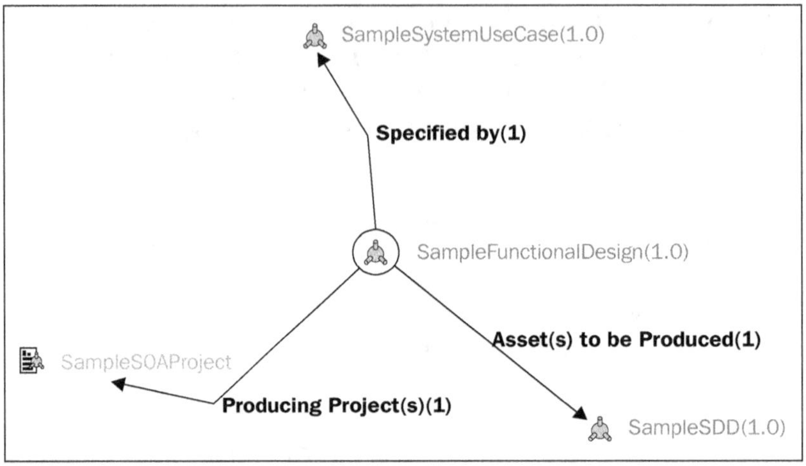

This third example is centered on the **SOA Design Standards(1.0)** Asset (note that this Asset was not displayed in any of the previous examples and it was accessed by performing another search). This is an important view as it shows all of the Governance Framework assets created specifically for Weir & Bell Telecom implementation, and how they all relate to each other. It can be seen that standards defined in the **SOA Design Standards(1.0)** are enforced by the policy **SOA Design Standard Enforcement Policy(1.0)**, that this standard in turn is based on the **Reference Architecture** and that the design patterns specified within this document apply to other documents (such as the **SOA Programming Standards**).

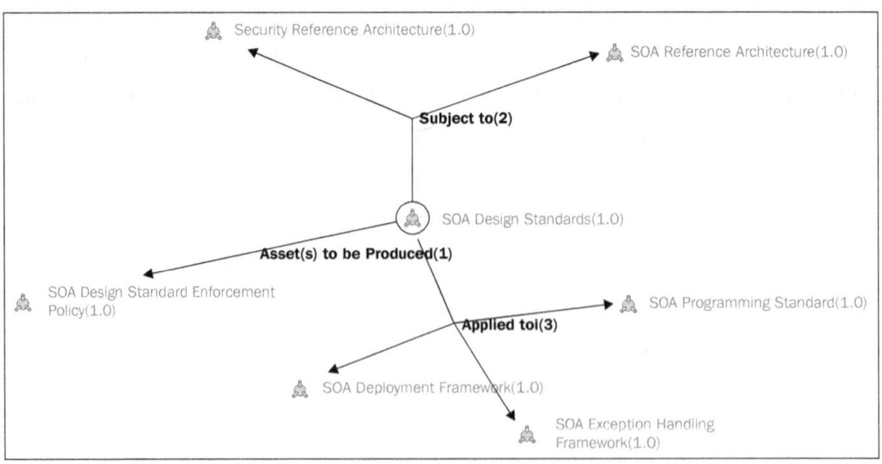

This last example shows how the Governance Framework assets created for the Weir & Bell Telecom implementation comply with the guidelines described in *Chapter 1, SOA Governance*. We can see how the **SOA Reference Architecture(1.0)** actually aims to support an **SOA Strategy and Roadmap(2.0)**, which in turn is based on the business strategy, and that it is the fundamental building block of the entire SOA Governance solution.

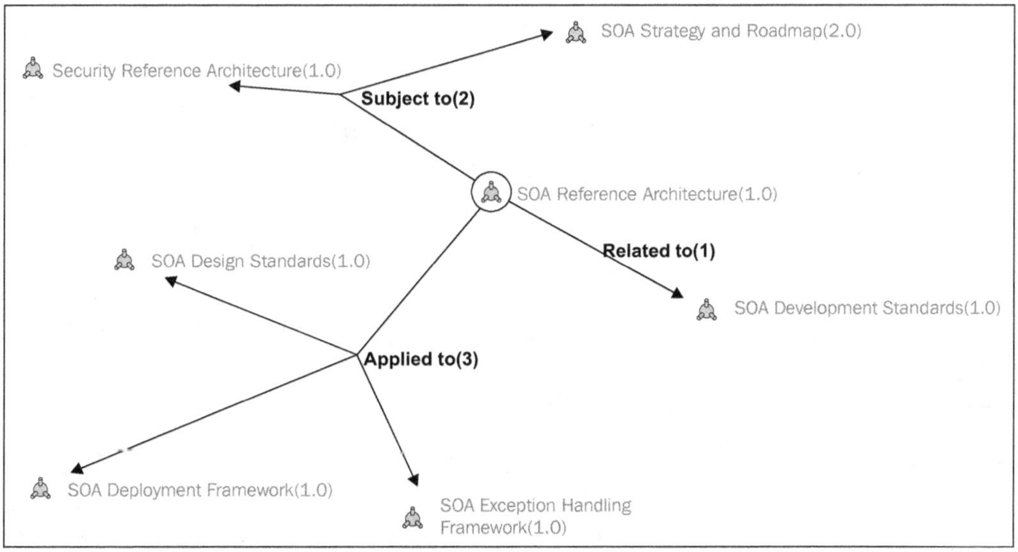

Summary

In this chapter, we have walked through all of the steps necessary to understand, define, and execute a Bootstrapping Strategy using the appropriate choice of the Harvester tool. We have demonstrated that the process of bootstrapping involves more than just executing the Harvester. In fact, we have shown how imperative it is to initially generate a complete profile of all existing Assets before defining a Harvesting Strategy. Such a strategy will be determined based on the status of all Assets and where they are located in the enterprise.

Furthermore, we have discussed the prerequisites that have to be fulfilled to successfully execute the Harvesting process and the post-Harvesting steps that are required to deliver a meaningful representation of the entire Asset landscape. This representation is critical to SOA Governance efforts as it becomes the single source of truth for all enterprise Assets.

The chapter has also covered some aspects of the *Chapter 6, Asset Lifecycle and Workflow*. These topics will be elaborated further in the following chapter.

6

Asset Lifecycle and Workflow

This chapter focuses on the Asset Lifecycle Management and workflow features of OER. The chapter elaborates further on the same requirements listed in *Chapter 4, Initial Configuration,* use case, however, it focuses on how design-time tools can be used in conjunction with a process and people to achieve the right level of governance.

Use case

Weir & Bell Telecom acknowledge that without some sort of enforcement of the defined standards and policies, it would be only a matter of time before things get out of control and governance becomes an issue again. To prevent this situation the architects at Weir and Bell came up with a target design-time Governance model:

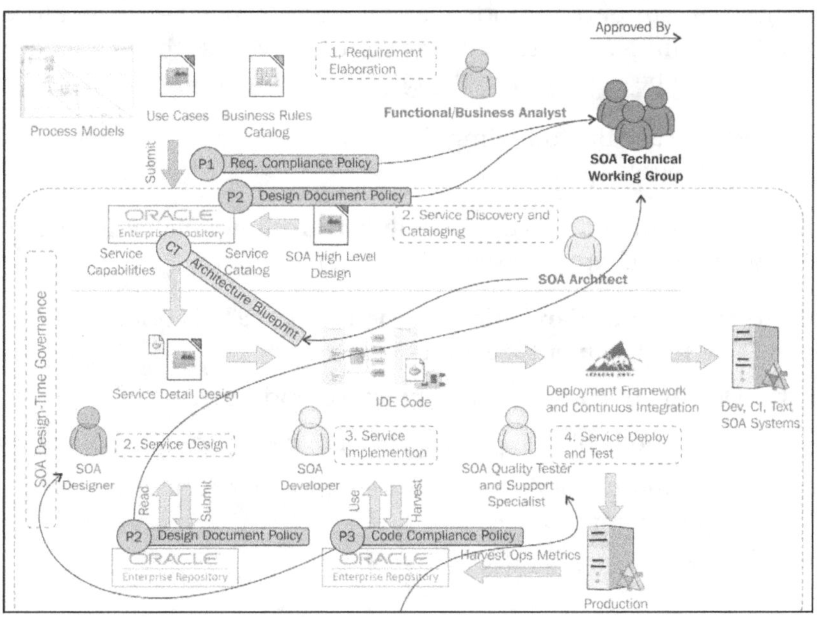

The model implies an Asset-centric Software Development Lifecycle (SDLC) whereby OER would be used to:

- Register all Assets created by the different actors throughout the lifecycles
- Once requirements have been captured, define a Bill of Materials that can be used later on by designers and developers to understand the scope of the requirements and the artifacts that need delivering
- Introduce human workflow for approvals either by individuals or groups
- Enforce design-time quality gates throughout the different stages of the Software Development Lifecycle

The subsequent sections describe how a gap analysis was done in order to understand what customizations were needed in the out of the box OER functionality and also how these customizations were implemented.

Implementing Policies

Assets compliance requirements can be enforced in OER with the utilization of Policies. Policies can be applied to one or many Assets. An Asset can have more than one policy attached to it. A policy in OER consists of one-to-many **Policy Assertions**. When a policy is applied to an Asset, all of the assertions within the policy must be true in order for Asset to comply with the policy.

Each assertion has a name, a description, and includes a technical definition. Technical definitions support additional metadata that may be needed to validate the assertion (for example, a particular Asset must have less than 1 percent defects before the service can be deployed to the next environment).

According to the use case the following Policies are needed in to order to support the target governance model:

Note that for your organization, you may define as many Policies as you required. For the purposes of this chapter we simplified it.

- **Requirement Compliance Enforcement Policy**: This policy is applied to **Asset Type** Requirement Documents to assert:
    - Document compliance to business and other enterprise templates
    - All sections of the documents have been properly completed
    - Traceability matrix exists for functional and nonfunctional requirements
    - There are no open issues or gaps

- **Design Document Compliance Enforcement Policy**: This policy is applied to **Asset Types** Design Documents to assert:
    - Adherence to enterprise architecture principles
    - Bill of Materials has been created capturing all needed artifacts
    - Data requirements have been captured
    - Compliance to design standards and design patterns
    - All relevant views (for example, static, dynamic, and sequential) are available and provide all levels of information required
    - All design decisions have been reviewed and approved
    - There are no open issues or gaps
- **Code Compliance Enforcement Policy**: This policy is applied to detail designs with the intention to assert:
    - Compliance to programming standards
    - Alignment to detail design
    - Unit Test has been executed successfully and there are no open defects
    - Deployment plans and other deployment pre-requisites have been successfully addressed.
- **Operational Compliance Enforcement Policy**: This policy is applied to detail designs with the intention to assert:
    - Release notes have been properly created and all deployment instructions are available
    - There is less than for example, 1 percent open defects (per testing stage) assigned to any Asset associated with the service

> Policies are made compulsory by introducing compliance checks throughout lifecycle stages of the Asset. Different checks can be introduced during code promotion between environments. For example, code should not be promoted to SIT before quality testing policies have passed, or to UAT before SIT policies have passed. This could be done manually or automated by extending a deployment framework to integrate with OER using the REX APIs.

Creating Policies

Policies are created in OER using the **Asset Editor**.

> Note that Policies can also be created from the **Assets** page; however, only a limited amount of attributes can be supplied using this page and therefore the **Asset Editor** will have to be used anyways.

Before creating Policies you should ensure that:

- Policies have been enabled and that the **Policy Management** Solution Pack has been successfully imported as described in the section *Installing Solution Packs* in *Chapter 5, Harvesting*.
- Policy rights have been granted to the desired roles as follows:
    1. Log on to OER as admin, and then navigate to the **Admin** page. From the **Basic Access Settings** menu, click on **Policies** and then click on the **Edit** button.

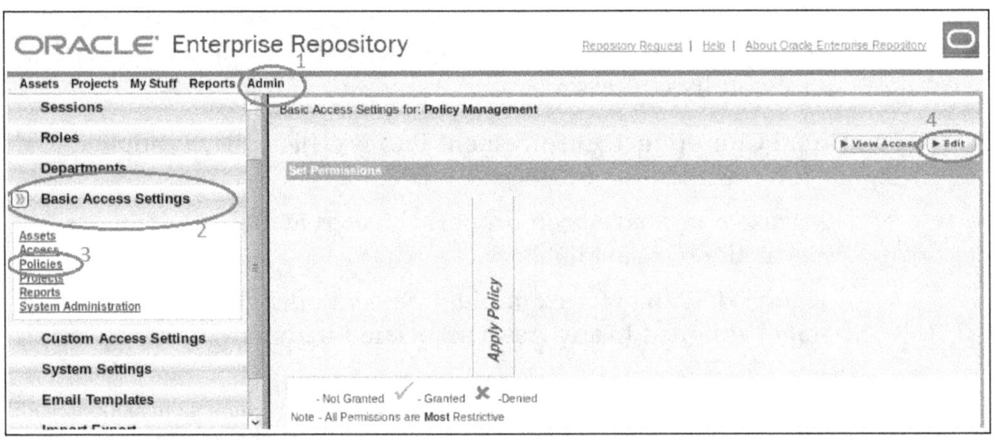

2. In the **Edit Access Settings** window, select **Show all available Roles** to display existing roles. Then select the roles for which **Apply Policy** rights will be granted. Click on the **Save** button. Now a user with any of these roles will be able to apply policies to Assets.

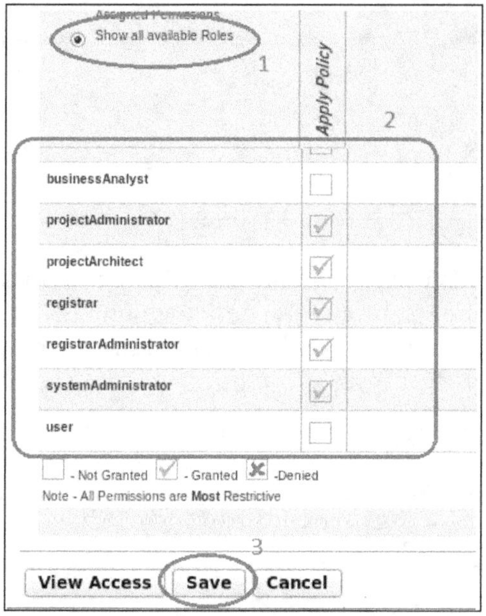

The next step is to create all policies as it has been identified. In this chapter we will explain how to create the Requirement Compliance Enforcement Policy. As the process of creating policies is fairly similar regardless of the policy requirements, the following steps could be reproduced to create the remaining polices.

> The Policy Compliance Solution Pack comes with many out-of-the-box policies that can be perfectly re-used.

The fastest way to create a policy is by using an existing **Policy Type** rather than creating one from scratch (although, this is still perfectly possible by using the **Type Manager**). This can be done as follows:

1. Log on to OER as admin and from the **Assets** page launch the **Asset Editor**.
2. From the **File** menu select **New**.

3. Enter the name of the policy and its version. Select **POL - Policy** as the **Type**. Select the desired **Initial State**. If you are an administrator, you can set the status as **Registered** if no further approvals are needed.

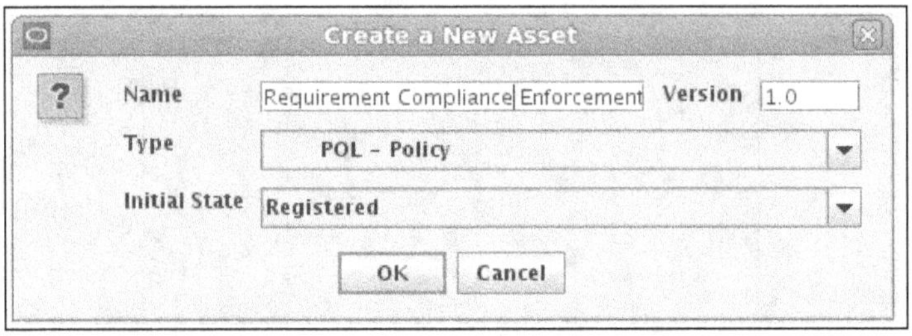

4. In the Asset details page enter as many details as possible as this will make it easier for someone to enforce the policy when needed. At the very minimum ensure that the **Name**, **Version**, **Description**, and **Policy Assertions** have all been populated accordingly.

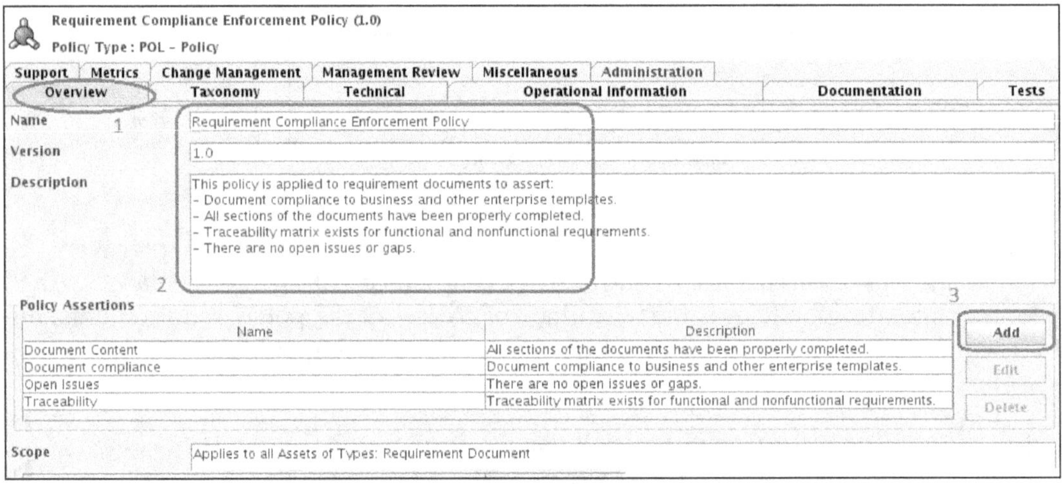

5. If there are any specific tests that must be executed in this policy, the same can be added from the **Tests** tab.
6. Save all changes made by clicking on the **Save** option within the **File** menu.
7. Repeat these types for all policies that need to be created.

Editing the Asset Types

Policies can only be applied to Assets for which the element **Applied Asset Policies** has been added to its corresponding **Asset Type**. This can be done as follows:

1. Log on to OER as admin and from the **Assets Page** launch the **Asset Editor**.
2. From the menu **Actions** select **Type Manager**.
3. Select the desired type that you wish to modify (in our example, **Requirement Document**).
4. Select the **Editor** Tab.
5. In the **Tabs** section, select **Overview**.
6. In the **Elements** section, click on the **Add** button.
7. In the new window, select **Applied Asset Policies** as the **Element Type** and click on the **OK** button.

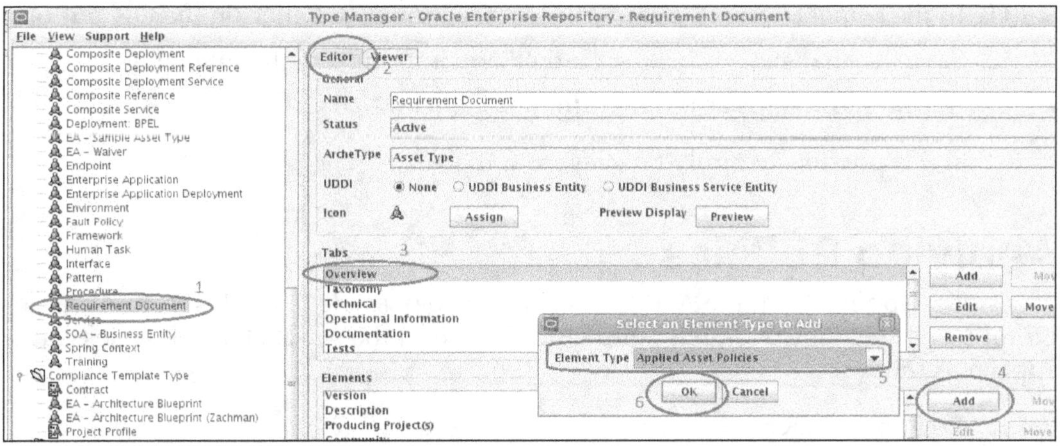

8. The Edit Applied Asset Policies window opens. Enter **Applied Asset Policies** and click on the **OK** button.

9. Click on the **Viewer** tab.

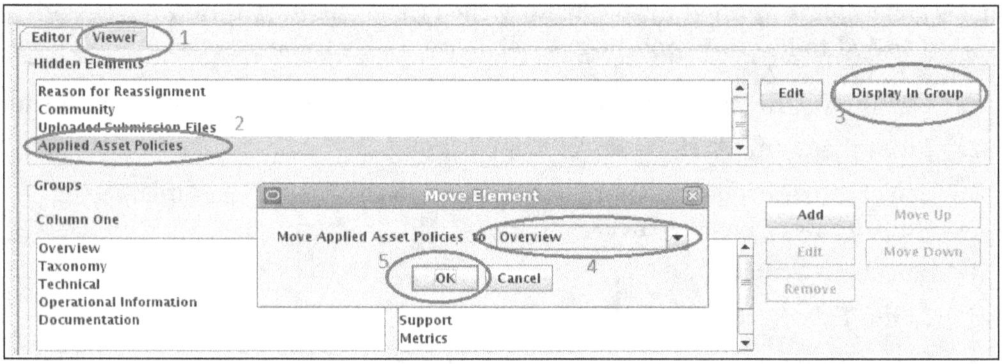

10. In the **Hidden Elements** section select the **Applied Asset Policies** element and click on the **Display In Group** button.
11. In the **Move Element** window, select **Overview** and click on the **OK** button.
12. Save the changes by clicking on the **Save** button from the **File** menu.
13. Repeat these steps as required for any Policies that have been created.

Note that it is possible to apply Policies from the

Applying Policies

Policies are applied from the **Assets** page. It is also possible to do this from **Asset Editor** by editing; however, it is simpler to do it from the **Assets** Page. Policies can be applied as follows:

1. Log on to OER as admin and go to the **Assets** page.
2. Search the Asset to which the policy is to be applied (in our example, we searched for use case document which is of type **Requirement Document**).

3. In the Asset details page click on the **Apply Policies** button.

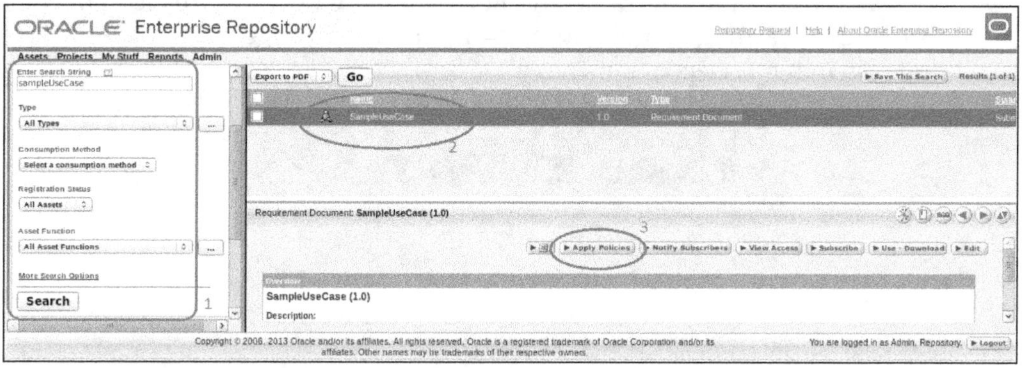

4. To display all available Policies click on **List All Policies**. All available Policies will appear in the **Available Asset Policies** box.
5. Select the policy you wish to apply (in our example, we want to apply the **Requirement Compliance Enforcement Policy** to the use case document Asset) and then click on **>>** to apply the policy and then click on the **Save** button.

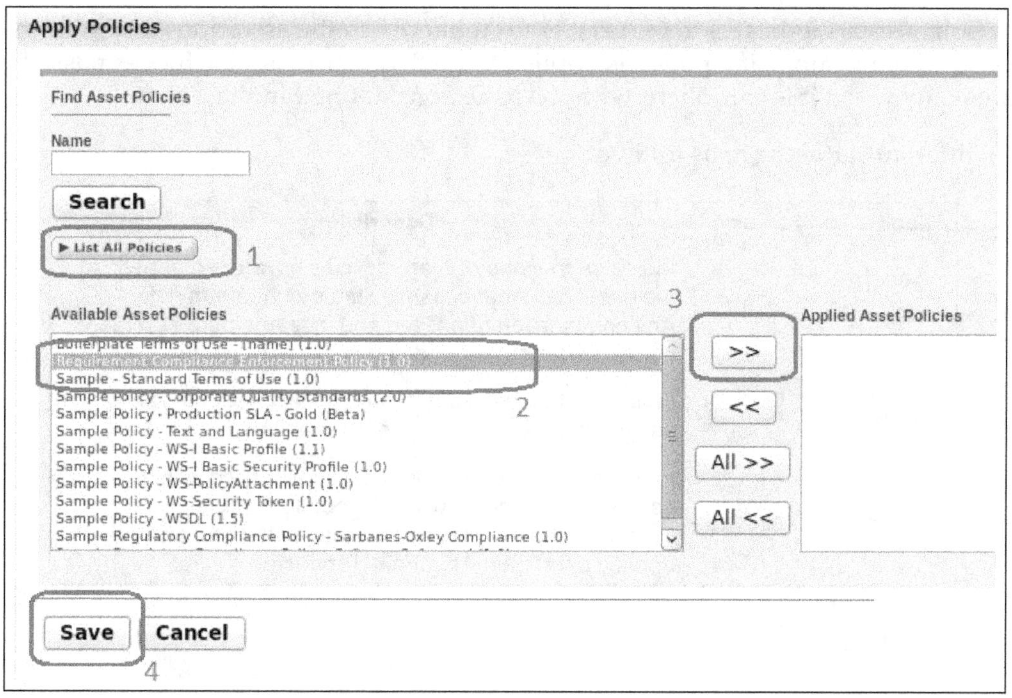

6. A confirmation message is displayed. Click on the **Close** button.
7. Refresh the Asset detail frame and notice that the Policy Status icon (a yellow icon with a warning symbol) appears in the results page next to the Asset and also in the Assets details page.

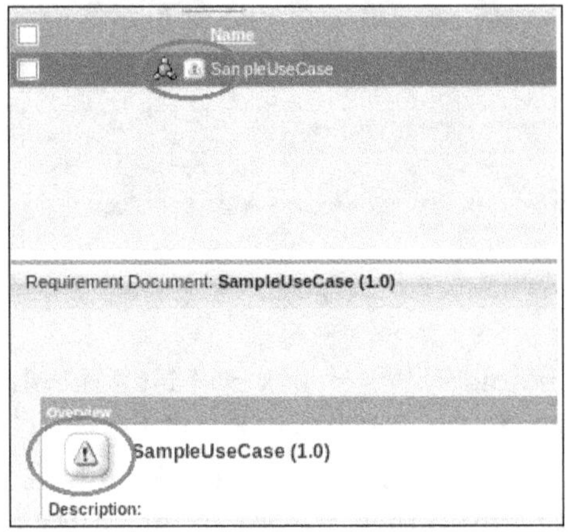

Policy status

The policy status indicates if an Asset is compliant with the assertions available in a policy. For example, if a policy is applied to an Asset, the Asset achieves passed status only when it is compliant with the assertions defined in the policy.

The different statuses are as follows:

Icon	Status	Description
	Applied	Indicates that one or more policies have been applied to the asset, and that pass/fail status is indeterminate. Any combination of passed and indeterminate assertion statements results in indeterminate asset status.
	Passed	Indicates that the asset is in compliance with every assertion statement within every applied policy.
	Failed	Indicates that the asset is not in compliance with all assertion statements within all applied policies. Failure to comply with any assertion statement within any applied policy results in Failed status.

Validating Policies

Policies can be validated manually through the **Asset Editor** or automatically using external tooling (that is, a customized workflow or BPM process) and the REX API's. The following is an example of how to manually validate a policy:

1. Log on to OER with any user with a role that has the **Apply Policy** grants.
2. Search for the Asset to validate the policy either from the **Assets** page or from the **Asset Editor**. If searched from the **Assets** page, find the Asset and then from the Asset details page click on the **Edit** button.
3. From the **Overview** tab of **Asset Editor**, scroll down and from the **Applied Asset Policies** select the policy to validate and click on the **Details** button.

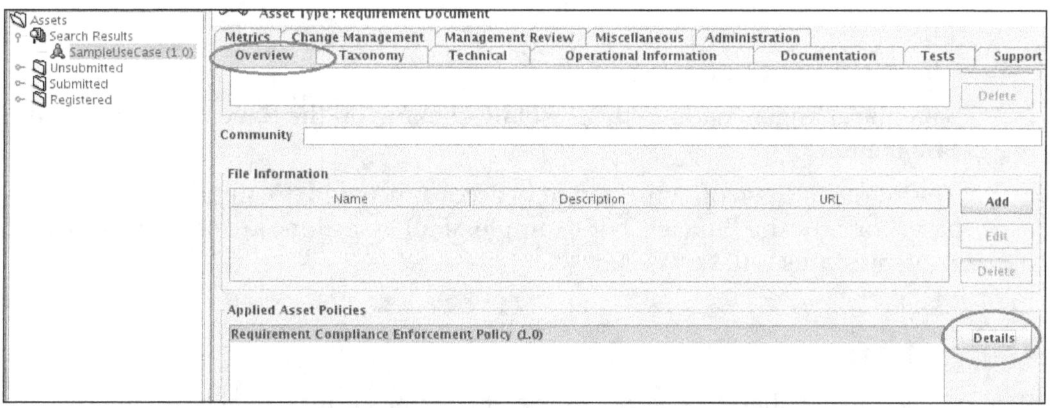

4. Select the **Assertions** to validate and click on the **Edit** button.

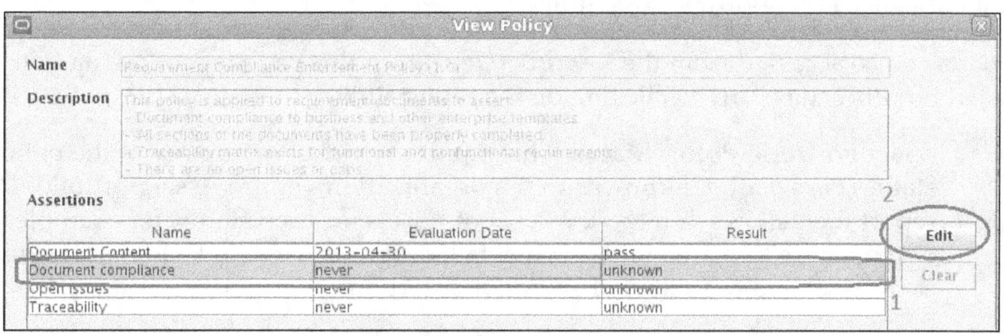

5. Enter the **Evaluation Date, Evaluation Value** (pass or fail), and some description on the evaluation in the **Evaluation Information** field.

6. Click on the **OK** button.

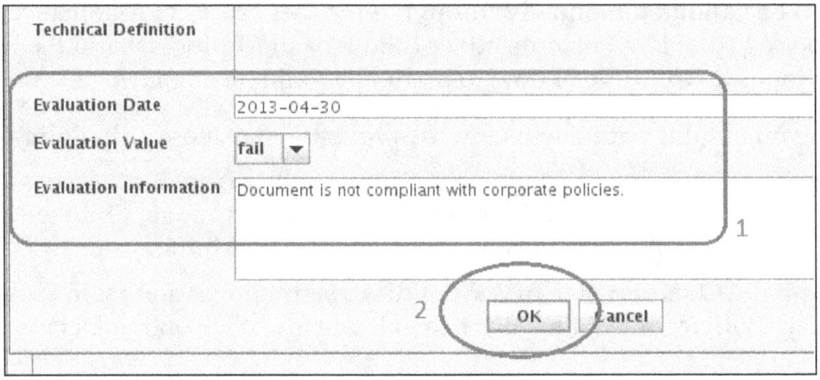

7. Click on the **OK** button again.
8. Save the changes made to the Asset by clicking on the **Save** button from the **File** menu.
9. The status of the icon will change in accordance with evaluation of the assertions for the Policies. For example, if all assertions are set to pass then the icon status will be **Passed**.

Reporting

When policies are applied to several Assets, it becomes unpractical to manually check the status of the Policies applied to Assets. For this purpose it is possible to leverage the reporting capabilities of OER and thus generate reports using the built-in BI Publisher 11*g* reporting capabilities.

Reports can be accessed from the **Reports** page. From this page the following policy related reports can be run by clicking on the report link:

- **Asset Portfolio Policy Status**: This report provides a summary of the policy status (**Pass, Fail, Unknown**) for an organization's entire Asset portfolio. The report then allows you to view a list of Assets for each status, for example, all of the Assets that are failing. The detailed reports list all policies applied to each Asset and the status of all policy assertions.

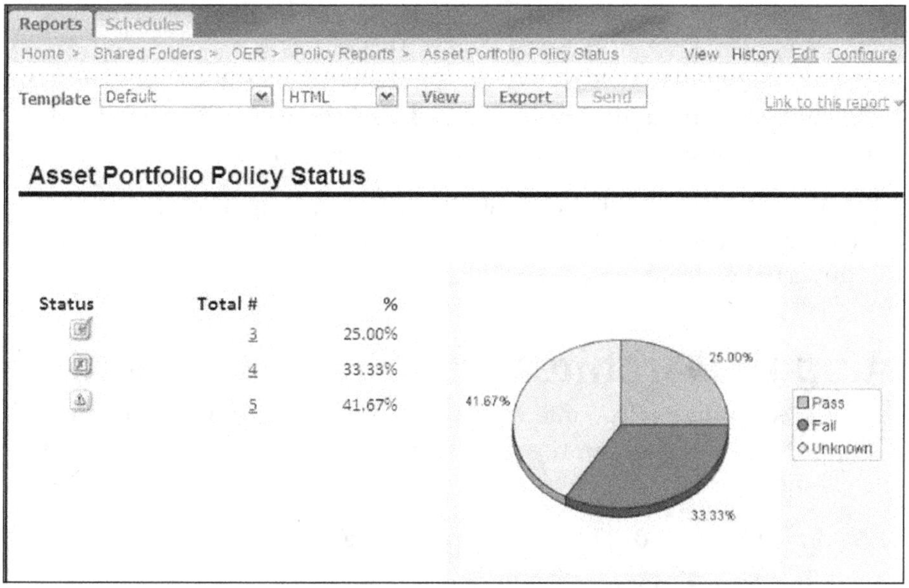

- **Policy Status**: This report provides a summary of all Policies in an organization's policy portfolio, and the number of Assets that are passing, failing, or have an unknown status. This report also shows a detailed list of the Assets that are governed by each policy, and the number of assertions that are passing, failing, or have an unknown status.

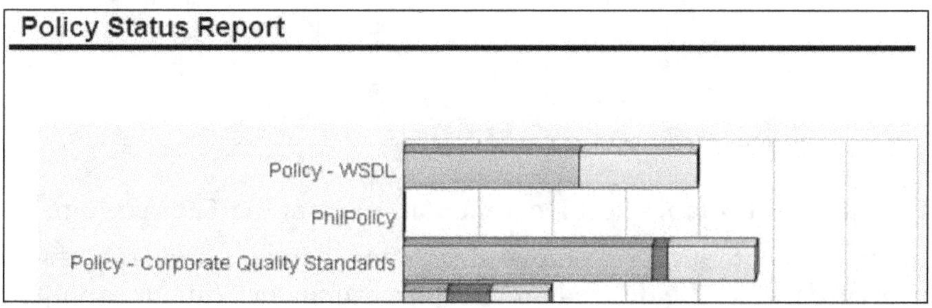

Implementing Architecture Blueprints

Architecture Blueprint is one of the three compliance templates available in OER PS6. In *Chapter 4, Initial Configuration,* it was explained how to create and apply a **Project Profile** compliance template to an existing project. The process of creating and applying an Architecture Blueprint is fairly similar to a project profile, however, its purpose is slightly different.

Architecture Blueprints can be used as the means to predefine which Assets apply to more than one project (for example, technical standards, require environments, frameworks, amongst others). This feature can be very useful for architects, for example, to convey architectural requirements and the **Bill of Materials** (**BOM**) to the downstream (or outsourced) teams in a noninvasive fashion.

In the following example, it will be shown how to create an Architecture Blueprint that will articulate the expected deliverables in accordance with Weir & Bell Telecom's governance framework.

Creating the Architecture Blueprint Asset Type

Although OER Solution Packs come with some Architecture Blueprints that can be used straight away, it will be shown how to copy and customize an existing compliance template:

1. Log on to OER as admin and from the **Assets** Page launch the **Asset Editor**.
2. From the **Assets** menu select **Manage Types**.
3. From the **File** menu select **New**.
4. Enter the **Type Name** and select **EA - Architecture Blueprint** as **Type for Defaults**. Then click on the **OK** button.

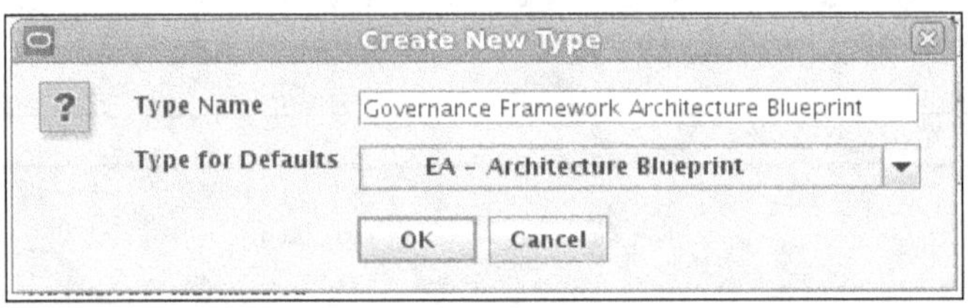

5. From the **Editor** tab, select **Documentation** from the **Tabs** section.
6. In the **Elements** section, remove all existing elements and add new ones in accordance to the desired architecture framework (in our example, we based this in the architecture deliverables defined for Weir & Bell Telecom's governance framework).

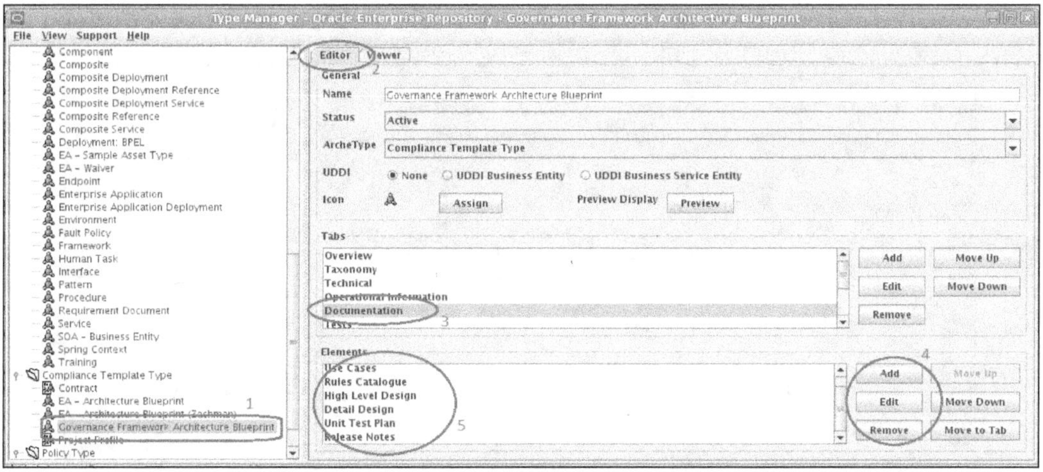

7. Once finished editing, save the changes made by clicking on the **Save** button from the **File** menu.

Creating an Architecture Blueprint

Now that the customized type has been created for the company's specific architectural deliverables, a specific Architecture Blueprint can be created and applied to specific projects. The following is an example of how to achieve this:

1. Log on to OER as admin and from the **Assets** page launch the **Asset Editor**.
2. From the **File** menu select **New**.
3. Enter the **Name** and **Version** of the Asset. Select **Governance Framework Architecture Blueprint** as **Type**, set the **Initial State** and finally click on the **OK** button.

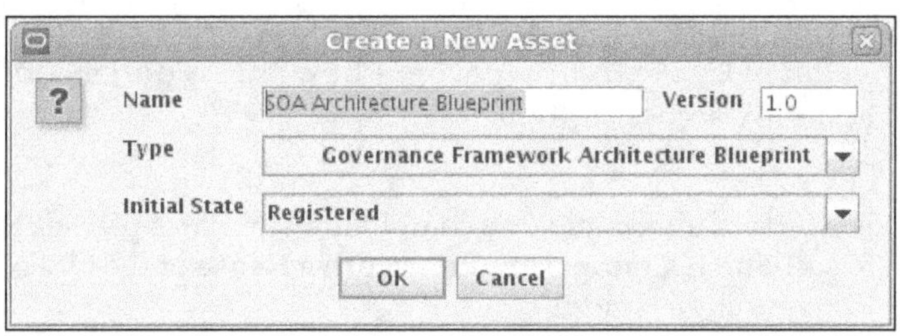

4. In the **Overview** tab include the basic details of the compliance template.

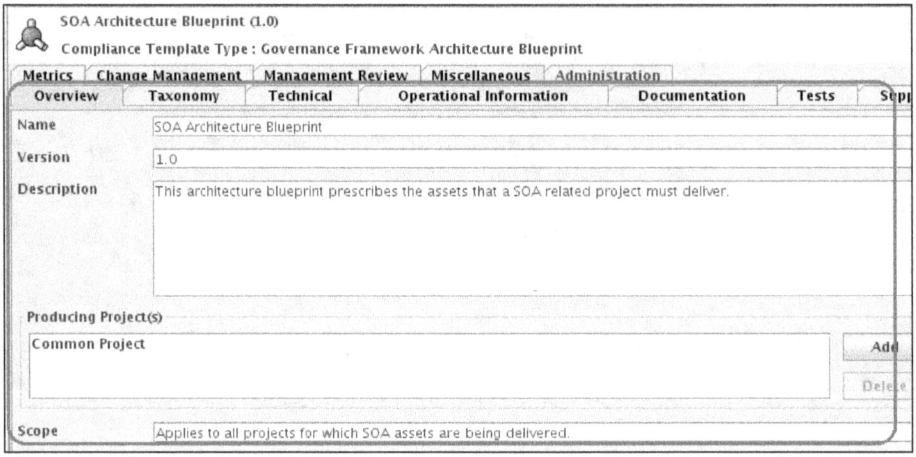

5. Most importantly in the **Targeted Project(s)**, add the projects for which this Architecture Blueprint will be applied by clicking on the **Add** button.

6. Once finished editing, save the changes made by clicking on the **Save** button from the **File** menu

Prescriptive re-use

It is possible with compliance templates to prescribe Assets to be used by the projects. *Chapter 4, Initial Configuration*, covered how this is done along with the configuration of complex access settings.

> For further information on compliance templates please refer to section 11, **Configuring Prescriptive Reuse** of the OER Configuration Guide.
>
> `http://docs.oracle.com/cd/E28280_01/admin.1111/e16580/compliance.htm#sthref725`

Report and compliance

OER comes built in with a reporting capability for compliance templates. Project Compliance reports provide the means for verifying project adherence to the Assets prescribed for use in compliance templates. The report can be run from the **Reports** page by clicking on the Project Compliance report link.

> For further information on compliance templates reporting please refer to section 11.6, **Running a Project Compliance Report** of the OER Configuration Guide.
>
> `http://docs.oracle.com/cd/E28280_01/admin.1111/e16580/compliance.htm#BBAGCHBG`

Understanding workflow

The first step to understand which customizations are needed is to do a gap analysis between the existing functionality and the desired functionality.

Let's start by understanding how the standard approval process works in OER by default:

- When an Asset is submitted through the Harvester or REX API, the status of the Asset can be defined as desired. However, note that the user provided when executing the Harvester or REX API must belong to the relevant role, as otherwise, the Asset submission will fail.
- When an Asset is submitted through the **Asset Editor** by any user with role Advance Editor, the status of the Assets is set to **Unsubmitted**. The Asset then needs to be approved by a user with the role of Advance Editor in order for the Asset to change its status to **Submitted - Pending Review**.

> Note that every time the status of the Asset changes, Event Managers throw an event. These events are then picked up by the workflow engine to execute a specified action.

- When an Asset is submitted through the web console by any user that has the role Basic User, the status of the Asset is set to **Submitted - Pending Review**. The Asset then needs to be approved by a user with the role Registrar in order for the Asset to change its status to **Submitted - Under Review**.

- When an Asset changes to the status **Submitted - Under Review,** it can then be registered by any user with Registrar role. Note that the registrar may decide at this point to delegate to another user registration of the Asset.

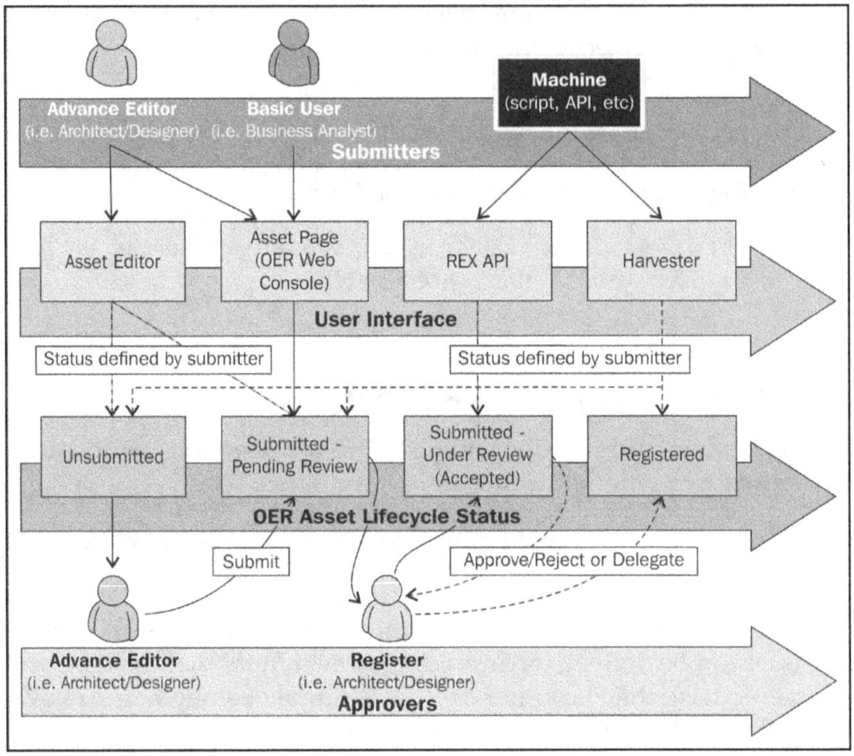

Although this functionality might be useful for some customers, in many other implementations the default behavior of the workflow functionality within OER needs to be customized in order to fit the customer needs. Furthermore, when the status of any Asset changes, it is possible to configure the Event Manager and BPM Workflows functionality of OER to automate or customize the out-of-the-box approval process. This can be very useful especially to address the following use cases:

- Multitiered approvals, for example, when approvals are needed from a design authority group
- Automated life cycle stage assignment, for example, when it is desired to automatically change the status of an Asset from build to release
- Automatic publishing of services to OSR depending on status, life cycle stage or any other categorization
- Implement custom Oracle BPM 11*g* processes based on different events

> Note that not all of the preceding use cases will be covered in this chapter. It is intended however, to provide information and references that can help in the implementation of the same.

The Event Manager allows for different types of events to be wired to OBPM automated workflows or if desired, to custom BPM 11*g* PS6 processes. The following diagram depicts some samples of events wire to workflows:

> Please refer to *Chapter 3, Introduction to Oracle Enterprise Repository*, for an architectural description OER workflows and Event Manager. You may also refer Event Manager to the Oracle OER Configuration Guide section 9.2.2, **Automated Workflows**.
>
> `http://docs.oracle.com/cd/E28280_01/admin.1111/e16580/oerwf.htm#CJHGDIJB`

Oracle classifies automated workflows as follows:

- **Community Assignment Flow**: It provides a way to automate the Asset acceptance, assignment, and registration processes by allowing the configuration of automated assignment rules and also provides the notion of federated registrars among different authorities.
- **Automated Acceptance and Automated Registration Flow**: In addition to using the Community Flows to automatically accept and register the Assets, a number of user roles can be used to accept and register Assets.
- **Multitier Approval Flow**: It structures the tab approval process in multiple steps called tiers. Asset approval tabs can be grouped into tiers, and the Multitier Approval Flow tracks each tier to verify whether all the tabs are approved by the designated approvers. As soon as the last tab in a tier is approved, the flow starts the next tier by assigning the Asset to the next level of designated approvers.
- **Metadata Change Flow**: It exposes a flexible framework where state changes or metadata changes can be wired to actions. The Metadata Change Flows come with a set of pre-bundled actions. New actions can be developed in the form of OER flows and can be plugged in.
- **Time-based Escalation Flow**: It tracks Assets in various states and notifies all interested parties. There are four different kinds of time-based escalation flows and each one can be configured individually.
- **Validation Expiration Flow**: It tracks expired Assets prior to the specified expiration date, as well as at the day of expiration, and sends warning notifications to all interested parties.
- **AutoSyncAlerToUddi Flow**: It moves a service from Oracle Enterprise Repository to Oracle Service Registry, based on a defined criteria (refer to *Chapter 8, Design-time Service Promotion and Discovery*, for further details).
- **BPM 11*g* Custom Processes**: Version 11.1.1.7 (PS6) of OER supports the creation of custom Oracle Unified BPM Suite 11*g* processes.

> Note that licensing restriction applies when using BPM 11*g*. For further info please refer to `http://docs.oracle.com/cd/E23943_01/doc.1111/e14860/products.htm#CDEHFEFG`

Workflow prerequisites

Before implementing an OER automated workflow, the following tasks must be completed:

1. Install OBPM 10.3.2 or BPM 11*g* PS6 if custom BPM processes are to be implemented.
2. Generate, edit, and install the automated workflows.
3. Configure the Event Manager.
4. Customize the desire workflows.

Please refer to the *Appendix, Installation Tips and Techniques* for detailed steps of the installation and configuration process for OER, OBPM, and the Event Manager. The following section covers the steps needed to customize workflows.

> The version of OER used in this book (OER PS6) introduces the possibility of utilizing custom Oracle BPM 11*g*. For the purposes of this book our objective in the chapter is to show the thought process needed in order to deliver a fit-for-purpose solution rather than using all features of the product. However, the OER configuration steps considered to be relevant have been described in more detail.

Gap analysis

Having understood the default behavior of the automated workflows, as well as the new requirements that need to be supported by the target governance model, the next step is do a gap analysis and identify what changes need to be made to the OER workflows.

Based on the use case described in the chapter, the following model identifies is the expected behavior that needs to be configured in the automated workflows in order to deliver the requirements of Weir & Bell Telecom.

> Please note that one site doesn't fit all so before making any changes it is critical that you understand what your company's specific requirements are and that these are properly captured in a structured way.

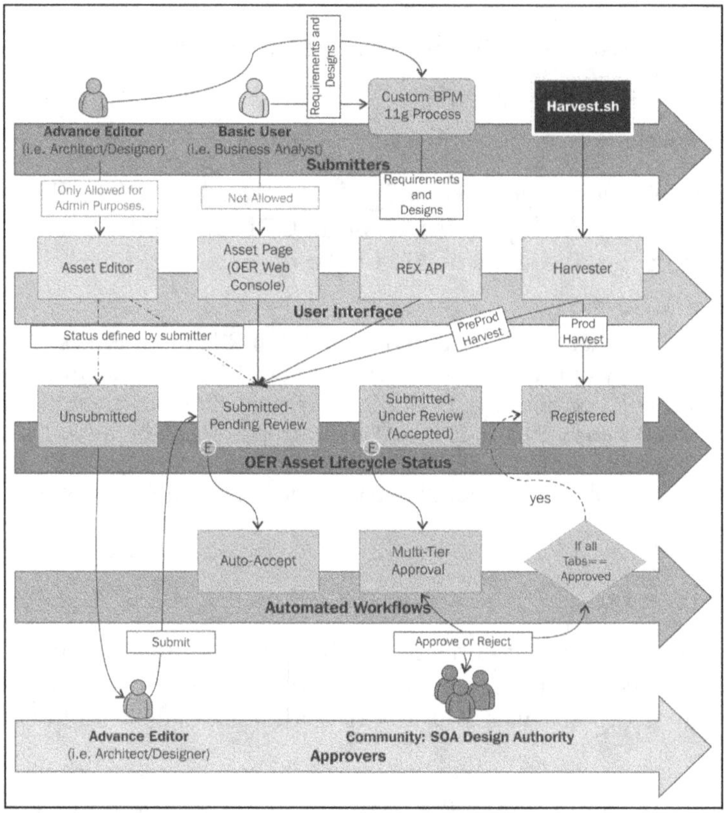

The model suggests that the following configurations and customizations are needed in OER and OER Workflows:

- A custom BPM 11*g* process needs to be created to allow the submission of Requirement Documents and Design Documents. The process would then undergo a custom approval workflow and once completed the Assets should be submitted into OER with a status of **Submitted – Pending Review** (please refer to section ***BPM 11g*** for further info).
- Assets should not be submitted either from the **Asset Editor** or the **Submit an Asset** page. The only exception to these rules is when for administration or troubleshooting purposes an Asset must be created via these tools.

- Once Assets reach the status of **Submitted - Pending Review,** an automated workflow should trigger multitier approval based on the different roles of the SOA Technical Working Group. At this stage the different approvers can verify the **Policy Assertions** and Asset them accordingly. Once all tabs of the Assets are approved, the Asset is automatically accepted and registered.
- New or modified Assets are harvested from preproduction with the status of **Submitted - Pending Review**. Periodically Assets are harvested from production with status of **Registered** (refer to *Chapter 4, Initial Configuration,* for additional information on Harvesting).

The following diagram shows the mapping between events and workflows that support the listed requirements:

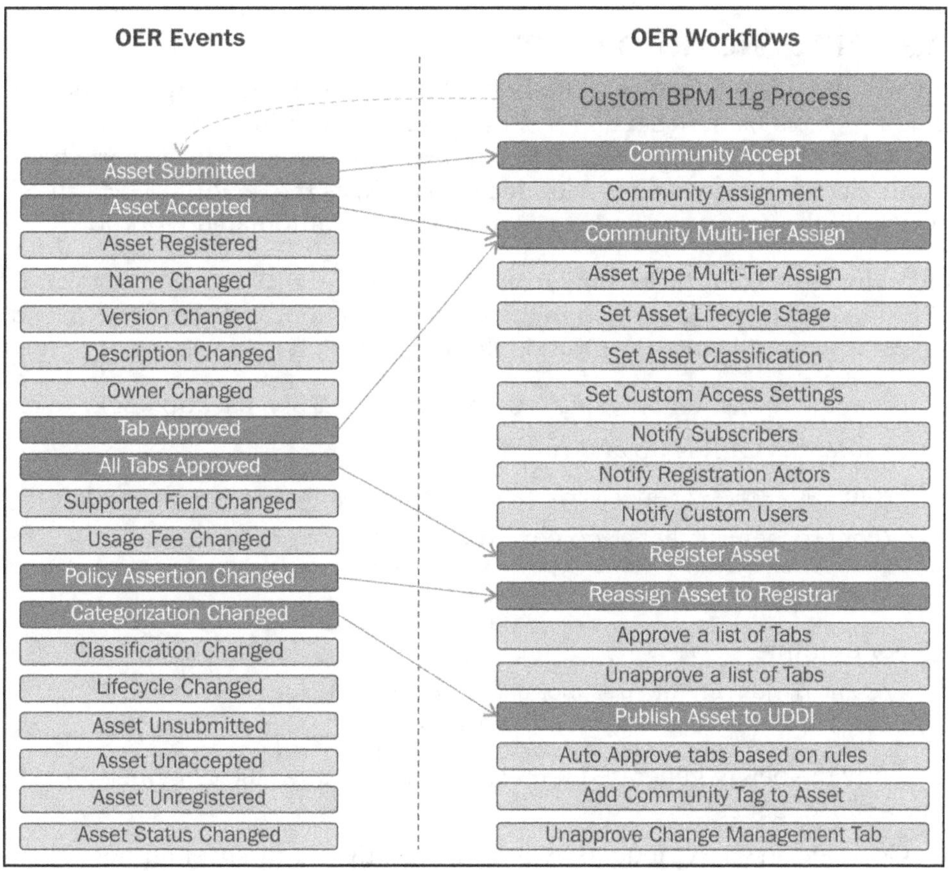

Configuring workflows

Configurations of the out of the box automated workflows are done in a file called `workflows.xml`.

This files needs to be generated using an OBPM Workflow Utility that comes with OER and then subsequently loaded into the OBPM OER engine.

> Note that this chapter assumes that an OBPM has been successfully installed and the OBPM OER engine has been configured. For further information on how to achieve this task please refer to *Appendix, Installation Tips and Techniques*.

Generating workflow.xml

During installation and configuration of OBPM, this toolkit is unzipped and placed under `<OBPM HOME>/OBPM_SetupScripts`. From this location the `script /config_gen.sh` can be executed to generate a new `workflow.xml` file. This is particularly important whenever new users are added into OER, as the `workflow.xml` file should be refreshed if the new users have to participate in an automated workflow.

The following is an example of how to customize the `workflow.xml` file to address the OBPM requirements identified in the previous section, and also how to load the new `workflow.xml` file into the OBPM OER engine:

1. From the folder `<OBPM HOME>/OBPM_SetupScripts` backup `workflow.xml`.
2. Ensure that OER is up and running.
3. From `<MW Home>/repository111/core/workflow-tools` execute:

   ```
   ./config_gen.sh http://<oer host>:<port>/oer/services/
   FlashlineRegistry <oer admin user> <oer password> <output
   directory>
   ```

   For example:

   ```
   ./config_gen.sh http://soabpm-server:7101/oer/services/
   FlashlineRegistry admin welcome1 .
   ```

4. Copy the newly generated `workflow.xml` to `<OBPM HOME>/OBPM_SetupScripts`.
5. Generate an encrypted password for the OER Admin user (either as described in *Chapter 5, Harvesting*, or from the following URL: `http://<oer server>:7101/oer/diag/encryptstrings.jsp`)

6. From <OBPM HOME>/OBPM_SetupScripts edit workflow.xml to include the encrypted password as follows:

    1. Change the <alerConnection> element details so the uri points to the OER server. For example,

```
<alerConnection>
  <uri>http://soabpm-server:7101/oer/services/
FlashlineRegistry</uri>
    <registrar>
      <user>admin</user>
      <password>encrypted password</password>
    </registrar>
</alerConnection>
```

    2. Include the encrypted password for admin users in all locations where user appears. For example,

```
<user>admin</user>
<password>v2_1.yCFfBmPBkrk=</password>
```

Configuring Community Flows in workflow.xml

Asset acceptance, assignment, and registration can be automated by configuring the Community Flows. By configuring a community, Assets within the community can be auto-accepted and upon approval of all **Asset Types,** the Asset will be registered. Communities are configured as follows:

1. Set the community for the producing projects in the <producingProjectSettings> tag.

```
<producingProjectSettings>
  <producingProject name="Common Project" community="SOA Design
Authority" id="50000"/>
  <producingProject name="Order To Cash Integration"
community="SOA Design Authority" id="50001"/>
</producingProjectSettings>
```

2. Set the community for all Asset Types that will be handled by the community in the <assetType> tag.

```
<assetType name="Service" community="SOA Design Authority"
id="154">
...
<assetType name="Requirement Document" community="SOA Design
Authority" id="50100">
...
<assetType name="Design Document" community="SOA Design Authority"
id="50100">
```

3. Based on an existing community (for example, SOA Center of Excellence) create a new community named SOA Design Authority and add the properties `autoAccept=true` and `autoRegister=true`. These two properties are needed so workflows autoaccept an Asset after submission and once all tabs are approved (based on the multitier approvers, defined in the multitier rules) it then autoregisters the Asset.

```
<communities name="SOA Design Authority" autoAccept="true"
autoRegister="true">

        ...
```

4. Set the multitier rules in both the community and the Asset Types as follows:

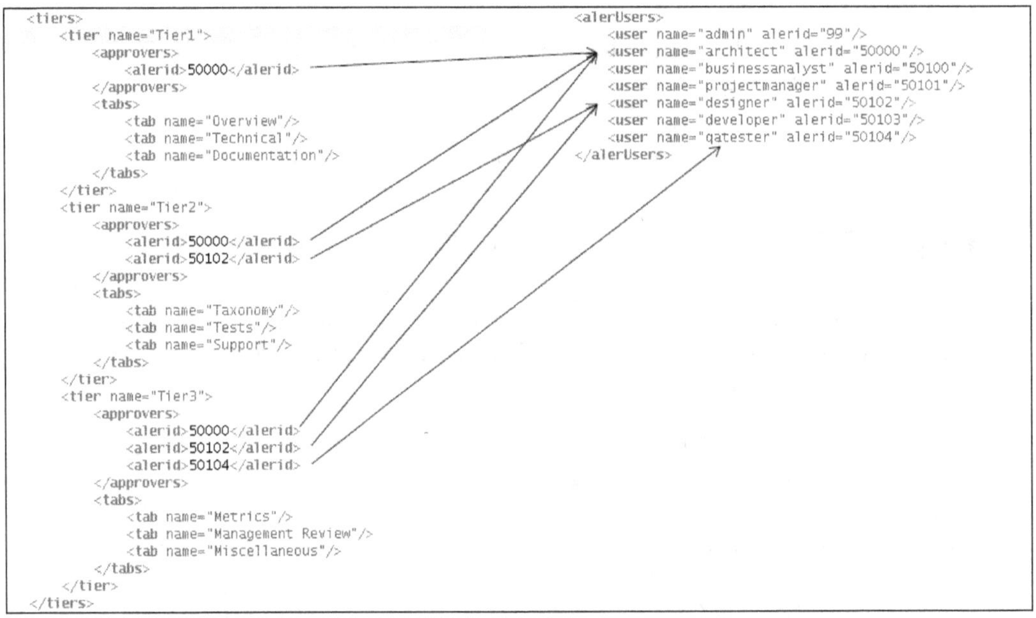

5. Wire the `AssetSubmission` event to the `CommunityAccept` workflow as follows. This wire will allow for the community rules to autoaccept the Asset.

```
<state name="urn:com:bea:aler:events:type:AssetSubmission">
    <action>CommunityAccept</action>
    <action>ApproveTabAction</action>
    <approveTabs>
        <tab name="Change Management"/>
    </approveTabs>
</state>
```

6. Wire the `AssetAccepted`, `AssetTabApproved`, and `AssetAllTabApproved` as follows so once all tabs are approved, the Asset is automatically registered.

```
<state name="urn:com:bea:aler:events:type:AssetAccepted">
  <action>MultiTier_Tier1_Assign</action>
</state>
<state name="urn:com:bea:aler:events:type:AssetTabApproved">
  <action>MultiTier_NextTier_Assign</action>
  <action>ResetChangeManagementTab</action>
</state>
<state name="urn:com:bea:aler:events:type:AssetAllTabApproved">
  <action>AllTabsApproval_Register</action>
</state>
```

7. Save the file and backup.

Refreshing workflow.xml

Once the changes have been made to `workflow.xml`, the file needs to be loaded into the OER BPM engine. This could be done in two ways:

- Stopping the OER OBPM engine and copying `workflow.xml` to `<OBPM HOME>/workflow/aler_egine` and then starting the engine.

> Note that this option is not good practice as it might interrupt ongoing workflows to finish.

- Loading the `workflow.xml` to the OER OBPM engine with the `refresh_workflow.sh` script as follows:

    1. From the folder `<OBPM HOME>/OBPM_SetupScripts` run:

    ```
    source setenv.sh
    ant -v copy-workflow-config
    ```

    2. Ensure that OER is up and running.

    3. From `<MW Home>/repository111/core/workflow-tools` execute:

    ```
    ./refresh_workflows.sh http://<obpm server>:9000/
    albpmServices/aler_engine/ws/RefreshConfigServiceListener
    aler_workflow_user <aler password>
    ```

  For example,

  ```
  ./refresh_workflows.sh http://soabpm-server:9000/albpmServices/
  aler_engine/ws/RefreshConfigServiceListener aler_workflow_user
  welcome1
  ```

Testing the workflow

Once all of the desired changes have been made to the automated workflows, these should be tested by submitting a new Asset and stepping through each step of the Asset life cycle and check that the behavior is consistent with the changes made in `workflow.xml`. For example:

1. An Asset of type Service is harvested with status **Submitted - Pending Review** and with a producing project set to, for example, Order to Cash Integration.
2. OER triggers the event `AssetAccepted`. In `workflow.xml` this event is wired to the `CommunityAccept` action and therefore the Community Accept flow is executed.

> Refer to section 9.6.4.1, **Configuring Community** of the OER Configuration Guide for further info on this flow: `http://docs.oracle.com/cd/E28280_01/admin.1111/e16580/oerwf.htm#CJHJEGAB`

3. The workflow checks if there is an `autoApprove` or `autoRegister` flag set for this Asset's `assetType` in `workflow.xml`. As none of these flags were set in `assetType`, it then tries to determine if these flags have been set for the community to which either the Asset or the project belongs to.
4. The workflow identifies from the `producingProjectSettings` of `workflow.xml` that the Asset belongs to the project Order to Cash Integration and therefore identifies that the Asset belongs to the community SOA Center of Excellence.
5. As defined in the community rules, the Asset is then auto-accepted.
6. Once an Asset is accepted the `AssetAccepted` event is triggered. In `workflow.xml` this event is wired to the `MultiTier_Tier1_Assign` the Asset is assigned to Tier 1 approvers as defined in the multitier rules for the community. In this example, the Tier 1 approver is only the architect.
7. As defined in the multitier rules of the community SOA Center of Excellence, the Tier 1 approvers are responsible for approving the tabs **Overview**, **Technical**, and **Documentation**.
8. The Tier 1 approvers should now see the Asset that needs approving in the `MyStuff` page.
9. The approver can click on the **Edit** button of the Asset to open the **Asset Editor** and then perform the necessary approvals.

10. Once the tabs **Overview**, **Technical**, and **Documentation** are approved, the event `AssetTabApproved` is triggered. In `workflow.xml` this event is wired to the `MultiTier_NextTier_Assign` action. This action triggers a flow that will reassign the Asset to the Tier 2 approvers (in our example, the architect and the designer) and subsequently to the Tier 3 approvers (architect, designer, and quality tester) once the **Taxonomy**, **Tests**, and **Support** tabs have been approved.
11. Once all of the remaining tabs are approved (**Metrics**, **Management Review**, and **Miscellaneous**), the event `AssetAllTabApproved` is triggered. The `AllTabsApproval_Register` action triggers the flow to register the Asset.

Debugging OBPM 10*g* workflows

The best way to debug OBPM 10*g* workflows is by using the OBPM 10*g* **Log Viewer**. To debug automated workflows using **Log Viewer** follow these steps:

1. Using a browser launch **OBPM Process Administrator** by entering the URL: `http://<OER Server>:8686/webconsole/faces/jsf/login.jsp`.
2. Log on with the `oer_bpm_admin` user. Note that this user was created during the configuration of OBPM 10*g*.

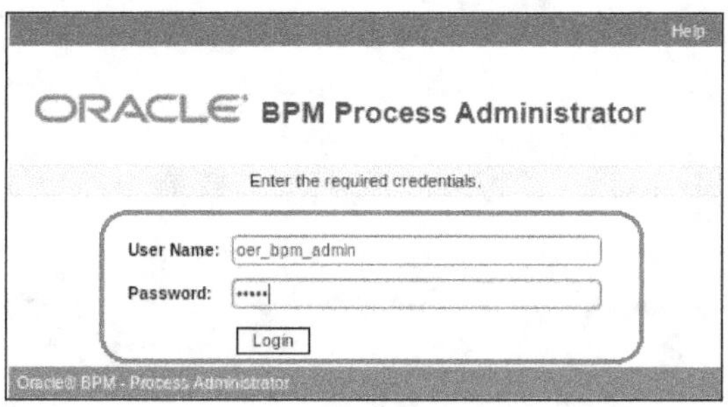

3. Click on the link **Engines** located on the left-hand side of the page. When the middle page refreshes click on **aler_engine**.

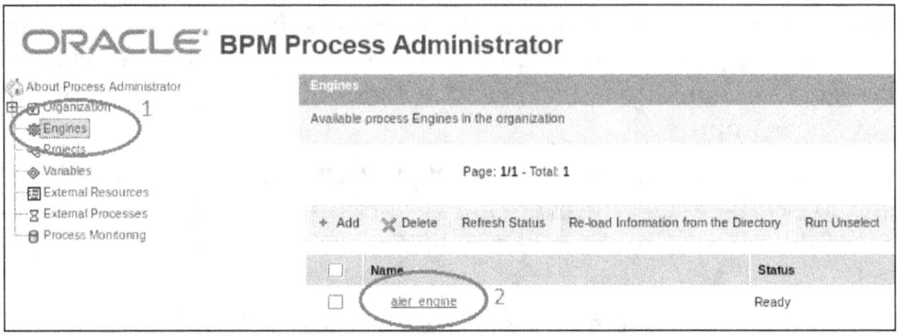

4. Click on the **Log Viewer** link located on the bottom right-hand side of the middle page.

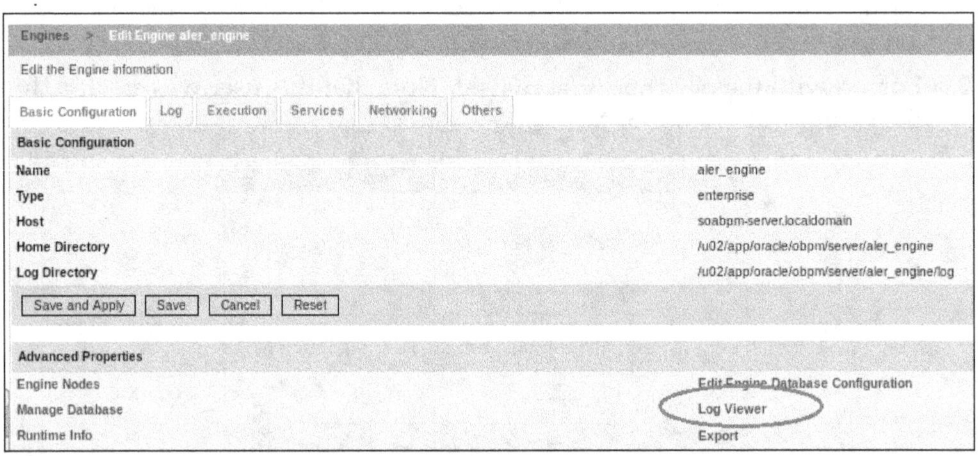

5. From the **Log Viewer** page, click on the **Launch Log Viewer** link located on the top right-hand side of the page. This will open up the **Log Viewer** applet.

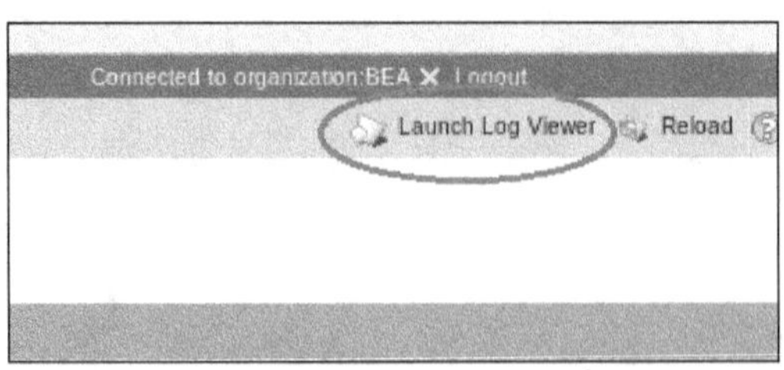

6. Click on **Get Engines** and then enter the user `oer_bpm_admin` and its password and click **OK**.

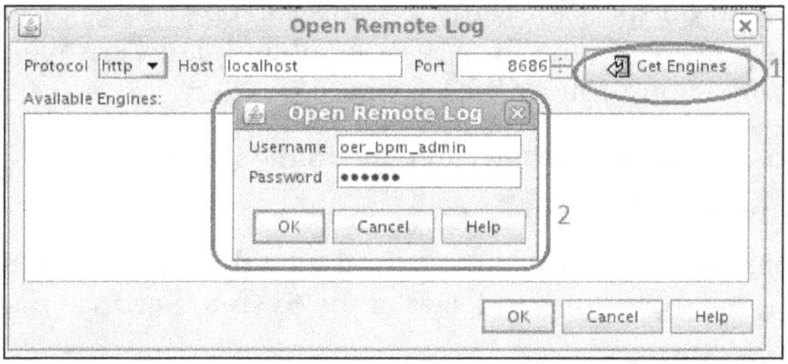

7. Click on **aler_engine** and then click on **OK**.

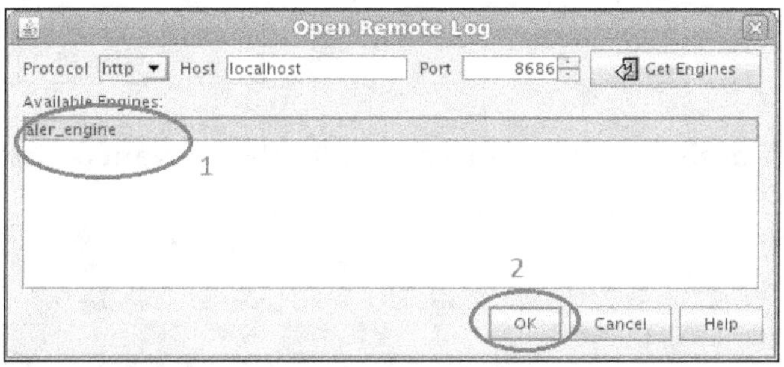

8. The **Log Viewer** window will open. Filter the OER logs by selecting the filters **Message** | **Begins with** and enter the text `OER` and then click on **Apply Filter**.
9. Select a message to view further details.

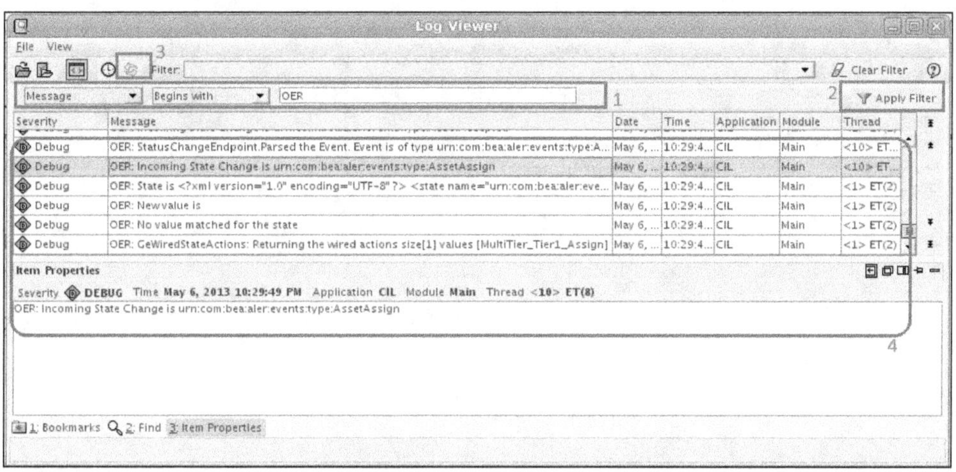

E-mail notifications

OER supports sending automatic e-mail notifications within the OER automated workflows and based on specific events. E-mails can be enabled or disabled as desired and also a variety of out of the box e-mail templates are available for use. To set up general notifications, follow these steps:

1. Log on to OER as admin and navigate to the **Admin** page.
2. Click on the **System Settings** menu option.
3. Enter the `cmee.registrar.email` in the **Enable New System Setting** field located on the top right-hand side of the **System Settings** page.
4. Click on **Enable**.

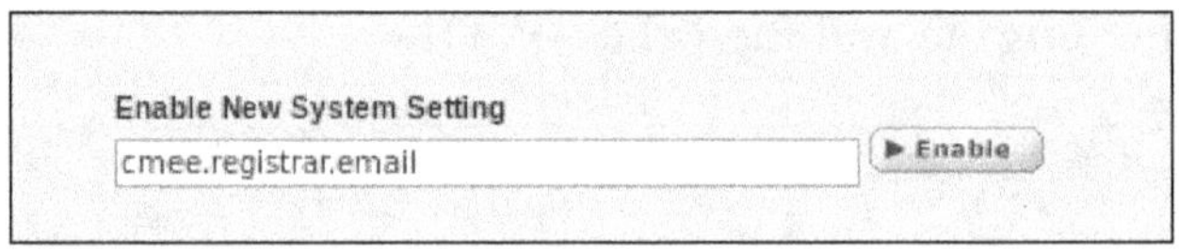

5. Enable the desired notifications and enter the relevant e-mail addresses.

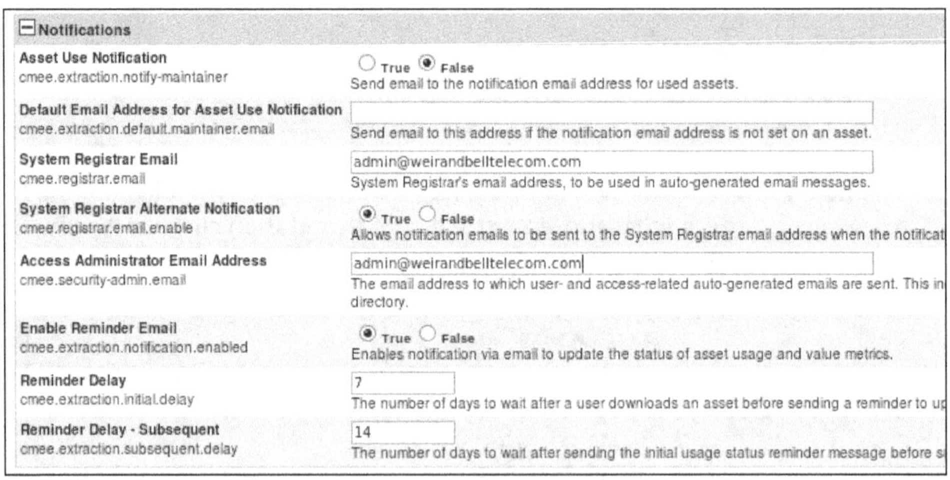

6. On the section **Email** enter the details of the **SMTP Server**.

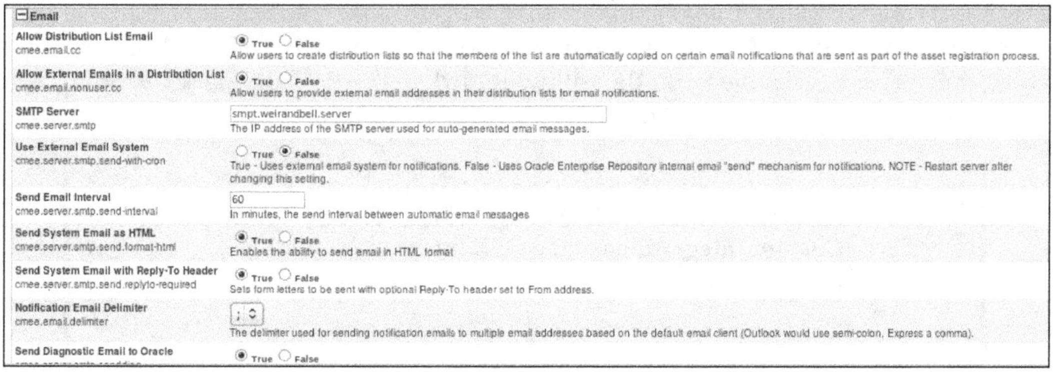

7. At the bottom of the page click on the **Save** button.

BPM 11*g*

Integration with custom processes developed using the Unified BPM Suite 11*g* is supported from Version PS7 (11.1.1.7) and above of OER. However, the implementation OBPM 10*g* is still required if it is desired to leverage the out-of-the-box OER automated workflows.

It is possible (and likely) that at a later stage (perhaps an individual patch or new patch set), Oracle will migrate these workflows to the Unified BPM Suite 11*g* at a later release, however, from a functional and conceptual perspective, the content described throughout the chapter should still be applicable.

> Please note that Oracle provides restricted licensing terms when implementing custom BPM 11*g*. For further information, please refer to `http://docs.oracle.com/cd/E23943_01/doc.1111/e14860/products.htm#CDEHFEFG`.

The general recommendation is to build a custom process with the Unified BPM Suite 11g rather than adding complex customizations to an out-of-the-box automated workflow.

> What this means in practice is that creating custom BPM 11*g* processes should be considered whenever a specific requirement cannot be addressed by simply changing `workflow.xml`.

When implementing BPM 11*g* custom processes please bear in mind the following considerations:

- Use of the REX API web service for inbound integrations. The WSDL of this service is accessible from the following url: `http://<hostname>:<port>/oer/services/RexAPI?wsdl`.

> Further information, REX is available in **Part IV Developing Custom Integrations** of the OER Integration Guide.
>
> `http://docs.oracle.com/cd/E28280_01/doc.1111/e15754/partpage3.htm#BHAGDECA`

- For OER outbound integrations (or callouts), custom BPM Suite 11*g* processes can subscribe to the Event Manager events. For this, configure the Event Manager to use WebLogic as the external JMS server and then make use of the out of the box JCA JMS adapter in BPM Suite 11*g* process to listen to events.

> Refer to section 9.7.2.1, **Enabling and Configuring an External JMS Server** of the OER Configuration Guide, for information on how to configure external JMS servers in OER.
>
> `http://docs.oracle.com/cd/E28280_01/admin.1111/e16580/oerwf.htm#CJHBGABIs`

- If you are interested in implementing custom BPM 11*g* processes refer to the documentation available in the Oracle Fusion Middleware 11.1.1.7 Documentation Library at `http://docs.oracle.com/cd/E28280_01/soa.html`.

Summary

Throughout the different sections of the chapter, it has been shown how to implement policies, compliance templates, and workflows to address requirements identified after doing a gap analysis between the out-of-the-box OER functionality and the desired target governance model. It was described in detail why it is imperative to the success of a governance implementation to have a clear and concise understanding of both the customer specific requirements and the scope of the features available out-of-the-box in OER.

The chapter also explained why and when OBPM 10*g* workflows are required and how the new OER PS6 features around support of the Unified BPM Suite 11*g* fit within a governance implementation.

The next chapter focuses on the use of the Oracle Service Registry and its integration with the Oracle Enterprise Repository.

7
Oracle Service Registry

This chapter will introduce the **Oracle Service Registry** (**OSR**), a fully v3-compliant implementation of the **UDDI** (**Universal Description, Discovery, and Integration**) specifications, and a key component of a **Service Oriented Architecture** (**SOA**). A UDDI Registry provides a standards-based directory for locating and invoking services and for managing service metadata such as security, transport, quality of service, and service endpoints.

We will discuss the purpose of the Registry and highlight the differences between OSR and the **Oracle Enterprise Repository** (**OER**). We will also discuss the product architecture and how the Registry can be employed to assist in the overall SOA Governance effort. It should be noted that it is not our intention to write a full tutorial for OSR and the reader should seek alternative sources of information for a more in-depth, step-by-step tutorial of the product.

We will also examine some of the theory that lies behind the UDDI specifications and how services can be classified in the Registry to assist consumer searches. Again, we will introduce some of the concepts behind UDDI, but a more detailed description can be found online at `http://uddi.org/pubs/uddi-v3.00-published-20020719.htm#_Ref8978020`.

OSR overview

The OSR provides a standards-based mechanism to classify, catalog, and manage services, so that they can be discovered and consumed by other applications, and is a key component of an SOA. The registry stores details of each service including metadata such as security, transport protocols, and quality of service:

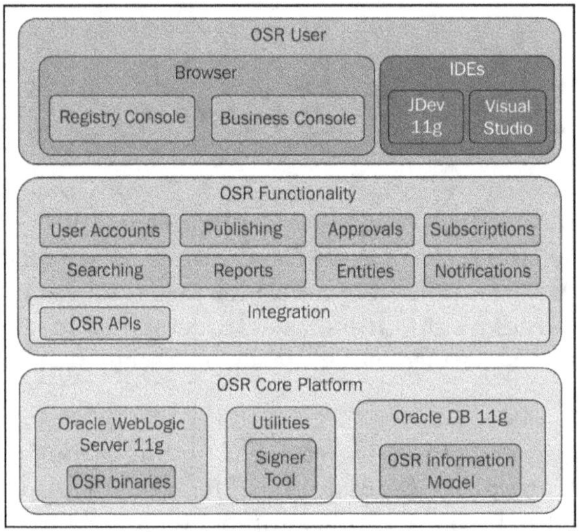

OSR is fully compliant with the UDDI v3 specification that describes details for the implementation of a service registry and associated programmatic interfaces. UDDI supports the description and discovery of:

- Businesses, organizations, and other Service Providers
- The services they publish
- The technical interfaces that may be used to access and manage these services.

OSR promotes service re-use by allowing consumers to easily locate published services using categorization rules (**taxonomies**) that are either industry-standard or specific to an individual organization. The registry provides information on security and transport protocols supported by a given service and the parameters required to invoke the service. OSR also supports versioning of services and endpoint virtualization. The latter allows services to be moved or migrated from one server or another, which can prove extremely useful particularly in the development environments where services are promoted between development, test, and production servers. URLs are resolved by the registry at runtime rather than developers embedding them into applications.

The OSR serves as an integration point for runtime tools such as **Oracle Service Bus** and **Oracle SOA Suite 11*g***. For example the Oracle Service Bus can automatically publish and subscribe to new or modified assets.

In addition, OSR supports the design time discovery of Assets using tools such as JDeveloper, which further supports and maximizes the discovery and re-use of existing published services, many of which can be created by external organizations.

The roles of OSR and OER

As discussed earlier in this book, OER is a fundamental component for effective design-time Governance (refer to *Chapter 3, Introduction to Oracle Enterprise Repository*). OER delivers critical information about current service capabilities to architects, SOA designers, and developers at design time, empowering them to make informed decisions for service re-use. All Design Time components and metadata are stored in OER.

OER provides a flexible meta-model for cataloging all assets within the SOA ecosystem and their dependencies and relationships to other artifacts. It is primarily used during the plan, design, and build phase of the lifecycle as a single source of truth for service and composite application development.

The OSR, on the other hand, acts as a reference point for services that have been deployed into the runtime environment. It is primarily used by components of the SOA infrastructure for programmatic, dynamic discovery and binding. OSR typically contains a subset of the metadata from the OER for runtime discovery. From a Service Provider's perspective, OSR also creates a service virtualization layer, providing a means to insulate applications from service failures or changes to service end points.

It must be stressed that, unlike OER, OSR only exposes a service interface. It does not show service dependencies, related assets and other important governance requirements. It is aimed at service consumers only.

OER and OSR can be synchronized using the **Oracle Enterprise Repository Exchange Utility**. OSR effectively bridges the gap between the design time and runtime environments via automated synchronization with OER, Oracle Service Bus, and Oracle SOA Suite.

OER's enterprise metadata repository capabilities together with the OSR's comprehensive support for UDDI v3 provide support for managing and governing the full SOA lifecycle. The tight coupling of OER and OSR gives organizations a means to manage their enterprise assets in order to provide visibility, reusability, and traceability throughout the enterprise.

UDDI principles

The UDDI specifications provide a standardized way to connect service publishers to service subscribers both within and between organizations. Businesses can discover each other and locate exposed service functionality using searches that are based on standard classifications. The UDDI specification, which is built upon existing standards such as **Extensible Markup Language** (**XML**) and **Simple Object Access Protocol** (**SOAP**), was collaboratively developed by a number of industry and business leaders.

A UDDI registry contains programmatically accessible descriptions of businesses and the services they support. Services can be classified by their support for industry-specific specifications and by taxonomy definitions, which are used for meaningful categorization of services. Identification systems are also employed for meaningful identification of businesses.

UDDI specifies a programming model (API) and data structures that define how consumers can communicate with the registry. All APIs in the UDDI specification are SOAP-based. Request and response semantics and error handling are described by the specification together with guidelines on convention and usage. Companion documents include the Data Structure and API Schema specifications that define the message and data semantics.

This section will introduce the reader to some of the UDDI theory that underpins OSR, including the UDDI data model. In practice, OSR hides the end user from much of the low-level plumbing by providing a user-friendly interface that wraps the underlying implementation. Behind the scenes, however, OSR is generating data that conforms to the standard UDDI data model explained as follows.

UDDI data model

The UDDI specification provides four core XML data structures to describe a Business and the Business Services that it provides. These are described in the following table:

XML Structure	Description
`businessEntity`	Provides details about a Service Provider.
`businessService`	Describes a Business Service that can be consumed.
`bindingTemplates`	Describes the technical details for the service, including a reference to the service's programmatic interface. Each `bindingTemplate` contains a reference to one or more tModels.

XML Structure	Description
`tModels`	Technical Models, or tModels for short, store metadata that describe a service, such as taxonomy, transports, and policies.

We will describe each of these structures in the sections that follow. The following diagram shows the relationship between these data structures:

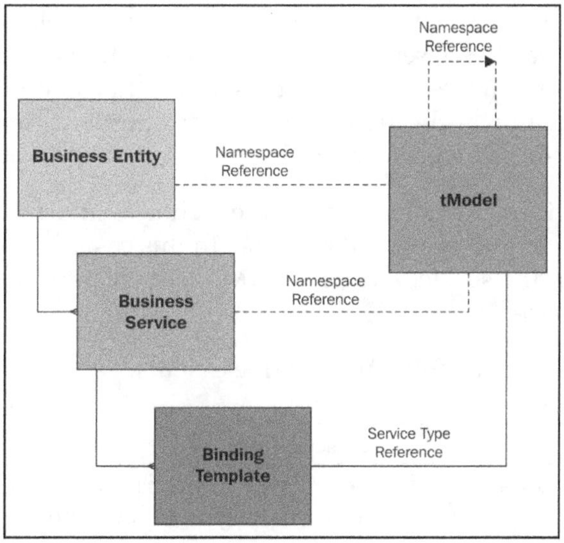

The preceding diagram illustrates the parent-child containment relationship between the **businessEntity**, **businessService**, and **bindingTemplate** structures. Thus, for example, a Business Entity can contain many Business Services whilst a Business Service belongs to a single Business Entity. All of the above UDDI data structures are expressed in XML and Oracle OSR stores these structures in a relational database from where they can be accessed using UDDI queries.

tModels can be referenced from all the other structures and from themselves. For this reason, tModels exist outside the parent-child containment relationships. The tModel plays a different role depending on the structure referencing it. The `businessEntity`, `businessService`, and `tModel` use a tModel to define a namespace or taxonomy, whereas the `bindingTemplate` uses a tModel to expose a technical interface. From an XML view point, the `businessEntity` is the root element that holds descriptive information about the business or organization it describes. Each contained `businessService` describes a logical service offered by that business or organization and a `bindingTemplate`, contained within a given `businessService`, provides the technical description of that service.

The tModel

A tModel represents a unique concept or construct in a UDDI Registry. In essence, tModels are XML data structures that store metadata for all UDDI entities. They can be used to describe the technical interface of a service or to represent metadata for other types of UDDI data structures such as Business Entities.

The UDDI specification provides a means to classify services that have been published to a registry so that they can be searched for by consumers. To achieve this end, there needs to be a way to describe how a service behaves and what specifications or standards the service complies to. At Model is used to define a **namespace** or **taxonomy** (classification) for a service, thus allowing a service to be queried based on consumer-specified criteria. For example, a consumer can search a registry for all SOAP-based web services.

Also, the UDDI provides a way to describe the technical interface for a service so that a consumer can bind to that service at runtime. In this case, a provider produces a Binding Template for the service, which is a tModel that is used to define a technical interface for that service.

A tModel is described by the following XML elements:

Element	Description
Name and Description	The name and description of the tModel, in different languages if required.
Overview Doc	An overview document is a reference to a document that specifies the tModel's purpose. For example, it can point to a WSDL for a web service.
Categories	tModels can be categorized as can all the UDDI entities.
Identifiers	The tModel can be associated with an arbitrary number of identifiers that uniquely identify it.

Business Entities

A Business Entity represents a Service Provider in UDDI. This can be an organization or a group of people responsible for a set of services. Also, it is used to represent a high level grouping of services; for example a development project, department, or organization.

A Business Entity is composed of the following elements:

Element	Description
Name and Description	Name and description of the Business Entity. This can be in a variety of languages if necessary.
Contacts	A list of contacts associated with the Business Entity. Contact details can include name, address, telephone number, and use type.
Categories	Set of categories that describe the Business Entity's features or quantities such as geographical area.
Identifiers	The Business Entity can be associated with a set of identifiers that can uniquely identify it such as a department number.
Discovery URL	Discovery URLs are additional links to documents that further describe the Business Entity.
Business Entities	This column defines links to other Business Entities and is used to model relationships between such business entities.

The following XML fragment shows an example of a Business Entity:

```
<businessEntity businessKey="uuid:
  E0F6D5A8-C446-4f01-49AB-70A45185A40"
  operator="http://weirbelltelecom.com" authorizedName=
    "Patrick Smith">
  <name>Weir & Bell Telecom</name>
  <description>Providers of Telecomunication Solutions</description>
  <contacts>
    <contact useType="general info">
      <description>General Information</description>
      <personName>Patrick Smith</personName>
      <phone>+44 78767766</phone>
      <email>psmith@weirbelltelecom.com</email>
    </contact>
  </contacts>
```

```
    <businessServices>
    ...
    </businessServices>
    <identifierBag>
      <keyedReference
        tModelKey="UUID:8609C81E-EE1F-4D5A-B202-3EB13AD01823"
        name="D-U-N-S"
        value="666999111" />
    </identifierBag>
    <categoryBag>
      <keyedReference
        tModelKey="UUID:C0B9FE13-179F-413D-8A5B-5004DB8E5BB2"
        keyValue="517110"
        keyName="Telecommunications Solutions" />
    </categoryBag>
  </businessEntity>
```

Business Service

The Business Service structure represents a logical service and contains descriptive information about the service in business terms. A Business Service is the logical child of a single Business Entity.

A Business Service is described by the following elements:

Element	Description
Name and Description	Name and description of the Business Service. This can be in a variety of languages if necessary.
Categories	Set of categories that describe the Business Services features or quantities such as service availability and version.

The following XML fragment shows an example of a Business Service entity:

```
<businessService serviceKey="uuid:
  G6A1B765-ABB3-4837-666D-4516203E5A2F"
  businessKey="uuid:E0F6D5A8-C446-4f01-49AB-70A45185A40">
  <name>Address Lookup</name>
  <description>A Web service to locate an address from a house
    number and post code</description>
  <bindingTemplates>
  ...
  </bindingTemplates>
  <categoryBag />
</businessService>
```

> A Business Service in a UDDI Registry does not necessarily represent a Web service. The UDDI Registry can register other service implementations such as EJB, CORBA and others.

Binding Templates

A Binding Template describes the technical details of a web service and provides details of how to consume the service. A Business Service can contain one or more Binding Templates. Binding Templates are described by the following elements:

Element	Description
Name and Description	Name and description of the Binding Template. This can be in a variety of languages if necessary.
Overview URL	Specifies the actual service endpoint including the specification of the protocol required to access the service
Categories	Set of categories that describe the Binding Templates features or quantities such as certification status (test, production) or versions.

An example Binding Template tModel is provided as follows:

```
<tModel tModelKey="uuid:5DD52389-B1A4-4fe7-B131-0C7EF73EE121">
  <name>AddressLookup</name>
  <description xml:lang="en">Interface for Web service for Address
    Look up</description>
  <overviewDoc>
  <description xml:lang="en">The service's WSDL document
  </description>
  <overviewURL>http://www.weirbelltelecom.com/services/interfaces/
    AddressLookup.wsdl</overviewURL>
  </overviewDoc>
</tModel>
```

Understanding UDDI taxonomies

Taxonomies are structures that can be used to organize information. UDDI employs taxonomies to classify entities in a consistent manner so that they can be located within a registry. For example, Service Providers use taxonomy to indicate that a service implements a specific domain standard, or that it provides services for a specific geographic area. These taxonomies make it easier for consumers to find services that match their specific requirements.

UDDI allows publishers to define multiple taxonomies to be used in a registry. Users can employ an unlimited number of appropriate classification systems simultaneously. The choice of which taxonomy is used can be left to the user or can be specified based on the role of the user. Tailored views of a UDDI Registry can be created with no customization by assigning user profiles to taxonomies and granting access via a controlled mechanism. Technical users might use taxonomies to group services by technical characteristics and/or functionalities whereas business users might navigate the same catalog filtering Assets based on Line of Businesses or process.

The first version of the UDDI specification defined three pre-built taxonomies that could be used to categorize businesses and services. These were NAICS, which is used to classify a business type, UNSPC for project and service categorizations and ISO-1366-2 that defines geographic classification. These taxonomies are internally checked by the UDDI Registry. The importance of meaningful categorization in UDDI is critical to allow organizations to find useful information and to locate and consume services.

Version 2 added the ability for organizations to define new, externally checked taxonomies that can be offered for public use in UDDI. These external taxonomy suppliers must support a "validate values" web service to provide external checking and validating of taxonomy values. Thus when a client wishes to associate a taxonomy value with a registry entry this must first be validated. Registration of an externally validated taxonomy can be accomplished only with the approval of a UDDI Business Registry operator.

Each taxonomy system is represented by a tModel and the classification of a particular entity within that taxonomy system is represented through use of an XML element called `categoryBag` as defined by the UDDI standard. A `categoryBag` is simply a collection of `keyedReference` elements that provide valid name-value pairs within the scope of a taxonomy system (referred to by its `tModelKey`).

Enterprise taxonomies

Enterprise taxonomies are specific to the particular enterprise or application. These taxonomies reflect specific categories such as company departments, types of application, and access protocols.

OSR allows users to define enterprise taxonomies. Users can also download and upload any taxonomy as an XML file. OSR offers tools for creating, modifying, and browsing taxonomies using either a web user interface or via SOAP API calls.

Checked and unchecked taxonomies

There are two types of taxonomies: **checked** and **unchecked**. Checked taxonomies are validated to ensure that only valid categories are used as specified by that taxonomy. They are usually used when the taxonomy provides all valid values required by the Registry. A checked taxonomy can be validated using an internal validation service that is available in OSR or by using an external validation service.

Unchecked taxonomies, on the other hand, do not prescribe any set of fixed values meaning that any name and value pair can be used for categorization of UDDI entities. Unchecked taxonomies are used for things such as volume, weight, and price amongst others.

A special case of the unchecked taxonomy is the **General Keywords** taxonomy. The UDDI General Keywords Taxonomy provides a way to informally define any number of unchecked taxonomies each consisting of a namespace identifier and an associated set of category values. It does not require the creation of a tModel. As with other taxonomies, the General Keyword taxonomy is used in `keyedReference` elements to categorize entities, but unlike other taxonomies, in the General Keyword taxonomy both the `keyName` and the `keyValue` attributes are semantically meaningful. The `keyName` identifies a particular value set and the `keyValue` specifies the value within that value set. With other taxonomies, the `keyName` plays no semantic role and is therefore essentially commentary.

For example, Weir & Bell Telecoms would like to classify services by the internal business unit that published the web service. They decide to use the General Keywords for this. The following is a fragment from the Business Service tModel shows how they achieved this:

```
<categoryBag>
  <keyedReference
  tModelKey="UUID:C0B9FE13-179F-413D-8A5B-5004DB8E5BB2"
    keyValue="517110"
```

```
      keyName="Telecommunication Solutions"/>
    <keyedReference
      tModelKey="UUID:C1ACF26D-9672-4404-9D70-39B756E62AB4"
      keyValue="wsdlSpec"
      keyName="Specification for a Web Service described in WSDL"/>
    <keyedReference
      tModelKey="Uuid:a035a07c-f362-44dd-8f95-e2b134bf43b4"
      keyValue="101"
      keyName="Datacentre Name"/>
  </categoryBag>
```

The `tModelKey` in the above XML snippet ending with `e2b134bf43b4` refers to the General Keywords taxonomy. The `KeyName` element refers to an internal classification specific to Weir & Bell - in this case `Datacentre Name`. The `KeyValue` element refers to the Data Centre Id – in this case `101`. By adding this category, service consumers are able to search the registry for web services developed by particular Data Centers.

A UDDI Taxonomy example

By way of an example, let us assume that Weir & Bell Telecom wishes to publish a service to a UDDI Registry that looks up an address based on a house number and post code. The development team needs to define an interface for the service (assuming that there is no interface already defined in the Registry, in which case they would have to implement the new interface in accordance with the interface definition). Firstly, the development team needs to create and register an interface using a tModel. This may look as follows:

```
<tModel tModelKey="uuid:5DD52389-B1A4-4fe7-B131-0C7EF73EE121">
  <name>AddressLookup</name>
  <description xml:lang="en">Interface for Web service for Address
    Look up</description>
  <overviewDoc>
    <description xml:lang="en">The service's WSDL document
      </description>
    <overviewURL>http://www.weirbelltelecom.com/services/
      interfaces/AddressLookup.wsdl</overviewURL>
  </overviewDoc>
</tModel>
```

This `tModel` represents the interface that will be developed and contains a unique identifier, together with a name and description and a pointer to the service implementation using the `overviewURL` element. In this case, the service is to be implemented as a web service, so this points to the service's WSDL file location.

Once the service is defined in the Registry, the development team can develop the service implementation that conforms to this interface. On completion the team will then also publish the service details to the Registry. Please note that we will show how to publish a service in subsequent chapters. The registration process involves creating an XML document that has a root of businessEntity. Inside this root element will be a businessService element that in turn contains a bindingTemplate that points to the above `tModel`, using its unique reference ID.

To invoke the new service, a consumer must locate the correct Business Entity in the Registry and determine the service implementation details. The consumer could search for all interfaces published by Weir & Bell; however, as the number of interfaces increases, or if the service is to be exposed to an external UDDI Registry via the internet, there needs to be a way of classifying a service so that consumers can search by a given category. In UDDI such categorizations are implemented using tModels. tModels can be searched to locate interfaces based on the functionality that they expose. To achieve this, a tModel describing the service classification is added as a child element to the parent tModel. The parent tModel describes the interface whereas the child tModel represents some classification scheme.

Continuing the example, Weir & Bell Telecom develops the `AddressLookup` service as a WSDL-based web service and exposes this in a Registry. The development team decides to categorize the service as a web service as follows:

```
<tModel tModelKey="uuid:5DD52389-B1A4-4fe7-B131-0C7EF73EE121">
  <name>AddressLookup</name>
  <description xml:lang="en">Interface for Web service for Address
    Look up</description>
  <overviewDoc>
    <description xml:lang="en">The service's WSDL document
      </description>
    <overviewURL>http://www.weirbelltelecom.com/services/
      interfaces/AddressLookup.wsdl</overviewURL>
  </overviewDoc>
  <categoryBag>
    <keyedReference
      tModelKey="uuid:c1acf26d-9672-4404-9d70-39b756e62ab4"
      keyName="Specification for a web service described in WSDL"
      keyValue="wsdlSpec"/>
  </categoryBag>;
</tModel>
```

As the example shows, the categorization is introduced into the Binding Template using one of the core pre-defined taxonomies called UDDI Types. This taxonomy provides a `tModel` called `uddi-org:types` (key is `uuid:c1acf26d-9672-4404-9d70-39b756e62ab4`).

You will also notice from the above XML snippet that the newly added categorization information, namely, the `wsdlSpec` tModel, is added into a `categoryBag` element using the `keyedReference` data structure. Once this is added, a consumer searching for `wsdlSpec` will see the newly created service in their list of results. Clearly such a search will bring back a lot of results and so further classifications will be required in this case.

> In practice, OSR shields the user from much of the complexity involved with defining tModels. Furthermore, in the context of a full Governance Implementation, OER would publish services directly into OSR.

Product architecture

OSR has a much simpler architecture than OER. The following diagram shows the conceptual architecture of the product. The sections that follow will elaborate on each of the application layers shown in the following figure:

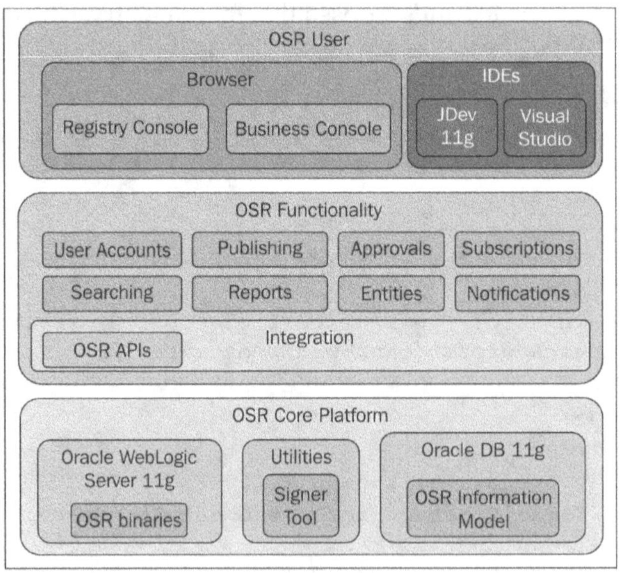

Core platform

OSR is essentially a set of web services and applications that implement and conform to the UDDI specifications. The Java-based web applications provide a framework for publishers to register services in a registry and for consumers to locate and consume these services.

The OSR installer supports a standalone-registry or multi-registry configuration. The default installation option provides a standalone registry and enables the creation of a new registry database.

For Discovery, Publication, or Intermediate installation options, multiple registry installations are required to support approval processes. A multi-registry deployment is appropriate for environments where organizations want to impose more control over the exposed registry content. Quality control processes are implemented by separating the registry into Publication and Discovery registries, with an Approval Process to control promotion of services from one to another. This approval process can be configured to use either manual or automated approval of promoted information. An Intermediate registry sits between one or more Publication Registries and a top-level Discovery Registry.

OSR can be clustered to provide increased scalability and resilience, and also configured to use external accounts in an LDAP repository.

> Detailed installation instructions for OSR can be found in **Oracle Fusion Middleware Service Registry Guide 11*g* (11.1.1.6.0)**. URL: `http://www.oracle.com/technetwork/middleware/registry/osr111productdocumentation-159992.pdf`.

Oracle DB 11*g*

A relational database is required to store data and metadata associated with an OSR installation. Although the preceding diagram shows an Oracle relational database, OSR is also certified against MSSQL or DB2. Installation options include the ability to create a new database or to populate a new schema in an existing database.

Oracle WebLogic Server 11*g*

Currently, OSR 11*g* is only certified with the Oracle's WebLogic Application Server. The primary recommendation when implementing OSR along with OER is to install a standalone topology of OSR 11*g* in its own Managed Server within the same WebLogic Domain as the SOA Suite, illustrated as follows:

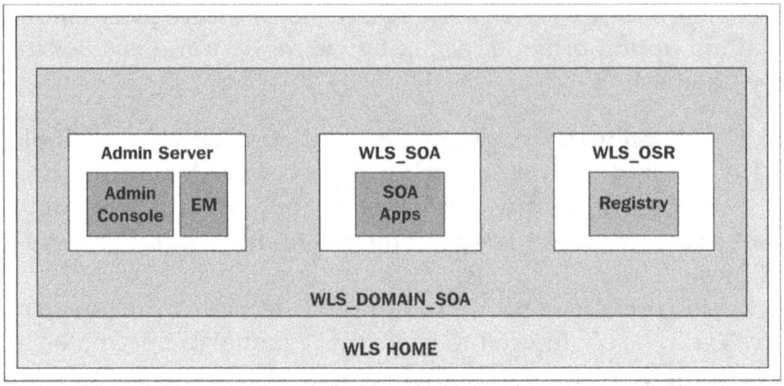

This setup has the advantage that it does not require a completely separate domain to be created for OSR. Since OSR is contained in a dedicated managed server, this configuration provides the administrator with the flexibility to configure and tune the registry independently in its own JVM. Alternatively, OSR can be installed in its own separate WebLogic Domain. In this architecture, OSR is completely independent of the SOA Suite and can be managed separately, meaning that the environment can be independently patched and backed up. The downside to this configuration is that there is an added overhead for creating and maintaining the extra WebLogic Domain for OSR.

For enterprise deployments, OSR should not be installed in the Admin Server since the Admin Server is meant for administrative applications such as Enterprise Manager and the WebLogic Console. Changing any configurations in this managed server can lead to unpredictable behaviors for the registry server. Smaller departmental or development environments can employ this configuration, but as a general rule OSR should be deployed in a separate managed server. This ensures that OSR does not conflict with existing applications and provides OSR with a dedicated JVM leading to better flexibility, availability, and scalability.

Replication

The content of a UDDI Registry can be replicated using a simple parent-child model. The registry replicates data according to multiple replication definitions that are defined using standard UDDI queries. The parent-child relationship is specific to the replication definition, so one registry might be the parent registry for one specific replication definition and a child for another. The security settings (ACL, users, and groups) are not subject to replication, but permissions can be configured on replicated data.

> When OSR is implemented alongside OER, the latter would be responsible for keeping the registries in sync and therefore this feature is not required in such a topology.

Signer Tool

One of the most important advantages of UDDI version 3 is its support for digital signatures. Without signatures a service consumer cannot verify whether the publisher of a Business Entity is really who they claim to be. When a publisher has signed the UDDI structure, however, consumers can verify that the registry information is unmodified and can confirm the publisher's identity.

The OSR Signer tool is provided to simplify signature manipulation. The tool's scripts are located in the bin directory of the OSR installation. The Signer is a graphical application that can be used to add, remove, and verify the signatures of UDDI structures you have published.

> More details of how to utilize this tool can be found in section **2.6.2 Signer** of the **OFM Service Registry Guide 11*g* (11.1.1.6.0)**. URL:
>
> `http://www.oracle.com/technetwork/middleware/registry/osr111productdocumentation-159992.pdf`.

OSR functionality

Having covered the product architecture for OSR, let us now turn our attention to the functionality provided by the tool in support of SOA Governance.

OSR fully implements the UDDI specification providing an open standards framework for exposing services and their associated metadata. OSR is used to provide an interface by which selected OER content may be accessed or published and serves as an integration point for runtime tooling such as Oracle Service Bus, Oracle SOA Suite 11*g*, and JDeveloper. Oracle Service Bus can automatically publish and subscribe to new or modified assets.

OER and OSR are synchronized using the Oracle Registry Repository Exchange Utility.

While OSR fully implements the core UDDI V3 standard, Oracle has additionally provided key extensions to the base standard to provide support for enterprise deployments. These include:

- Advanced security that provides a mechanism for defining granular access control for registered components. Component publishers can specify find, get, modify, and delete access permissions for every published object.
- Data accuracy and quality enforcement mechanisms to ensure that component registrations are accurate and up-to-date. OSR clearly defines responsibility for every registered component. It offers component promotion and approval mechanisms for promoting components between development, QA, and production environments.
- Subscription and notification mechanisms for automatically notifying registry users about changes to components to which they subscribe.
- Selective replication among multiple registries allowing for automated propagation between different registries. For example, between internal and external registries.
- Advanced Taxonomy management for enforcement of well-defined taxonomies.
- Powerful management for granular control, logging, and auditing of the publishing and discovery processes.
- OSR provides maximum performance and scalability for a UDDI Registry by efficient implementation of the web services stack and database algorithms, and by supporting load balancing and clustering mechanisms.

OSR user interaction

Users interact with OSR using two-key functional components and their associated user interfaces. These are the **Registry Control** and the **Business Service Control**. These consoles provide a user interface that wraps UDDI web service implementations, allowing the user to search, maintain, and publish components to the registry.

Registry Control is aimed at developers familiar with Business Entities and tModels. It allows users to create tModels, define taxonomies, browse and publish registry content, create subscriptions, and manage security. **Registry Control** is also the primary console for administrators to perform registry management.

Business Service Control provides a much simpler user interface for less-technical users who are unfamiliar with tModels and other complex attributes. UDDI functionality is exposed through easy-to-use and customizable publication wizards. Developers, architects, and business users can browse the registry from different perspectives to locate services and artifacts using business-relevant abstractions of SOA information such as schemas, interface local names, or namespaces.

Services can be published and discovered using both configurations.

OSR Registry Control (ORC)

The registry console is the primary user interface for advanced users and for administrators to perform registry management. The console provides users with more fine-grained access to the UDDI Registry information model, allowing them to add and amend tmodels and other UDDI artifacts including taxonomies.

Registry Control can be found at `http://<hostname>:<port>/<context>/uddi/web`. The host name and port are defined by the administrator when OSR is installed. The default port is `7101` or `8888`, depending on application server settings. Accessing this URL provides access to a home page from which the user can log into the registry (or create a log in account) and search and amend the registry. The home page is shown as follows:

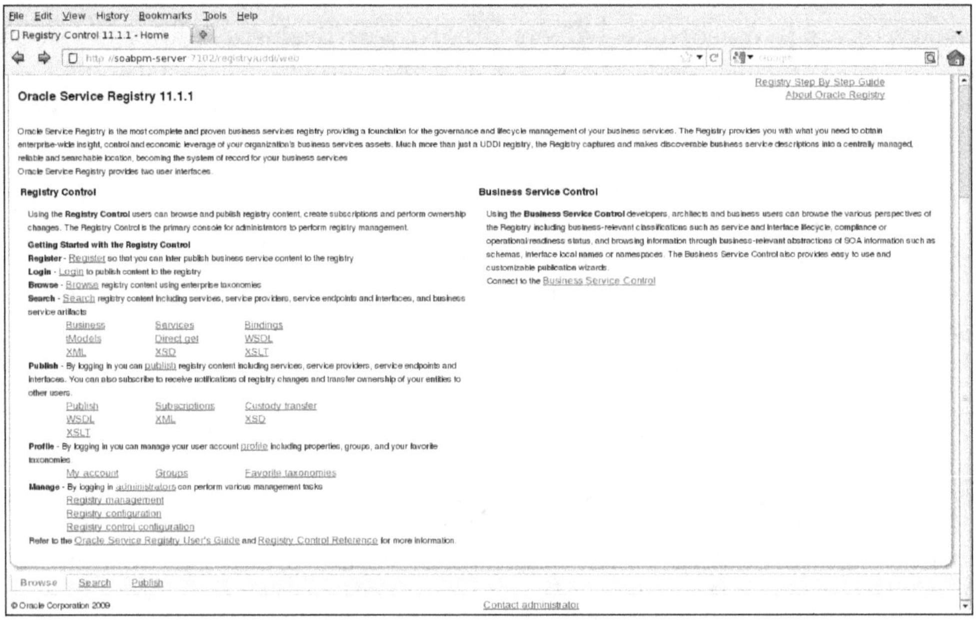

Registry Control supports the following functionalities:

Function	Description
Browse	This link allows users to browse UDDI entities.
Search	This tab allows users to search the registry. Users can perform queries on UDDI entities, search for services, Binding Templates, tModels, and related Business Entities. The **Menu** option also allows users to browse taxonomies. Entities are queried directly using their entity key if it is known in advance (business, service, Binding Template, and tModel).

Function	Description
Publish	This tab allows users to publish UDDI structures (`businessEntities`, `businessServices`, `bindingTemplates`, and `tModels`). Users can also assert relationships between Business Entities, subscribe interest in receiving information about changes made to the registry, transfer ownership of selected UDDI structures (Custody Transfer), and publish WSDLs to the registry.
Profile	Users can use this link to maintain user account properties, account groups, and favorite taxonomies.
Manage	This tab is used by the Oracle Service Registry administrator to perform management tasks. Refer to the Administrators Guide for more information.

Example of using ORC – adding a Business Entity

Before any artifacts or services can be published to the registry, we have to publish a Business Entity for the Service Provider. In this section we will provide an example of using ORC by creating a new Business Entity.

1. The user should first log into the ORC and then click on the **Publish** link. The following screenshot illustrates that, by right-clicking on the **Businesses** node in the tree navigator, we can add a new Business Entity. In this case, we are going to add `Weir & Bell Telecom` as a Business Entity:

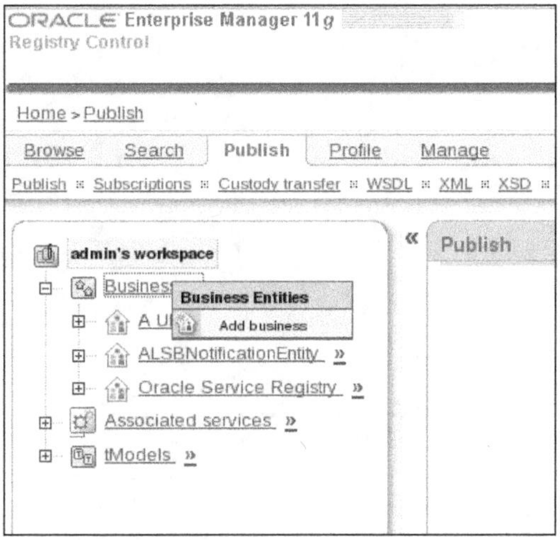

2. The user then enters the **Publish** wizard. The following screen is used to specify the **Name** and **Description** value of the new Business Entity. We can also add a custom **Business Key** value for search purposes:

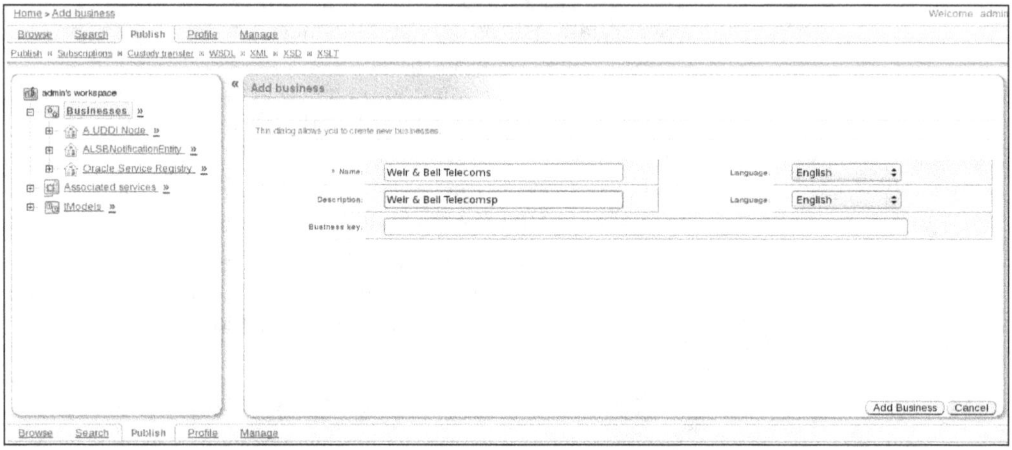

3. Once the details have been entered, click on the **Add Business** button to create the new Business Entity. A screen similar to the one shown as follows will appear showing the newly created entity:

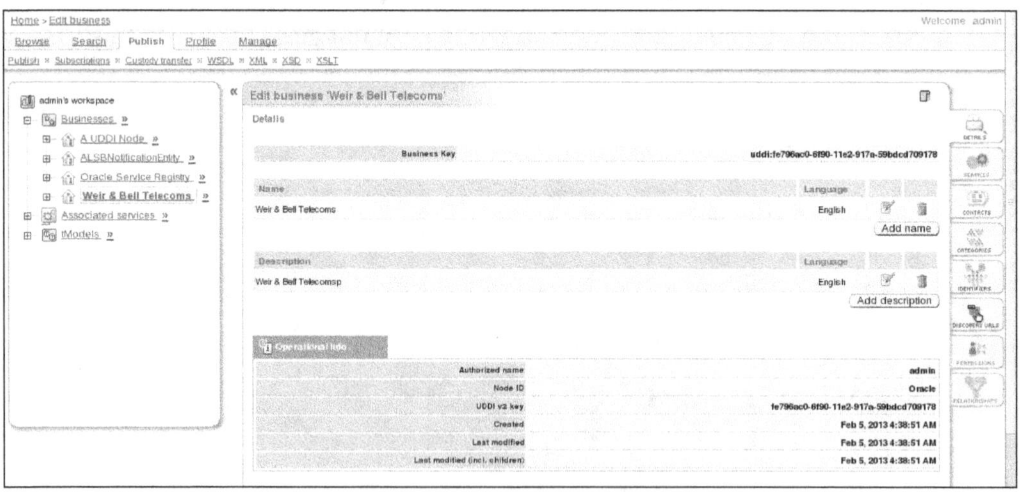

> A similar interface is available in **Business Service Control**, but is wizard-driven for less technical users.

OSR Business Services Control (BSC)

This section provides a high level overview of the functions that can be performed under **Business Control Service**.

Business Service Control can be found at the following URL: `http://<hostname>:<port>/<context>/uddi/bsc/web`. The host name and port are defined when OSR is installed. The default port is `7101` or `8888`, depending on the application server setting. The context is specified during the installation and defaults to registry.

A user must have an OSR account before they can publish data to the registry. The following section details the account setup process.

Maintaining user accounts

A user must create an account before publishing data to the Registry. An account can be created from the **Business Service Control** console (or the **Registry Control** console) as follows:

1. Click on the **Create New Account** link illustrated as follows:

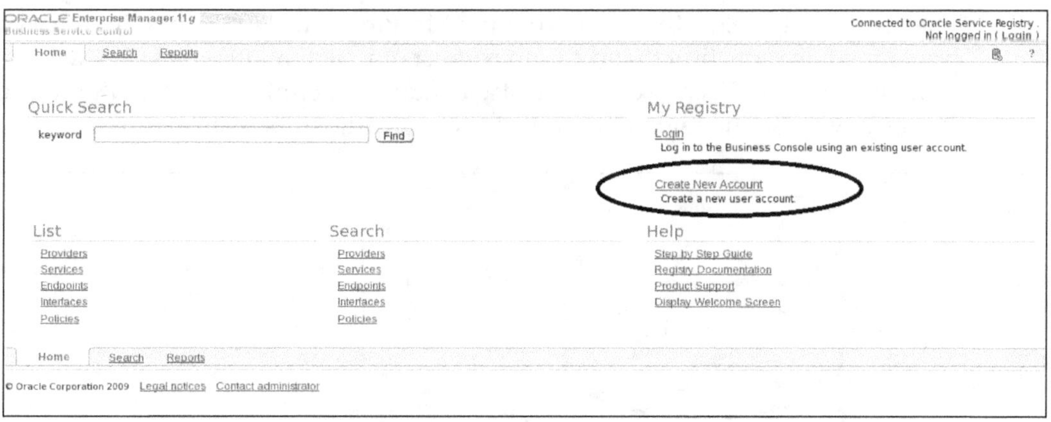

2. Then the user enters their details illustrated as follows:

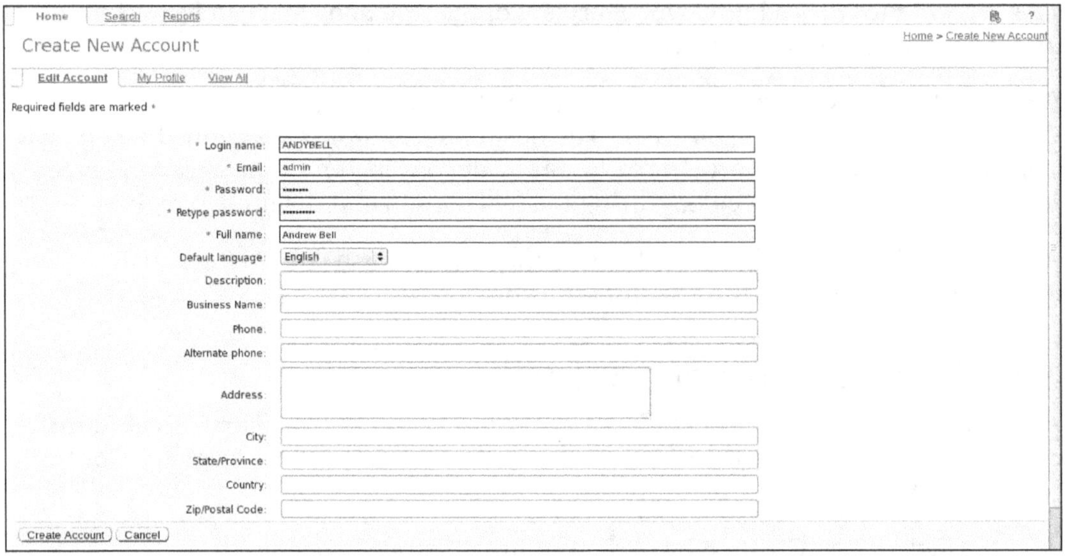

3. The user should select their role from the **My Profile** tab. OSR contains a list of predefined user profiles that differ in respect of which main menu tabs will be available to them. Each user profile also contains a definition of default formats for result views. The registry administrator can adjust these as required:

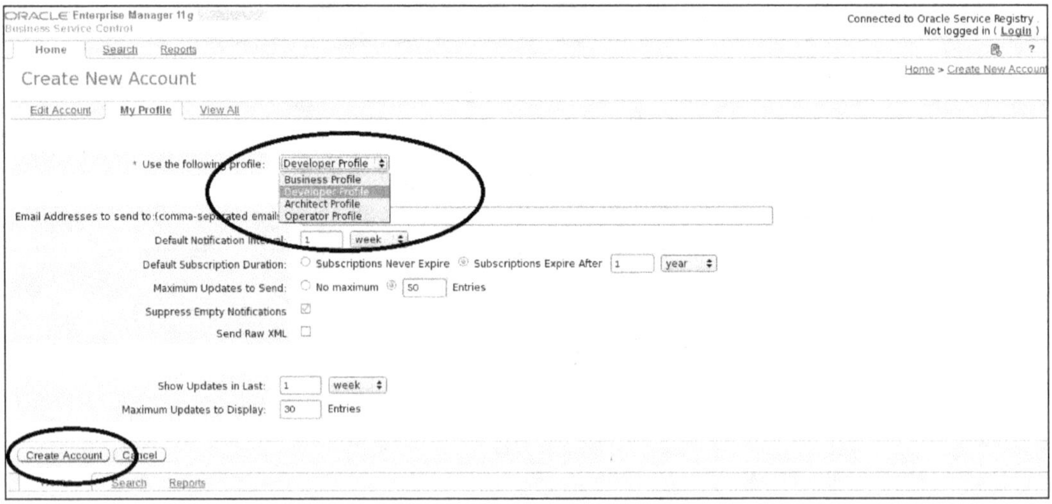

4. And finally, once the user has entered their details they should click on **Create Account**.

OSR Administrators can maintain accounts from the ORC including group membership and permissions.

> Please refer to section **Registry Configurations and Permissions** of the OSR **OFM Service Registry Guide 11*g* (11.1.1.6.0)**. URL: `http://www.oracle.com/technetwork/middleware/registry/osr111productdocumentation-159992.pdf`.

Searching

Business Service Control allows users to search OSR for services and related metadata. Searching functions are located under the **Search** menu tab and allow consumers to search for **Providers**, **Services**, **Endpoints**, and other artifacts that have been published to OSR.

The following screenshot shows the **Search** tab as selected by a user:

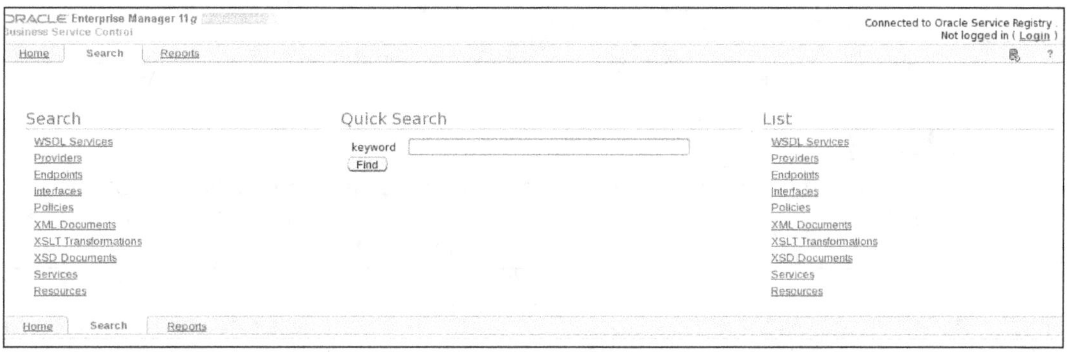

Properties for search criteria are used in conjunction with one another. The search function returns all records that satisfy any of the search criteria property values.

The following screenshot shows the options available for searching that include **Keywords**, **Local Name**, and **Namespace**, among others:

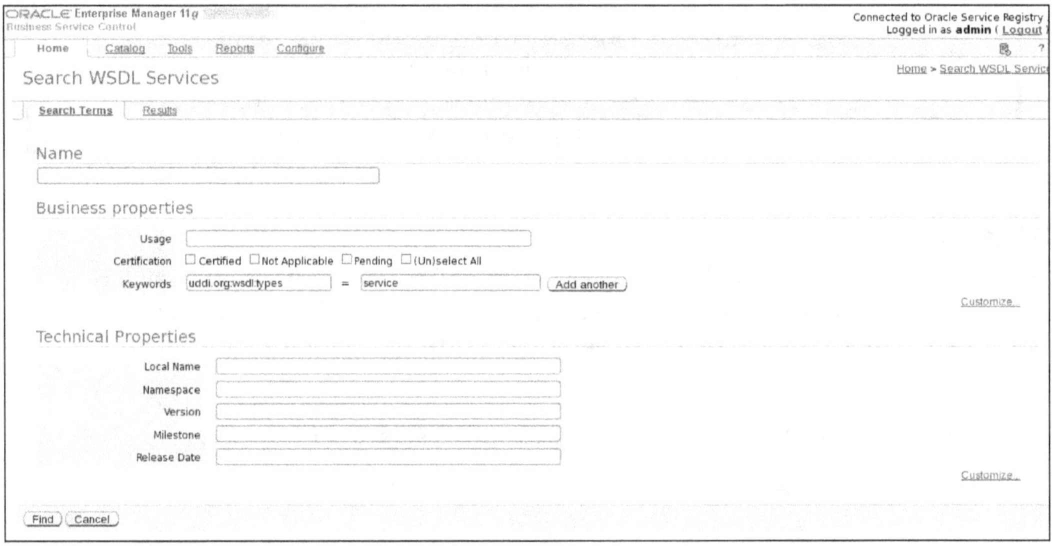

Publishing

Under the **Catalog** main-menu tab, users can use publishing wizards to publish entities to OSR:

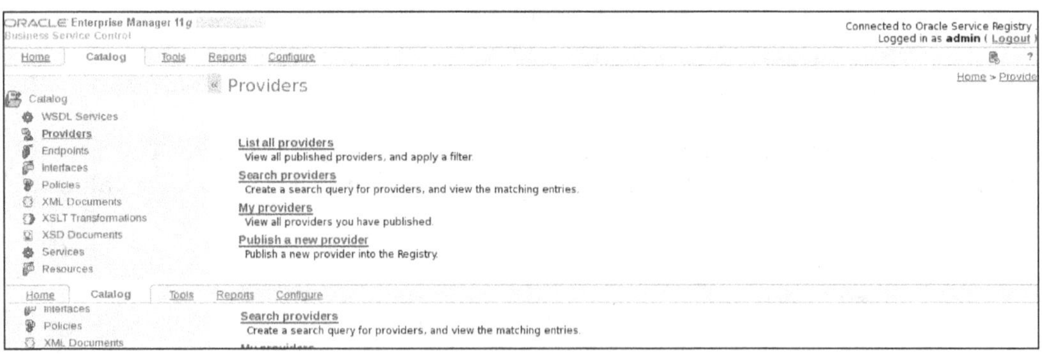

The following entities can be published from this tab:

Entity	Description
Providers	A two-step publishing wizard allows users to enter a provider's name and description, taxonomy classification, and contacts.
Services	A four-step publishing wizard guides the user through publishing a service, its interfaces, and its endpoints.
Interfaces	A wizard for publishing and republishing service interfaces.
Resources	This node allows users to publish WSDL files, XML files, XML schemas, and XSL transformations.

Notification and subscription

Any UDDI Registry user can subscribe to a set of UDDI entities and monitor their creation, modification, and deletion. The UDDI Registry notifies the user whenever any entity that matches the subscription query changes even if the change itself causes the entity to not match the query any more. The following entities can be monitored: providers, services, interfaces, and endpoints, as well as resources (WSDL, XML, XSD, and XSLT).

The notification can be synchronous or asynchronous. Synchronous notifications occur when the interested party explicitly asks for all changes that have happened since the last notification. Asynchronous notifications are periodically run at a configurable interval and notify interested parties whenever the matched entity is created, modified, or deleted.

The following screenshot shows a user adding a subscription to **Holiday request service**:

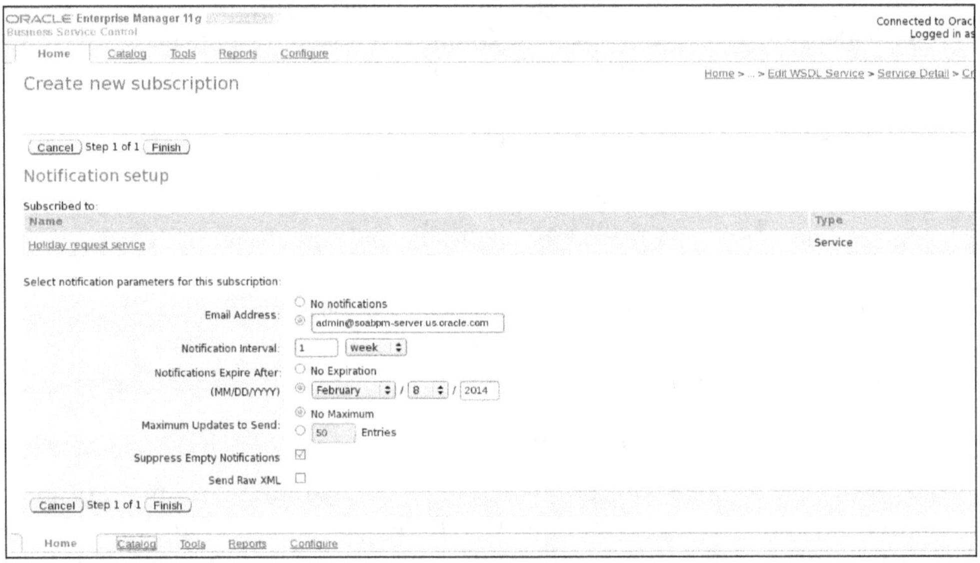

Users can establish a subscription based on a set of entities in which they are interested or on a specific search query. Users can receive notifications about modified structures via e-mail or they may view the modified entities under the **Tools** main-menu tab in the **My Subscription Results** section.

The approval process in OSR

The approval process governs the consistency and quality of data stored in OSR. It involves the creation of two registries. One registry is used to publish entities for verification by a supervising party and the other is a Discovery Registry, which is open to consumers and only contains data that has been approved and promoted from the Publication Registry.

The approval process includes two types of users. A requester seeks approval for data to be promoted to the Discovery Register. An approver is a user or a group given the ability to review published information in the Publication Registry. The approver can grant or deny approval in order to promote that data to the Discovery Registry. Every user can ask for approval; however, to have data considered for promotion, a user must have the administrator-assigned approver privilege. An approver group can be created with multiple users assigned.

> When implementing OSR alongside OER, this feature is not required as all approvals should take place within OER. Furthermore, the OSR standalone topology must be used when implementing OSR together with OER.

Reports

The **Business Service Control** console contains a set of predefined reports under the **Reports** main-menu tab. A registry user can browse and execute these reports:

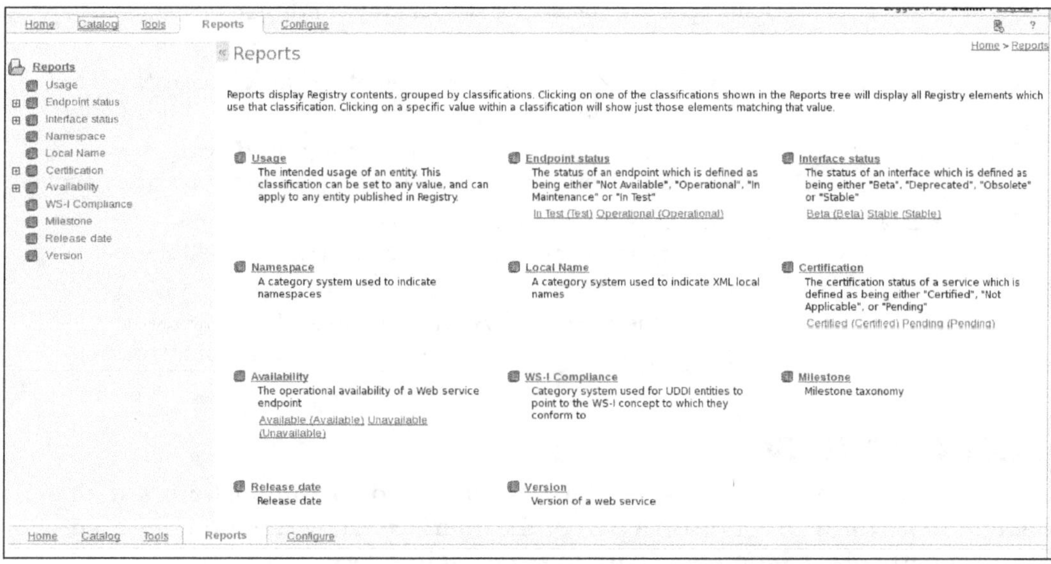

The **Business Service Control** console includes the following predefined reports:

Report Functionality	Description
Usage	This report shows services, resources, endpoints, and interfaces categorized by the `systinet-com:taxonomy:usage` taxonomy
Endpoint status	This report shows endpoints categorized by the `systinet-com:taxonomy:endpoint:status` taxonomy
Interface status	This report shows interfaces categorized by the `systinet-com:taxonomy:interface:status` taxonomy.

Report Functionality	Description
Namespace	This report shows services, endpoints, interfaces, and resources categorized by the `uddiorg:xml:namespace` taxonomy.
Local Name	This report shows services and endpoints categorized by the `uddi-org:xml:localName` taxonomy.
Certification	This report shows services categorized by the `systinet-com:taxonomy:service:certification` taxonomy.
Availability	This report shows endpoints categorized by the `systinet-com:taxonomy:endpoint:availability` taxonomy.
WS-I Compliance	This report shows endpoints and interfaces categorized by the `ws-i-org:conformsTo:2002_12` taxonomy.
Milestone	This report shows services categorized by the `systinet-com:versioning:milestone` taxonomy.
Release date	This report shows services categorized by the `systinet-com:versioning:releaseDate` taxonomy.
Version	This report shows services categorized by the `systinet-com:versioning:version` taxonomy.

OSR security

In OSR, roles are tied to permissions. Permissions, used by administrators, define the right to perform an action on a part of the interface. They represent the ability to process a particular method on a particular UDDI interface.

Permissions are very different from **Access Control Lists**, which is the other mechanism for enforcing rights in OSR. Access Control enables the administrator to control access to the basic UDDI data structures such as businessEntity, businessService, bindingTemplate, and tModel. Access Control on OSR is provided by the Access Control List (ACL). An ACL is based on permissions given to a user or group. An ACL ensures that a given user can access only the information that has been made available to the user by the Registry administrator or other users.

Thus, Access Control Lists limit the visibility of entities and so restrict access to the underlying UDDI data structures stored in OSR. Permissions, on the other hand, limit users through the visibility of interfaces.

> For more details on permissions and ACLs, please refer to chapter **6 Permissions** of the **OFM Service Registry Guide 11*g* (11.1.1.6.0)**.
> URL: `http://www.oracle.com/technetwork/middleware/registry/osr111productdocumentation-159992.pdf`.

Using OSR with OER

Without doubt, OER is Oracle's flagship product for design-time Governance, providing rich management features for controlling SOA Assets and their dependencies as well as support for approval and publishing of Assets.

OSR compliments OER by also providing support for runtime governance, but the observant reader may well have noticed a number of overlaps between the two products in the design-time Governance space. For example, both OER and OSR support Asset approvals, service lifecycle via promotions between environments, and the categorization of Assets using taxonomies.

While this chapter has focused on the rich functionality provided by OSR, the reader may be keen to understand how Oracle envisages the two products working hand-in-hand. The following section sets out to answer some of those questions.

Topology options

As explained earlier in this chapter, OSR can be installed in standalone or multi-registry mode. In organizations where OSR and OER co-exist, the recommended topology is to install OSR in standalone mode and to use OER to manage Asset approval and Asset promotion to multiple environments.

OSR and OER can co-exist in the same WebLogic Domain and the same managed server. However, at the time of writing, a system bug prevents OSR from functioning properly when OER events are turned on.

Thus, our recommendation is to install OSR in standalone mode within its own dedicated managed server and as part of the SOA domain.

Asset approvals

As described previously in the chapter, OSR has inbuilt functionality to support Asset approvals. However, the implementation is quite heavy weight, requiring SSL and the installation of multiple registries: one or more Intermediate Registries and a Discovery Registry. Oracle recommends using OER for approvals instead as these are better supported and more lightweight. The following diagram shows how OER can be used to promote Assets between environments using the approvals process:

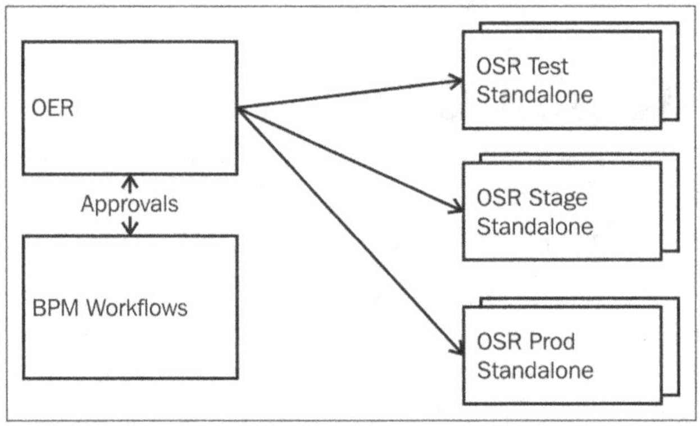

As can be seen in the preceding diagram, OER handles approvals and promotions of Assets across all environments.

Closed-loop governance

OSR can be employed to monitor service utilization and to provide runtime metrics for service usage. These metrics can feed back into OER to help make more informed Asset management decisions such as defining SLAs.

OSR can also be used to enforce runtime control on Assets, ensuring adherence to SLAs, policies, and performance requirements. Once again, information can be sent back to OER to assist in design-time decision making.

When used with the SOA management packs, Oracle Enterprise Manager can also provide OER with runtime performance metrics using prebuilt integrations with OER APIs:

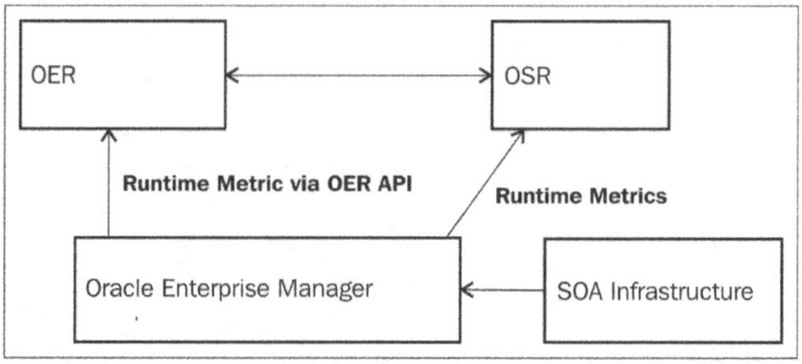

Managing taxonomies

As we have seen in previous sections, OSR can be used to define new taxonomies or utilize standard prebuilt UDDI taxonomies. However, categorization is better served earlier on in the Asset lifecycle by employing OER to categorize all SOA Assets. Consequently, it is considered best practice to use OER to master all taxonomies rather than OSR when the two products are co-deployed. These taxonomies should be defined prior to service publication to a registry. Generally speaking:

- OER should be used as the single source of truth for taxonomies. Approved taxonomies can be propagated to OSR using supplied utilities. This eliminates the need to create custom taxonomies in OSR.
- Service classification schemes should be determined before services are published to the registry.
- The service providers should not use the default OSR taxonomy. Furthermore, the administrator should remove all unused taxonomies from OSR.
- Taxonomies should be kept simple and business focused to encourage their use in the registry. This is because a registry is only as good as the ability to search it based on a sensible classification scheme.

The following diagram shows how OER taxonomies are mapped to OSR:

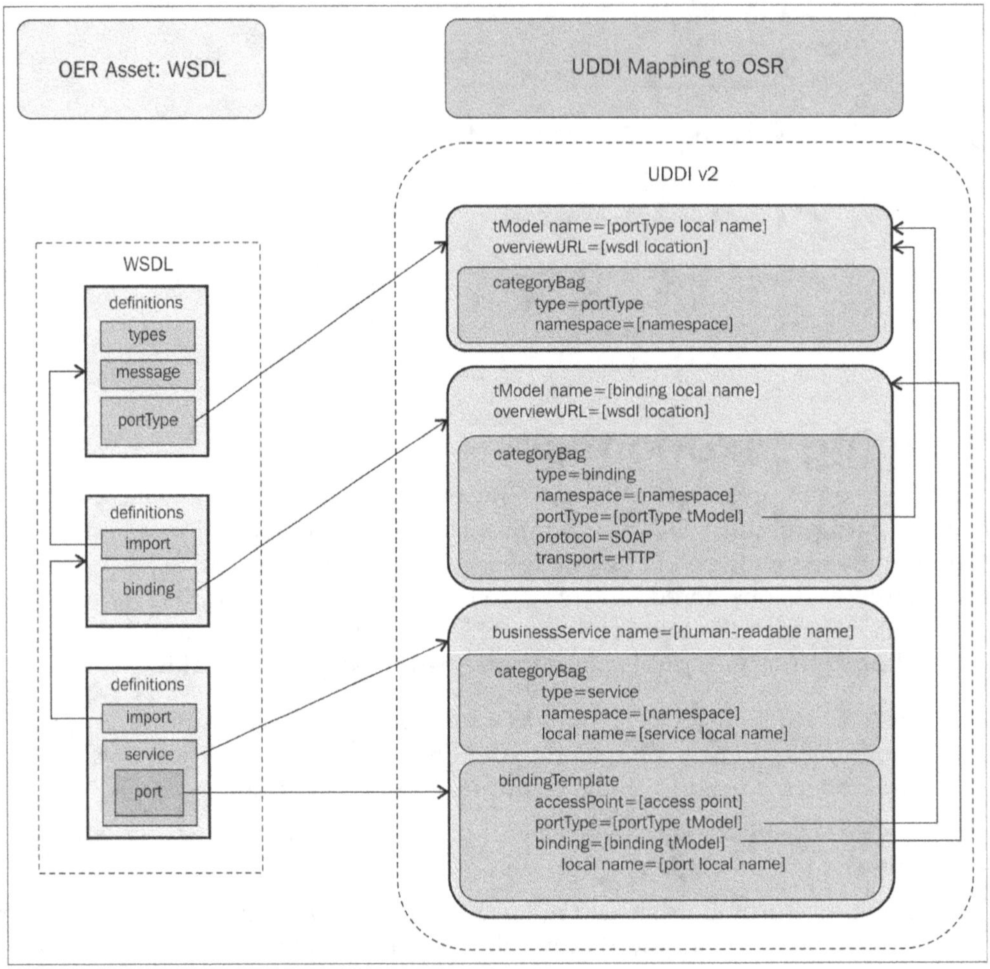

Summary

Oracle Service Registry (OSR) is a fully V3-compliant implementation of the UDDI (Universal Description, Discovery, and Integration) specifications. OSR stores data and metadata for all published services and is therefore a central place where service consumers can search for existing services. This search capability greatly improves service re-use across and between enterprises.

OSR can be employed with or without OER to store, classify, and manage metadata about services using taxonomies that define, among other things, security, transport, and quality of service. It also provides a virtualization layer, abstracting actual service implementation end points from the runtime container.

While OSR can be deployed and used without OER, and vice versa, the real-value proposition in terms of SOA Governance is to utilize both together. The rich functionality provided by OER can be employed to define and classify SOA Assets, manage their dependencies, and to promote them to OSR for consumption. Thus OSR, in effect, stores and exposes an approved subset of data from OER.

Furthermore, OSR can be programmatically searched by internal consumers or even consumers outside of the organization using the standard UDDI APIs. This provides a powerful mechanism to expose service functionality to third parties in a controlled manner.

In the next chapter we will develop and explore a use case that shows how OSR can be used to locate and consume externally exposed services, and how services can be promoted between environments using OER.

8
Design-time Service Promotion and Discovery

In order to create supply chain management efficiencies, Weir & Bell Telecom decided to expose web services for consumption by trusted third party suppliers. By offering web services to suppliers, Weir and Bell were able to streamline important supply chain processes and hence reduce the transaction costs for tasks, such as supply re-ordering, in a way that does not lock them into any particular supplier. Weir & Bell Telecom promote externally callable services for discovery via a private **UDDI** registry that is located in their **Demilitarized Zone** (**DMZ**). Third party suppliers are given access to this registry in order to locate and consume services.

In this chapter, we will demonstrate how Weir and Bell expose services using **OSR** for runtime resolution and how integration can be achieved between **OER** and OSR for service promotions. While outside the scope of this book, we will also discuss the role played by **Oracle API Gateway** (**OAG**) in runtime governance.

Use case

Weir & Bell Telecom have identified a number of areas in which they can improve and streamline the supply chain management activities by exposing internal services directly to third party suppliers. This will allow partners to integrate with their internal purchasing and supply chain systems directly, reduce costs, and improve the third party experience significantly. The services expose functionality such as submit purchase orders, cancel orders, and view order status amongst others.

The architecture team at Weir & Bell has decided to expose external services using an UDDI registry that they will host privately in their DMZ. The reason for this is that they only want to expose services to selected third party vendors and retain control over who can have visibility into service offerings. By using their own registry as opposed to a global registry (such as `uddi.org`), Weir & Bell is able to apply strict controls on who is registered to access service details.

The following diagram shows the architecture used to expose the services:

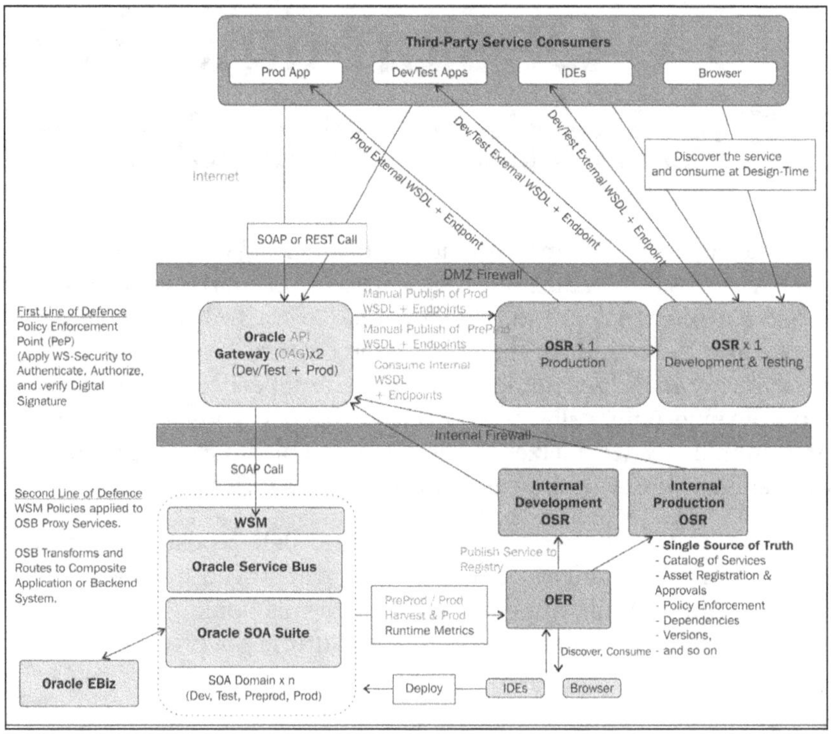

Service design artifacts are stored and governed in OER, which is used to enforce policies during service development. When services are approved for development, the internal IT team at Weir & Bell implement the services and ensure that they are fully system, integration, and performance tested. When a service is ready to be exposed to external parties, its Asset lifecycle status is changed in OER and the service is automatically published by an OER Asset registration workflow to an internal development registry. From here, the service **WSDL** is further consumed by security development staff, who apply appropriate internal and external security policies, and the resulting external WSDL is manually entered into an external registry wherein it can be consumed and tested by third parties. Similarly, a production registry is used for services that are integration-tested and ready for publication to a production registry, which exposes services that fully integrate with Weir & Bell live application systems.

Weir & Bell Telecom has decided to utilize the **Oracle API Gateway** (**OAG**) appliance to expose external services and to enforce first line security using **Policy Enforcement Points** (**PeP**). OAG provides vital protection between untrusted and trusted networking zones, enforcing DMZ-class security, and comprehensive threat defense mechanisms at the service perimeter of a SOA environment. Protection offered here includes XML schema validation, payload analysis (to prevent XML bombs), and enforcement of **WS-Security** and **OAuth** policies amongst others.

The services exposed are a mix of **REST** and/or **SOAP** services with binding details defined in the binding template in OSR.

> Note that OAG is a subject matter that is beyond the scope of this book, so we will not cover the product in detail in this section.

Security for internal web services exposed to the DMZ is further enforced using **Oracle Web Services Manager**, which sits alongside the service and implements standard security policies such as WS-Security. This provides a second line of security to augment OAG.

> Note that implementation of runtime governance using WSM is covered in *Chapter 9, Implementing Basic Runtime Governance*.

As stated, services that are consumed externally are exposed and secured by OAG. OAG exposes a WSDL that reflects the WS-Security policies that are applicable to the service and that the consumer code must adhere to when binding to the service. This book was written using **OER Patchset 6 (11.1.1.7)**, which does not support direct harvesting of the OAG Assets, so it was decided that OAG WSDLs should be manually registered into OSR and that these would then subsequently be harvested into OER using the **Oracle Registry Repository Exchange Utility**. OER is used for design-time Governance.

> Note that Weir and Bell decided to employ a registry for internal services consumed from the DMZ by OAG and for OAG services exposed to third parties. Internally consumed services do not utilize a UDDI registry since there are other mechanisms in place to manage endpoints, such as at deployment-time using a deployment framework. Furthermore, service discovery is internally supported with OER.

Runtime metrics are fed back to OER from OEM and **Business Transaction Manager** (**BTM**) providing important operational feedback to policy makers and ensuring that all the service SLAs are met. These topics are covered in *Chapter 9, Implementing Basic Runtime Governance*, and *Chapter 10, Extending Runtime Governance*.

The steps necessary to make an internal service externally discoverable and consumable can be summarized as follows:

1. A candidate service is discovered from a use case as part of the analysis phase and entered into OER as a potential service. The SOA Design Authority will consider the service and approve as required. Following approval, the **High Level Design**, **Service Detailed Design**, **XML schemas**, and WSDLs are all created following an OER centric SDLC as described in *Chapter 5, Harvesting*, and *Chapter 6, Asset Lifecycle and Workflow*, of this book.

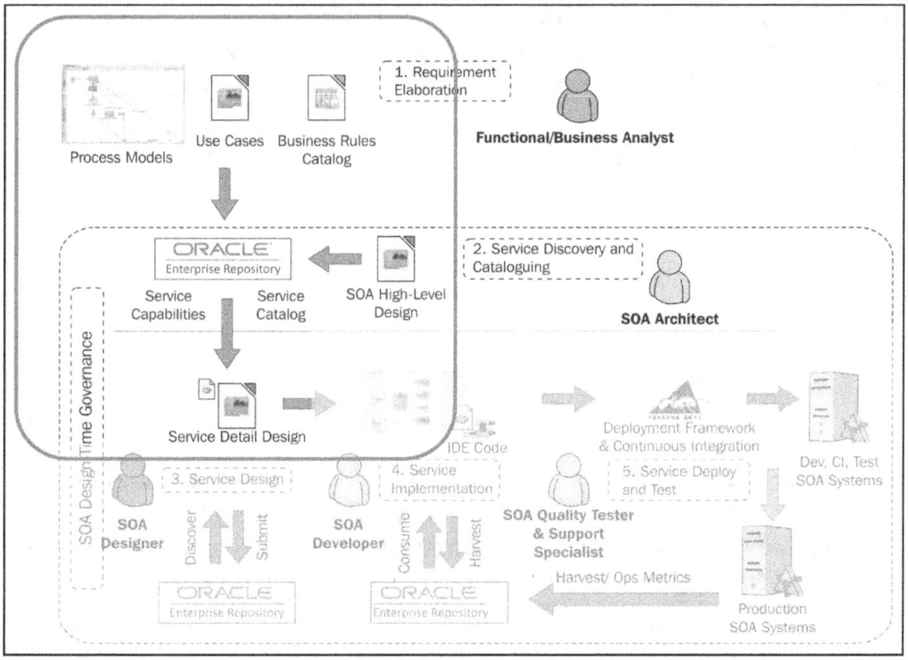

2. The internal composite application is then developed in SOA Suite 11*g* by the development team. For the Weir and Bell use case, the composite application makes use of the **Oracle for Applications adapter** to consume relevant PL/SQL procedures that are contained in Weir & Bell Telecom's ERP system. The latter was implemented using eBusiness Suite R12.

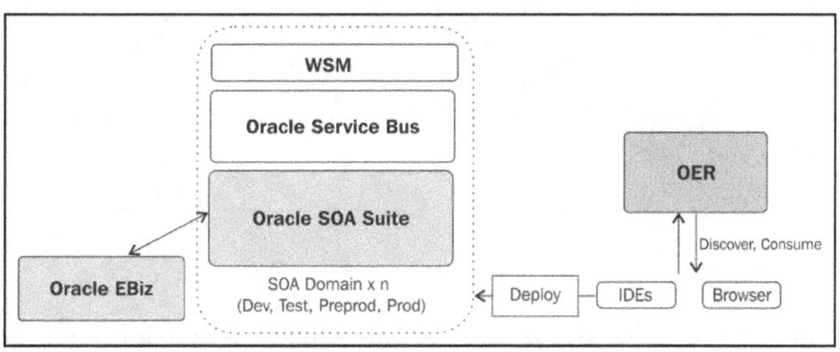

[Note that Weir & Bell Telecom adopted **Oracle Application Integration Architecture (AIA) 11*g*** foundation pack as their accelerator framework for integration with Oracle Applications. *Chapter 11, Extending Governance with AIA 11g*, covers the utilization of OER in governing AIA 11*g* Assets.]

3. Once the service has been developed as a SOA Suite 11*g* composite application, a **Business Service** is created in OSB to wrap this service. In AIA terms, this would be an **Enterprise Business Service** or **EBS** for short.

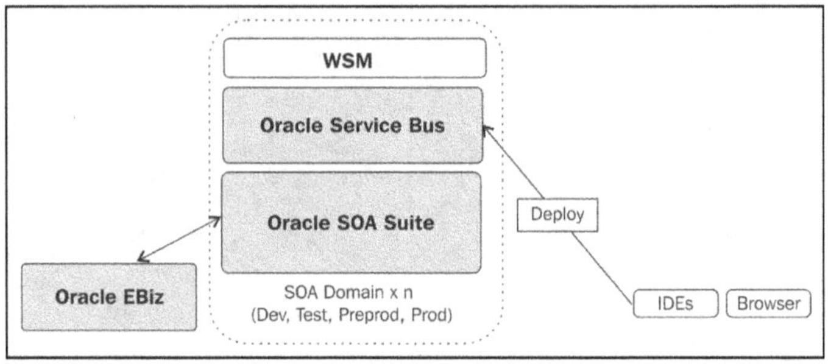

4. A **Proxy Service** is created in OSB to transform from the canonical schema used by the EBS service (basically Enterprise Business Message and Enterprise Business Object) into a denormalized and simplified **Application Business Message** or **ABM** for short.
5. A WSM policy is implemented in OSB to enforce authentication and authorization for the internal services exposed to OAG. A system account is created using the **WebLogic Admin Console**, which should be used whenever OAG consumes the OSB service.

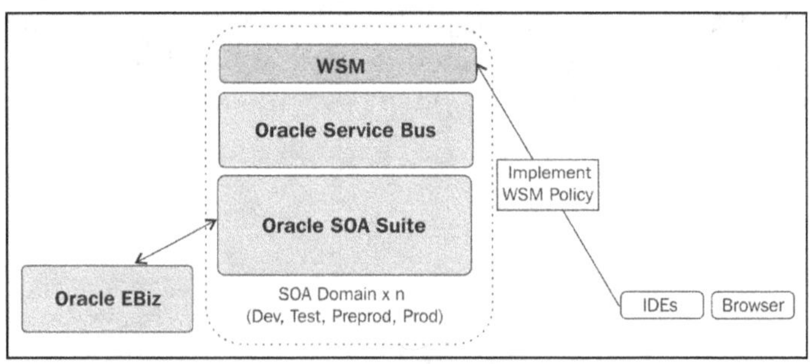

[Note that implementation of runtime governance using WSM is covered in *Chapter 9, Implementing Basic Runtime Governance*.]

6. Each component is unit-tested with a combination of the SOA Suite 11*g* Test Suite and SoapUI.

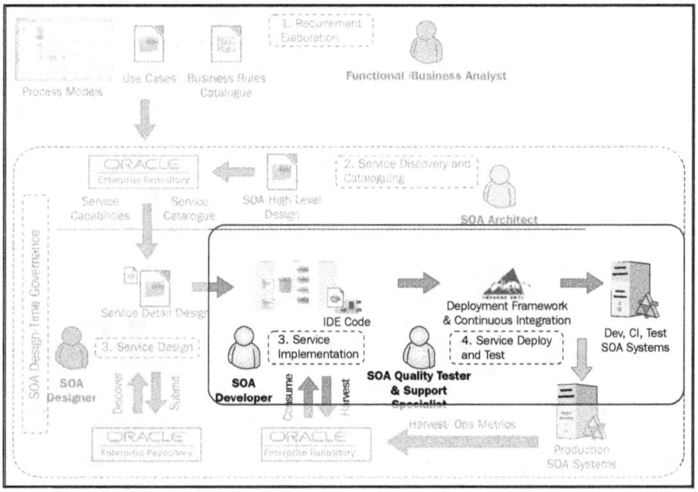

7. Once unit testing concludes, the internal services are included into the **Continuous Integration** solution. The **Continuous Integration** solution was built using **Jenkins** (`http://jenkins-ci.org/`).
8. The internal services are rolled out for testing into the **System Integration Testing (SIT)** environment and subsequently into the **User Acceptance Testing (UAT)** environment.
9. Once SIT and UAT testing is completed, the SOA Suite 11*g* composites and the OSB services are harvested into OER with a status of **Submitted - Under Review**. This can be done in a number of ways; however, for this use case, it was decided to do it by triggering the command-line harvester utility from within the Weir and Bell deployment framework. This allowed only the harvest services to be deployed instead of all the available services in the environment.

10. At this point, an OER publishes into the **Internal Development OSR** any service with status **Submitted - Under Review**.

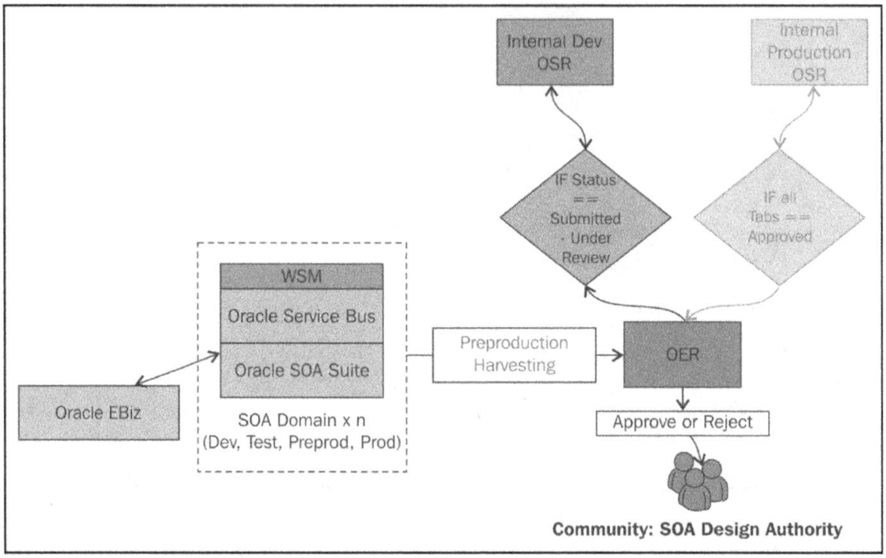

> Although it is possible to harvest these Assets using the OER JDeveloper and Eclipse plugins, harvesting at the development phase is not generally recommended. This is because OER can become cluttered with outdated Assets that are in many cases no longer relevant or valid. Furthermore, in this use case it was decided that services should only be made available in OER after SIT and UAT completion. Individual company requirements will dictate at what stage of the lifecycle Assets are submitted to OER.

11. Once **Performance Testing** concludes, the internal services are ready to be exposed from OAG to external parties. At this point, all the policies and other workflow approvals must take place in OER. Once all the necessary approvals take place, an Asset reaches the **Registered** status in OER.

12. Once a service reaches the **Registered Asset** status in OER, an automated workflow is triggered that will set the lifecycle stage of the Asset to **Stage 4 - Release** and will automatically register only the OSB proxy services into the internal OSRs.

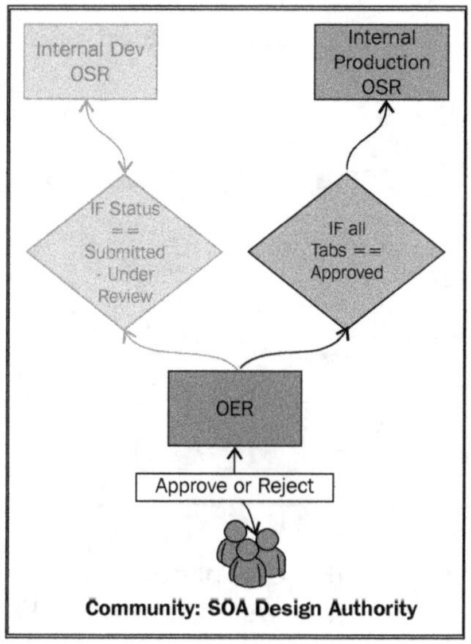

> Note that OER was configured such that only the OSB service WSDL is published to the service registry after the service has been successfully tested.

13. The OAG developers are then able to locate the relevant internal service endpoints in OSR and consume them from OAG in order to apply further security policies to them as required. The OAG developers then create a Policy Enforcement Point (PeP) that can securely expose the OSB proxy service to the Internet for third party consumption.

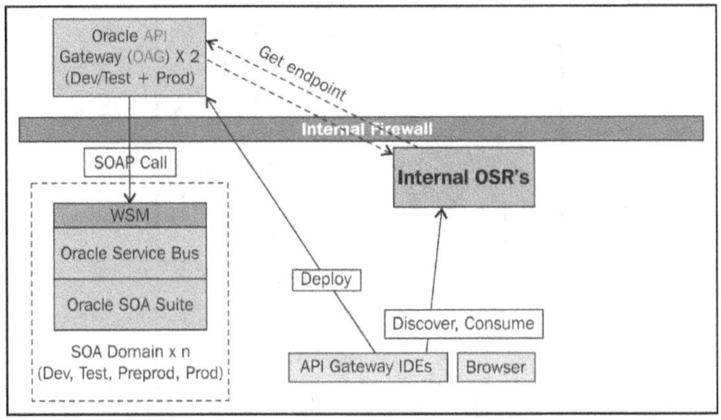

14. Once the OAG development is completed and tested, the OAG WSDL for the external services is manually registered into the **Development and Testing OSR** under the **Business Entity** specifically created for external parties. The services are then integration tested by the suppliers.

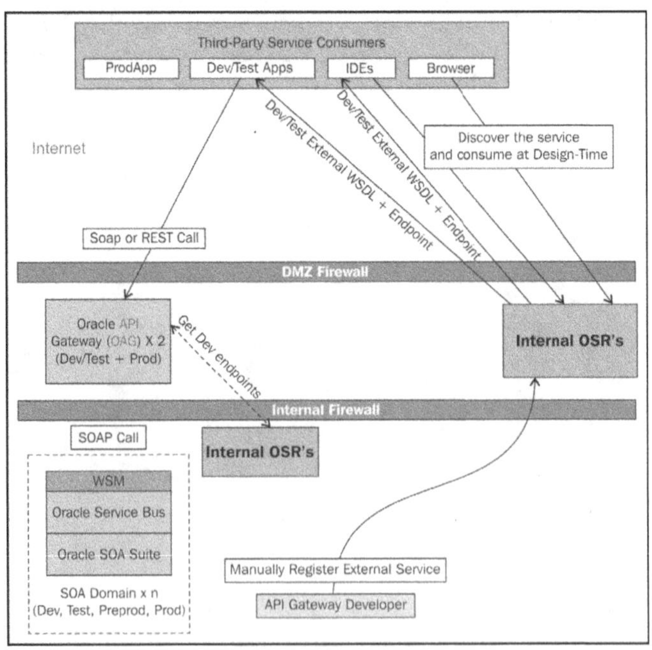

15. Once the internal services are tested by the suppliers, they are ready to be deployed into **Production**.
16. Finally, once the **OAG Service** is promoted into the production environment, the external WSDL is manually registered into the production OSR.

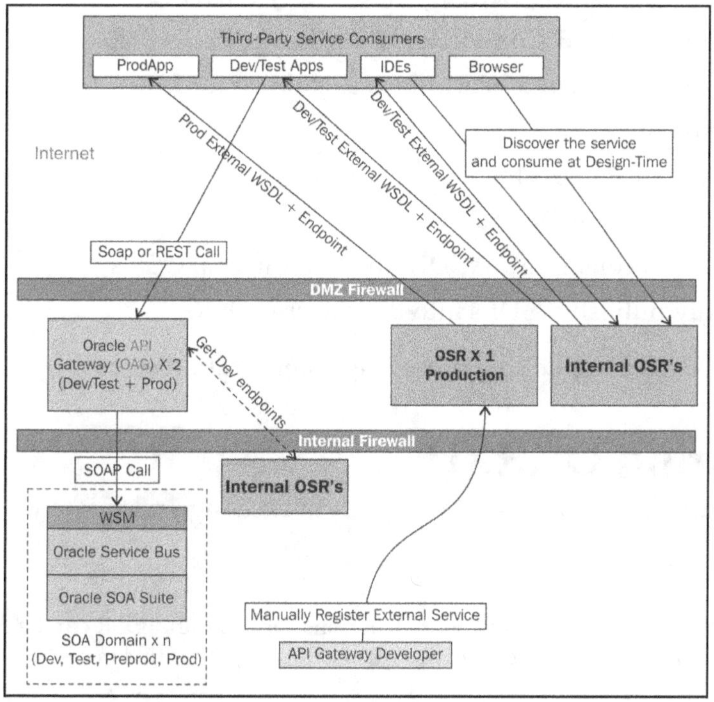

The following sections will demonstrate how to perform steps 9, 12, and 13 and the configuration pre-requisites that are required in order to facilitate the OER-OSR integration.

> Note that many of the preceding steps were only mentioned for reference purposes and a detailed explanation of how to perform these tasks will not be covered by this book.

Configuration steps

In order to implement the previous use case, the administrator must perform the following configuration steps:

- Configure the **Oracle Registry Repository Exchange Utility** (**ORRXU**)
- Configure the **OSR Connection Details**
- Configure **Automated Workflows** to publish to OSR
- Configure `Workflow.xml`
- Configure the **Harvester**
- Approve assets in OER
- Use OAG to consume a WSDL from the internal OSR's
- Manually publish WSDLs into the external OSR.

This section describes each of the preceding configuration steps.

Configuring ORRXU

This section describes how to configure OER to exchange metadata with OSR using the exchange utility.

> Note that installation instructions for OER and OSR can be found in *Appendix, Installation Tips and Techniques* of this book.

The **Oracle Registry Repository Exchange Utility** can be used to:

- Publish services and endpoints from design-time environments to OSR and to harvest runtime services back to OER.
- Harvest runtime services to OER for governance.
- Automatically publish services to OSR using Oracle Business Process Management 10*g* automated workflows that are built in OER based around the Asset's lifecycle status changes. For example, a workflow may be triggered when a service has its status changed to indicate that it is now ready for release to **Production**.
- Capture runtime metrics from Oracle Business Transaction Manager. This will be covered in later chapters.
- Capture service performance data contained in OSR back to the repository to better inform service providers of service usage.

Before we can execute the utility, we need to configure the connections to OER and OSR. The following sections will show you how to do this.

Configuring ORRXU.XML connection details

Connection details are contained in a file called `orrxu.xml`, which is located in the directory `<OBPM HOME>/workflow/aler_egine`. You will need to edit this file to set endpoints appropriate to your environment.

Open the `orrxu.xml` file and modify the following XML section to point to your OER instance and specify the appropriate credentials.

```
<repository>
  <uri>http://<OER SERVR>:7101/oer</uri>
  <credentials>
    <user>admin</user>
    <password>*****</password>
  </credentials>
</repository>
```

You should provide an encrypted password in the preceding code as described in earlier chapters.

In the preceding example, `uri` should point to the OER URI, using the following format:

```
http://<host>:<port>/<OER web app name>
```

Here `host` and `port` are the machine IP and port that are hosting OER.

> Note that, as with the harvester product, it is recommended that you execute the **Repository Exchange Utility** tool with a specifically created user that has basic access settings for Assets, in this case **View**, **Edit**, **Accept**, and **Register**.

Configuring the OSR environment details

The OSR environment-specific details are also configured in `orrxu.xml`. In here, a configuration can be made to publish one or more OSRs. The first step is to create one or more registry nodes with appropriate connection details.

For each registry in your architecture, you must configure the URLs to the appropriate UDDI APIs as follows:

```
<registries>
  <registry name="INTERNAL-DEV-OSR">
 <inquiryURI>http://<SERVER>:<PORT>/registry/uddi/inquiry</
   inquiryURI>
 <publishURI>http://<SERVER>:<PORT>/registry/uddi/publishing</
   publishURI>
 <securityURI>http://<SERVER>:<PORT>/registry/uddi/security</
   securityURI>
    <credentials>
      <user>admin</user>
      <password>*****</password>
    </credentials>
  </registry>
  <registry name=" INTERNAL-PROD-OSR ">
 <inquiryURI>http://<SERVER>:<PORT>/registry/uddi/inquiry</
   inquiryURI>
 <publishURI>http://<SERVER>:<PORT>/registry/uddi/publishing</
   publishURI>
 <securityURI>http://<SERVER>:<PORT>/registry/uddi/security</
   securityURI>
    <credentials>
      <user>admin</user>
      <password>*****</password>
    </credentials>
  </registry>
</registries>
```

As can be seen in the preceding code snippet, we have initially configured two registries, namely `Internal Development OSR` and `Internal Production OSR`. You will notice that we have configured the URI endpoints to various registry components, namely the inquiry service, the publish service, and the security service.

To set these values correctly for your environment, you will need to locate the UDDI API URLs from the OSR console. To do this:

1. Log into the registry console (`http://<SERVER>:<PORT>/registry/uddi/web`) and select the **Search** link:

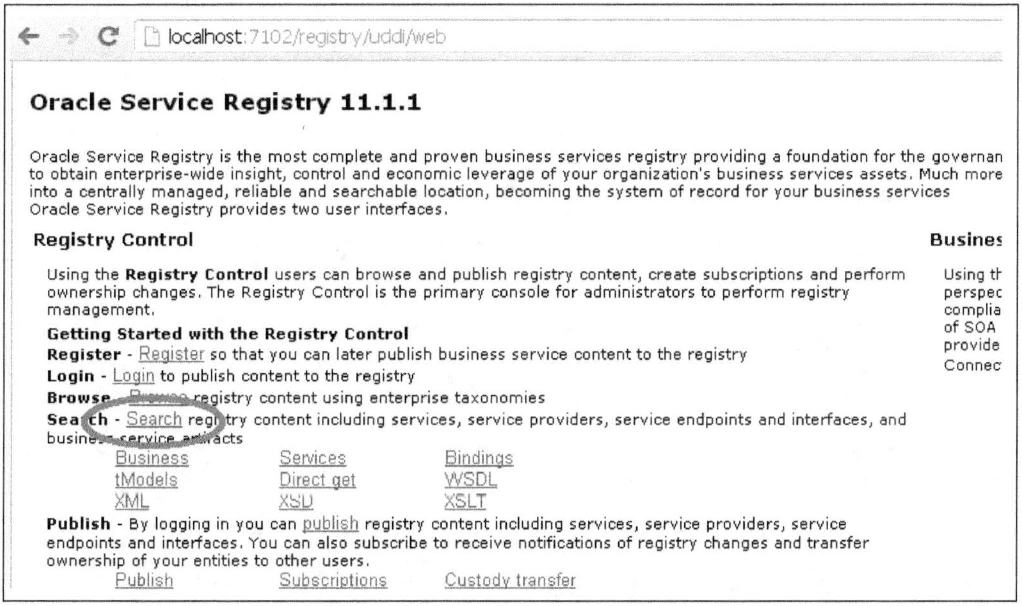

2. From the **Search** screen, enter the search criteria `UDDI_Inquiry_SoapService` in the **Service name** field:

3. Click on the **Find Service** button. The results should be shown as follows:

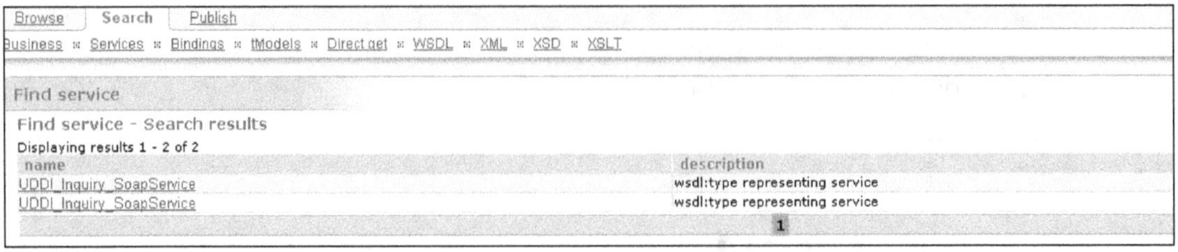

4. Finally, click on the link representing the name and the details of the service will appear as follows:

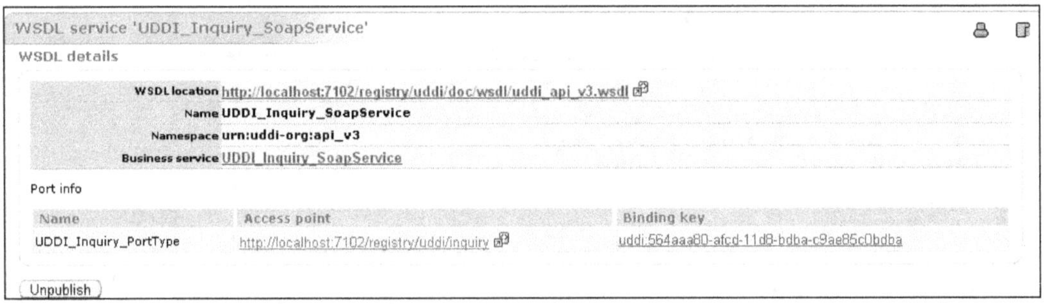

> The WSDL location identifies the endpoint for the inquiry service that is used for browsing the registry.

5. Open the WSDL and ensure that it contains an entry for each of the following services `UDDI_Inquiry_SoapService`, `UDDI_Security_SoapService`, and `UDDI_Publication_SoapService` as shown in the preceding screenshot. If it does then the same URL can be used for each service. Otherwise, you must repeat the process for the security and publication services.

```
<?xml version="1.0" encoding="UTF-8"?>
<definitions name="UDDI_API_V3"
xmlns="http://schemas.xmlsoap.org.wsdl/"
xmlns:soap="http://schemas.xmlsoap.org.wsdl/soap"
xmlns:api_v3_binding="urn:uddi-org:api_v3_binding"
xmlns:tns="urn:uddi-org:api_v3"
targetnamespace="urn:uddi-org:api_v3">
```

```
<documentation>
  Copyright 2001-2005 Systinet Corp. All rights reserved.
  Use is subject to license terms.

  WSDL  SOAP/HTTP binding for UDDI V3 Security, Publication and
Inquiry APIs.
</documentation>
<import namespace="urn:uddi-org:api_v3_binding" location="uddi_
api_v3_binding.wsdl"/>
<service name="UDDI_Security_SoapService">
  <port name="UDDI_Security_PortType" binding="api_v3_
binding:UDDI_Security_SoapBinding">
    <soap:address location="http://localhost:7102/uddi/security"/>
  </port>
</service>
<service name="UDDI_Publication_SoapService">
  <port name="UDDI_Publication_PortType" binding="api_v3_
binding:UDDI_Publication_SoapBinding">
    <soap:address location="http://localhost:7102/uddi/
publishing"/>
  </port>
</service>
<service name="UDDI_Inquiry_SoapService">
  <port name="UDDI_Inquiry_PortType" binding="api_v3_binding:UDDI_
Inquiry_SoapBinding">
    <soap:address location="http://localhost:7102/uddi/inquiry"/>
  </port>
</service>
</definitions>
```

6. The `<soap:address>` location attribute may contain `urn:unknown-location-uri`. If this is the case, the WSDL file must be updated on the OSR machine. To do this, login into the machine hosting OSR and edit the WSDL file so that it contains the correct URLs for accessing the inquiry, security, and publishing services. The WSDL documents can be found in `/opt/oracle/osr/doc/wsdl`. Enter the SOAP address to match the `UDDI_INQUIRY_PortType` as determined.

Configuring automated workflows to publish to OSR

Services are published to OSR based on the metadata attributes such as Asset status or Asset lifecycle stage. It is up to your specific implementation to define which attribute to use. In our use case, we used the Asset status; however, in the subsequent sections we describe how to do this configuration regardless of the approach taken.

Data that passes to and from OSR has to be mapped to the UDDI entities (see *Chapter 7, Oracle Service Registry*, for more details on UDDI). All the mappings are contained within the `UDDIMappings.xml` file that is also located under `<OBPM HOME>/workflow/aler_egine`.

The following metadata entities are mapped in `UDDIMappings.xml` and handled by the ORRXU:

- All services, SCA composites, and any custom services of any OER Asset Type developed by end users.
- Business Entities that have created and published the services.
- Endpoint Assets that describe a service's access point. These are mapped to UDDI Binding Templates (see *Chapter 7, Oracle Service Registry*, for more details on binding templates).
- OER Categorizations, which are mapped to **UDDI tModels** using the UDDI Category Bag (see *Chapter 7, Oracle Service Registry*, for more details on tModels).
- The status of the service is added to the Category Bag of the Business Service in OSR.
- Service keys are the keys that remain consistent across all the registries stating that the service is promoted to and from OER. Where services are published from OSR to OER, OER uses that service key whenever it promotes services to other service registries.

> Note that the services without an HTTP transport are not published to the UDDI Registry. For further details on how metadata is exchanged with OSR, please refer to *Section 10.3.2* of the *OER Configuration Guide* (`http://docs.oracle.com/cd/E28280_01/admin.1111/e16580/oereu.htm#BGEHDBEB`).

Next, we need to specify the connection to the registry that is to be published to. We do this by editing the `orrxu.xml` file and entering values for the `<destinationRegistries>` element. The following snippet demonstrates an example configuration that shows how to use the `<destinationRegistries>` element to refer to one or more destination registries. These elements specify where the selected services from OER will be deployed.

In our use case, we also want to query Assets based on their lifecycle stage. As such, Assets that reach the lifecycle stage of **Stage 4 - Release** should be released to the internal registry.

```
<destinationRegistries>
  <destinationRegistry name="INTERNAL-PROD-OSR">
    <endpointAssetLifecycleStatus>Stage 4 -
      Release</endpointAssetLifecycleStatus>
  </destinationRegistry>
</destinationRegistries>
```

Each destination registry element can optionally contain an **endpointAssetLifecycleStatus** property that filters service endpoints by the **Asset Lifecycle Stage Categorization** type. This ensures that only service endpoints that match the given **Asset Lifecycle Stage Categorization** are published to the specified registry.

It is necessary to create different configuration files configured to point at each registry. Depending on the lifecycle, the services can be moved to different registries based on the Asset lifecycle triggers.

Setting the Repository Query

In order to publish services to the registry, it is necessary to create queries that `orrxu.xml` will use to locate the services that are to be published. This section shows the reader the basics for creating such queries. Queries can be created in a number of ways and you can specify one or more queries that **Repository Exchange Utility** should use. A query can locate services in the following ways:

- By name
- By registration status
- By categorization
- Using a filter

For this use case we will query by `filter` and `status`. For more details on how to create other queries, the reader should refer to *Section 10.2.3.3* of the *OER Configuration Guide* (`http://docs.oracle.com/cd/E28280_01/admin.1111/e16580/oereu.htm#BGEHDBEB`).

When the `<registrationStatus>` element is configured, only the services with the specified status are published. For this use case, we want to publish services to the internal registry when their status is set to **Registered**.

To create this query, we will set the element in `orrxu.xml` as follows:

```
<registrationStatus>Registered</registrationStatus>
```

So, the `orraxu.xml` file will now look as follows:

```
<query>
  <!--Query: the services to publish-->
  <repositoryQuery>
    <services>
      <service name="%"/>
    </services>
    <!--Search criteria for the registration status of the service in
OER -->
    <registrationStatus>Registered</registrationStatus>
```

Querying by filter

Finally, we need to filter by Asset Type since we only require the OSB endpoint to be published to the internal registry.

Filters allow us to query Assets using either metadata or WSDL location.

To create a filter, the user must edit the `orrxu.xml` file and create a `filter` element. The following `filter` element can be used to filter by Asset Type—in this case to query for an OSB proxy service only.

```
<filter
type="metadata.internal.introspector.store/sync/Service_Type"
value="Proxy Service" />
```

> For more details, the reader is referred to *Section 10.2.3.3.4* of the *OER Configuration Guide* (`http://docs.oracle.com/cd/E28280_01/admin.1111/e16580/oereu.htm#BGEHDBEB`)..

Configuring the OER categorization to UDDI Mapping

Before publishing Assets to OSR, OER categorizations need to be mapped in the **UDDI Mappings** file, `UDDIMappings.xml`.

> Note that this file is mapped to UDDI by default during installation. Therefore, this file will only need customizations if new categorizations have been added and that need to be mapped to UDDI, for example, lifecycle stage.

For example, the following snippet shows a mapping used to map a custom OER Asset Lifecycle Stage to UDDI categorizations:

```
<uddi:uddiSettings xmlns:uddi="http://www.bea.com/aler/integration/
config/uddi">
  <categorizationMappings>
    <categorizationType
      alerCategorizationTypeName="AssetLifecycleStage"
      alerCateqorizationTypeId="112"
      uddiCategoryTModelKey=
        "uddi:bea.com:aler:categorization:AssetLifecycleStage">
      <categorization alerCategorization=
        "Stage 4 - Release to Preproduction"
        uddiKeyName="Stage 4 - Release"
        uddiKeyValue="Stage 4 - Release to Preproduction" />
```

An OER categorization will be honored in OSR if a corresponding mapping is present in the UDDI Mappings file. Otherwise, the categorization will be ignored. Therefore, if a new Asset Categorization is created in OER, you must regenerate the UDDI Mappings file for that Categorization in order for it to be honored in OSR.

> Further details can be found in the *OER Configuration Guide* in *section 10.2.4* (`http://docs.oracle.com/cd/E28280_01/admin.1111/e16580/oereu.htm#BGEHDBEB`).t.

Configuring Workflow.xml

Chapter 6, Asset Lifecycle and Workflow, introduced the pre-built Asset registration workflows that support and automate the registration of Assets and form an integral part of the overall governance process. The processes and workflows are modeled and executed in the OBPM 10*g* component of OER. These processes can be run out-of-the-box with little configuration, and can be tailored to support different use cases.

One such workflow, `PublishAssetToUDDI`, supports the synchronization of OER and OSR. Assets and their metadata can be published to OSR by wiring events that are triggered when these Assets are registered or their status in the lifecycle is changed to the execution of ORRXU. By using workflows to invoke ORRXU, synchronization of OER and OSR can be fully automated.

To execute the workflow, we need to ensure that the event that represents the taxonomy being approved at **Stage 4 – Release** is wired to an action to call the `PublishAssetToUDDI` workflow. This is done by editing `workflow.xml` (see *Chapter 6, Asset Lifecycle and Workflow,* for further details) and entering the following xml snippet:

```
<state:name="urn:com:bea:aler:events:type:AssetTabApproved"
value="Taxonomy">
  <action>PublishAssetToUDDI</action>
  <alrrxConfigFileName>orrxu.xml</ alrrxConfigFileName>
  <alrrxMappingFileName>UDDIMappings.xml</alrrxMappingFileName>
</state>
```

The addition of this event-action pairing will cause the `PublishAssetToUDDI` workflow to be executed when the all the approvals have been granted by the approvers (see *Chapter 6, Asset Lifecycle and Workflow,* for further details).

To avoid having to manually change the **Asset Lifecycle Stage** to **Stage 4 – Release**, the following snippet can be added to `workflow.xml` so that, when the **Documentation** tab is approved, the **Asset Lifecycle Stage** is automatically set to **Stage 4 – Release**.

```
<state:name="urn:com:bea:aler:events:type:AssetTabApproved"
value="Documentation">
  <action>ChangeAssetLifeCycle</action>
  <assetLifecycle>Stage 4 - Release</assetLifecycle >
</state>
```

> Further details on how to configure these automated workflows can be found in *Chapter 6, Asset Lifecycle and Workflow*, and *section 10.3.1.1* of the *OER Configuration Guide* (`http://docs.oracle.com/cd/E28280_01/admin.1111/e16580/oereu.htm#BGEHDBEB`).

Prior to executing the workflow, ensure that the following files are available under `<OBPM HOME>/workflow/aler_egine`:

- plugins
- `orrxu.xml`
- `orrxu.properties`
- `log4fl.properties`
- `types.properties`
- `UDDIMappings.xml`

Note that the `orrxu.xml` and `workflow.xml` files should be configured as per the previous section.

Configuring the harvester

Chapter 5, Harvesting, of this book introduced the **harvester** as the tool used to gather the metadata about services deployed in the SOA ecosystem. Once the OSB proxy has been deployed, we need to harvest the endpoint back into OER.

For details on how to configure the harvester tool the user should refer to *Chapter 5, Harvesting*.

For this use case, the administrator needs to configure the **Repository** connection details for the command line. This is done by editing the `HarvesterSettings.xml` file. You will recall that we will harvest both the SOA composite information and the OSB business and proxy services. The latter should use the harvester that ships with OSB only. Locate the appropriate `HarvestingSettings.xml` file and set the repository connection details illustrated as follows:

```
<repository>
  <uri>http://localhost:7101/oer</uri>
  <credentials>
    <user>harvester</user>
    <password>*****</password>
  </credentials>
</repository>
```

Here it is necessary to provide the login details to the repository. Note that the password should be encrypted using the Oracle supplied encryption tool as described earlier in the book. In this case, we created a special user called `harvester` so that we could identify those Assets that have been automatically harvested.

We also need to configure the host details for the OSB server in order to harvest the OSB proxy. The following snippet shows how to connect to the OSB server:

```
<remoteQuery>
  <serverType>OSB</serverType>
  <projectName>%</projectName>
  <uri>http://<SOA Server>:7001/</uri>
  <credentials>
    <user>weblogic</user>
    <password>v2_1.G+NTr3az8thaGGJBn0vwPg==</password>
  </credentials>
</remoteQuery>
```

Here, we specify the server type as OSB and provide credentials on how to log into the OSB server.

Harvesting

Having deployed our OSB proxy to the SIT environment, we need to harvest the deployment details such as the service endpoint. This will ensure that OER masters all details of our deployed Assets.

Harvesting has already been dealt with in *Chapter 5, Harvesting*, of this book and the user should refer to this chapter to understand how to install, configure, and use the harvester tool. As stipulated earlier, we would recommend that harvesting only takes place late in the lifecycle; in our example, we harvest from pre-production and production. Note that depending on your particular requirements you may decide to take a different strategy towards harvesting.

> In our use case, we decided that harvesting should not take place in the development environment as this is too volatile and we risk cluttering OER with outdated or superseded metadata. Consequently, harvesting should be done via the command line and not using the Jdeveloper or OSB plugins.

When harvesting OSB proxies, please ensure that you use the harvester that came with the OSB installation.

In order to harvest, the user must set entries in the `HarvesterSettings.xml` configuration file that provide details of how to connect the deployed SOA infrastructure and how to connect to OER. Here, you will also specify the status at which the services are harvested—in our case, `Submitted - under review` when harvesting from pre-production and `Registered` when harvesting from production. Once these configuration values are set, the user can execute the harvester using the command line.

The following snippet shows how to set the harvested status of the Asset:

```
<!--Registration status to set on created Assets in OER.
  The Valid Registration states are 1) Unsubmitted 2)Submitted -
Pending Review 3)Submitted - Under Review 4)Registered -->
  <registrationStatus>Submitted - Pending Review</registrationStatus>
```

Once the harvester configuration settings are configured, the harvester can be invoked and Asset metadata is harvested back to OER. Please refer to *Chapter 5, Harvesting*, for further details.

Approving Assets in OER

As described, Assets that are harvested from the testing environments will have been submitted with a status of `Submitted - Under Review`. The service will then need to be reviewed and registered. The `Registration` process will ensure that all the appropriate policies have been applied to the Asset. For details on how the service is accepted and registered, please refer to *Chapter 6, Asset Lifecycle and Workflow*, of this book, which details the Asset lifecycle and its approval processes.

Using OAG to consume a WSDL from OSR

Once a service has been deployed to the internal registry, the OAG developer can access the WSDL and create the Policy Enforcement Point (PeP) in OAG. The developers, in effect, will produce a proxy WSDL which will be used to access the service via the Oracle Enterprise API Gateway (OAG). The gateway will enforce security policies and protect Weir and Bell against threats such as XML bombs, denial of service attacks, and other external threads.

> For more information on security threads and security web practices, we recommend referring to the *Open Web Application Security Project* (`https://www.owasp.org`).

To access the service endpoint from the internal registry, the user must first configure the connections between OAG and OSR. This section describes how to configure the OAG Policy Studio to connect to OSR in order to browse the service data held in the registry. The Gateway itself does not connect to OSR but rather the Policy Studio connects to OSR in order to consume a service WSDL. The Policy Studio, however, must be connected to a Gateway in order to access the registry.

For details on how to determine the required repository URL settings, please refer to the section on Setting up the OSR Connection Details for OER. Once this configuration has been performed, log into the OAG Policy Studio and select the **Web Services Repository** node. Right-click on it and select **Browse UDDI Registry**. You will see the following screen:

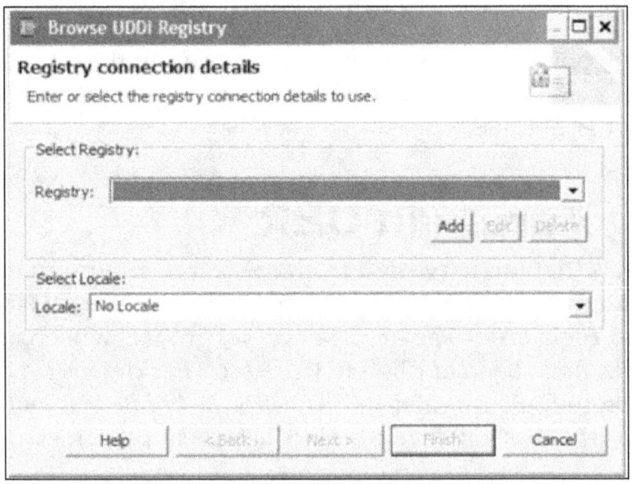

Click on the **Add** button to add a new registry connection. Select **UDDI v3**, and enter the WSDL URLs for the inquiry, publishing, and security services that were found previously into the **Inquiry URL**, **Publish URL**, and **Security URL** fields as follows:

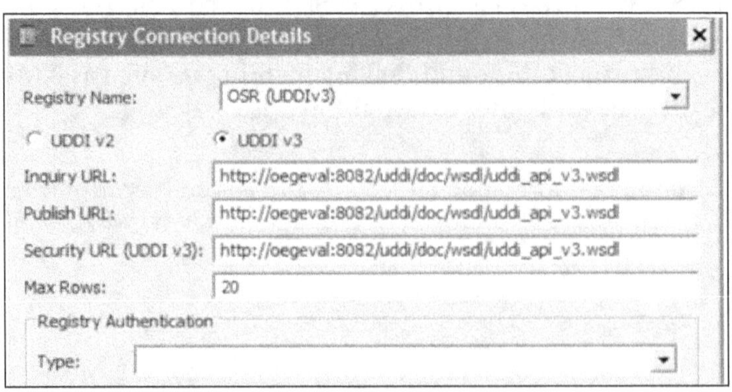

In the **Registry Authentication** fields enter the `username` and `password` for registry access.

Finally, click on **OK** and you are ready to browse OSR and consume service endpoints. This book will not provide details on how to create PePs for services and the reader should refer to the Oracle documentation that can be located at the following URL: `http://docs.oracle.com/cd/E39820_01/index.html`.

The gateway developer is able to create PePs that encompass the underlying service and the external bodies used to access the exposed services. The PePs implement protection steps, such as WS-Security, and utilize features of OAG to protect internal Assets against external threats.

Manually publishing WSDLs into the external OSR

Once the PeP is created, the developer can then enter the PeP endpoint into the external registry so that it can be consumed by the third party suppliers. Please note that it is possible to publish endpoints directly into OSR from OAG but this subject is beyond the scope of this book.

For completion, the OER administrators may wish to harvest the PeP endpoints from the external registries back to OER. Details of this can be found in *Chapter 5, Harvesting*, which details how to harvest Assets.

Summary

In this chapter, we have expanded on a use case in which Weir and Bell has employed OSR to expose services to trusted third party suppliers. Services are initially created in OER, which is used for all the aspects of design-time Governance including the enforcement of key policies and standards. Once the service is implemented and tested, it can be published to registries for consumption.

We have shown how to configure the connections between OER and OSR and demonstrated how to publish services using the Oracle Registry Repository Exchange Utility. We have also shown how to harvest deployed services using the harvester tool.

We also briefly introduced Oracle API Gateway and showed how services could be consumed from OSR in order to secure services and reduce the risk to Weir and Bell from denial of service attacks and XML bombs.

In the next chapter, we will discuss how to implement the basic runtime governance using the standard tools that ship with the Oracle SOA and Governance products. Runtime security and service monitoring are also introduced.

9 Implementing Basic Runtime Governance

This chapter will demonstrate how to implement basic Runtime Governance using the standard tools that are shipped with the Oracle SOA and Governance products. The chapter will describe how to use **Oracle Web Services manager** to implement security policies for running services, how to monitor services and policy compliance using **Oracle Enterprise Manager Fusion Middleware Control**, and also how to harvest runtime metrics into OER therefore achieving **close-loop governance**.

> This chapter assumes that **Web Service Manager Policy Manager (WSM-PM)** has been installed in the WebLogic domain alongside SOA Suite and OSB.

Use case

This use case extends *Chapter 8, Design-time Service Promotion and Discovery* and details on how to implement Runtime Governance for the deployed services. These services enable Weir & Bell to enhance its supply chain process by exposing key business services for consumption by the third parties.

Exposing services into untrusted networks for the third parties to use implies that extra security measures have to be taken into consideration, to protect Weir and Bell core systems from unauthorized access and other external threads such as:

- **Denial of Service** attacks (**DoS**)
- Malicious SOAP or REST requests
- **XPath** and XQuery injections

- XML Injections
- Cross-site encrypting (XSS)
- Other threads such as the OWASP top 10 (`https://www.owasp.org/index.php/Category:OWASP_Top_Ten_Project`)

In order to enforce security and protect internal systems from such threats, Weir and Bell decided to implement three lines of defense:

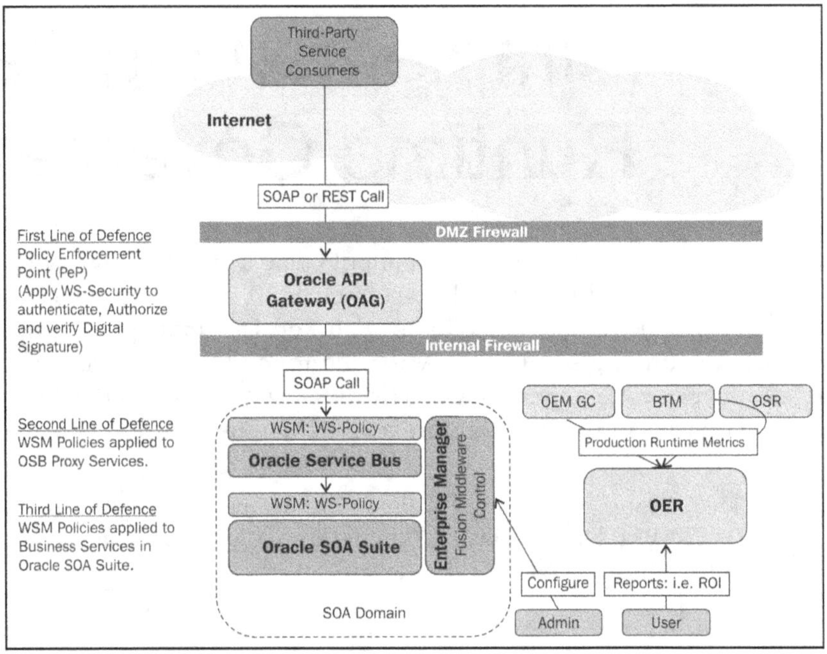

- **First Line of Defense (or Perimeter Security)**: Located in the **Demilitarized Zone** (**DMZ**), Oracle's API Gateway was introduced to serve as a **Policy Enforcement Point** (**PeP**), and protect the internal services against all major external threads. **Oracle API Gateway** (**OAG**) advanced security features such as advance throttling capability, multi-protocol conversions (for example, native transformation between SOAP and REST/JASON, among others), support for all major security standards such as WS-Security, WS-Policies, and OAuth, made it an ideal fit to support this requirement.

> This book does not cover the implementation of OAG. We recommend referring to the Oracle API Gateway site for further information on this product: `http://www.oracle.com/us/products/middleware/identity-management/api-gateway/overview/index.html`

- **Second and Third Line of Defense (or Green Zone)**: Located in the internal network, Web Service manager was introduced as an extra layer of security between the DMZ and the internal services. The idea behind adding an extra layer of security was not only to protect against systems located in the DMZ that may have been compromised, but also to protect against internal security threads. While these are usually less sophisticated than structured external threads, they still pose a considerable threat to the enterprise.

Furthermore, Weir and Bell recognized that the lifetime of a service does not end once it is deployed into production. By continuously monitoring the performance of a service and capturing meaningful runtime metrics in OER, it is possible to determine whether a service is delivering its desired value, and whether it requires either improvement or retirement.

Subsequent chapters will describe how to:

- Use Oracle Enterprise Manager Oracle Fusion Middleware Control and the WebLogic Console to monitor the health of an SOA infrastructure and its services
- Implement Web Service Manager Security policy to Oracle SOA Suite and OSB services

Harvesting of runtime metrics into OER will be covered in the next chapter.

Monitoring via consoles, an overview

Oracle delivers several consoles that can be used for the purpose of monitoring; however, each console has its purpose and its own strengths. It is therefore important to understand the capabilities and constraints within these consoles before defining a support model. The following list provides a summary of the consoles that are available out of the box within the products:

- **Oracle Enterprise Manager Fusion Middleware Control**: This console delivers an SOA infrastructure, monitoring the capabilities for a single WebLogic domain. Through this console, an administrator would be able to perform tasks such as:
    - Creation and deletion of partitions
    - Managing the composite state (activating, retiring, starting, stopping, and setting the default composite version)
    - Deletion and termination of composite instances

 - Deployment, undeployment, and redeployment actions for SOA composite applications.
 - Export of a deployed SOA composite application to a JAR file.
 - Manual initiation of SOA composite application test instances from the Test Web Service page.
 - Recovery from faults in SOA composite applications, service components, service engines, and business events.
 - Manual recovery of failed messages in BPEL processes.
 - Automated unit testing of SOA composite applications.
 - Attachment of policies to SOA composite applications, service components, and binding components.
 - Incoming and outgoing notification messages in human workflow.
 - Subscriptions to business events and testing of event publications.
 - Publication of web services to the **Universal Description, Discovery, and Integration** (**UDDI**) registry.
 - Disabling of business monitors (BPEL sensors, BPEL monitors, and BPMN measurements).
 - Storage of instance and callback message data in Oracle Coherence distributed cache on Oracle Exalogic platforms.
 - Management of the Oracle SOA Suite plugin introspected by Oracle Virtual Assembly BuilderSource: `http://docs.oracle.com/cd/E28280_01/admin.1111/e10226/soasuite_intro.htm#CEGFCGAH`.

> This console is not to be confused with **Oracle Enterprise Manager Cloud Control 12*c*** (formerly known in previous versions as **Oracle Enterprise Manager Grid Control 11*g***) that delivers multi-domain and multi-environment monitoring capabilities.
>
> For further information on monitoring SOA services with **Oracle Enterprise Manager Fusion Middleware Control** please refer to section *6 Monitoring SOA Composite Applications* of the *Oracle Fusion Middleware Administration Guide for SOA and BPM Suite* `http://docs.oracle.com/cd/E28280_01/admin.1111/e10226/soacompapp_mon.htm#CJHGFICD`

- **OSB Console**: This console delivers extended monitoring and management capabilities specifically for Oracle Service Bus. Some of the most notable capabilities of this console are:
    - Gather statistics about message invocations, errors, performance characteristics, messages passed, and SLA violations
    - Send SLA-based alerts as SNMP traps, enabling integration with third-party ESM solutions
    - Support for logging selected parts of messages for both systems operations and business auditing purposes
    - Search capabilities by extracting key information from a message and use as it as a search index

> For further information on using the OSB Console, please refer to the *Oracle Fusion Middleware Administration Guide for OSB* `http://docs.oracle.com/cd/E28280_01/admin.1111/e15867/intro_console.htm`

- **WebLogic Console**: This console is mainly used to manage a WebLogic domain, including the domain administration server and all of its managed servers and clusters. The WebLogic Console is a great tool for managing the WebLogic infrastructure and also for monitoring the server health of the applications running in it. However, the console is not focused on managing an SOA infrastructure and, although monitoring services is possible, administrators should use the more intuitive Enterprise Manager Fusion Middleware Control. So in summary, this tool should be used for administration of WebLogic domains and its servers and clusters, but when it comes to managing services, Enterprise Manager is the recommended option.

> For further information on the WebLogic Console, please refer to the WebLogic *Administration Console Online Help* `http://docs.oracle.com/cd/E23943_01/apirefs.1111/e13952/core/index.html`

- **JRockit Mission Control**: JRockit Mission Control is a utility that comes as part of the JRockit JDK and that allows for in-depth monitoring of Java Virtual Machines. It includes tools to monitor, manage, profile, and eliminate memory leaks in your Java application without introducing the performance overhead normally associated with these types of tools. This tool is usually used during performance tuning of your system or for general monitoring purposes of the JRockit JVM's supporting the different SOA infrastructures.

> For further information on the JRockit Mission Control please refer to `http://docs.oracle.com/cd/E15289_01/doc.40/e15067/intro.htm#CEGIAGIG`

- **Business Activity Monitoring (BAM)**: Unlike any of the previously mentioned consoles, BAM is really an application that delivers a comprehensive framework to create user-friendly dashboards that are updated in near real-time. The main difference between BAM and any other console is that in order for BAM to deliver useful content, sensors need to be added into the desired SOA composites that are specifically configured to gather (or sense) information, and send it to a BAM data source that would then be used to generate different dashboards with any desired different dimension. BAM is a powerful tool if used properly, and it can be used for a series of use cases such as monitoring Key Performance Indicators in near real-time, service SLAs, and any other meaningful business-driven dashboard.

> For further information on BAM please refer to the Oracle Business Activity Monitoring documentation `http://www.oracle.com/technetwork/middleware/bam/documentation/documentation-089589.html`

In addition to the consoles mentioned previously, there are two additional tools that although do not come as part of the main SOA Suite product installation, do add a lot of value to an SOA Governance implementations:

- **Oracle Enterprise Manager Enterprise Edition**: OEM Grind Control 11*g* (OEM GC) or its latest version OEM Cloud Control 12*c* (OEM CC) is a powerful tool, to monitor an entire Oracle solution and all of its technology stacks. Depending on what part of the stack is to be monitored, different management packs may be required. Management packs are add-ons to the base product, and enable OEM to fully monitor and manage different technologies.

- **Oracle Business Transaction Manager (BTM)**: This tool allows for the SOA business transactions to be monitored end-to-end, regardless of which system is executing the transaction. By making use of the observers deployed into the different systems involved in operating a transaction (for example, OSB, SOA Suite, JMS queues, J2EE applications, or even .NET applications), BTM generates at runtime a full end-to-end view of the transaction and then allows for different monitoring capabilities such as SLA alerts, exception handling to mention a few, to be configured.

> Both tools will be covered in greater detail in the next chapter.

Monitoring services with Fusion Middleware Control

This console delivers a wide variety of functions that can be used to monitor and manage the SOA composites through the entire lifecycle, once a service has been deployed. It can also be used to monitor performance of the server using several metrics.

> Unfortunately this tool cannot be used to monitor the OSB services. For this, you will have to use the OSB console or other tools that will be cover later in the chapter.

In this section we will focus on showing how to:

- Monitor the health of the SOA infrastructure
- Monitor the performance of SOA composites
- Monitor composite instances

Monitoring the health of the SOA Infrastructure

To monitor the health status of the different managed servers within a specific SOA WebLogic domain, follow these steps:

1. Log in to Fusion Middleware Control with the WebLogic user from the URL: `http://<SOA admin server host>:<port>/em`

2. On successful authentication, the landing page will show a dashboard of the SOA infrastructure components within that WebLogic domain. The dashboard on the left-hand side shows the health of the individual applications deployed on the servers, whereas the dashboard on the right-hand side shows the status of the managed servers supporting all SOA applications. In this example, the BAM managed server is down and therefore is shown with a red arrow:

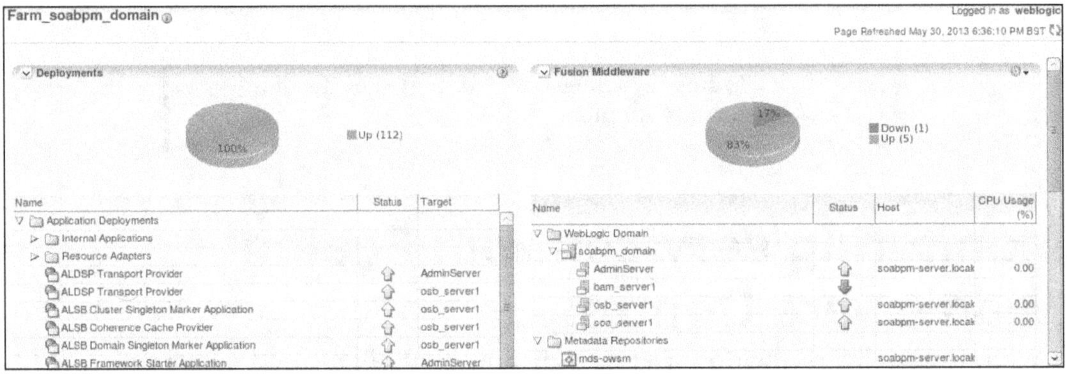

3. Click on an individual application or server, to drill down into further levels of detail. For example, click on the **soa_server1** link to see further details regarding this server's performance such as **Request Processing Time (ms)** or **Requests (per minute)**:

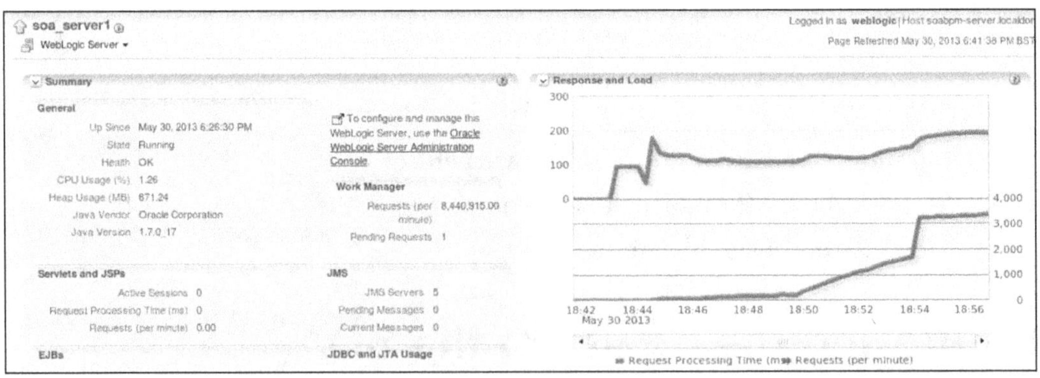

Monitoring SOA Composites performance

Composite performance can also be monitored within Fusion Middleware Control. To do so:

1. From the main **Farm** menu, expand the **SOA** folder. Then right-click on the **soa-infra** item and select **Monitoring**, and then select either **Performance Summary** or **Request Processing**.

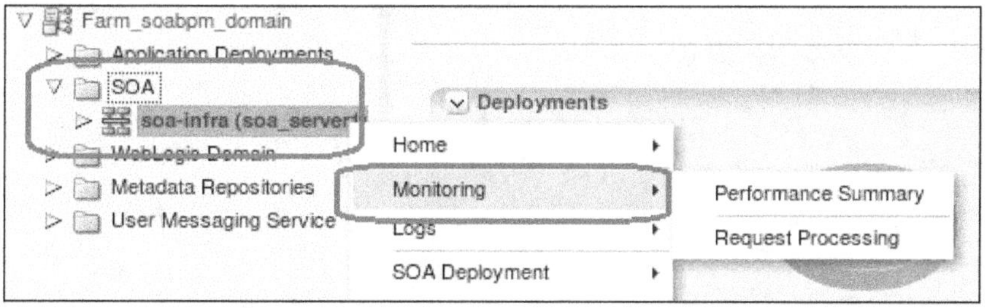

2. If **Performance Summary** is selected, then a page with two main dashboards will appear. One displays the **Total number of composites since server startup** and the other shows the **Total number of faults since server startup**. To show more metrics in the graphs, the **Metric Palette** can be opened by clicking on the **Show Metric Palette** button. From the **Metric Palette**, it is possible to select a wide variety of metrics such as **Composite Policies**, **Composite Instances** among many others:

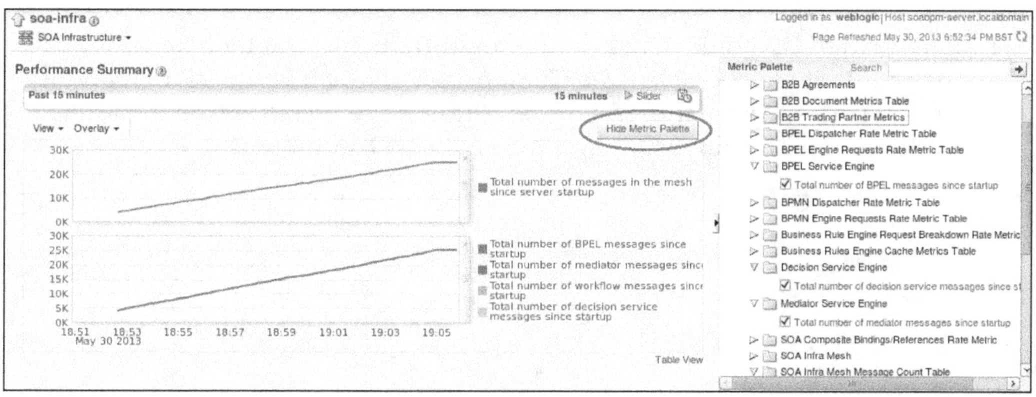

3. If **Request Processing** is selected then a page with three main containers will appear, showing different statistics for the **Service Engines** (for example, BPEL, BPMN, and Mediator engines), **Service Infrastructure**, and **Binding Components** (for example, inbound and outbound services and JCA adapters).

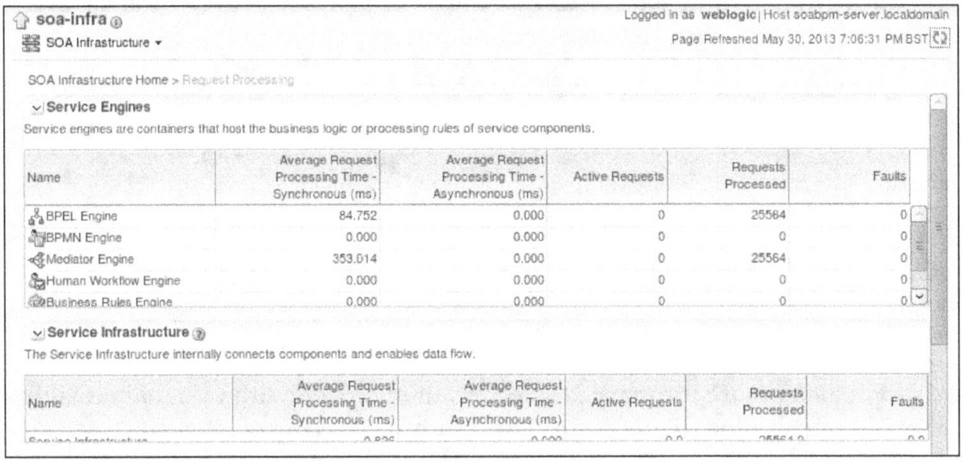

Monitoring SOA Composite instances

SOA composite instances can also be monitored, visualized, searched, or managed from within Fusion Middleware Control. To do so:

1. Under the **SOA** folder, click on the **soa-infra** item. And then on the right-hand side container, select the **Composite** for which you wish to monitor the instances. Alternatively, you can click on the **Instances** tab to monitor all instances for all composites available in the SOA domain.

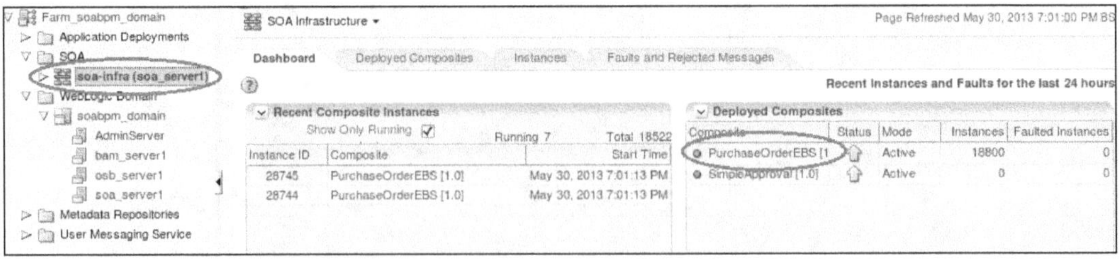

2. If you click on an individual composite, then the composite main page will open showing the **Dashboard** tab. From this tab, a summary of recent and faulted instances is available. However, by clicking on the **Instances** tab, it is possible to conduct advanced searches on all available instances (and their state) for the composite, and based on specific criteria such as time, different IDs, and even composite name.

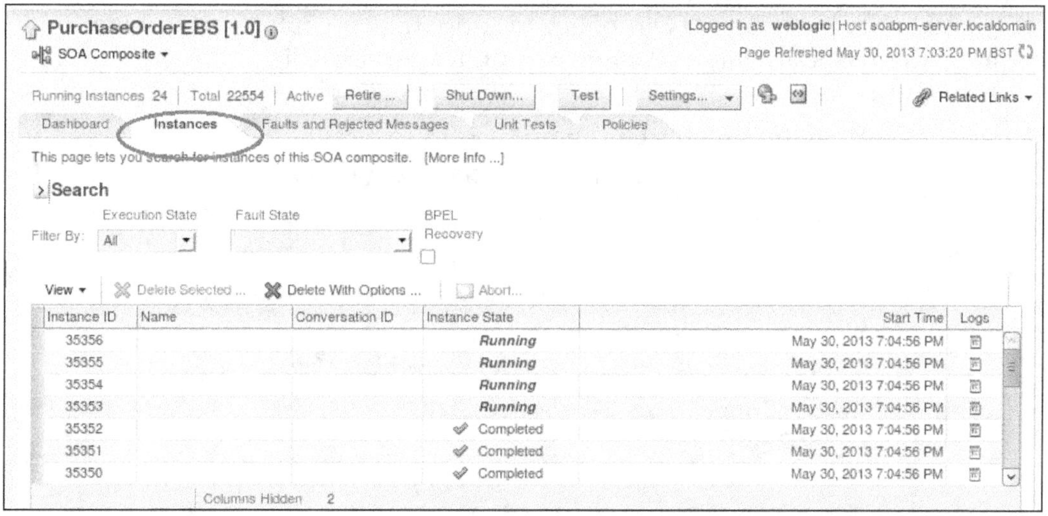

WSM, a quick overview

Oracle Web Services Manager is a component of the SOA Suite that allows the central implementation and enforcement of policies to service endpoints, service engines, and Java services in general. Policies that can be implemented include:

- WS-Policies
- WS-Security
- WS-Addressing (for call backs)
- WS-Transactions
- MTOM
- WS-RM
- And also custom policies

Policies can be attached at design-time using JDeveloper or at runtime using Oracle Enterprise Manager Fusion Middleware Control. Some policies (for example, security policies) are best applied through Fusion Middleware Control as through this console, using policy sets, policies can be attached globally to all composites deployed. Other policies that are more ad-hoc (aimed at addressing specific use cases) are best attached through JDeveloper. For example, an MTOM policy is usually attached during design-time stages, when a designer or developer might wish to make use or try an MTOM policy to support, in an optimized fashion, a requirement to handle a large attachment within a service call.

> For further information on WSM we recommend:
>
> *OFM Security and Administrator's Guide for Web Services*
>
> `http://docs.oracle.com/cd/E28280_01/web.1111/b32511/toc.htm`
>
> For further information on developing custom policies please refer to:
>
> *OFM Extensibility Guide for Oracle Web Services Manager*
>
> `http://docs.oracle.com/cd/E28280_01/web.1111/e13882/toc.htm`

Implementing WSM policies in Composites

In the following example we will show how **policy sets** are used to attach policies to multiple composites at once, and also how policies can be individually attached.

1. Log into OEM Fusion Middleware Control with the WebLogic user.
2. Expand the **WebLogic Domain** menu and right-click on the **soabpm_domain option**. Select **Web Services** and then **Policy Sets**:

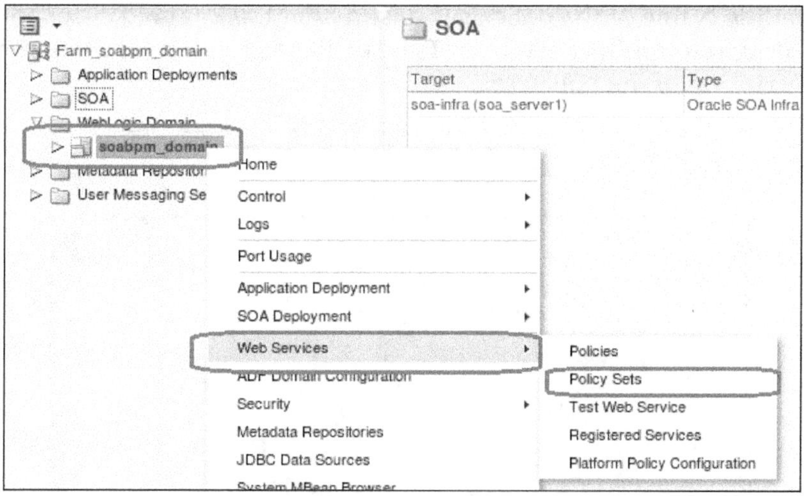

3. Once the SOA domain page opens, click on the **Create** button to create a new policy set. This will launch a wizard that will walk through the steps required to create the policy set:

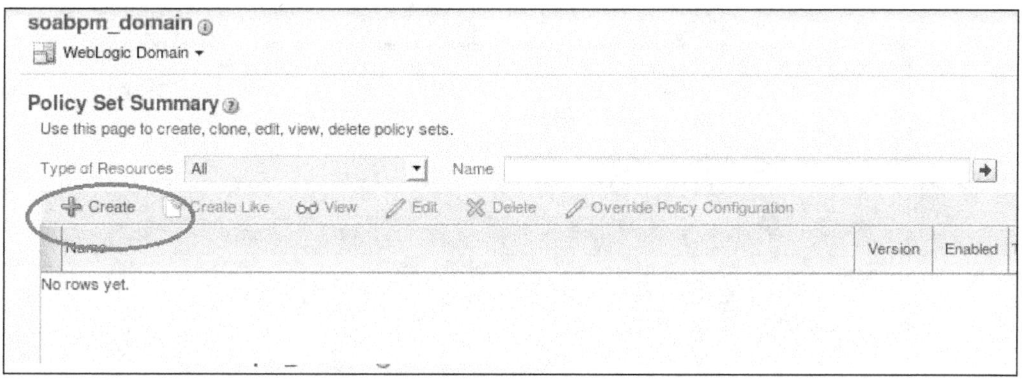

4. Enter the **Name** of the policy set, ensure that the **Enabled** checkbox is selected, select **SOA Service** as **Type of Resources,** and if desired enter a **Description** of the policy set:

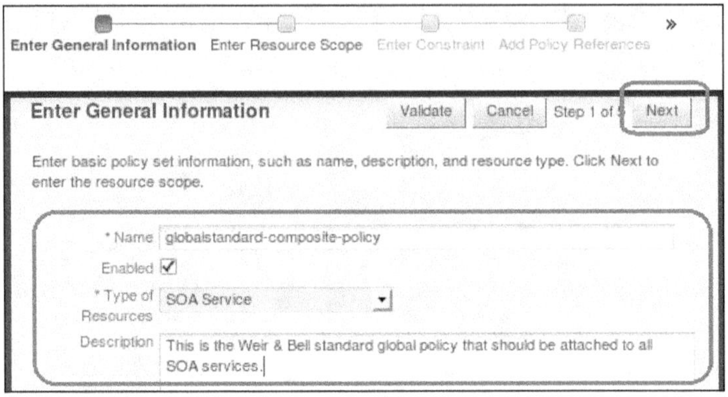

5. In the **Enter Resource Scope** page, define the pattern that will be evaluated by the SOA Suite to determine whether the policy set is to be applied at runtime to a composite:

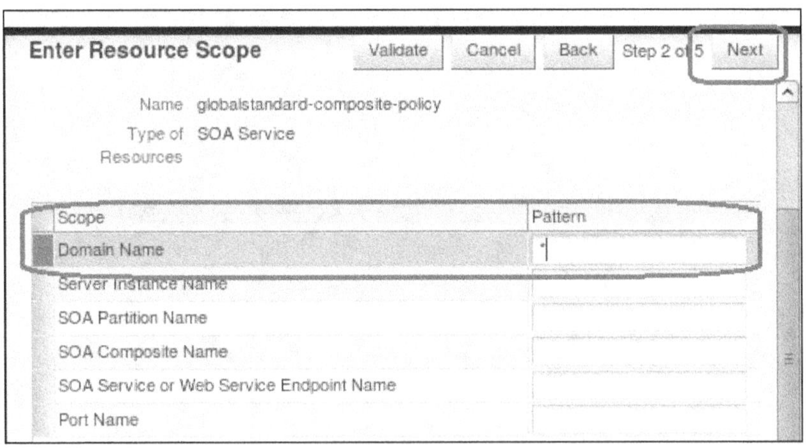

> Any composite for which the pattern evaluation results in true, will be applied with this policy set. In our example, we used a wildcard (*) so all the composites deployed in the SOA Suite server are applied with this policy set. This is a powerful feature since it allows a single set of policies to be consistently applied to a set of composites, thus taking this concern away from development teams.

6. If desired, define the constraint expressions that should be evaluated. Constraints are used to specify environment-specific constraints, such as applying a policy set depending on whether a service is exposed to an internal or external network. In our example, we did not have such a requirement so we avoided creating constraints by simply clicking on **Next**:

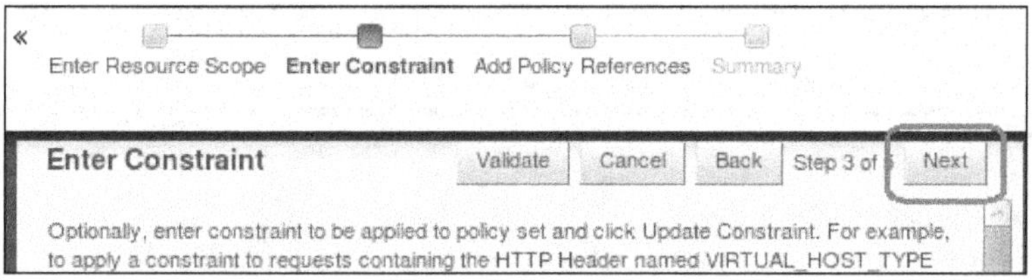

> For further information on constraints please refer to the *Specifying Run-time Constraints in Policy Sets* section of *OFM Security and Administrator's Guide for Web Services*.
>
> `http://docs.oracle.com/cd/E28280_01/web.1111/b32511/policy_sets.htm#CIHCJDFB`

7. Scroll down to the **Available Policies** section and select the policy or policies that should be attached to the composites. Click on **Attach** on each policy selected:

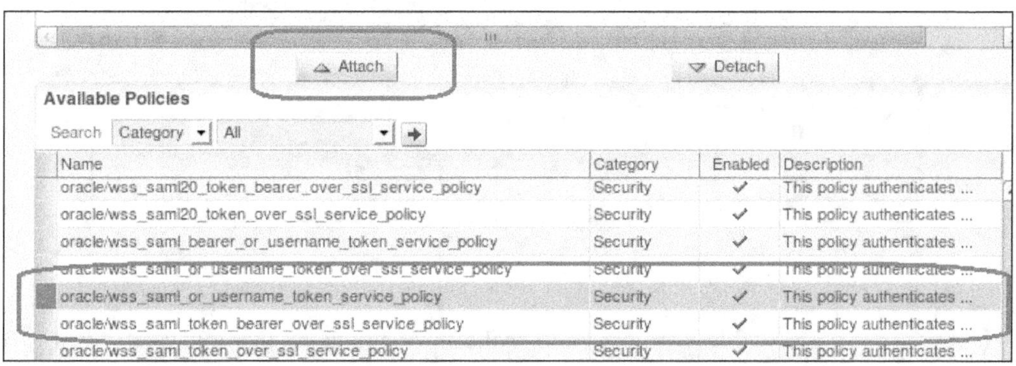

> In our example, we are attaching the policy **wss_saml_or_username_token_service_policy**. This policy will allow for either a SAML token or a username and password to be passed in the security header of a SOAP message.

8. Once all desired policies have been attached, click on **Next**:

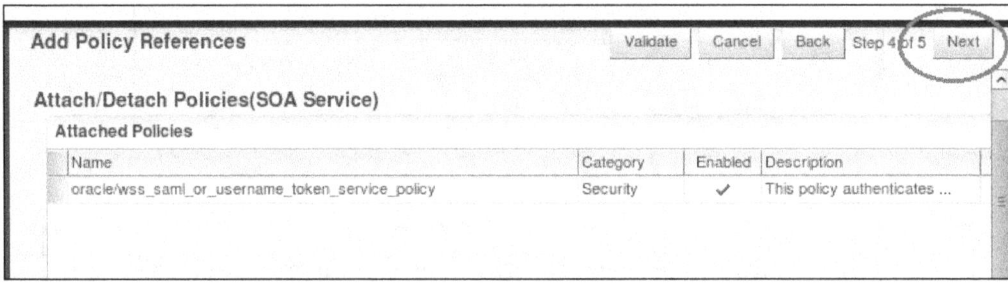

9. Review the **Summary** of the Policy Set, and finally click on **Save**:

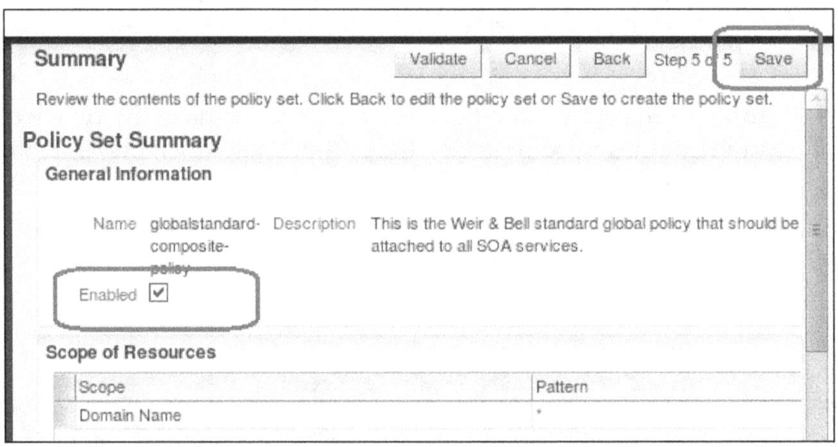

> It is possible to go back and make amendments to the policy set, before it is actually saved.

10. After saving the policy set, a yellow information box should appear in which you are informed that the policy was successfully created:

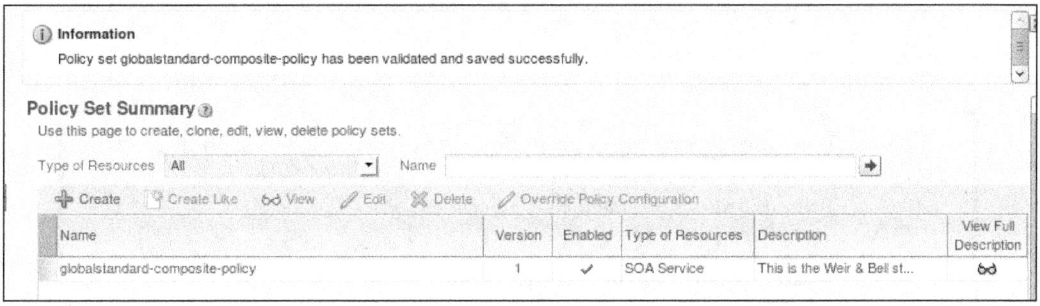

11. Click on any composite available within an SOA partition. In our example, we want to verify if the recently created policy set was applied to the composite **PurchaseOrderEBS**. To do so, navigate to the composite page, click on the **Policies** tab, and then from the **Attached To/Detach From** menu select a service endpoint (for example, **PurchaseOrderEBS**). By selecting this option it is possible to see what policies have been globally or directly attached to the service endpoint:

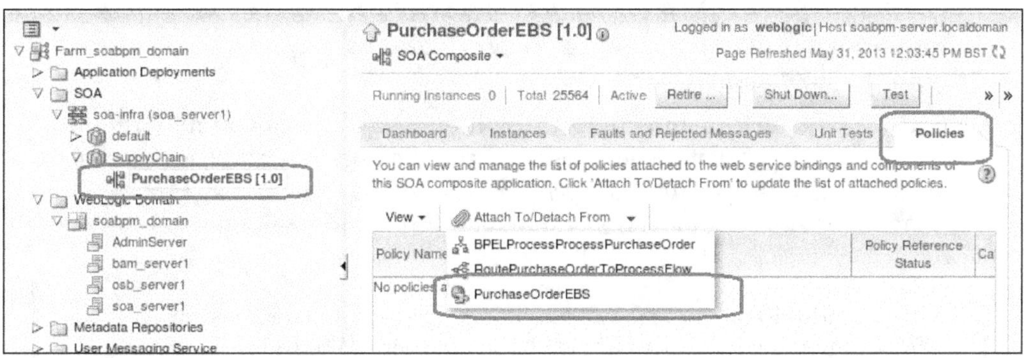

12. A pop-up window will open, showing what policies are globally or locally attached. This shows how all policies attached to the policy set have been attached to the service endpoint:

> From this page it is also possible to directly attach policies into the service endpoints. It is important to note that, by default, a policy that is directly attached takes precedence over a policy that is globally attached.

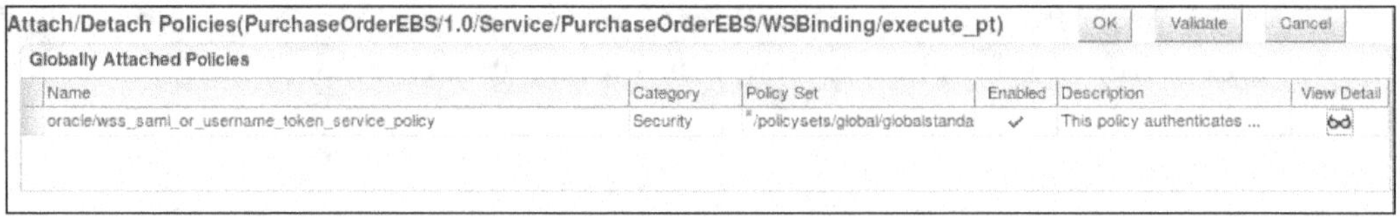

> For more information on Policy Sets please refer to section *9 Creating and Managing Policy Sets* of the *OFM Security and Administrator's Guide for Web Services*.
>
> `http://docs.oracle.com/cd/E28280_01/web.1111/b32511/policy_sets.htm`

Implementing WSM Policies in OSB

Note that, before Oracle Web Services Manager 11*g* can be implemented to secure OSB services, certain pre-configuration steps must be done. These steps are:

- Ensuring that WSM and Fusion Middleware Control are properly configured to work with OSB. For this you may refer to section *50.2 Setting Up and Using Oracle Web Services Manager with Oracle Service Bus* of the Developers Guide for OSB: `http://docs.oracle.com/cd/E28280_01/dev.1111/e15866/owsm.htm#CHDDEAJG`.
- Creating a Keystore and configuring it on EM. For this you may refer to the *Configuring Keystores for Message Protection* section of *OFM Security and Administrator's Guide for Web Services*: `http://docs.oracle.com/cd/E28280_01/web.1111/b32511/setup_config.htm#BAJJHHII`.

> Additionally, the following link is a good video demonstration showing how to secure OSB services using WSM 11*g*: `https://blogs.oracle.com/owsm/entry/osb_security_using_owsm_11g`

Note that the following sections assume that this configuration has been successfully completed.

Expanding on the example described in the previous section, *Implementing WSM Policies in Composites*, we will demonstrate how a WSM **username client policy** can be attached to the **OSB Business Service** consuming the PurchaseOrderEBS composite, and subsequently how to secure the **OSB Proxy Service** fronting the same business service.

Configuring the policy in a Business Service

Sometimes, it is necessary to call the SOA composites from OSB for which WSM security policies have been applied. In these scenarios, it is easy to comply with such policies by attaching the equivalent client policy of the server policy applied to the target composite. In the following example, we will show how to attach the **wss_username_token_client_policy** to an OSB Business Service that consumes an SOA composite that has been secured with the **wss_saml_or_username_token_service_policy**.

> Although it is possible to attach WSM policies using the Eclipse IDE, in this example we will show how policies can be attached at runtime using the OSB console.

1. Log in to the OSB console using the WebLogic user and URL: `http://<osb managed server url>:<osb managed server port>/sbconsole`
2. On the top right-hand side of the screen, under the **Change Center** section, **Create** a new session:

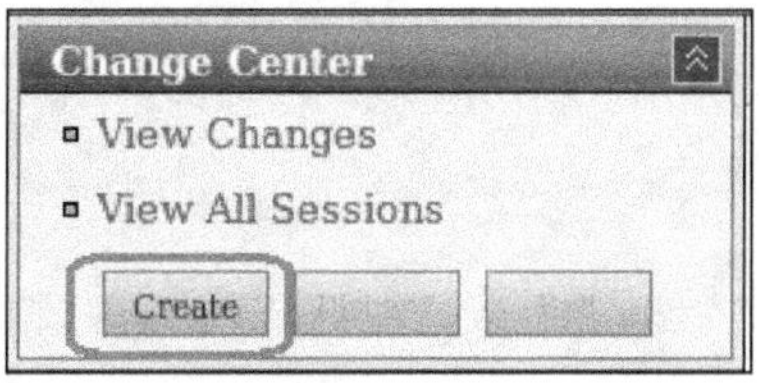

3. Under the **Operations** menu, click on **Resource Browser**:

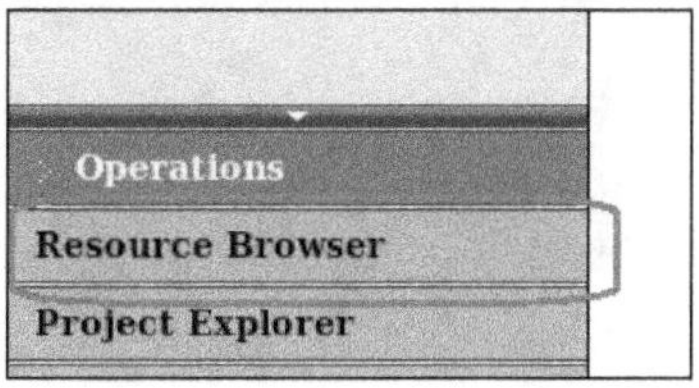

4. Under the **Service** section located on the right-hand side of the screen, click on the **Business Services** link, and then on the central page click for the business service to which the policy will be applied:

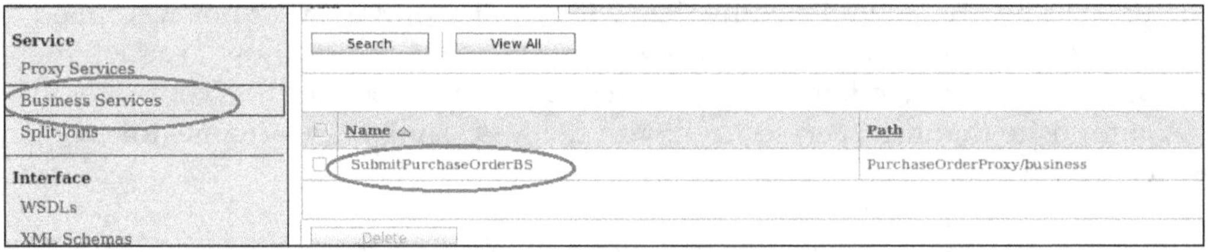

5. Click on the **Policies** tab. Ensure that the option **From OWSM Policy Store** under **OWSM Policies** is selected, and then click on the **Add** button:

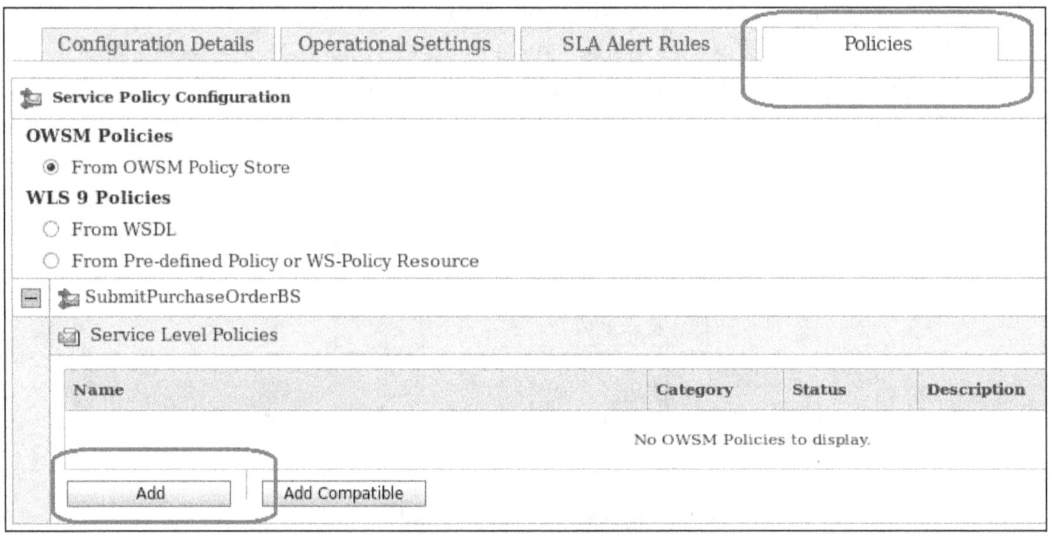

6. Search for the policy you wish to be attached. In our example, we searched using wildcards (`*`) for any WSM policy that contained the text `username` in the policy name. Once a policy has been selected click on **Submit**:

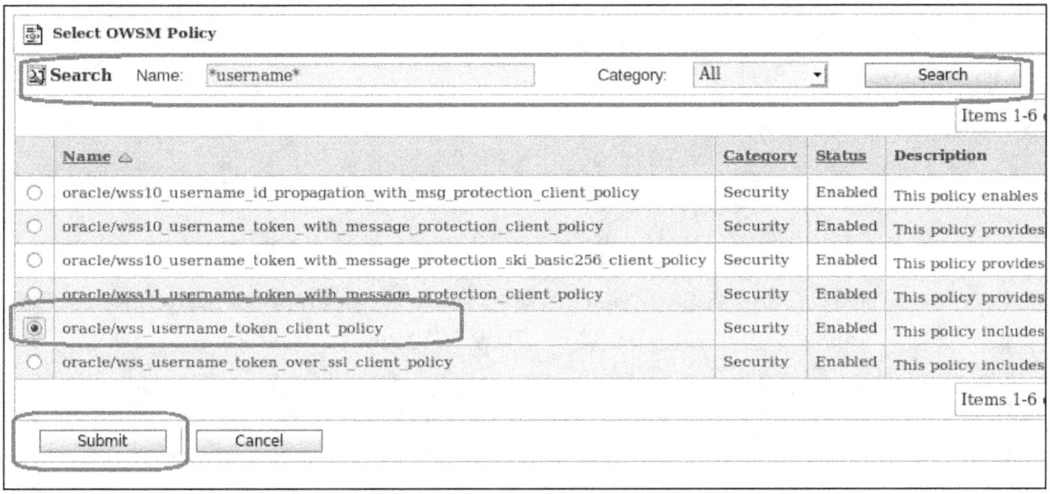

7. Ensure that the selected policy appears under the **Service Level Policies** section. Then click on **Update**:

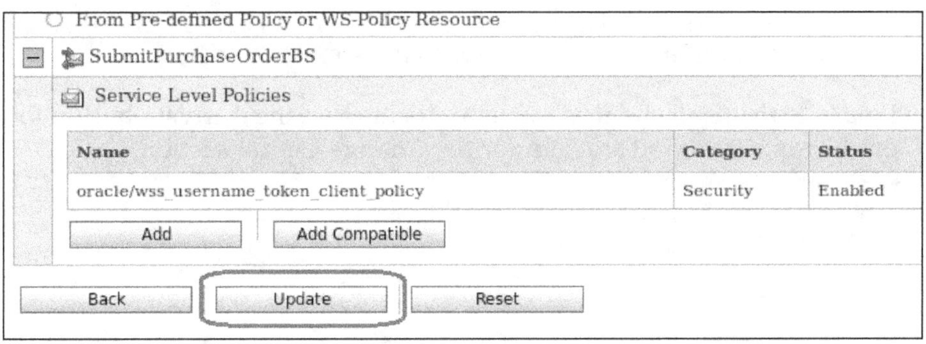

8. Click on the **Security** tab. In the **csf-key** field, enter the name of the key used when configuring WSM to work for OSB. Then click on **Update**:

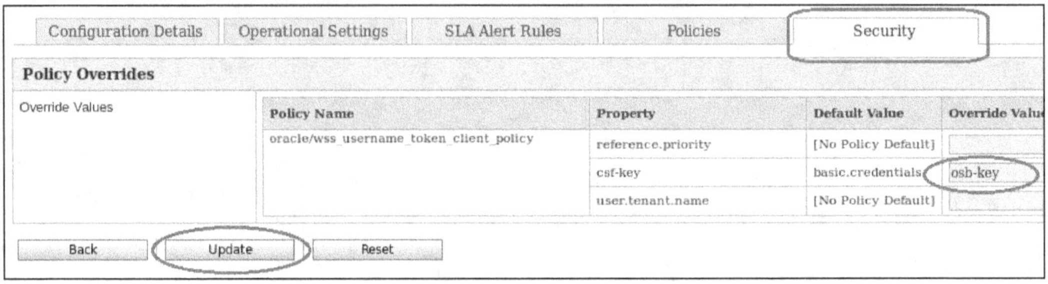

> This section assumes that WSM has been configured to work with OSB. For information on how to do this you may refer to:
>
> Section *50.2 Setting Up and Using Oracle Web Services Manager with Oracle Service Bus* of the *Developers Guide for OSB*:
>
> `http://docs.oracle.com/cd/E28280_01/dev.1111/e15866/owsm.htm#CHDDEAJG`
>
> Section *Configuring Keystores for Message Protection* of the *OFM Security and Administrator's Guide for Web Services*:
>
> `http://docs.oracle.com/cd/E28280_01/web.1111/b32511/setup_config.htm#BAJJHHII`

9. Finally activate all changes made by clicking on the **Activate** button located on the top right-hand side, under the **Change Center** section.

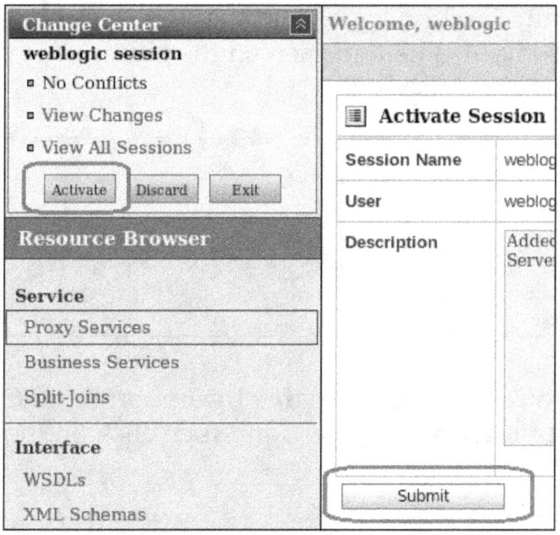

The implementation of WSM Client Policies allows OSB Business Service to comply (without any extra coding) with policies implemented in target services. In this example, the **WSM Username Client Policy** allows the OSB Business Service to invoke an SOA Composite that is secured using the WSM SAML or Username Service Policy. The application of this policy does not require any complex mappings or coding, in order to include the username token into the SOAP header of the message.

Configuring the policy in an OSB Proxy Service

The next step is to implement a second line of defense, by applying a WSM security policy to the OSB Proxy Service. This will add an additional layer of security, therefore ensuring that any calls coming from the DMZ (for example, the API Gateway) are from the trusted parties.

1. Log in to the OSB console using the WebLogic user and the URL: `http://<osb managed server url>:<osb managed server port>/sbconsole`.
2. On the top right-hand side of the screen under the **Change Center** section, **Create** a new session.
3. Under the **Operations** menu click on **Resource Browser**.

4. Under the **Service** section located on the right-hand side of the screen, click on the **Proxy Services** link and then on the center page and click on the proxy service to apply the policy to:

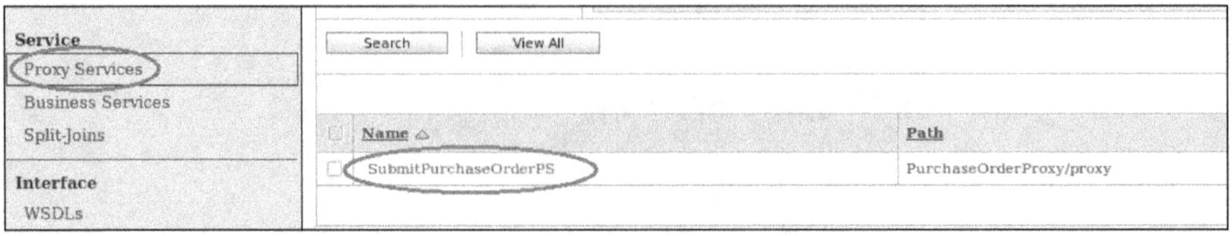

5. Click on the **Policies** tab. Ensure that the option **From OWSM Policy Store** under **OWSM Policies** is selected, and then click on the **Add** button:

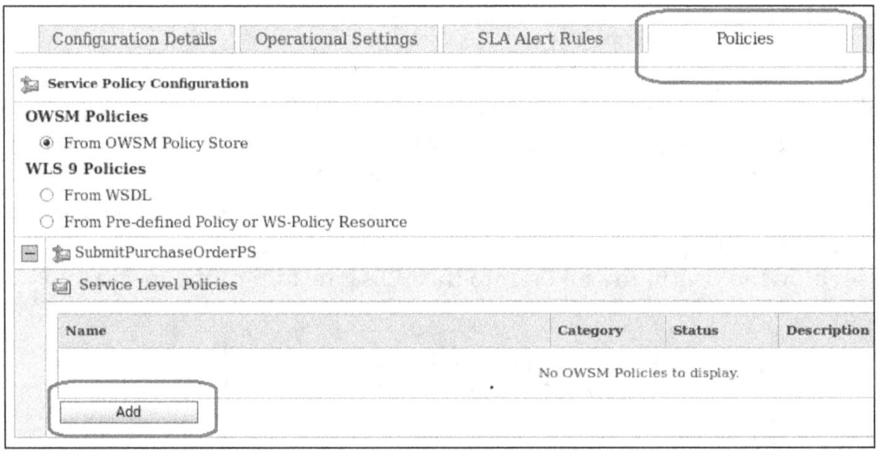

6. Search for the policy you wish to be attached. In our example, we searched using wildcards (*) for any WSM policy that contained the text **username** in the policy name. Once a policy has been selected click on **Submit**:

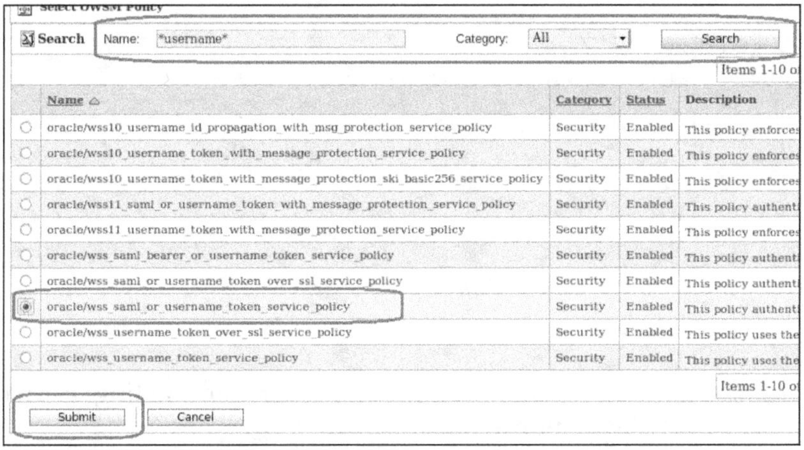

> In this case, we are attaching a service policy instead of a client policy.

7. Ensure that the selected policy appears under the **Service Level Policies** section. Then click on **Update**:

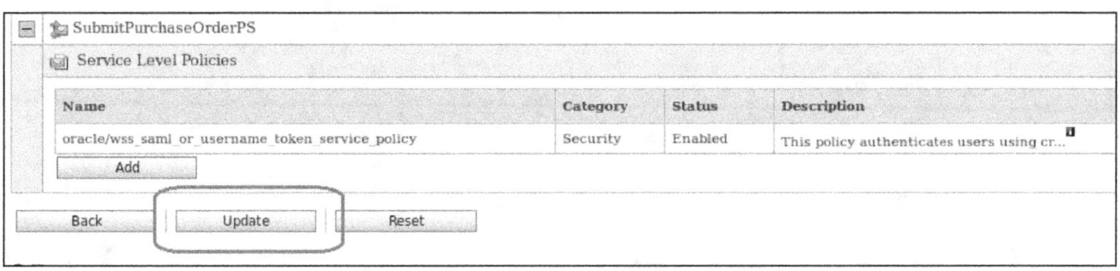

8. Activate all changes made by clicking on the **Active** button located on the top right-hand side under the **Change Center** section.

9. Test the proxy service using SoapUI or a similar tool. The following example shows that, by making an invocation to the proxy service using a non-existent username in the WS-Security username token that OSB responds with a SOAP fault:

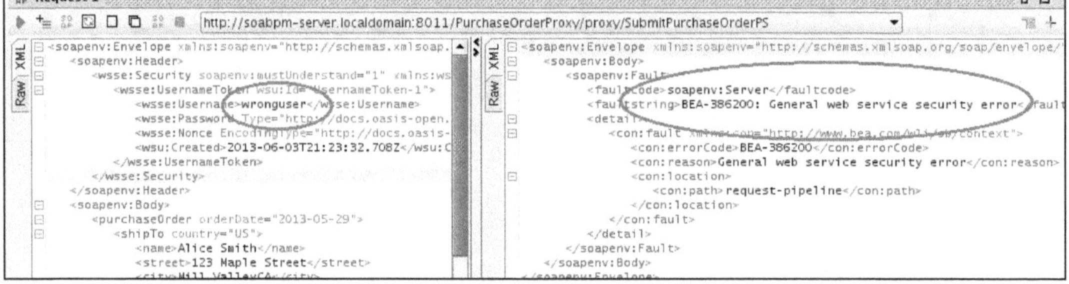

10. The next example demonstrates that by sending an existing username, we get a successful SOAP response from OSB:

> In order for the OSB to send a successful response, the WSM service policies attached to both the Proxy Service as well as the composite endpoint must have resulted in a successful evaluation.

Summary

This chapter has described how the standard features available out of the box within the SOA Suite product can be utilized and configured to address complex use case requirements. It has also discussed the different consoles that are available with a basic installation of the product, and what the benefits and purposes of these consoles are.

Furthermore, we have described in detail how Oracle Fusion Middleware Enterprise Control can be used to now monitor the performance of the SOA domain and the composites within it. We have also discussed how **Web Service Manager Policies** and Policy Sets can be applied to different service endpoints.

This chapter has also shown how Web Service Manager Policies can be implemented in **Oracle Service Bus Proxy** and **Business Services**, and highlighted what dependencies must be completed in order to achieve such a configuration.

The next chapter will describe how Runtime Governance can be extended with the implementation of **Oracle Enterprise Manager** (**OEM**) and **Business Transaction Manager** (**BTM**).

10
Extending Runtime Governance

This chapter focuses on additional tooling such as **Oracle Enterprise Manager** and **Business Transaction Management**. It shows how they can be used to further enhance runtime Governance to deliver a comprehensive and complete solution to SOA infrastructure monitoring including SLA notifications and alerts and service management, amongst others.

The chapter will also describe how to configure OER to capture runtime metrics generated from these tools that can be used to enrich the Asset metadata available within OER. The chapter will also show how this data can be used to tune and improve Assets and therefore close the loop between runtime and design-time Governance.

> Note that, for the practical sections within this chapter, it is assumed that there is an environment available that contains an installation of OEM 12*c* and SOA Suite 11*g*. For details about the OEM 12*c* installation steps please refer to the **OEM 12 Basic Installation Guide** `http://docs.oracle.com/cd/E24628_01/install.121/e22624/toc.htm`.

Use case

Just as with many other organizations, Weir & Bell Telecom used a wide variety of tools to monitor their technological landscape and provide support to their IT operations and ITIL processes. However, the fact that many different tools were being used presented its own challenges since it made business-as-usual tasks, such as fault detection, problem solving and root cause analysis, and creating a service ticket far more difficult than they should be.

Weir & Bell recognized that, by not having a unified and integrated set of tools to support their IT systems, they were failing to realize a huge opportunity to save costs. Some of the reasons why this was believed to be true included:

- Each layer of the stack was monitored using its own specific tool. Therefore, support staff had to view several consoles in order to troubleshoot an issue.
- Each environment (development, system test, user acceptance test, preproduction, production, DR, and others) had its own set of instances of the monitoring tools for each layer of the stack. This further complicated troubleshooting since, for example, OEM Fusion Middleware Control is only capable of monitoring a single WebLogic domain and OEM Database Control is only capable of monitoring a single instance of an Oracle database. For this reason a support engineer had to look at each environment's specific console in order to detect issues as there was not a single view across all environments.
- While scripts were utilized to automate many troubleshooting tasks across the environment, with time, maintenance of the plethora of scripts became a problem is its own right with very few individuals possessing the knowledge to modify such scripts. Furthermore, the scripts lacked the capability to correlate issues across the layers of the technology stack.
- When issues were identified, tickets had to be manually created in the service management tool; Weir & Bell used Remedy for this purpose.

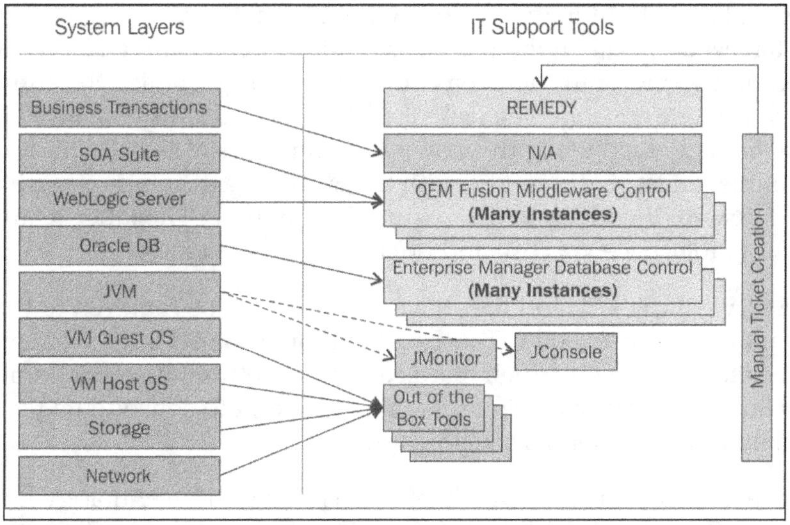

Moreover, because a SOA transaction can spam several systems, issues were exponentially magnified when supporting a SOA infrastructure. For example, on those occasions when service consumers received SOAP Faults, several teams within the Weir & Bell IT support function had to correlate errors across multiple consoles in order to identify the root of the problem, as illustrated in the following diagram:

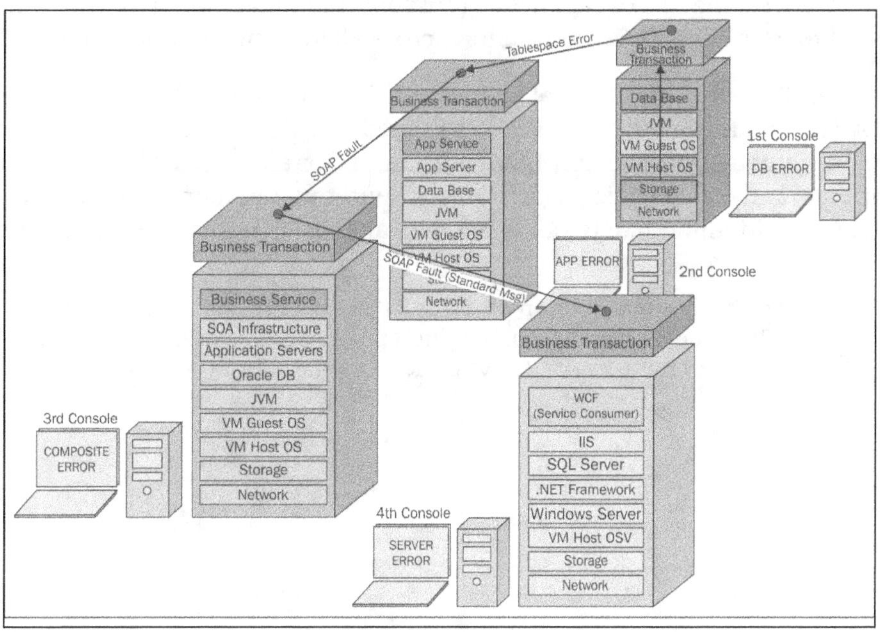

Each team could see a fault in its own individual console; for example the DBAs could see a tablespace issue in the DB server and the SOA team an error caused by an application service, but there was no capability to visualize the entire SOA transaction in a single console. The lack of such global visibility meant that several teams had to engage, each using their own tools and consoles, in order to conclude that, for example, an issue did not lie with the SOA infrastructure or with an application, but with the file system housing the database. The latter resulted in an error because a tablespace was full and not able to autoextend.

The unnecessary complexity and the sheer number of steps required to troubleshoot an issue meant that Weir & Bell's IT support and operational costs were much higher than they needed to be. Weir & Bell realized that something had to be done to reduce costs and to improve service levels and so they decided to consolidate their IT support and monitoring tools as a key priority.

Given the increased footprint of Oracle products in their IT technology landscape, Weir & Bell architects evaluated the different Oracle solutions available that could help solve their particular support and monitoring requirements. It did not take long to identify that Oracle Enterprise Manager (OEM) configured with a number of **Management Packs** had the capability to address all of Weir & Bell requirements.

The SOA Management Pack was of particular interest given that it promised to deliver the features needed around monitoring several SOA domains within a single console; moreover, the use of Business Transaction Management (BTM) would allow Weir & Bell to monitor a SOA transaction across all systems involved in it.

In addition, OEM came with several connectors that allowed OEM to integrate with external service management tools such as Remedy, which was used as the ITIL service management tool. The OEM Remedy connector allows OEM to automatically create, update, and/or close tickets in Remedy, without any manual intervention. This feature alone could immediately deliver significant cost benefits to Weir & Bell.

> For further information please refer to the **Plug-ins** tab of the OEM 12*c* Cloud Control Documentation page `http://docs.oracle.com/cd/E24628_01/nav/plugins.htm`

Monitoring solution

The first step for Weir & Bell IT operations and their architecture team was to map each layer of the stack against the system responsible for its management and monitoring. The following layers were considered (from bottom to top):

- **Network**: Basically the seven layers of the OSI model. Anything from physical cabling, switching and routing appliances, firewalls, IDS and IPS, load balancers, firewalls, and other network devices.
- **Storage**: The Storage Area Network (SAN) and its related infrastructure such as the Switched fabric and iSCSI SAN devices.
- **VM host OS**: The underlying virtualization platform that supports the deployment of virtual machine instances.
- **VM guest OS**: Individual virtual machine instances and its operating system.
- **JVM**: One or more Java Virtual Machines.
- **Oracle DB**: One or several Oracle databases.
- **WebLogic Server**: One or several WebLogic Servers.
- **SOA Suite**: One or several SOA suite domains.
- **Business transactions**: A single atomic transaction that spans several systems.

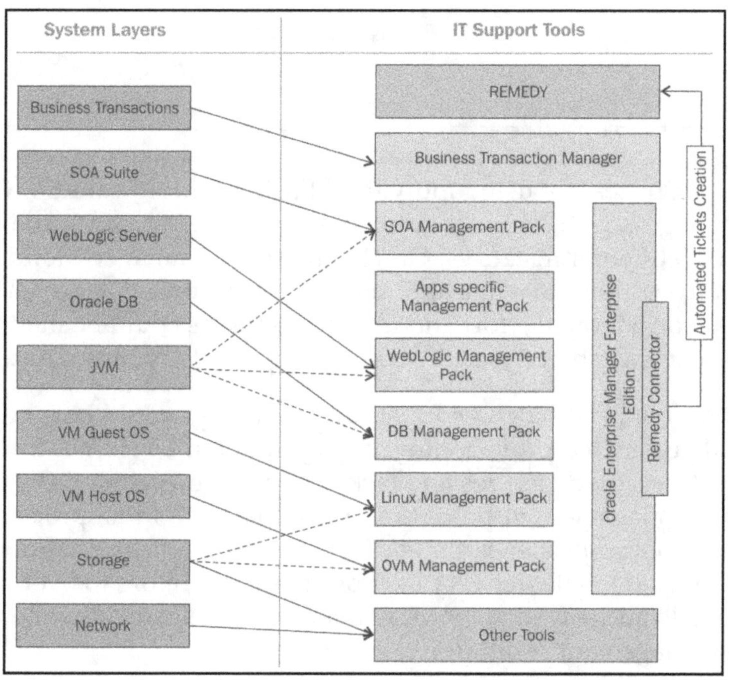

As the diagram suggests, Weir & Bell opted to use a variety of Management Packs to monitor the different layers of the stack. The Remedy Connector was used to integrate OEM with their existing service management solution and therefore automate tasks around ticket creation. However, Weir & Bell opted to retain their existing tooling for the network (bottom) layer.

OEM implementation

To monitor their SOA Suite domains and other WebLogic systems, Weir & Bell produced the following high-level architecture:

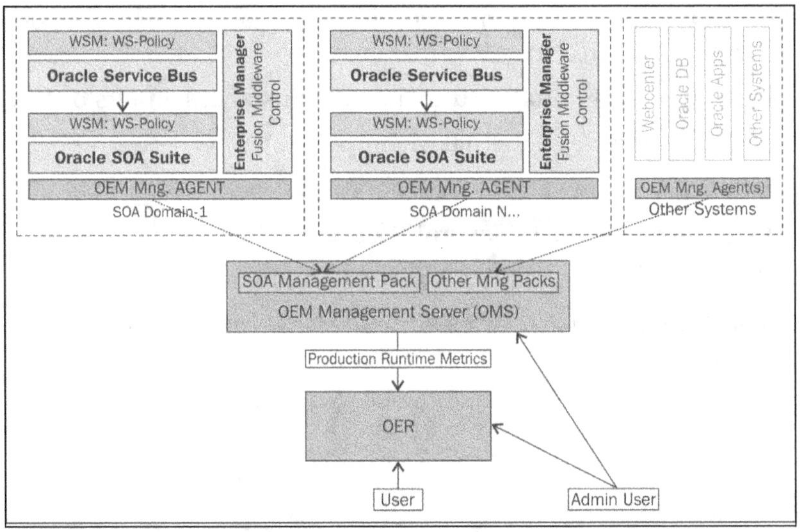

The idea was that, instead of using individual Fusion Middleware EM Control instances to manage each SOA Suite domain, the Oracle Databases and other WebLogic and WebCenter instances, Oracle Enterprise Manager Cloud Control 12*c* would be used to centrally manage and monitor all of these instances. Weir & Bell recognized that considerable effort and thus cost savings could be made by simply avoiding having to switch between several consoles to do typical day-to-day tasks.

Furthermore, Weir & Bell recognized that further savings could be made by making use of the OEM automated provisioning, configuration management, and patch deployment features. Inefficiencies and lack of control in Weir & Bell's provisioning and configuration management processes meant that individual projects had to deal with a series of inconsistencies and discrepancies between environments. These issues often led to late delivery of projects and therefore to over spend. The use of OEM to help address some of these issues was welcomed by the project and configuration management community.

Further details regarding OEM and its features will be covered in the section *Oracle Enterprise Manager overview*.

BTM implementation

In order to solve the issue of visibility over a business transaction that spanned multiple systems, Weir & Bell implemented Business Transaction Management. BTM observers were deployed into each server that participated in the transactions to monitor all of the individual transactions taking place in each server. BTM Monitor server collects raw data from all observers and distributes it to central servers. The BTM Central Servers are responsible for further processing of the data (basically making sense of the data), building up the single transaction view based on complex pattern matching algorithms, enforcing SLAs, implementing exception handling rules, and presenting all of the information in a user-friendly user interface.

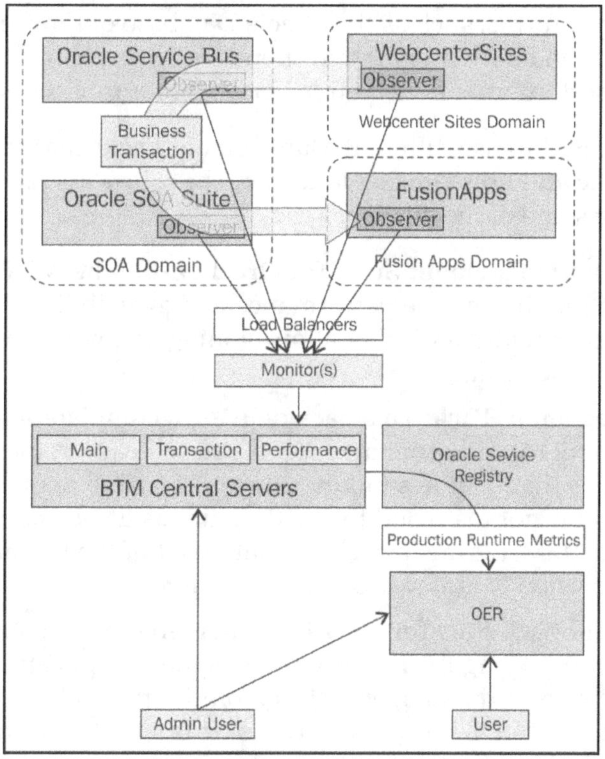

Further details regarding BTM and its features will be covered in the section *Business Transaction Management overview*.

Oracle Enterprise Manager overview

Oracle Enterprise Manager (OEM) is basically a management suite that allows enterprises to centrally manage and monitor almost all layers of the stack across a variety of systems within an enterprise's IT landscape.

Cloud Control 12*c* is the latest version of OEM and it provides many improvements and several bug fixes over previous versions of the product. For this reason, if you are planning to implement OEM the recommended version, at least at the time of writing, is OEM Cloud Control 12*c*. Its predecessor, OEM Grid Control 11*g*, is generally considered to be a much less stable version and is no longer available for download from the **Oracle Technology Network** (**OTN**) or from `edelivery.oracle.com` (it can only be downloaded by creating a ticket in the Oracle Support website).

Although OEM is not by any means the only product of its kind available in the market, it delivers several benefits and advantages especially when it is used to monitor Oracle platforms, such as the Oracle Database or Oracle SOA Suite. Nevertheless, OEM can be used to monitor non-Oracle product, IBM DB2, Microsoft SQL Server, Microsoft Internet Information Server, amongst others.

OEM can be configured to use different Management Packs that connect to and manage other Oracle and non-Oracle platforms. The following list provides summary details of some of the available packs:

- **Application Management Suite for Oracle E-Business Suite**: It provides support for monitoring the performance and availability of the E-Business Suite. It also provides tools that allow cloning of environments to assist with deployment and scaling.
- **SOA Management Pack**: This pack delivers a complete solution to manage and monitor SOA infrastructures. As discussed earlier, the main advantage of this pack is that it allows monitoring and management of several SOA domains and is not restricted to one domain (as EM Fusion Middleware Control). In OEM 12*c* this pack is available out of the box after installing as part of the Fusion Middleware Management feature.
- **Management Pack Plus for Identity Management**: This pack provides features for managing the Identity Management applications that extend beyond the standard management capabilities that ship out the box with the products. In OEM 12*c* this pack is available out of the box after installing as part of the Fusion Middleware Management feature.

- **WebLogic Server Management Pack Enterprise Edition**: This pack facilitates detailed monitoring and management of the WebLogic server platform that underpins many of the Oracle products. In OEM 12*c* this pack is available out of the box after installing as part of the Fusion Middleware Management feature.
- **Business Intelligence Management Pack**: This pack provides capabilities for configuration management, application performance management, and service level management for Oracle Business Intelligence Enterprise Edition and Oracle Business Intelligence Applications.
- **Oracle Diagnostics Pack and Oracle Tuning Pack**: These two packs combine to support database performance monitoring and tuning. Almost every database requires this level of support eventually as data grows. In OEM 12*c* this pack is available out of the box after installing as part of the Database Management feature.
- **Oracle Linux Management Pack**: This pack allows the monitoring and management of Linux servers, including patching, performance tuning, and provisioning tasks.
- **Oracle VM Management Pack**: This pack provides support for the central monitoring and management of the Oracle Virtualization technology. It aids the collection of key metrics and facilitates performance monitoring as well as configuration management and automatic provisioning of virtual instances.

Some of these packs are available out of the box while others are available for download and will require installation.

> OEM, as a standalone product, does not require the purchase of a license. However, the usage of a pack to monitor a target server is subject to license terms. Use of some of the packs is allowed with the standard license when you purchase a suite of Oracle products. However, it is strongly recommended that you engage with an Oracle representative before installing and using a pack to ensure that your organization is making use of a licensed product.

In addition to the Management Packs, OEM is capable of integrating with other IT service management tools such as BMC Remedy, CA Service Desk, HP Operations and Service Manager, and IBM Tivoli Enterprise Console (amongst others) through the use of connectors. Using these connectors, it is possible to automatically create, update, close, or reopen ticket for incidents created in Enterprise Manager.

For more information on OEM Enterprise Edition Cloud Control 12*c* and the available Management Packs, please refer to Oracle's OEM documentation page. `http://docs.oracle.com/cd/E24628_01/nav/management.htm`

At a high level the architecture of OEM 12*c* is as follows:

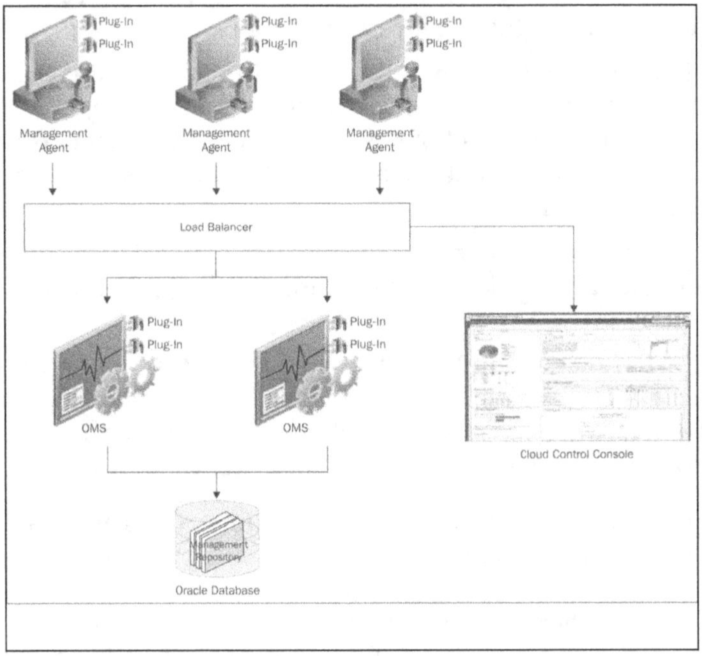

The components of the architecture are summarized as follows:

- **Management Agent**: A component that is deployed on each monitored host. It is responsible for monitoring all of the targets running on those hosts, communicating that information to the middle tier Oracle Management Service, and managing and maintaining the hosts and their targets.
- **Management Service**: It is a web-based application that interacts with the Management Agents and the Management Plug-ins to discover targets, monitor and manage those targets, and store the collected information in a repository for future reference and analysis. Oracle Management Service is also responsible for rendering the user interface.

- **Management Repository**: It is a storage location where all of the information collected by the Management Agent is stored. It consists of objects such as database jobs, packages, procedures, views, and tablespaces. The Oracle Management Service uploads the monitoring data it receives from the Management Agents to the Management Repository. The Management Repository then organizes the data so that it can be retrieved by the Oracle Management Service and displayed in the console.
- **Management Plug-ins**: (Licensable as Management Packs) are application extensions used for managing and monitoring other Oracle and non-Oracle technologies, such as the Oracle Database, Oracle Fusion Middleware, and Oracle Fusion Applications. The Plug-ins (or packs) installed out of the box are:
    - **Oracle Database**: It enables the administrator to monitor and manage one or many Oracle Databases, Oracle Real Application Clusters (Oracle RAC), Oracle Automatic Storage Management (Oracle ASM), and so on.
    - **Oracle Fusion Middleware**: It enables administrator to monitor and manage one or more Oracle WebLogic domains, Oracle WebLogic clusters, Oracle WebLogic Servers, Oracle SOA Suite, Oracle Web Tier, Oracle GlassFish, and so on.
    - **My Oracle Support**: It enables authentication into My Oracle Support from within the console. My Oracle Support facilitates searches of the knowledge library for notes and documents, the creation of service requests, and the creation of patch plans and templates, for patching monitored targets.
    - **Oracle Exadata**: It enables to monitor and manage Oracle Exadata targets.
- **Console**: It is basically the user interface of OEM that is used to monitor and manage all of the target servers.

> For further information please refer to the OEM 12*c* Cloud Control Documentation online at `http://docs.oracle.com/cd/E24628_01/index.htm`.

SOA Management Pack Enterprise Edition overview

The SOA Management Pack Enterprise Edition is a licensable package (or simply a license term) that, when purchased, provides the user with the right to install and use the following products:

- **SOA Management Pack**: Use of Oracle Enterprise Manager to monitor one or many SOA Suite instances. This pack is available by default when installing Oracle Enterprise Manager Cloud Control 12*c* (referred to as the Fusion Middleware Plugin).
- **Business Transaction Management** (**BTM**): This product, formerly called AmberPoint, is a separate binary and must be downloaded and installed separately.

> There is often confusion around what the SOA Management Pack actually is. The confusion is mainly because although, a license for a product named SOA Management Pack Enterprise Edition can be purchased, in actual fact there isn't a single binary for such a product. When a license for this product is purchased the user gets the right to install and use the two main binaries, SOA Management Pack that is part of the Oracle Enterprise Manager binaries and Business Transaction Manager, which is a separate binary. Each binary must be downloaded and installed separately.
> For further information we recommend referring to the main Oracle page for this pack, but also liaising with an SI with subject expertise on Oracle licenses or with Oracle itself. `http://www.oracle.com/us/products/middleware/soa/management-pack/overview/index.html`

So in summary, with the purchase of the SOA Management Pack Enterprise Edition license a user has the right to:

- Install the Oracle Enterprise Manager along with the SOA Management Pack and use it to manage the SOA infrastructure.
- Install and use Business Transaction Management to monitor SOA transactions across the entire SOA infrastructure.

> Note that each of the previous products can also be licensed separately. Whether or not it makes sense to do so depends on your licensing arrangements with Oracle and how the product is physically deployed.
>
> Furthermore, if BTM is to be used to monitor transactions originating on a WebLogic Server (without SOA Suite) or another non-Oracle application server, the following management packs will be required: WebLogic Server Management Pack Enterprise Edition and Management Pack for Non Oracle Middleware.
>
> Note that these topics although mentioned for information purposes are not covered in this book.

Overall the main features and benefits of the SOA Management Pack Enterprise Edition are as follows:

Feature	Description
Centralized management console	Provides administrators managing SOA environments with a consolidated browser-based view of all the servers being monitored.
Discovery and service modeling	Provides discovery of the Oracle SOA Infrastructure and SOA composites.
Exception handling	Allows for definition of tests to measure and record availability and performance of services also allowing for historical trending, troubleshooting, and root cause analysis. Also provides an error hospital of process instances with drilldowns into instance details.
Infrastructure management	Monitors the availability and performance of the SOA environment and all of the infrastructure components. Both current and historic availability of targets is recorded for troubleshooting and root cause analysis.
Configuration management	Collects configuration information for the BPEL Process Manager server and processes, WebLogic domains and OSB. The parameters can be refreshed, saved, or compared with another target. Different versions of the same target can also be compared.
Deployment automation	Allows for the automated deployment of SOA composites, WSM policies, and OSB proxy/business services.

Feature	Description
Adapter metrics	Provides throughput and error metrics for different adapters in graphical format.
Service level management	Enables the monitoring of services from the end-user's perspective using service tests or synthetic transactions, model relationships between services and underlying IT components, and reports on achieved service levels.
Application Dependency and Performance (ADP)	ADP analyzes Java EE, SOA, and Portal applications to capture the complex relationships among various application building blocks in its Application Schema model — the core of the Oracle intelligent platform. These dependencies can then be visualized in the form of a diagram.
Historical analysis and reporting	Stores the collected metric and configuration data in a central repository, thereby enabling administrators to analyze metrics through various historical views and facilitate strategic trend analysis and reporting.
Dehydration store	Shows the performance of the database that is used by the SOA Infrastructure. Using this data, the SOA administrator can identify problems resulting in performance bottlenecks.

Further information about the SOA Management Pack Enterprise Edition can be found in Part IV **Managing Oracle SOA** of the OEM 12*c* Getting Started with OFM Management.

`http://docs.oracle.com/cd/E24628_01/install.121/e24215/part_soa.htm#sthref247`

BTM architecture overview

BTM's architecture is based on a series of distributed components (Observers, Monitor Servers, and Central Servers) that constantly interact in order to capture, process, analyze, and present transactional data in a human-readable fashion.

The following diagram shows a high-level architecture view of BTM:

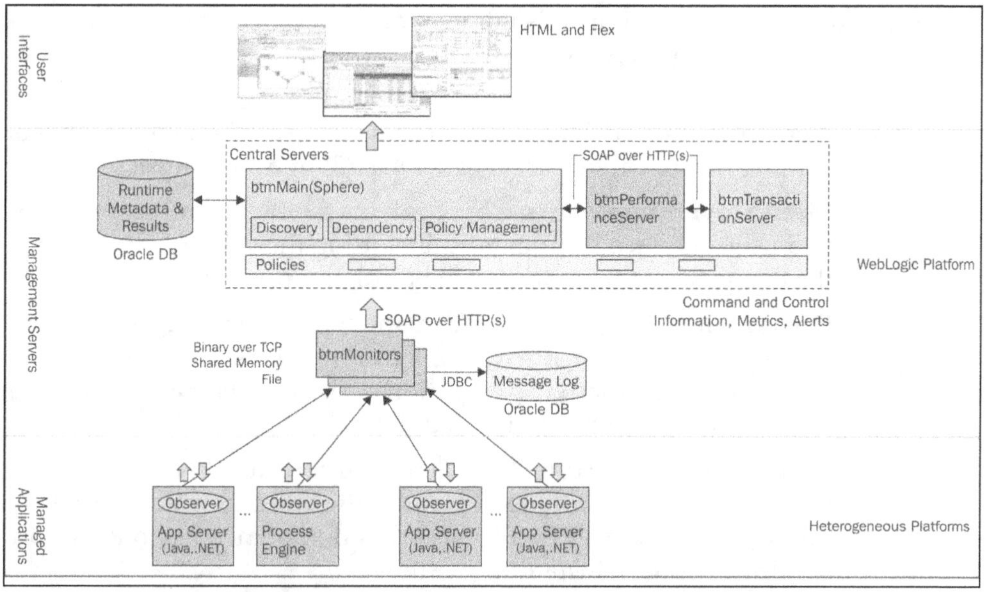

As can be appreciated from the above diagram, BTM consists of:

- **Observers**: They are basically agents that are deployed into the application server(s) that host the business application(s) that participate in a SOA transaction and therefore require monitoring. Observers can monitor several types of components and there are different types based upon the system or application that they monitor. For example, in the case of Weir & Bell Telecom, the following observers were used:
    - `BTMObserver_Wls_10.3_JavaEE_*.zip`: It is an observer for Java EE on WebLogic 10.3.x.
    - `BTMObserver_Wls_10.3_Soa11gR1_*.zip`: It is an observer for Oracle SOA Suite on WebLogic 10.3.x.
    - `BTMObserver_Wls_10.3_Osb11gR1_*.zip`: It is an observer for Oracle Service Bus 11*g*R1 on WebLogic 10.3.x.
    - `BTMObserver_Wls_10.3_FApps11gRUP1_*.zip`: It is an observer for Oracle Fusion Applications.

- **Monitors (btmMonitor.ear)**: They collect the data sent from the observers (such as performance data and measurements amongst others) and post processes it. A Monitor is basically an EAR archive that has to be deployed into an application server. For large volume configurations, a complex topology of multiple monitors can be configured (either as singletons or replicates) along with load balancers in order to achieve maximum performance and availability.

  In production environments it is not recommended to deploy monitors into the same application server as the Central Servers. Doing so may result in performance issues.

- **Central Servers (Sphere)**: All central servers are also EAR archives that are deployed into an application server. There are 3 types of central servers:
  - **Main Server** (btmMain.ear): It contains all the central system services and user interface components, including the sphere. The Sphere is the component that manages the BTM environment.
  - **Performance Server** (btmPerformanceServer.ear): It is responsible for gathering measurements from measurement sources (monitors) and performing time-based aggregation of data. It also provides a query interface to access the monitored data.
  - **Transaction Server** (btmTransactionServer.ear): It is responsible for monitoring transaction instances. Configures the system to collect appropriate data and performs correlation of message data to form a single transaction instance.

Similar to the monitor servers, central servers should be deployed individually and into their own application servers.

> Further information on BTM is available in the section **Associated Products** of the OEM 12*c* Cloud Control documentation page at `http://docs.oracle.com/cd/E24628_01/nav/assoproducts.htm`.

Monitoring SOA Suite with OEM 12*c*

As discussed earlier in the chapter, there are several features available in OEM to monitor Oracle SOA Suite domains. Whenever OEM is being implemented to monitor SOA infrastructures, the administrator must first identify and add target middleware domains containing SOA infrastructure components that require monitoring.

In order to have increased visibility over the monitored targets, it is important to set up additional features such as the Application Dependency and Performance (ADP) and **JVM Diagnostics (JVMD)** servers and agents.

The following is a step-by-step description on how to:

- Add OEM 12*c* middleware targets to monitor SOA infrastructures
- Configure ADP to have better visibility of the SOA targets and its internal application's inter-dependencies

Adding a Middleware target in OEM

Follow these steps to add an OEM 12*c* middleware target that contains the SOA Suite domain:

1. Log on to OEM 12*c* console through the URL:

```
https://<OEM 12c Server>:<port, if default: 7803>/em.
```

2. If logging in for the first time, it is recommended to define a preferred My Home page. Defining a My Home page will automatically redirect the user after logging on to the predefined page. In our example, we have set **SOA** as the My Home page. The My Home page may also be accessed through the **Favorites** menu. Multiple homes may be added to the **Favorites** menu from the option **Manage Favorites**:

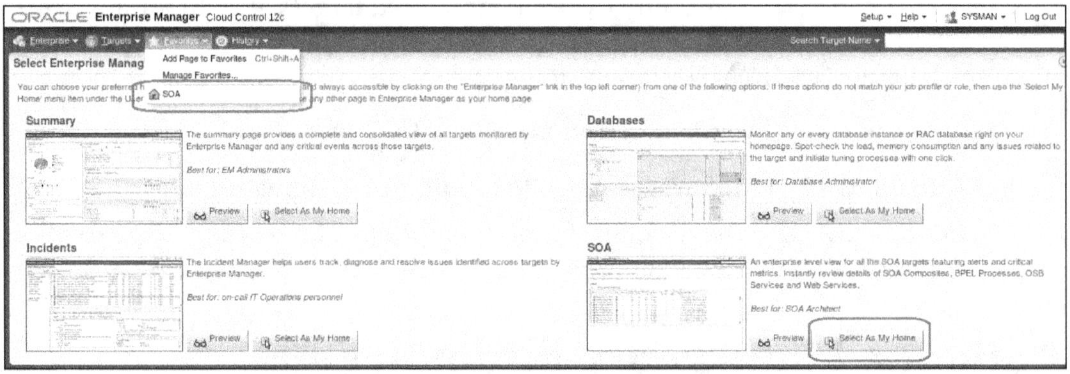

3. The **SOA Home** does not show any composites or services at this stage. This is because no middleware targets have been added that contain SOA infrastructures:

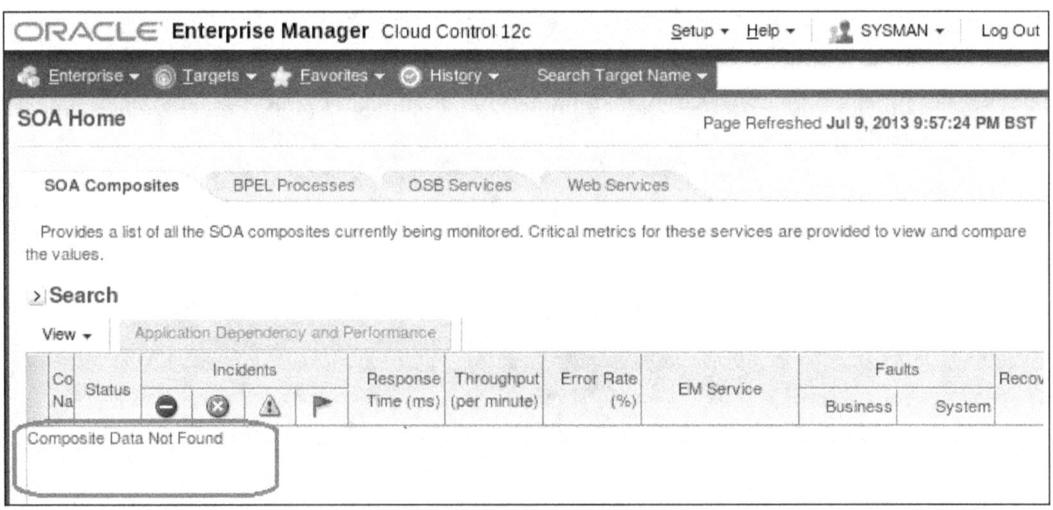

4. To add a target, select **Middleware** from the **Targets** menu:

5. From the **Middleware** home page, click on **Add** and then select **Oracle Fusion Middleware/WebLogic Domain**:

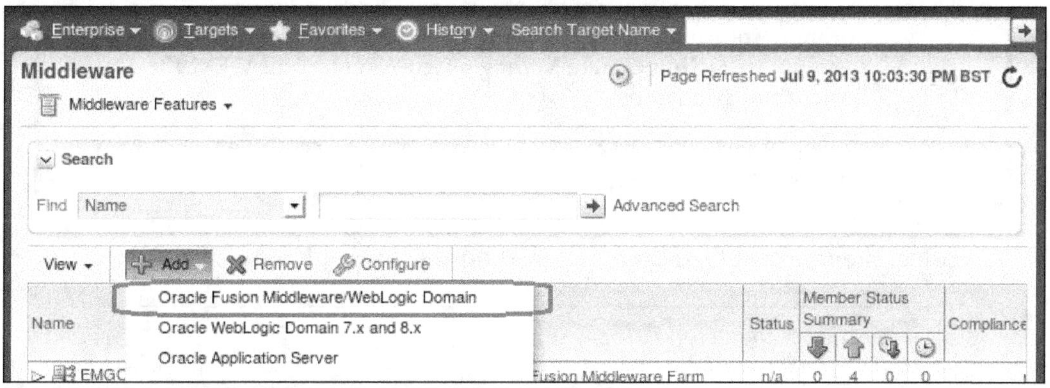

6. Enter the details for the WebLogic SOA domain and then click on the Search icon next to the **Agent** field. Note that as a prerequisite to achieve this step an **Oracle Management Agent** (**OMA**) must have been installed successfully into the target hosts of the SOA domain:

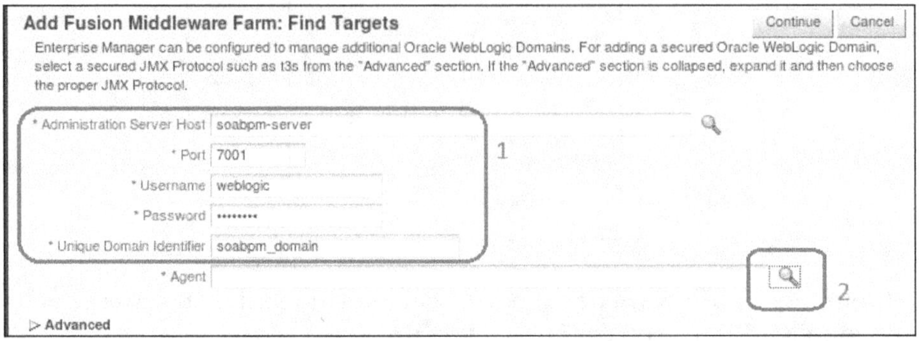

> For more information on Installing OAM agents please refer to section 7 **Installing Oracle Management Agent** of the OEM 12*c* Basic Installation Guide.
>
> `http://docs.oracle.com/cd/E24628_01/install.121/e22624/install_agent.html`

7. Select the relevant OAM agent based on the **Target Name** or **Host**:

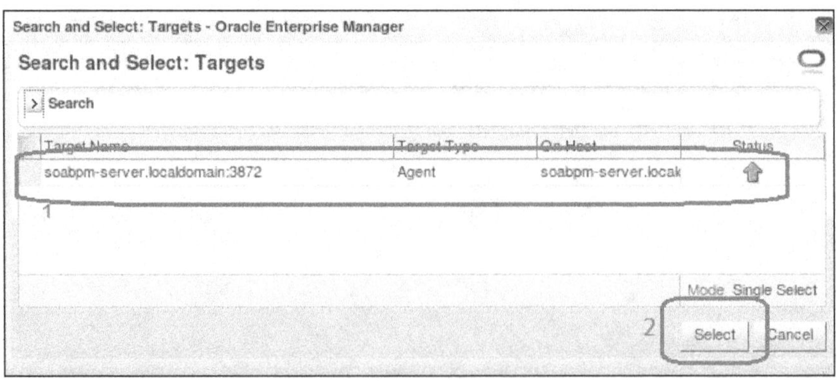

8. A **Confirmation** page will be displayed. Ensure that all Targets have been successfully identified and then click on the **Close** button:

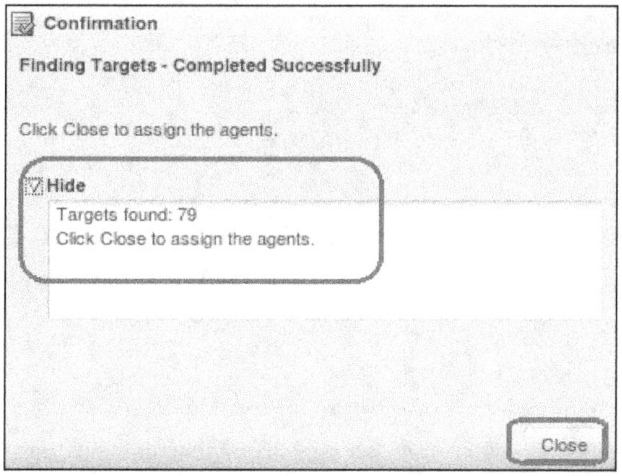

9. Click on **Targets And Agent Assignments** to view all targets assigned to the agent. You may override the default agent assignment if required from the column **Configure Agent**:

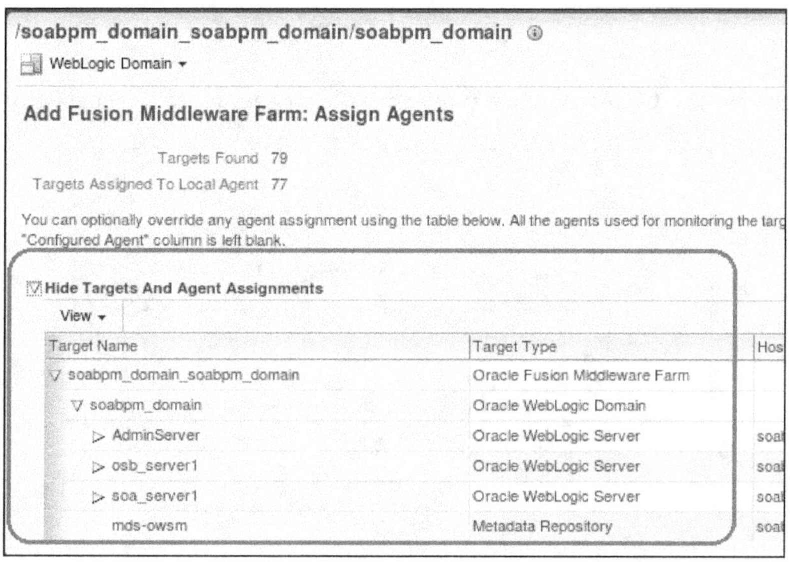

10. On the same page click on the **Weblogic Domain Global Properties** and enter the details describing the target domain:

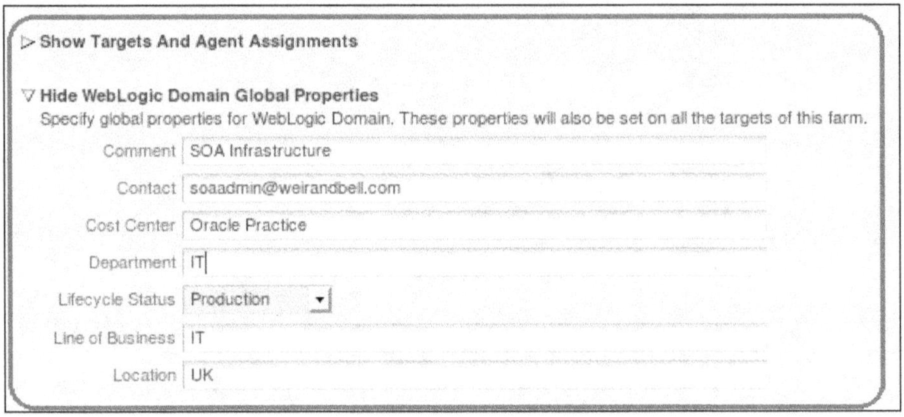

11. Click on the **Add Targets** button.

12. Check on the **Confirmation** page that all targets were successfully added.

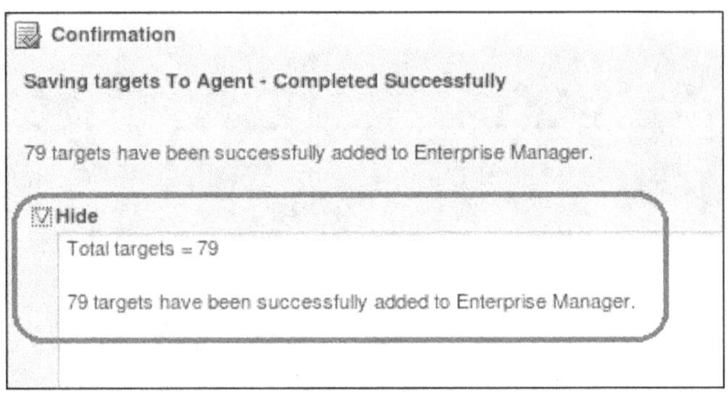

13. Click on the **OK** button.

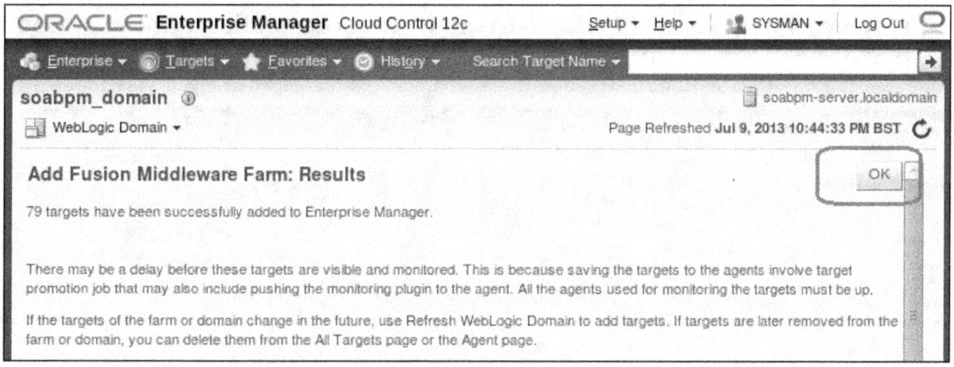

Note that there might be a delay before the targets are actually visible.

14. Now the new SOA domain should appear on the **Middleware** page that is accessible from the **Targets** menu. Click on the new monitored SOA domain to see further details on the target.

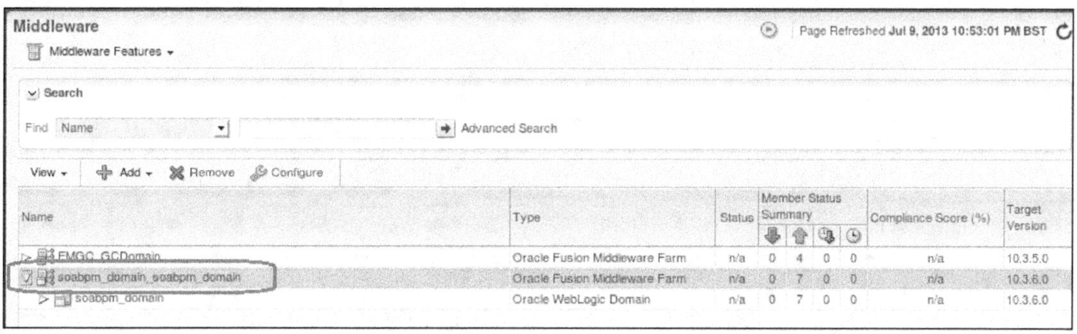

15. The monitored domain home page opens. As can be appreciated, this page is similar to the EM Fusion Middleware Control landing page. However, from OEM 12*c* there are no restrictions on the number of domains that can be monitored:

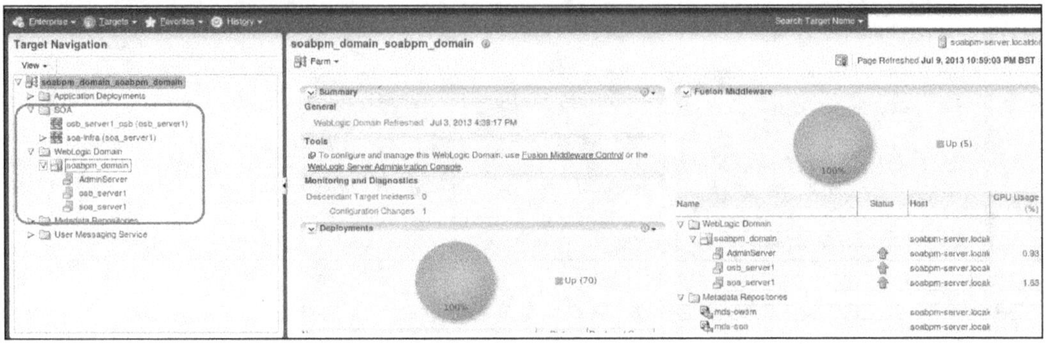

16. Now if you go back to the **SOA Home** by clicking on the **SOA** option from **Favorites**, all composites and services from all monitored SOA domains will appear along with useful statistics on their performance, errors, and faults (amongst others).

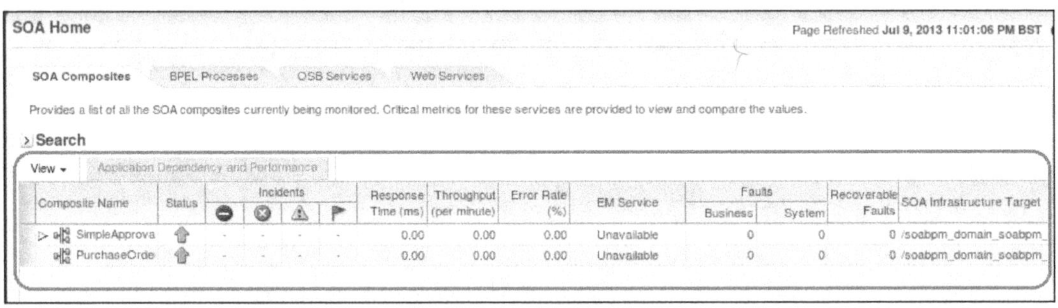

For more advanced topics please refer to the OEM 12*c* documentation page.

http://docs.oracle.com/cd/E24628_01/index.htm

Visualizing application interdependencies in OEM

Another very useful feature of OEM is the Application Dependency and Performance (ADP). ADP is an **Application Service Management** (**ASM**) platform for visualizing complex application relationships and further application performance statistics on the monitored servers. ADP helps eliminate manual and repetitive tasks usually required to conduct such tasks.

From the OEM 12*c* console, there are four main steps that need to be completed to configure ADP:

- Create an ADP Manager Engine
- Deploy ADP Agent
- Create ADP Manager Schema
- Enable Request Monitoring

Creating ADP Manager Engine

ADP Manager is the core analytical engine of the ADP. ADP Manager performs real- time complex mathematical modeling and statistical calculations using the data collected from the ADP Java Agents.

The following steps describe how to create the ADP Manager Engine:

1. From the **Setup** menu (located on the top-right hand side of the OEM console) select **Application Performance Management**:

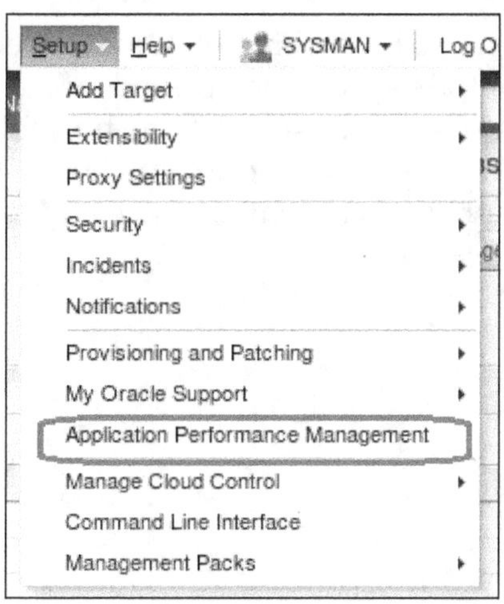

2. From the Application Performance Management home page, click on **Add** and then select **Application Dependency and Performance Engine**:

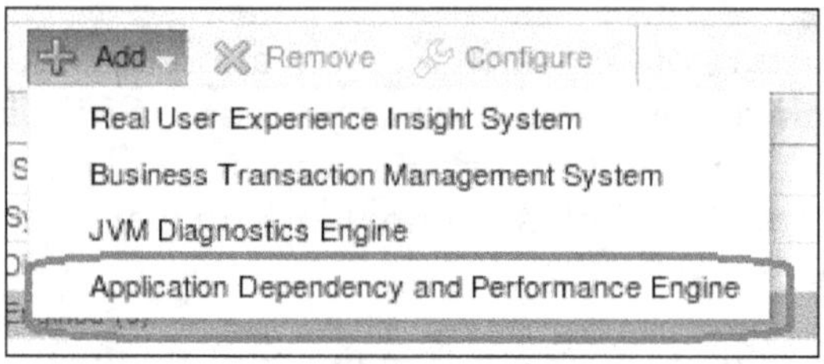

3. The option **Create a managed server** is selected by default. Check that the details entered by default are applicable in your scenario. From this same page, enter the host and domain credentials as described in the subsequent steps:

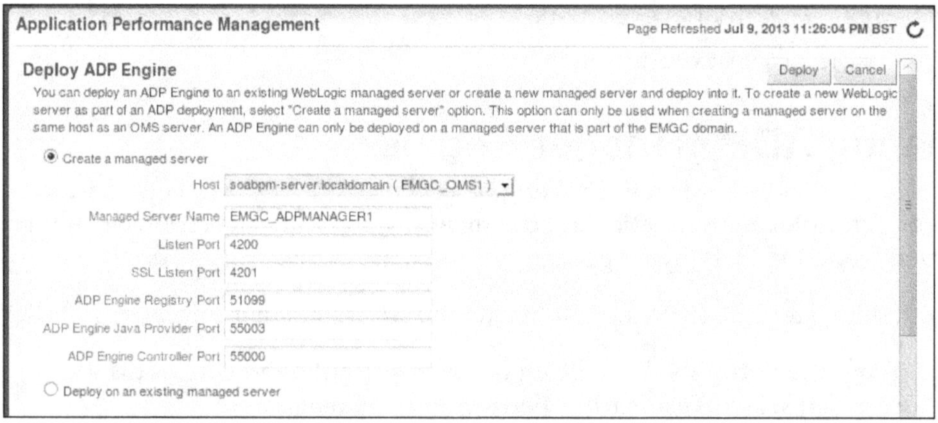

4. Add the host credentials by clicking on **Oracle Weblogic Administration Server Host Credentials**. Select the option **New** to add new credentials. Note that the credentials entered must be for the host to which the managed server will be deployed (in our example, the same host where OEM 12*c* sits). Then click on **Test** to ensure that credentials were added correctly.

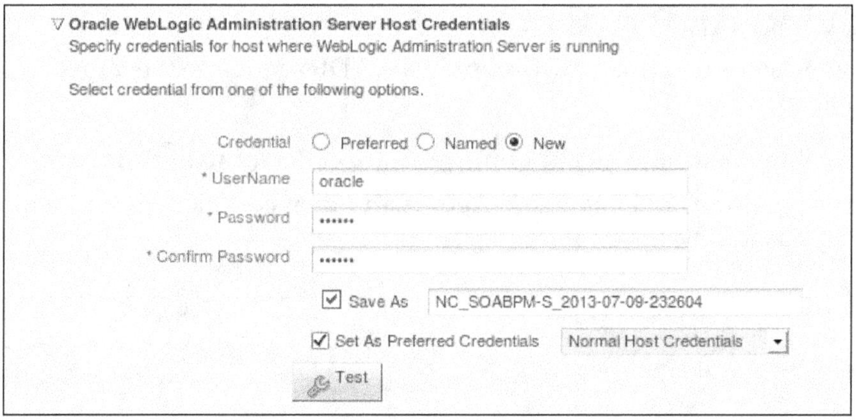

5. Enter the WebLogic domain credentials by clicking on the **WebLogic Server Domain Credentials**. Note that the credentials entered must be for the WebLogic user of the OEM 12*c* domain. Click on **Test** to check that the credentials were entered correctly.

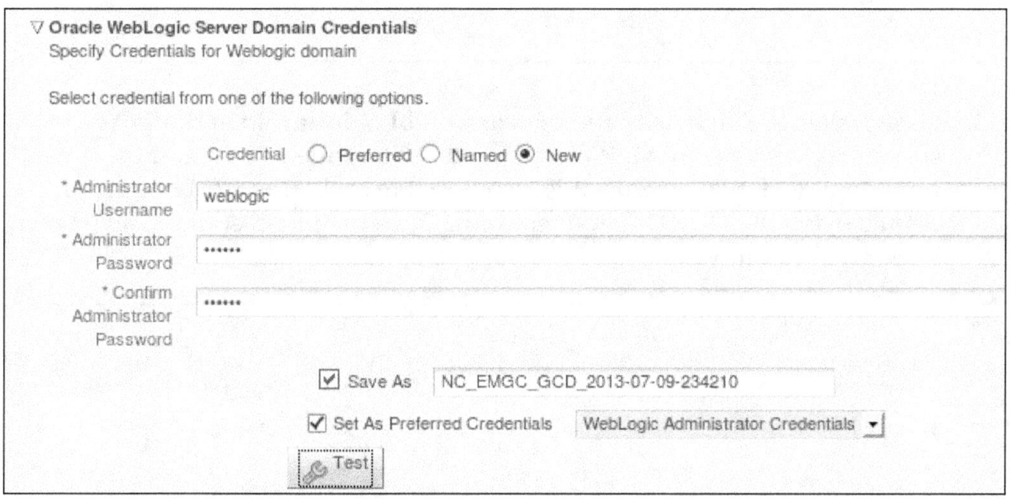

6. Finally click on the **Deploy** button.

Deploying ADP Agent

The following steps describe how to deploy the ADP agent into the target SOA domains:

1. From the **Setup** menu click on **Application Performance Management**.
2. Click on **Manage Diagnostic Agents** and then complete the subsequent six steps as follows:

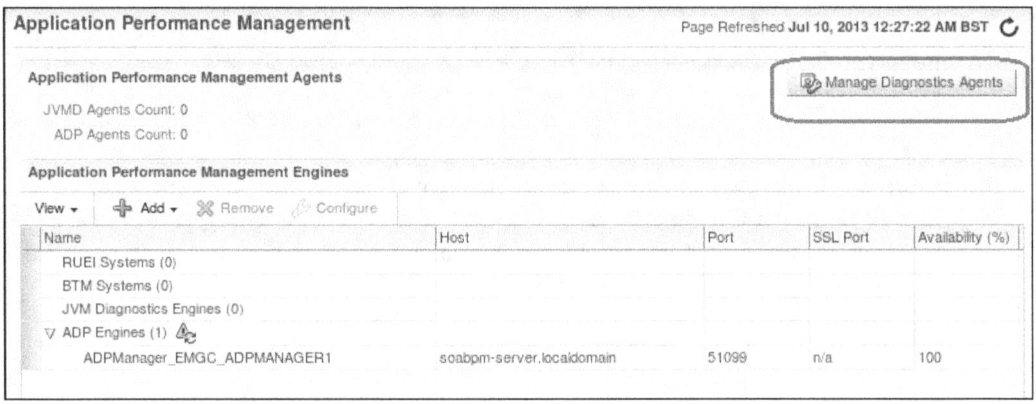

3. Assign the ADP agents to the relevant WebLogic admin and managed servers in the column **ADP Detail**. Note that, while in the example it was only deployed ADP agents, it is also possible to deploy JVM diagnostic agents using the **JVMD Detail** column. Once the target servers have been selected click on **Next**:

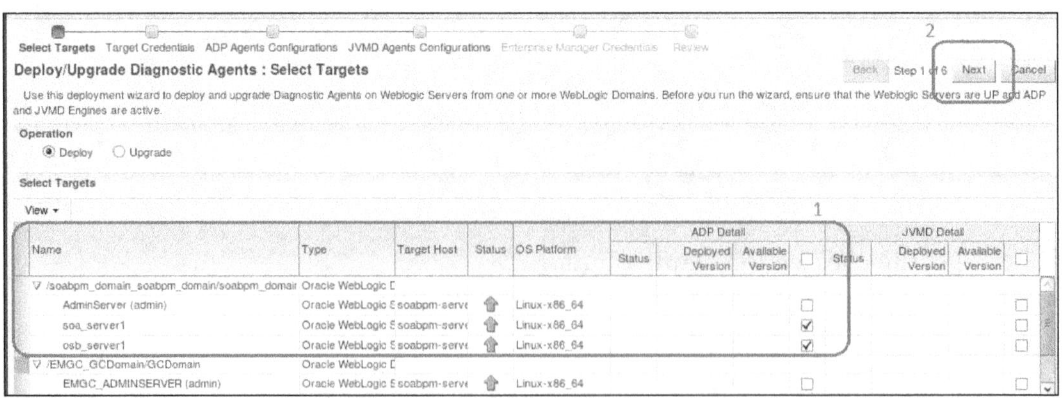

4. Select the target WebLogic domain and enter the WebLogic domain and host credentials (credentials are entered in the same fashion as step 4 of the *Creating ADP Manager Engine* section). Click on **Apply** once credentials have been entered and then click on **Next**.

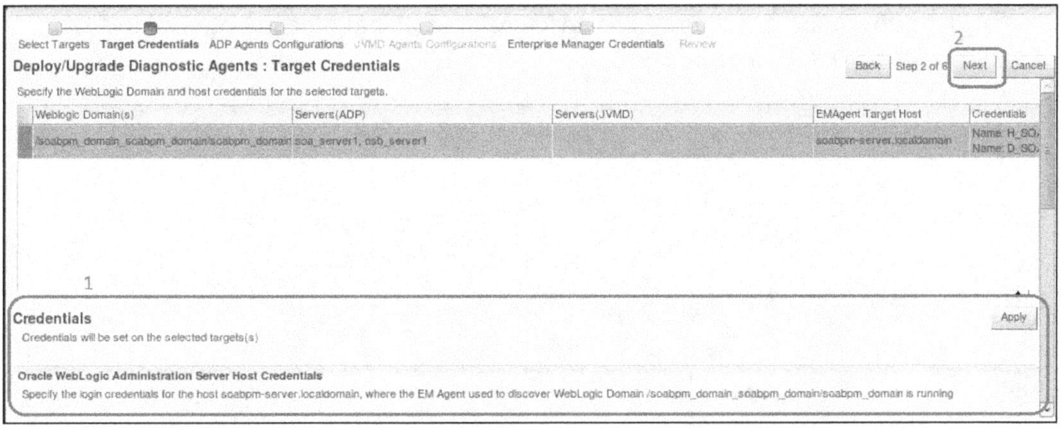

5. Select the target domain and then click on **ADP Agent Configuration**. On the **Available ADP Engine(s)** field, select the ADP engine created earlier. Click on the **Apply** button and then click on **Next**.

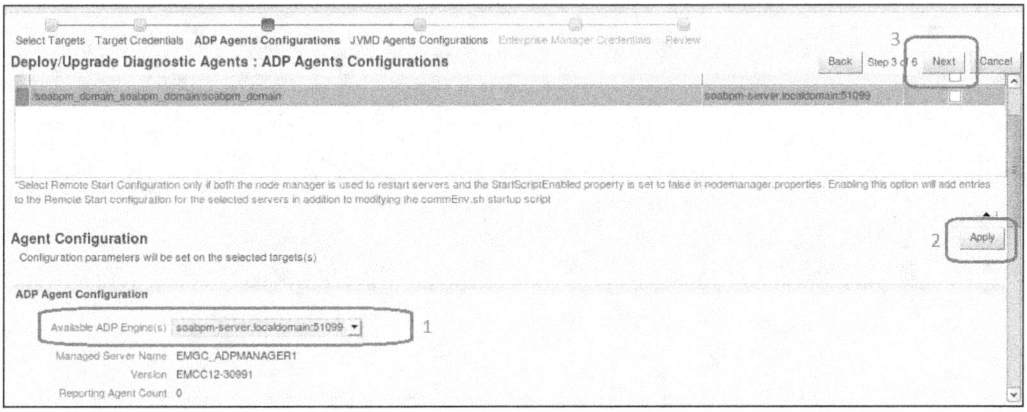

6. Now enter the **Oracle Management Server** (**OMS**) WebLogic domain and host credentials. Note that, because these credentials were previously created in step 4 of **Creating ADP Manager Engine** section, it is not necessary to create the credentials again. Instead, from the **Credentials** field select **Named** and then select the credentials previously created from the **Credential Name** dropdown list. Click on **Save** once credentials have been entered and then click on **Next**.

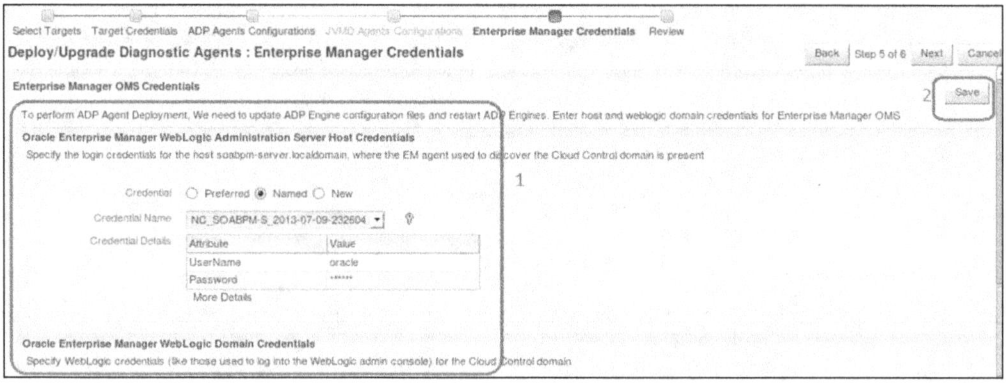

7. From the **Targets** table, verify that all target server settings are correct and then click on **Deploy**. Otherwise it is possible to go **Back** and correct the settings.

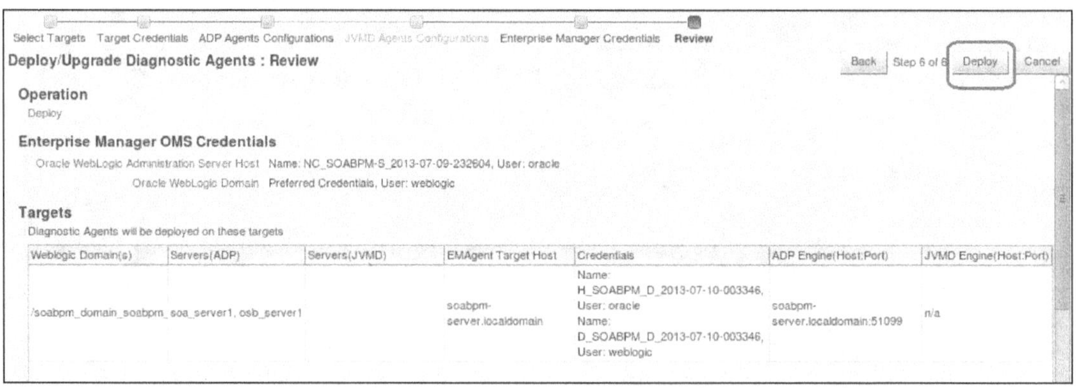

8. The deployment of the agent will occur in the background in a job created by OEM. Click on the ADP Agent Deployment link to see the progress of the job. Once the job has finished, restart the target WebLogic domain admin and managed servers.

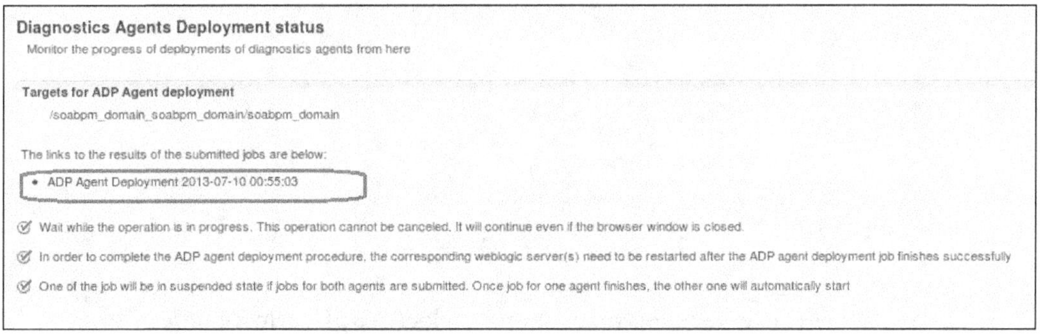

Creating and configuring ADP DB

ADP manager requires a separate database schema to store its analyzed data and application models. There could be several managers in an ADP deployment and each ADP manager database is created subsequently by the creation of the engine itself.

Following are the steps to create and configure the ADP Manager database:

1. Using the `sysdba` user (or another user with `CREATE` and `GRANT` rights) create the `adp` user as following:

```
CREATE USER adp IDENTIFIED BY <password>;
GRANT CONNECT, RESOURCE to adp;
```

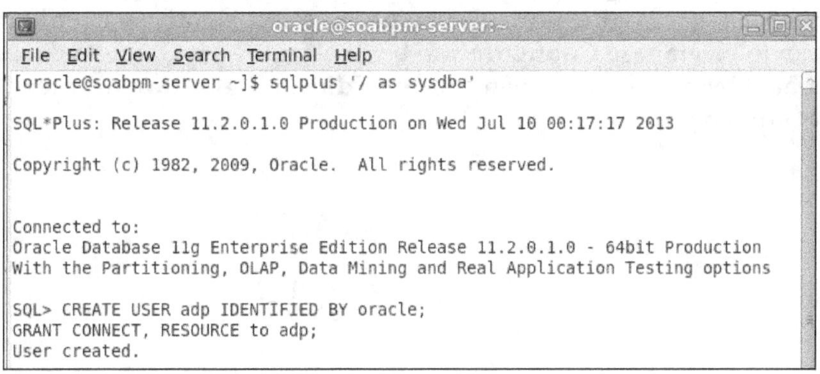

2. Then from the OEM 12*c* console, navigate to the **Middleware** home.

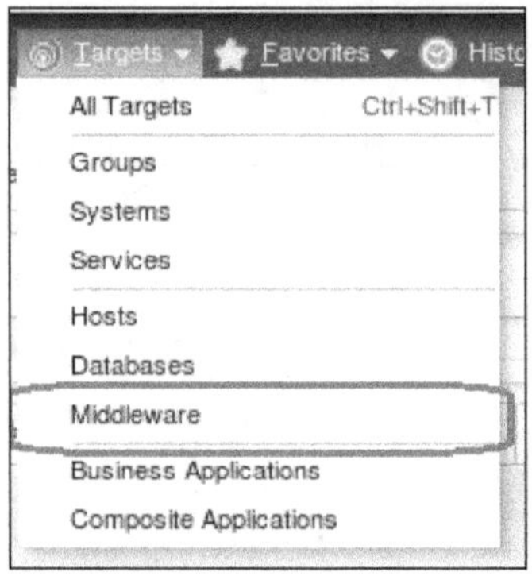

3. From the **Middleware Features** menu, select **Application Dependency and Performance**.

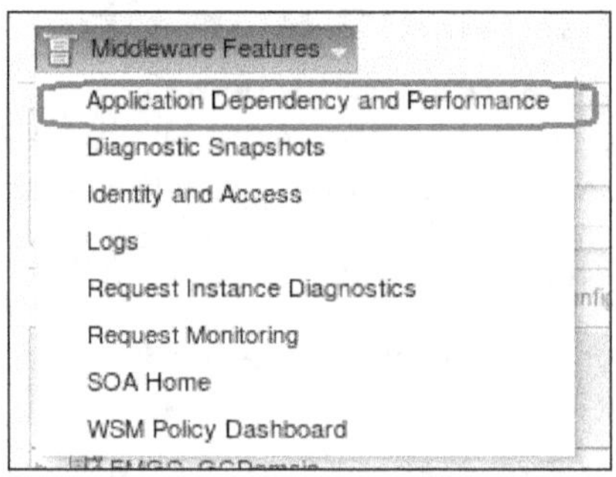

4. Click on the **Configuration** tab. Then, under the **Configuration** menu for the ADP Manager Engine previously created, select **Database Configuration**. From the **Database Configuration** box, select the **MyOracle** database (created by default) and then click on **Edit Configuration** to enter details of the adp schema.

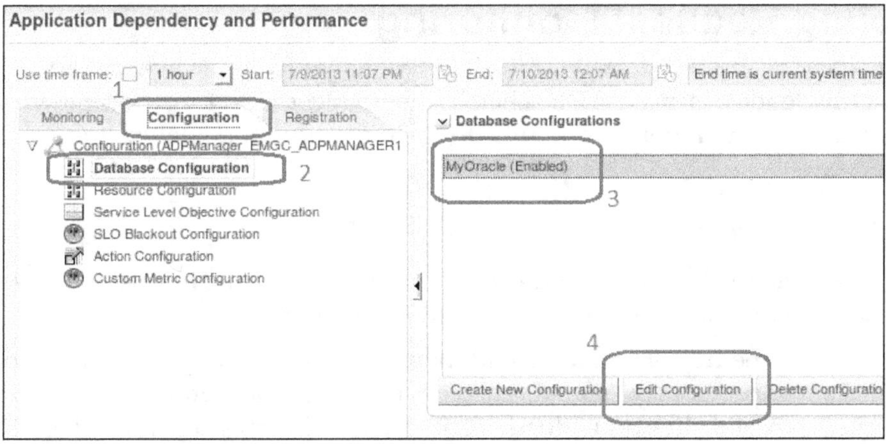

5. Enter the details of the recently created ADP schema along with the details of the database and then click on **OK**. Note that the **Driver Name**, **URL Format**, **Connector Type**, and **Connector DBMS** may remain as defaulted.

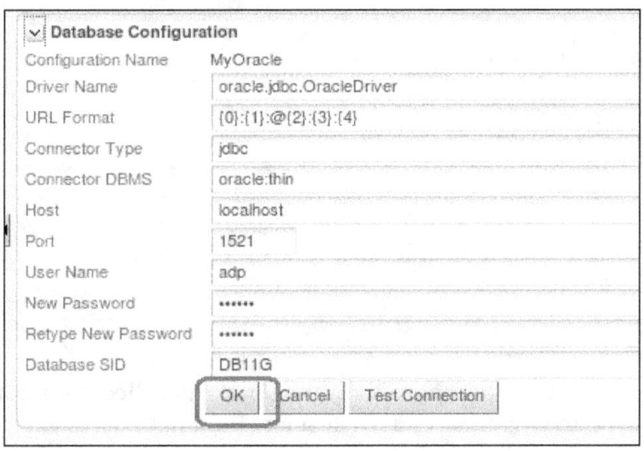

Enabling Request Monitoring

Once the data has been collected by the ADP Manager from the agents and subsequently loaded into the ADP schema, the Request Monitoring Framework processes the collected metrics and uses them to monitor and analyze the target servers.

Following are the steps to enable Request Monitoring:

1. Go to the **Middleware** home and then, from the **Middleware Features** menu, select **Application Dependency and Performance**.
2. Click on the **Registration** tab and then, under the **Managers** menu, select ADP Manager previously created. Then select the **Enable Request Monitoring** checkbox and click on **Upload**. Verify that an OK message is received; otherwise, navigate back to the **Application Performance Management** page from the **Setup** menu to troubleshoot the ADP Manager Engine.

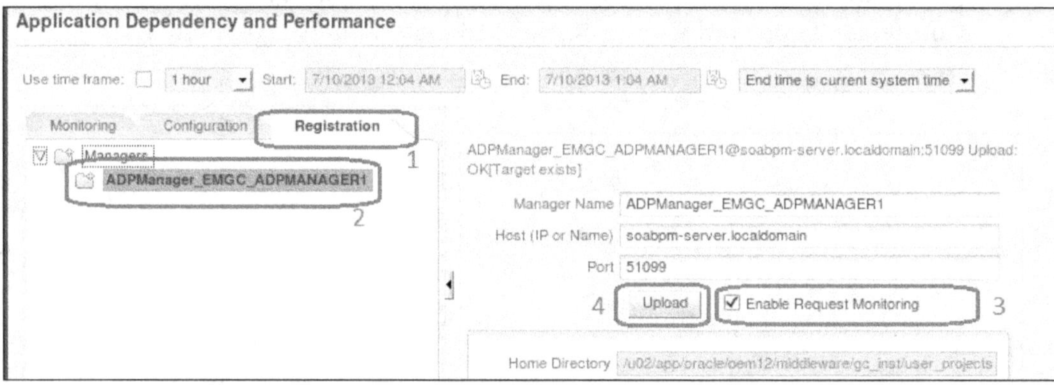

> To ensure that this ADP Manager starts collecting request monitoring data, you must select the **Enable Request Monitoring** checkbox.

3. Once Request Monitoring is enabled, it should be possible to start making use of the ADP features available. To do so click on the **Monitoring** tab and then expand the **OEM ADP Manager** menu. Several options will be available under this menu.

For example, to visualize the target WebLogic Domain topology, expand **Resources** and then click on the desired target domain. Finally on the center page click on the **Topology** tab.

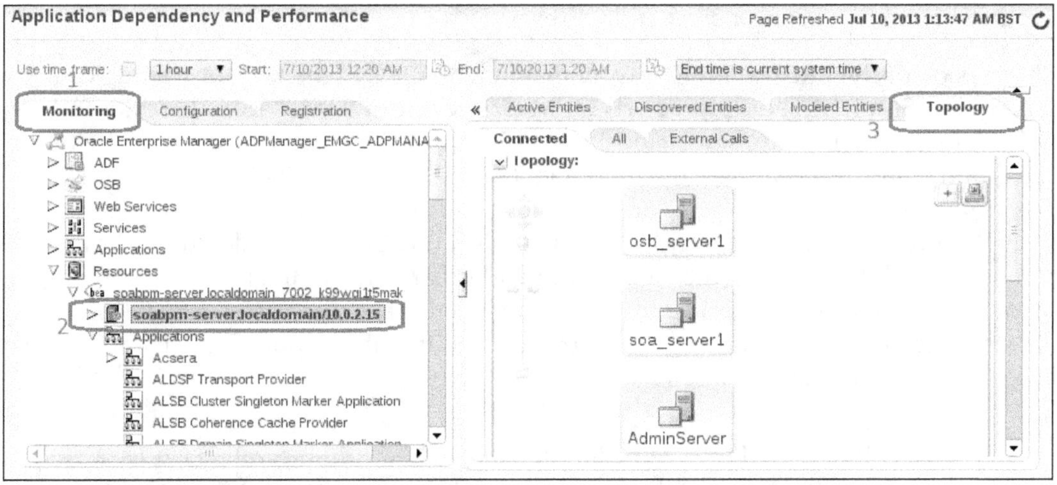

4. Equally, if you wish to see the OSB services available and their relationship, click on the **OSB** option and then on the center page click the **OSB Topology** tab.

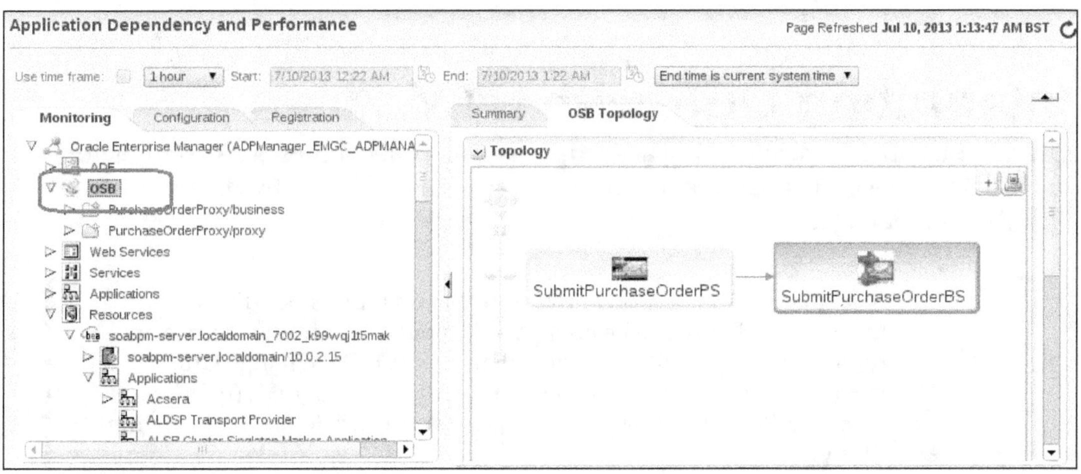

Integrating OER with OEM

OER 11*g* supports the collection of performance and runtime metrics from OEM using the OER Integration Utility. This feature allows important runtime data to be captured from SOA composites and OSB services.

The version of the Integration Utility available with OER at the time of writing of this book (PS6-11.1.1.7) only supports OEM Grid Control 10*g* R3 (10.2.0.5) and OEM Grid Control 11*g*. Both these versions of OEM have already been superseded by OEM 12*c* Cloud Control and are no longer available for download either from the Oracle Technology Network (OTN) site or from the e-Delivery site (`edelivery.oracle.com`). For this reason, it was decided that the addition of extensive details on how to configure the Integration Utility would not add great value to the reader. However, because this is a fundamental feature of the Oracle Governance providing Close-Loop Governance, it is expected that the Integration Utility will support OEM 12*c* in a later patch set or major release of OER.

> If you would like more information on how this integration works and the steps required to configure utility for the supported version of OEM, please refer to section 6 **Enterprise Manager Integration Utility** of the OER Integration Guide.
>
> `http://docs.oracle.com/cd/E28280_01/doc.1111/e15754/eminteg.htm#CHDFBHDF`

Integrating OER with BTM

Oracle Enterprise Repository 11*g* also supports the collection of SOA composite and OSB service performance and runtime metrics as gathered by Business Transaction Manager.

> Note that the integration between BTM and OER is not direct. Instead, BTM needs to be configured to publish runtime metrics and rogue services into OSR. Subsequently, the OER Exchange Utility needs to be configured to collect these metrics from OSR (refer to *Chapter 6, Asset Lifecycle and Workflow*, for further details on using the utility).

As of the version of OER used in this book (PS6-11.1.1.7), the integration with BTM is only supported for versions of BTM prior to 11*g* (basically the former Amberpoint product). In other words, BTM 11*g* and BTM 12*c* versions are not supported.

> If you would like more information on how this integration works and the steps required to configure it for the supported version of BTM, please refer to section 7 **Integration with Amberpoint** of the OER Integration Guide at `http://docs.oracle.com/cd/E28280_01/doc.1111/e15754/amber.htm#CCHGFAHH`.

Summary

This chapter started by describing the different support and monitoring challenges faced by Weir & Bell Telecom. It illustrated the problems encountered by the support team for having such a highly diversified and ungoverned support and monitoring solution in place. Such complexity increased the time taken to identify problems and diagnose faults. The cost of managing such an environment was inevitably carried by the business.

The chapter then elaborated on how Weir & Bell Telecoms' IT support and architecture departments put together a business case for Oracle Enterprise Manager and Business Transaction Manager by listing the benefits that implementing these tools would bring to the business.

The chapter went on to describe the technology architecture of these tools and how Weir & Bell Telecoms implemented them to address their support and monitoring challenges. Subsequently, two practical implementation use cases were presented that described in detail how to configure OEM 12*c* to monitor a WebLogic domain containing the Oracle SOA Suite, and also how to make use of the Application Dependency and Performance feature of OEM 12*c* to deliver an Application Service Management (ASM) solution.

The chapter ended by giving a brief description on the versions of OEM and BTM supported for integration with OER and also references for instructions on how to achieve these integrations.

The next chapter will elaborate on the business case for implementing Oracle Application Integration Architecture (AIA) Foundation Pack and will describe how Process Integration Packs (PIPs) help accelerate and de-risk the implementation of a Master Data Management (MDM).

11
Extending Governance with AIA Foundation Pack 11*g*

This chapter describes some of the data quality challenges faced by organizations and emphasizes the importance of having an effective **Master Data Management** (**MDM**) strategy in place to address these issues. The chapter elaborates on how MDM in conjunction with **Service Oriented Architecture** and the Oracle **Application Integration Architecture** (**AIA**) **Foundation Pack** (**FP**) delivers a solution to the data quality challenges while maintaining the benefits of SOA.

The chapter further describes how prebuilt **Process Integration Packs** (**PIPs**) available in the AIA FP can accelerate the implementation of an MDM solution and dramatically reduce the effort and risk involved in such deliveries.

A practical use case of AIA is also presented that shows how to harvest AIA assets into the **Oracle Enterprise Repository**.

> This chapter illustrates different MDM challenges only as a vehicle to highlight the use and benefits of implementing AIA FP along with OER. There are several other books available on the web that covers the topic of MDM in far more detail.s

For the practical sections of the chapter it is assumed that an environment containing an installation of the SOA Suite 11*g* and the AIA 11*g* Foundation Pack is available. For details about installing the AIA Foundation Pack refer to **Installation and Upgrade Guide for Oracle Application Integration Architecture Foundation Pack** `http://docs.oracle.com/cd/E28280_01/doc.1111/e17949/toc.htm`.

Use Case

Following the successful adoption of SOA, Weir & Bell Telecoms continued to face many data quality issues, most significantly around customer data. Weir & Bell Telecoms' architects had hoped that by adopting SOA, all of their data issues would be resolved. However, despite building their SOA services to the highest standard, the data served by the services had fundamental quality issues meaning that service consumers could not rely on it.

The architects began to realize that without adopting strict data-quality principles in tandem with the SOA infrastructure, all that was being achieved was high-quality services delivering poor-quality data. This paradox meant that the & Bell architects had to rethink their delivery strategy as SOA on its own wasn't a "silver bullet" to address all of their data integration challenges as they had mistakenly first thought it to be.

A fundamental issue faced by Weir & Bell Telecoms was that they didn't have a single view of their customers. Each application had its own view of the customer and even when SOA interfaces were built to synchronize the customer data, there were still several discrepancies and inconsistencies in the customer data. This lack of a single customer view presented real problems for the marketing department and reduced the capacity for up-selling and cross-selling. It also prohibited Weir & Bell Telecoms from presenting customers with personalized product offerings, tailored to suit their individual needs. In a highly aggressive market in which their more-agile competitors were already introducing tailored customer offerings, Weir & Bell Telecoms was on the verge of losing market share.

The following diagram summarizes the customer data integration flows between Weir & Bell Telecoms core systems. Although interfaces were built following best practices and high standards, fundamental data issues were still present:

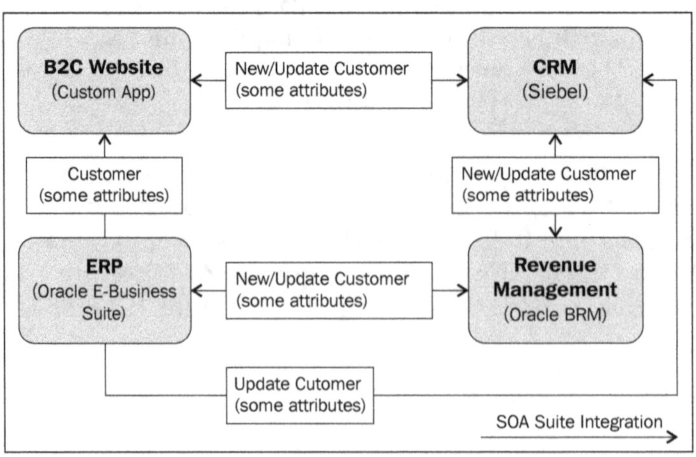

The Weir & Bell Telecoms' architects quickly established that their data quality issues were not attributable to their SOA architecture.

SOA infrastructures do not store any operational data. In fact, the issue was a problem with managing and governing data, and as such was basically a **Master Data Management** (**MDM**) problem. Consequently, the architects created a roadmap that articulated a strategy towards implementing a full MDM. MDM subject-matter experts were also recruited to assist in defining the strategy and high-level design. The strategy defined an incremental approach to be followed in order to address all identified data quality issues and prioritized problem areas that required immediate attention, such as customer data.

Once defined, the next step was to decide on the technology stack to underpin the solution. A **Request for Proposal** was sent out to different vendors and a number of products were considered.

In the end, the Oracle MDM was chosen. Weir & Bell Telecoms was very impressed with the proposition presented by the Oracle **MDM Suite** and this also fitted in with the overall I.T strategy that had focused mainly on Oracle software. The architects were particularly interested in implementing the Oracle **Customer Hub** that could help to build a single view of the customer, thereby exploiting the full potential of the information already available. Additionally, Weir & Bell Telecoms could make use of **Oracle Data Quality** family of products to steward, profile, match and merge, and audit their data.

The decision made had a buy-in from the architecture community and also from the main business stakeholders. Having the right level of sponsorship from the business was critical in order to secure the necessary funding. However, another challenge was identified. In order to gain maximum benefit from the introduction of the Customer Hub, it had to become the master for all customer data. To achieve this, the Hub needed to constantly collect and replicate customer data from all relevant systems. This seemed like an onerous task as Weir & Bell Telecoms had several systems that employed customer data and building the required interfaces was not a trivial task.

However, after conducting some research, the architects identified the existence of a number of PIPs. PIPs are prebuilt SOA interfaces implemented by Oracle and based on the AIA FP. PIPs are constructed to address end-to-end integration challenges in processes such as "Order to Cash", "Procure to Pay", "Record to Report", and MDM. In most cases PIPs can be implemented out-of-the-box with little extensions thus saving many man-hours of work.

Additionally, since the AIA FP is actually an add-on module for the SOA Suite, the Weir & Bell Telecoms' architects saw a fantastic opportunity to leverage their existing Oracle SOA 11*g* infrastructure thus saving considerable hardware costs. Moreover, by implementing the Oracle **Customer MDM Integration Base Pack** PIP, Weir & Bell could accelerate and derisk the implementation of the Customer Hub.

The architects referred to the PIPs documentation in order to better understand the architecture of the Customer MDM Integration Base Pack. Subsequently a view was created depicting how much of the PIP could be used out of the box and what extensions would be required:

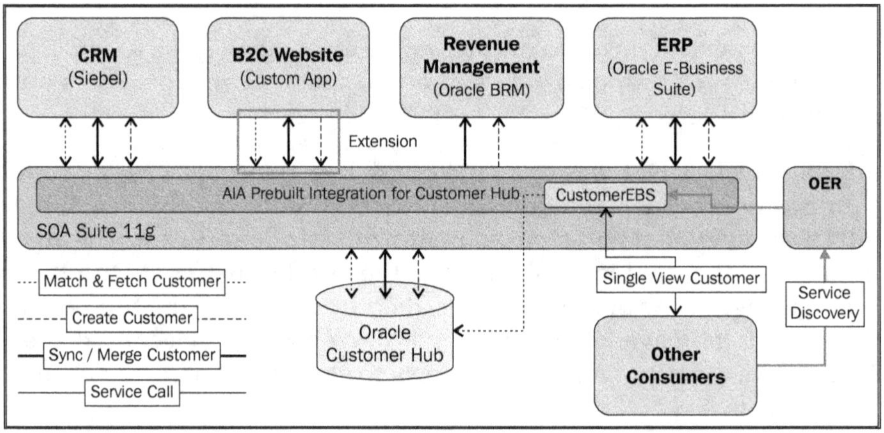

The view showed that very few extensions were required as most of the systems used by Weir & Bell Telecoms matched the endpoints assumed by the PIP. It was a win-win situation. They could not only accelerate the MDM rollout, but also, because the PIPs were SOA-based, other systems could plug to the hub more easily.

Moreover, by implementing the PIP, they also benefitted from all of the features and metadata artifacts available when installing the AIA FP, including the use of Oracle Enterprise Repository to promote service visibility, service re-use, and policy enforcement. By using the out-of-the box JDeveloper plugins, business services, **Web Service Description Language** (**WSDL**), and schemas, they considerably reduced development costs, and by adopting the AIA standards and service taxonomies, they matured their SOA adoption by enforcing the industry's best practices.

> This chapter will not cover the Oracle MDM suite or Oracle Data Quality products in detail. The chapter makes use of the MDM and data quality challenges faced by Weir & Bell Telecoms as a channel to position PIPs and the AIA FP. For further information on Oracle's MDM and Data Quality products please refer to `http://www.oracle.com/uk/products/applications/master-data-management/overview/index.html`.

AIA Foundation Pack overview

The AIA FP is Oracle's "accelerator framework" for implementing SOA-based system integrations. AIA FP and its prebuilt integrations such as PIPs were originally created to facilitate and accelerate the integration between different Oracle applications such as Siebel, E-Business Suite, PeopleSoft, and JD Edwards, among others. Customers looking to simultaneously implement and integrate several Oracle applications gain huge benefits from employing PIPs, as these significantly reduce the effort and risk involved with building interfaces to support business processes. Given Oracle's aggressive and continuous growth by acquisition, AIA FP and prebuilt integrations have become fundamental to rapidly integrate newly acquired products with their existing apps portfolio.

The AIA FP contains a variety of design-time and runtime artifacts that can be used when defining, designing, building, testing, and deploying SOA solutions. The following diagram presents an overview of the different components that build up the AIA FP:

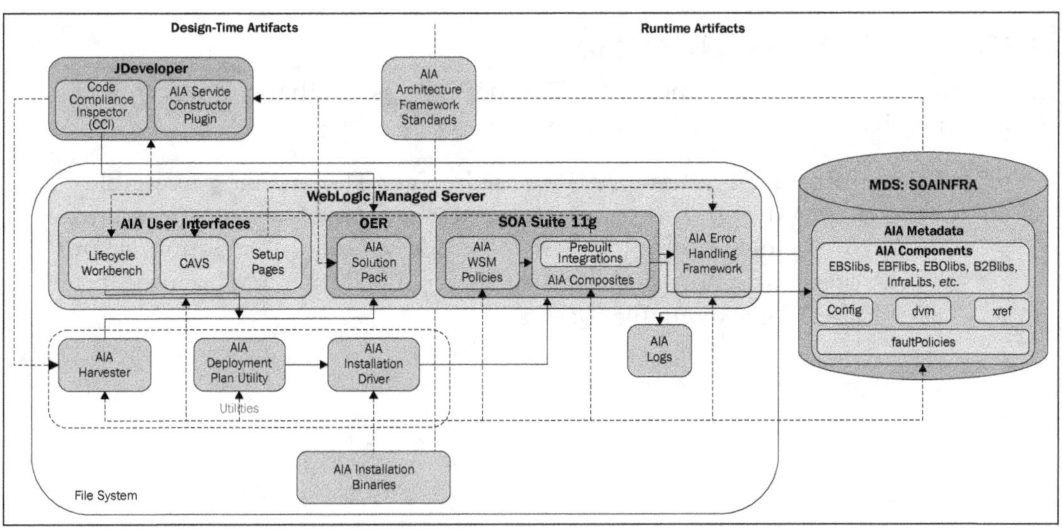

The AIA FP consists of:

- AIA Architecture Framework Standards
- Service Constructor JDeveloper Plugin
- Code Compliance Inspector (CCI)
- Lifecycle Workbench
- Composite Application Validation System (CAVS)
- Setup Pages
- AIA Message Resubmission Utility
- AIA Solution Pack
- AIA Harvester
- AIA Deployment Plan Generator
- AIA Installation Driver
- AIA WSM Policies
- AIA Composites
- AIA Prebuilt Integrations
- AIA Error Handling Framework
- AIA Metadata

The preceding components will be described in the following sections.

Design-time artifacts

These artifacts include tools, libraries, and other AIA assets that support the design-time phase of a project. These tools are:

- **AIA Architecture Framework Standards**: Consist of artifacts available for use during design-time governance stages. These include a reference architecture, a methodology, reference process models, conventions, and the AIA object library, which is basically a collection of XML artifacts such as XSD's and WSDLs, available for use.

> For more information on the AIA architecture framework refer to:
>
> **AIA Concepts and Technologies Guide**:
>
> `http://docs.oracle.com/cd/E23943_01//doc.1111/e17363/toc.htm`
>
> **AIA Reference Process Models User's Guide**:
>
> `http://docs.oracle.com/cd/E28280_01/doc.1111/e17368/toc.htm.`

- **Service Constructor JDeveloper Plugin**: JDeveloper plugin used to automate the creation of AIA services. At present this plugin only supports the creation of **AIA Business Connector Services (ABCS)** that will be described later in the chapter:

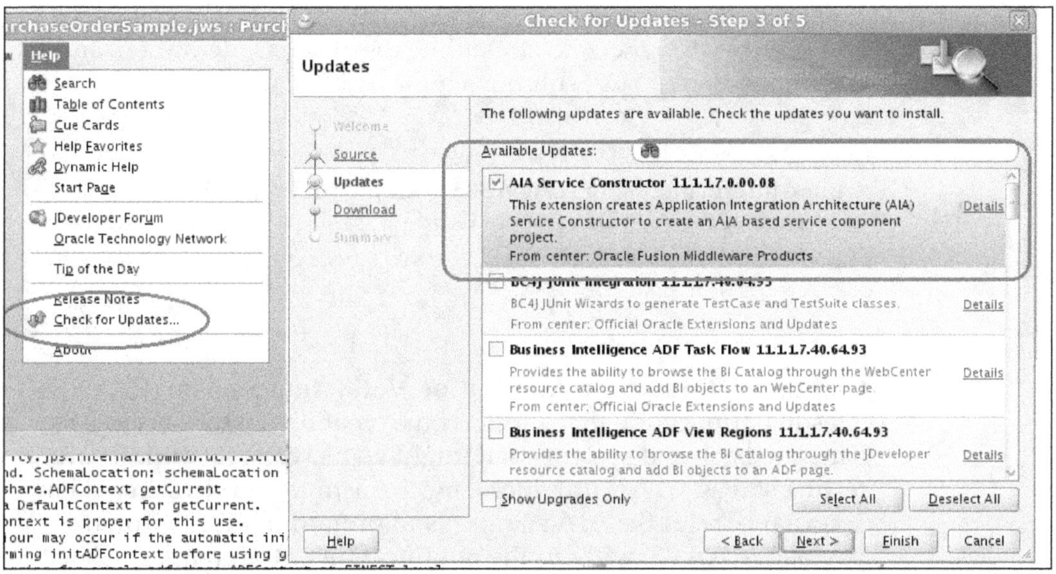

> For more information refer section **4 Working with Service Constructor of the AIA Developers Guide**:
>
> `http://docs.oracle.com/cd/E28280_01/doc.1111/e17364/workingwservcon.htm#BABBEHEI.`

- **Code Compliance Inspector** (**CCI**): JDeveloper plugin that can be used to check that code in SOA projects is compliant with AIA standards and best practices.

> For more information on CCI please refer to section **20 Using the Code Compliance Inspector** of the **AIA Infrastructure Components and Utilities User's Guide** `http://docs.oracle.com/cd/E28280_01/doc.1111/e17366/chapter20.htm`.

- **AIA User Interfaces**: A number of web applications aimed at supporting a project through the different AIA development lifecycle phases. The main web applications are:
    - **Lifecycle Workbench**: This application provides a comprehensive console that can be used by business analysts, solution architects, and services designers, to streamline the analysis, definition, and decomposition of SOA solutions built with AIA.

> For more information refer section **3 Working with Project Lifecycle Workbench** of the **AIA Developers Guide**.
>
> `http://docs.oracle.com/cd/E28280_01/doc.1111/e17364/workingwplw.htm#CHDEIHFG`.

-
    - **CAVS**: The **Composite Application Validation System** (**CAVS**) is a testing application that supports the creation of stub services to simulate back end systems that might be unavailable during early testing stages. CAVS provides a mechanism for services created in accordance with the AIA standards to programmatically route a payload to CAVS, without the modification of the composite itself.

> For more information on CAVS refer to the **AIA Infrastructure Components and Utilities User's Guide**.
>
> `http://docs.oracle.com/cd/E28280_01/doc.1111/e17366/toc.htm`.

- **Setup Pages**: Basically a configuration page to set up error notifications, error codes, routing configurations, and application registries, among others.

For more information on setup pages refer to the **AIA Infrastructure Components and Utilities User's Guide**.
`http://docs.oracle.com/cd/E28280_01//doc.1111/e17366/toc.htm`

- **AIA Message Resubmission Utility:** It allows browsing through a list of faults and resubmitting them based on specific criteria:

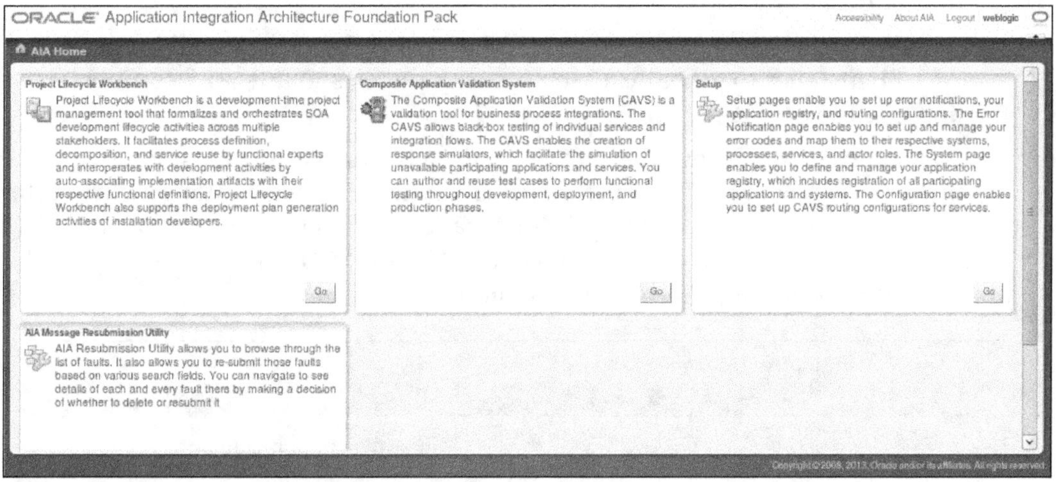

- **AIA Solution Pack**: This pack seeds OER with all of the asset types, categorizations, and metadata required to fully govern AIA solutions and assets. This component will be covered in more detail later in the chapter.
- **AIA Utilities**: A series of utilities available for post installation use with the AIA FP. The main utilities are:
    - **AIA Harvester**: A command line utility tailored for harvesting AIA services and assets into OER.
    - **AIA Deployment Plan Generator**: An Ant utility that takes the **Bill of Materials** file (`BOM.xml`), generated from the **Project Lifecycle Workbench** pack, as input and generates a **Deployment Plan** file (`<projectCode>DP.xml`) and a **Harvester Settings** file (`HarvesterSettings.xml`), based on the information supplied in the BOM.

- **AIA Installation Driver**: An Ant utility that reads a deployment plan generated from the Deployment Plan Generator and deploys all SOA artifacts specified in the plan to the target servers contained in the installation driver properties file (`AIAInstallProperties.xml`).

> The use of these tools will be covered later in the chapter.

Runtime artifacts

These artifacts include tools, libraries, and other AIA assets that support the runtime phases of a project. The supporting tools include:

- **AIA WSM Policies**: A **Web Service Manager** policy set created by the AIA FP installer to globally attach security policies to any AIA composite deployed to a SOA server.
- **AIA Composites**: A number of SOA Suite 11*g* AIA composites deployed into the SOA Server. These include: AIA utility services deployed during the AIA FP installation, AIA Prebuilt Integrations, and custom developed AIA services that follow the AIA FP lifecycle. The following screenshot shows the AIA composites deployed after installation of the FP:

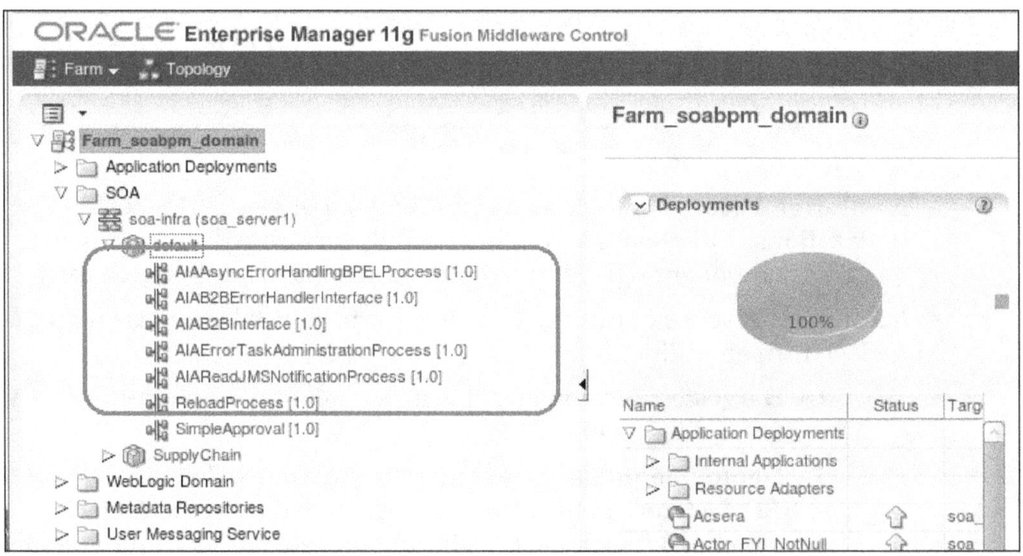

- **AIA Prebuilt Integrations**: Prebuilt integration solutions created by Oracle with the AIA FP. There are two types of Prebuilt Integrations:
    - **Direct Integrations**: Basically point-to-point integrations that manage data flows and data synchronizations between applications
    - **Process Integration Packs (PIPs)**: Integration accelerators that combine one or more integration styles, such as data-centric integration, web services, reference data query, and/or process-centric integrations, to deliver end-to-end integration solutions

> For a list of all available prebuilt integrations please refer to Oracle's AIA documentation page `http://docs.oracle.com/cd/E38316_01/index.htm`.

- **AIA Error Handling Framework**: This provides a complete common error handling solution for services developed following the AIA standards. As can be appreciated from the figure, the main features of the AIA Error Handling framework are:
    - Support for other technologies such as **Oracle Data Integrator (ODI)** and Oracle B2B
    - Support for the main types of faults, such as system, remote, and business faults
    - Configurable error notifications
    - Integration with **Human Workflow** using the SOA/BPM Suite **Worklist Application**
    - AIA specific error logger

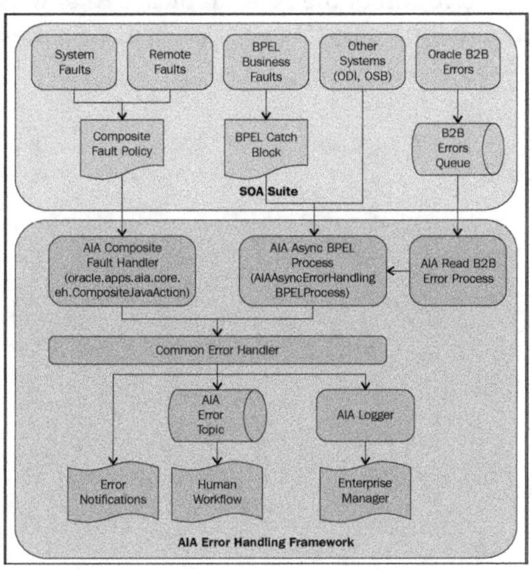

> For more information on the AIA Error Handling Framework please refer to section **13 Introduction to Oracle AIA Error Handling** of the **AIA Infrastructure Components and Utilities User's Guide**: `http://docs.oracle.com/cd/E28280_01/doc.1111/e17366/chapter13.htm`.

- **AIA Metadata**: A set of XML artifacts that mainly consist of AIA, specific XSDs, WSDLs, and other XML files, that are stored in the SOA Suite **Metadata Service** repository (**MDS**). The principle component of the AIA Metadata is the **AIA Components**. AIA Components contains the main XML libraries available for use in AIA FP. **Enterprise Business Object(s)** (**EBO**) and **Enterprise Business Message(s)** (**EBM**) are examples of AIA XSDs available for use in the object libraries. **Enterprise Business Service(s)** (**EBS**) is an example of AIA WSDLs Assets available for use in the service libraries.

> For a full list of the AIA Metadata content refer to section **2.1.3.5 Content of $AIA_HOME/AIAMetaData** of the **AIA Developer's Guide** at `http://docs.oracle.com/cd/E28280_01/doc.1111/e17364/bldgintflows.htm#BACBBAIC`.

The following sections describe in more detail some of the key components of the AIA FP.

> For a full description of the AIA FP please refer to 3Oracle's AIA documentation page: `http://docs.oracle.com/cd/E28280_01/aia.htm`.

AIA development lifecycle

Services built with the AIA FP follow a specific development lifecycle as illustrated in the following diagram:

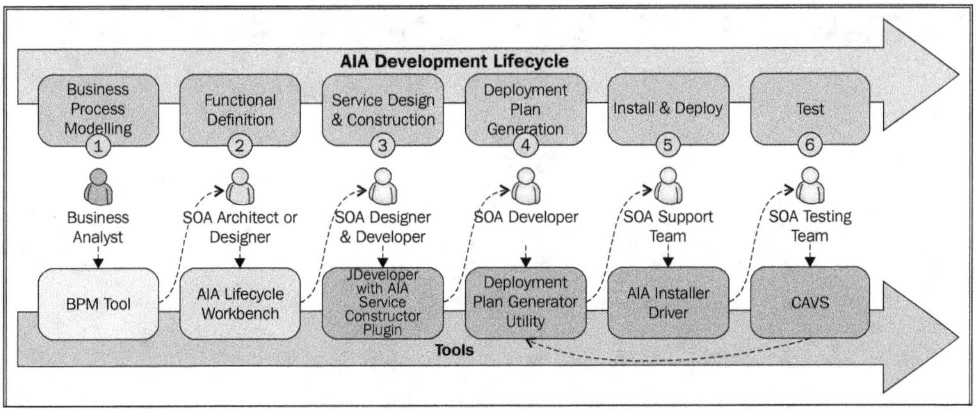

The AIA methodology follows a top-down approach that can be summarized as follows:

1. Business requirements are captured by Business Analysts using a BPM tool. At the time of writing this book, Oracle's documentation shows the **Business Process Analysis Suite (BPA)** as the preferred tool to conduct this analysis; however, this decision might change in the near future. The requirements are captured in the form of process models at levels 1 to 4.

> In future releases of the AIA FP it is very likely that the use of BPA will be superseded by another Oracle product. BPA Suite is in fact a rebrand of the **IDS Scheer ARIS** product. Shortly after the acquisition of IDS Scheer by Software AG back in 2009, Oracle announced that support for BPA Suite would end in the mid-term.

2. An SOA architect decomposes the requirements into different business tasks using the **Project Lifecycle Workbench** (http://<soa managed server>:<port>/AIA). The tasks are entered into a project as follows:

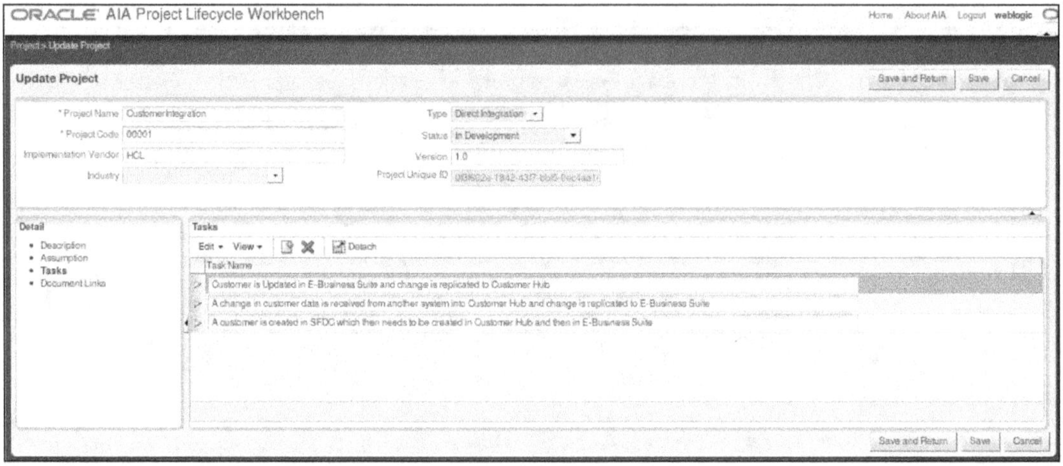

3. Service Design and Construction occurs as following:
    1. An SOA designer defines the different AIA services that are required to satisfy each business task. This activity is accomplished by adding several components under **Service Solution Component**; a collection of these components realizes the functionality specified by a given business task:

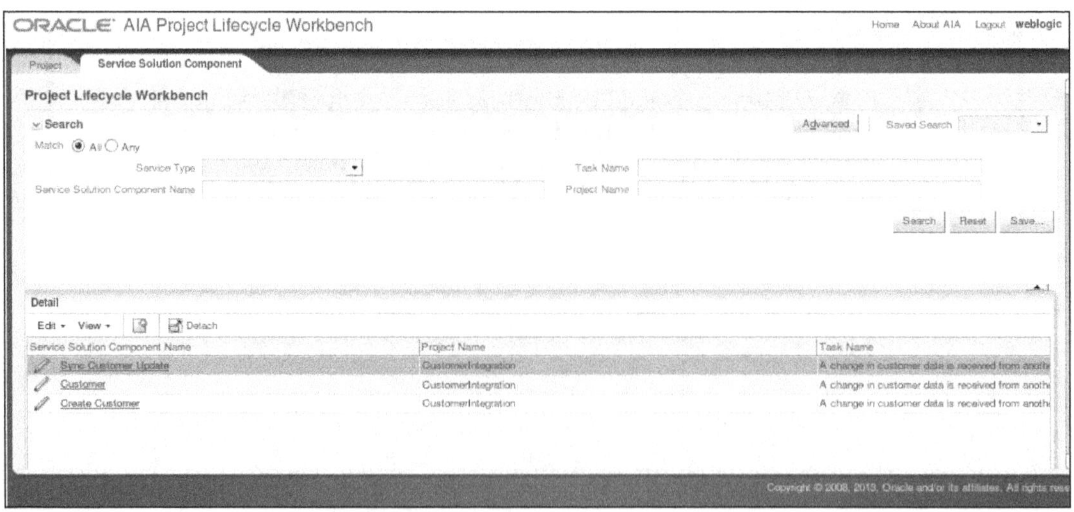

> At this point it is possible to search OER for potential re-use of existing assets.

2. Using JDeveloper with **AIA Service Constructor** plugin, an SOA developer browses through the different active requests (basically service solution components waiting to be developed) and then chooses a task to work on:

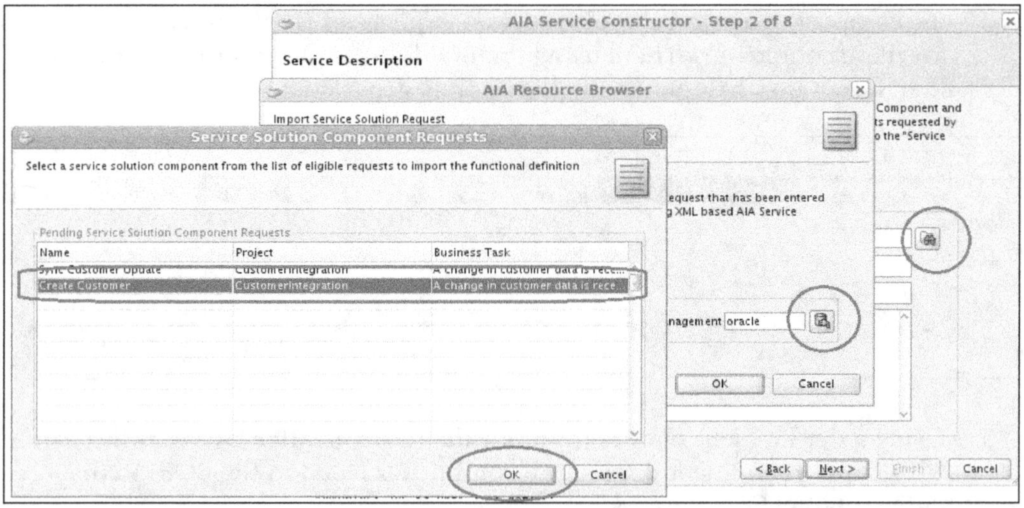

3. The developer generates and/or updates the relevant composites and adds the required annotations into the composite metadata:

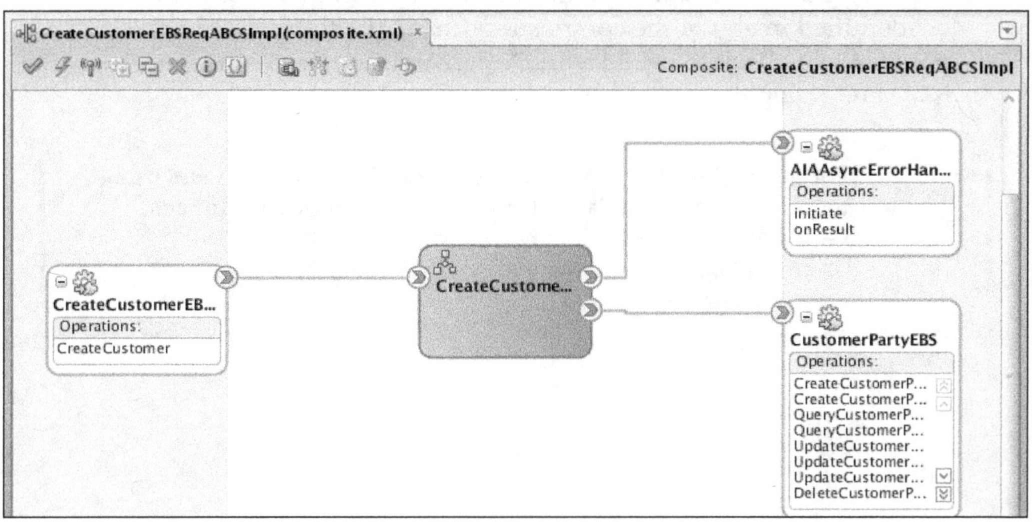

4. The developer harvests the built composites using the AIA Harvester utility back into the **Project Lifecycle Workbench** or alternatively into OER.

> Further details are available in the section *Harvesting AIA Assets.*

4. Back in **Project Lifecycle Workbench**, an SOA developer chooses which of the composites are to be deployed, and exports a **Bill of Material** (**BOM**) file for these composites. Then, using the BOM file as input for the Deployment Plan Generator, a deployment plan is thus generated:

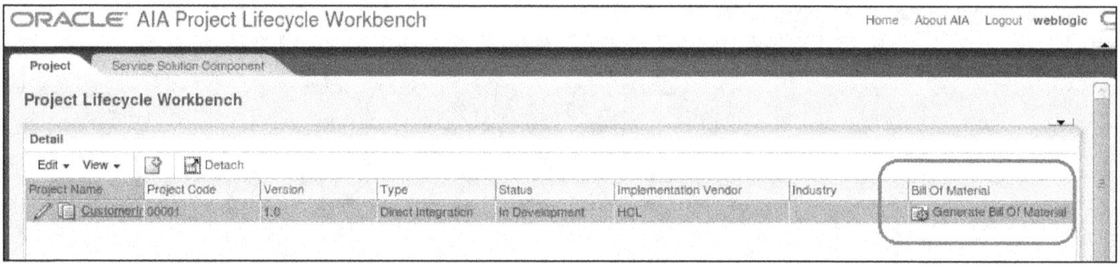

5. Using a deployment plan as input for the **AIA Installer Driver** utility, an SOA support engineer deploys all composites listed in the BOM to the defined target SOA servers.
6. Optionally the SOA Testing team may wish to perform tests on the AIA composites using the CAVS before releasing the composites into the integration or user acceptance testing environments. Should a defect be identified in any of the composites during the testing stage, it is possible to go back to the Service Design and Construction phase to fix the issue and redeploy.

> For detailed instructions on designing and building services using the AIA Foundation Pack please refer to the **AIA Developer's Guide** at `http://docs.oracle.com/cd/E28280_01/doc.1111/e17364/toc.htm`.

AIA reference architecture

The AIA reference architecture consists of a **Conceptual Service Architecture** and an **AIA Shared Service Library**. These architectural assets provide the foundations for AIA and enable the adoption of the core SOA design principles such as:

- **Reusability**: Designed and built assets that can be re-used across the enterprise now or in the future
- **Granularity**: Ability to identify the optimal granularity for the functionality delivered by a service and its service operations
- **Modularity**: Ability to break down a problem into smaller and distinct services that can be unit-tested in isolation and that expose well defined and standard interfaces
- **Composability**: Ability to create solutions by bringing together existing services that could themselves be made up of composed services
- **Loosely Coupling**: Service contracts are independent of application schemas or application
- **Standards-compliance**: Services are created based on industry standards and expose standard interfaces
- **Discoverability**: Services contain self-describing metadata that allows them to be identified and interpreted

AIA Conceptual Service Architecture

The AIA Conceptual Service Architecture is summarized in the following diagram:

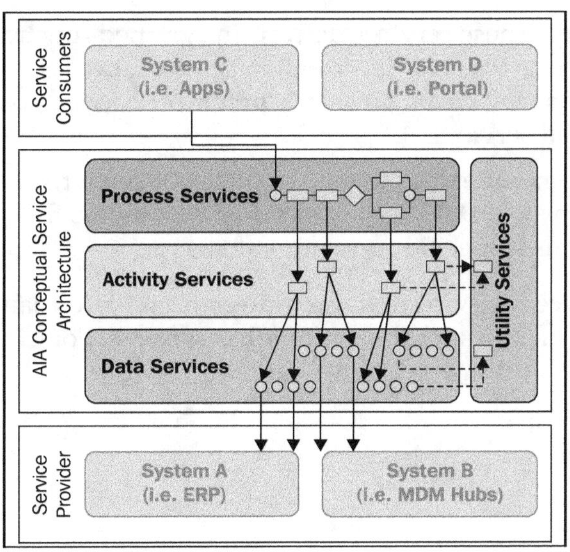

This architecture consists of:

- **Process Services**: These are services that automate business processes that span across multiple information systems and that require the orchestration of human and automated tasks as well as technical orchestration and use of business rules. Process Services are coarse grained in nature and their scope is limited to the business process that they support. Services can be short-lived or long-running, potentially spanning several months or even years.

  Process Sales Order is an example of a Process Service as it usually requires credit checks and address checks against the customer, human workflow for approvals depending on the sales order amount, availability to promise checks, creation of the order, and frequent notification of the order status to the customer and other systems.

- **Activity Services**: These services deliver a well scoped (yet still coarse-grained) business task that might require interaction with different systems. Activity Services support Process Services by providing the functionality needed to complete each task within the process.

  Customer Credit Check is an example of an Activity Service as it delivers a specific business task in support of a broader business process but in itself it may require interaction with more than one system (for example different credit agencies).

  Another example of an Activity Service is the Customer Business Service. This service would usually provide CRUD (create, read, update and delete) capabilities. The functionality is delivered by orchestrating and aggregating data from multiple systems that hold customer data.

- **Data Services**: These services deliver fine grained functionality and interact directly with the backend information systems. Data Services provide decoupling as they create an abstraction layer between backend systems and coarse grained services.

  Create Customer, Read Customer, Update Customer, and Delete Customer are all examples of Data Services as they encompass fine grained business functions against specific backend systems.

- **Utility Services**: Services that provide common error handling, diagnostic, and logging facilities for the use of other services. For example BAM services or exception handling or logging services.

AIA Shared Service Library

The **AIA Shared Service Library** is basically a **Logical Service Architecture** derived from the AIA Conceptual Service Architecture. The following diagram depicts it:

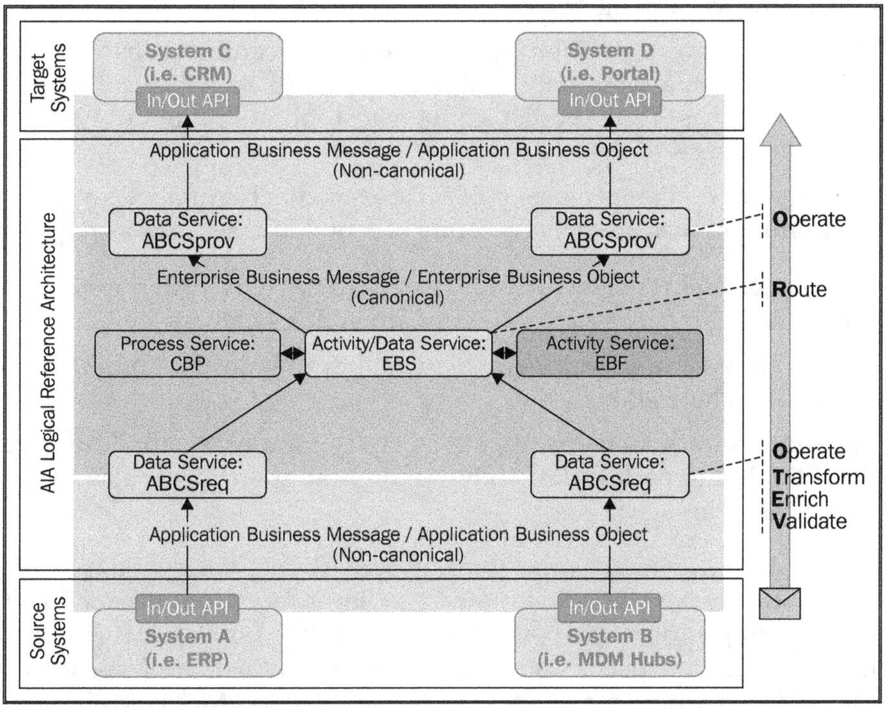

As can be seen from the preceding diagram, the AIA Share Service Library consists of a number of service artifacts. These artifacts define the **AIA Service Taxonomy** and are the building blocks for solutions delivered using AIA.

- **Composite Business Process (CBP)**: A Process Service is ideally implemented as a BPMN 2.0 process using the BPM Suite 11*g*. However they can also be implemented as BPEL processes using SOA Suite 11*g*.

  CBPs are application agnostic as they only interact with an EBS to complete their tasks and also to implement a canonical schema.

> Oracle is positioning BPEL as a technical orchestration component that can be used in support of the business process to perform more technically challenging tasks. BPM Suite is Oracle's strategic product to support organizations that implement Business Process Management (BPM) solutions.

- **Enterprise Business Service (EBS)**: EBSs are considered both Activity Services as well as Data Services as they expose coarse grained operations in support of specific business tasks. They also provide support for CRUD-like operations against first-class entities such as Customer, Sales Order, Purchase Order, Invoice, among others.

  EBS services are application agnostics and their contract is based on a canonical schema. EBSs only deal with EBF, CPB, or ABCS. EBSs are typically implemented as SOA Suite 11*g* composite applications and use the Mediator to route requests to other services.

  EBS services don't make use of BPEL as they don't actually do any service orchestration. Instead, they consume EBF or ABCS services as required.

- **Enterprise Business Flow (EBF)**: These are the Activity Services responsible for delivering business tasks and implementing business logic.

  EBF services are application-agnostic as they only deal with EBS services in technical orchestrations.

  EBFs are typically implemented as SOA 11*g* composites applications using the BPEL PM to perform the technical orchestrations. They also implement a canonical schema.

- **Application Business Connector Service (ABCS)**: They are a type of Data Service that exposes the fine-grained business functions provided by the participating applications. ABCS are responsible for transforming messages from application-specific format or **Application Business Message (ABM)** into AIA's canonical format or **Enterprise Business Message (EBM)**.

  ABCS services are also responsible for implementing the VETO pattern. This means validating (validating semantics and data), enriching (getting additional data required that may be required), transforming (from ABM to EBM), and operating on a message (calling out).

  ABCS services are typically implemented as SOA Suite 11*g* composite applications using mainly Mediator and BPEL components. BPEL is used to enrich the message. Mediator is used to transform and operate. Validation often involves the implementation of WSM policies and other checks such as semantic validations.

There are two types of ABCS:

- **ABCS Requesters (ABCSreq)**: Responsible for receiving client messages in application-specific semantics (ABM) and then validating the message, enriching it, transforming it into an EBM, and calling out to an EBS.
- **ABCS Provider (ABCSprov)**: Responsible for exposing fine-grained backend system functionality. They receive EBM messages from an EBS, transform them to ABM, and then persist them to backend systems.

> **For Weir & Bell Telecom, the PIP was extended with additional ABCS requesters to integrate a custom web application with the Customer Hub. The new ABCS requesters were created with the AIA Service Constructor.**

- **Application Business Flow (ABF)**: In some integration scenarios introducing several layers of abstractions to an interface cannot be justified. For such scenarios, AIA supports point-to-point integrations by delivering **Direct Integrations** using Application Business Flows (ABF):

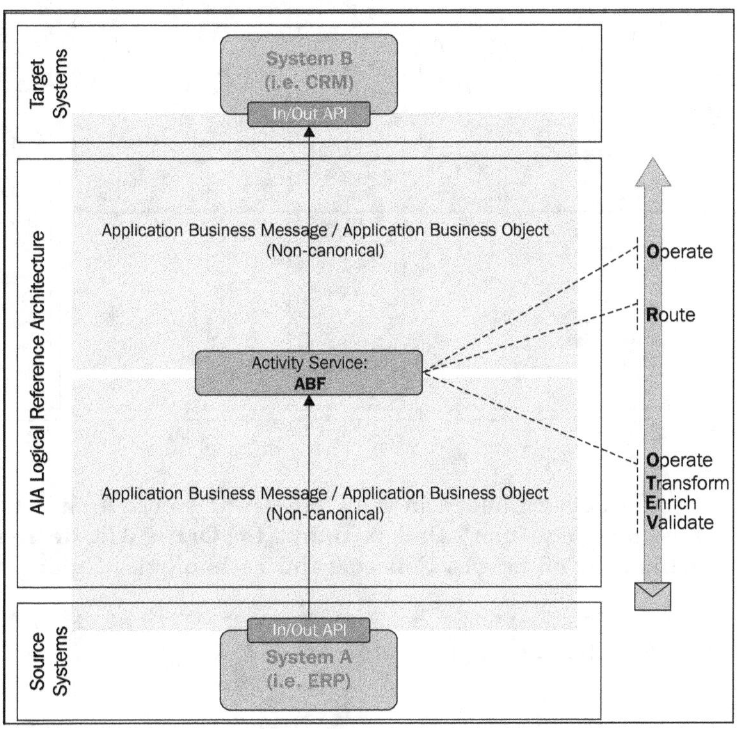

> Although Direct Integrations may result in better business outcomes for some specific integration scenarios, the abuse of this pattern may result in higher operational costs for mid and long term. Therefore, before deciding to implement Direct Integrations we strongly advise you to evaluate the short, mid, and long term benefits of it.

AIA services implement the **VETORO** integration pattern. This pattern is a variant of the industry-standard pattern VETO, which stands for Validate, Enrich, Transform, Operate. AIA introduces an extra **Route** and **Operate** step resulting in the VETORO variant.

Following is an example of an end-to-end interface implemented with AIA:

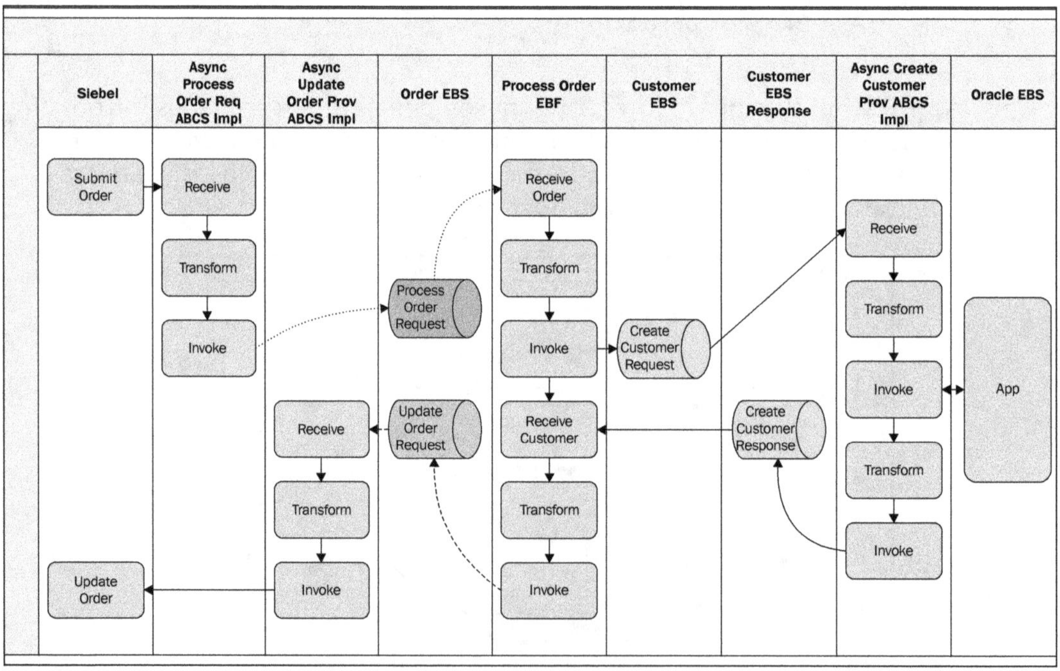

> For more detailed information on the AIA Reference Architecture please refer to section **1 Understanding the Oracle AIA Reference Architecture of the AIA Concepts and Technologies Guide**.
>
> `http://docs.oracle.com/cd/E28280_01/doc.1111/e17363/chapter01.htm#sthref9.`

AIA EBMs and EBOs

At the core of any integration, regardless of the architectural style or technology, there must be a message that contains the data required to action a business function. In AIA terms, these messages are referred to as **Enterprise Business Messages (EBMs)**. EBMs are exchanged by the different AIA services in order to transfer messages between the participating applications.

Strictly speaking, EBMs are envelopes that contain the business data that the participating applications are interested in. For this reason EBMs contain certain metadata in an **EBM Header** that would facilitate the transport of the message to the relevant destinations. This is comparable to how the postal service works. In order to send a letter an envelope must contain a recipient name and address. Without this information the envelope will never reach the destination (chances are that it will never leave the postal office and the message will get lost). Optionally, envelops may contain a return address so it can be returned to the sender's address in case of non-delivery.

An example of an EBM that supports the creation of a customer would be `CreateCustomerPartyEBM` and the corresponding response would be `CreateCustomerPartyResponseEBM`.

The business data that makes an EBM message relevant for the participating applications are contained in data objects referred to as **Enterprise Business Objects (EBOs)**. Using our previous analogy, this would be equivalent to the actual letter inside the envelope. Examples of EBOs could be a `CustomerPartyEBO`, `SalesOrderEBO`, and `ItemEBO`, among others. EBOs contain all of the relevant business data required by the participating applications or by the service to perform business logic.

EBMs and EBOs work hand-in-hand and during the transportation of the message they are coupled. Again, going back to our analogy, there wouldn't be much point in delivering an envelope that doesn't contain a letter. Equally, a letter would never be delivered without an envelope containing the recipient's address (perhaps the stamp could be considered as a metric used in cloud services to charge integration based on usage, but that's a topic for a different book).

Both EBMs and EBOs are defined using **XML Schema Documents (XSDs)**. Furthermore, EBMs and EBOs are built using common semantics and frequently implement the Canonical Scheme and Schema Centralization patterns. Individual applications on the other hand normally use their own specific data formatting for messages referred to as **Application Business Messages (ABM)** that contain **Application Business Objects (ABOs)**. It is the responsibility of ABCSs to transform ABMs/ABOs to EBMs/EBOs and vice versa.

The following diagram illustrates, at a high level, the anatomy of an EBM message:

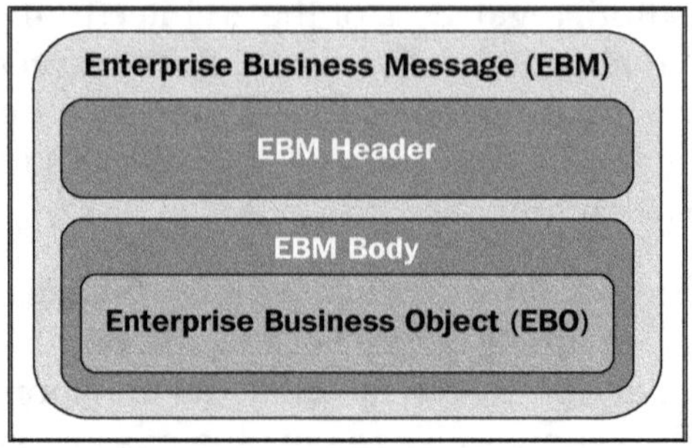

In a nutshell, an EBM message consists of:

- **EBM Header**: This carries important metadata that might be needed by the transporting party to ensure message delivery. Some of the information that can be included in the header includes:
    - Information about the message originator
    - Information about the message destination
    - Unique identifier of the message
    - Error handling information
    - Timestamps
    - Verbs (for example, create or update)
- **EBM Body**: Basically a place holder for the EBO.
- **EBO**: The business object containing the relevant business data. Since certain messages may require specific data items that cannot be held in a single EBO, it is possible to create a **context-specific EBO** that contains elements from multiples EBOs.

EBMs as well as EBOs are agnostic of the underlying transport mechanism. EBMs can be sent using a variety of transport protocols such as HTTP, JMS, RMI, and others. However, since AIA services are implemented as SOAP web services and defined using the WSDL, the preferred transport is HTTP. The following diagram illustrates how an EBM messages fits in a standard HTTP/SOAP message:

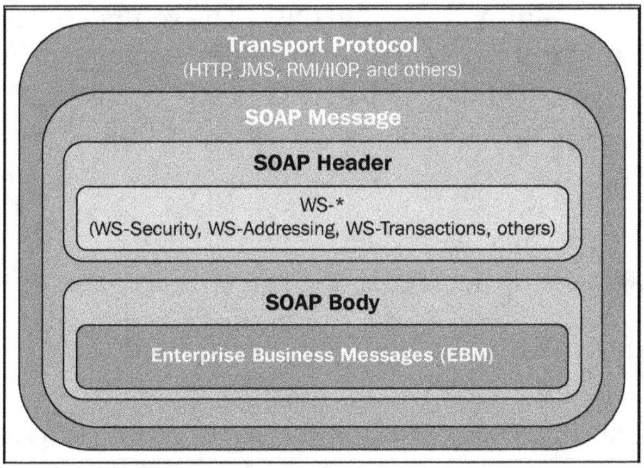

Implementing SOAP web services provides many benefits because AIA can rely on additional standards such as WS-Security to implement security (authentication, authorization, encryption, and signatures), WS-Addressing for asynchronous web services and WS-Policy for implementing several other policies.

Integrating AIA Foundation Pack with OER

As briefly described earlier in the chapter, AIA Foundation Pack can be integrated with OER. This integration allows for AIA assets to be harvested and discoverable via OER, including all of the prebuilt AIA assets available after installing the AIA Foundation Pack.

The steps to integrate the AIA FP with OER are:

1. Ensure that an installation of the AIA FP and OER is available.

> For details about installing the AIA Foundation Pack refer to **Installation and Upgrade Guide for Oracle Application Integration Architecture Foundation Pack** `http://docs.oracle.com/cd/E28280_01/doc.1111/e17949/toc.htm`.
>
> Refer to *Appendix, Installation Tips and Techniques* for more information on installation and configuring OER.

2. Import the AIA Solution Pack into OER. The solution pack will import into OER all prebuilt assets and assets types available in AIA FP after its installation:
    - Enterprise Business Service (EBS) WSDL files
    - Application Business Connector Service (ABCS) WSDL files
    - Enterprise Business Object (EBO) XSD files
    - Enterprise Business Message (EBM) XSD files
3. Configure an **AIA Artifact Store**. This is required to allow access to EBO and EBM HTML documentation.
4. Enable remote **Java Database Connectivity** (**JDBC**) in WebLogic Server. This is required to allow content to be harvested to the **Project Lifecycle Workbench** database from the developer's workstations.

The following sections illustrate how to perform the preceding steps.

Importing the AIA Solution Pack into OER

For OER to recognize AIA Assets and Asset Types, the following files must be imported to OER using the Import utility:

- **AIA-Types-Solution-Pack.zip**: This file contains the core AIA asset type's definitions.
- **AIA-ABF-Solution-Pack.zip**: This file contains the asset type's definitions for **Direct Integrations**.
- **AIA-Assets-Solution-Pack-part1 & 2.zip**: These two files contain a definition for all the out-of-the-box assets available in the AIA Foundation Pack after installation. Importing these file **bootstraps** OER with all AIA assets available in MDS.

These files are imported into OER as follows:

1. Logon into OER using the **Admin** account.

   `http:<oer server>:<port>/oer.`

2. Go to the **Admin** page:

3. Under the **Import Export** menu, click on **Import / Export Client** to open the Import/Export utility:

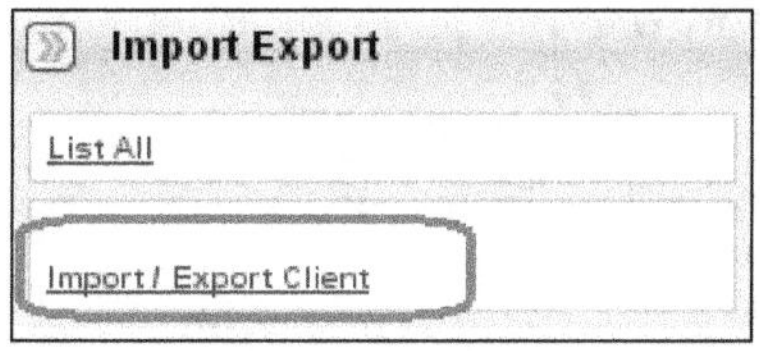

4. Click on the **Import** tab, and **Browse** to `$AIA_HOME/Infrastructure/LifeCycle/solutionpack/` where **$AIA_HOME** is AIA installation directory (for example, `/u02/app/oracle/middleware2/aiafp`).
5. Select the file to import then click on **Next**:

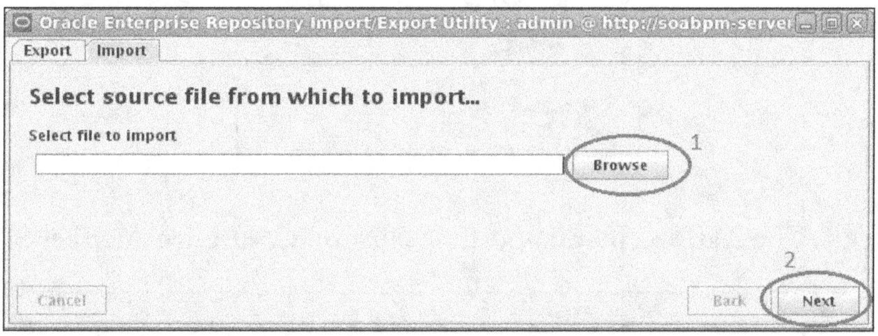

6. Ensure that all files were successfully imported and then click on **Finish**:

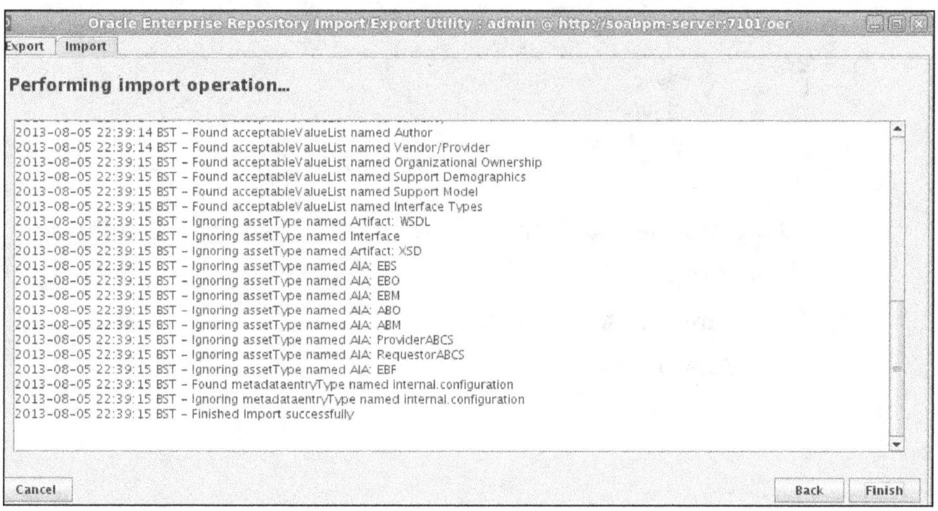

7. Repeat these steps for the remaining files.

Configuring the AIA Artifact Store

Once OER has been bootstrapped with the AIA assets, an **AIA Artifact Store** must be created so the **HTML reference pages** available for some of the AIA assets are accessible from OER.

The AIA Artifact Store is created as follows:

1. Logon into OER using the Admin account.

   `http:<oer server>:<port>/oer.`

2. Go to the **Assets** page.
3. Open **Asset Editor** by clicking on **Edit / Manage Assets**:

   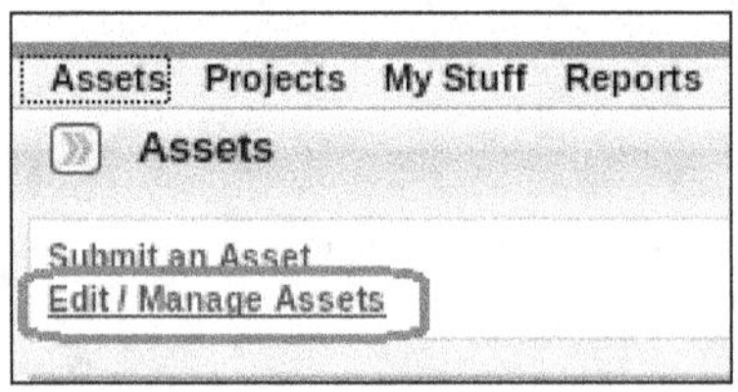

4. Click on the **Actions** menu and then click on **Configure Artifact Stores**:

   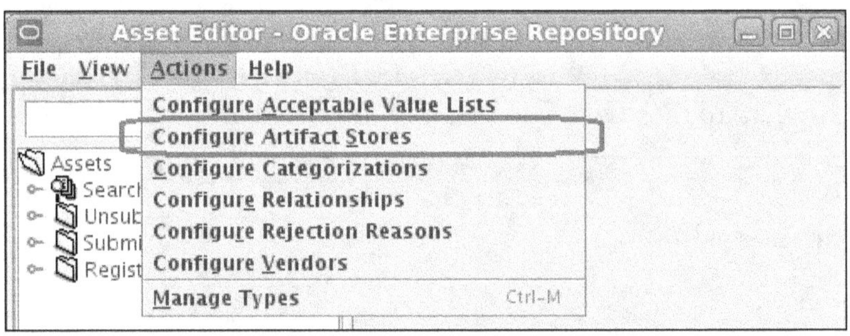

5. Click on **Add** and then enter the AIA Artifact Store details as follows:
   - **Type**: `HTTp`
   - **Hostname**: `<AIA Server>:<port>`
   - **Path**: AIA/faces

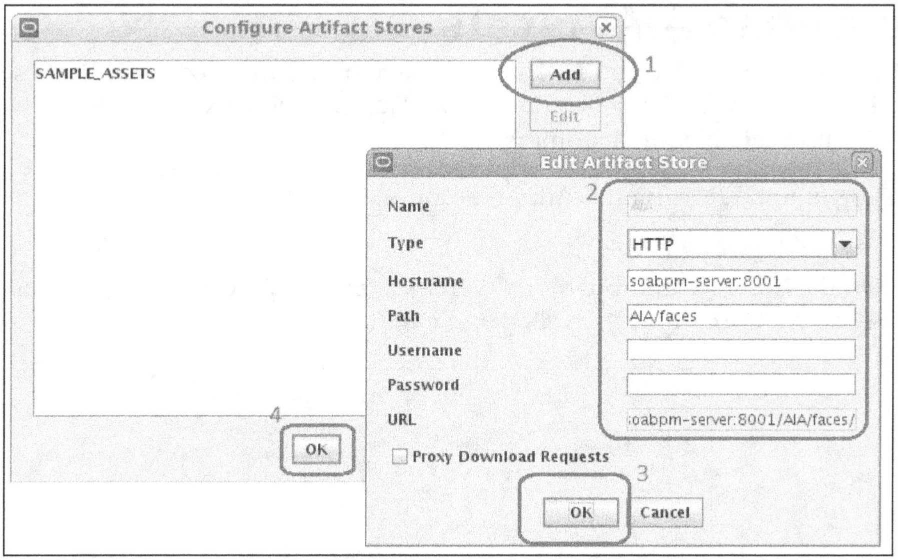

6. Click on **OK**.

Enabling Remote JDBC

Remote JDBC connections are enabled in the AIA server as follows:

1. Connect to the AIA server using a terminal client (for example SSH).
2. Go to the domain `$MW_HOME/user_projects/domains/soabpm_domain/bin` where **$MW_HOME** is the middleware home where SOA Suite has been installed. (for example `/u02/app/oracle/middleware/user_projects/domains/soabpm_domain/bin`).
3. Using a text editor open the file `setDomainEnv.sh`.
4. Search for **WLS_JDBC_REMOTE_ENABLED="-Dweblogic.jdbc.remoteEnabled= false"** and set the value to `true`:

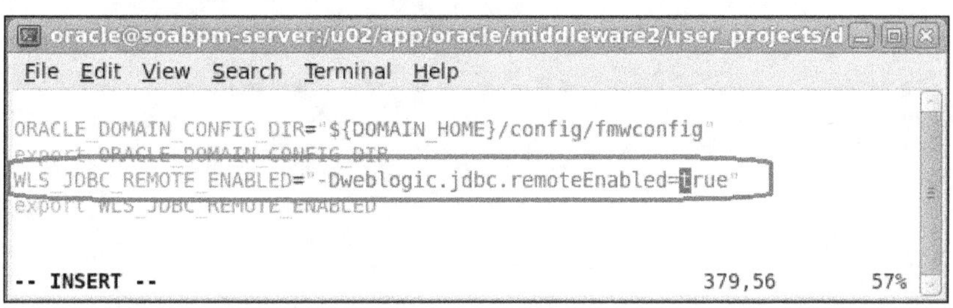

5. Save the changes and restart the Admin server.

Discovering AIA Assets

Once the AIA Solution Pack and AIA assets have been imported in OER, these become immediately available for discovery. The following example shows how to search for EBS available for customers.

1. Log onto OER using the Admin account, `http:<oer server>:<port>/oer`
2. Go to the **Assets** page.
3. On the **Enter Search String** field enter `Customer`. From the **Type** dropdown select **AIA: EBS** and then click on **Search**:

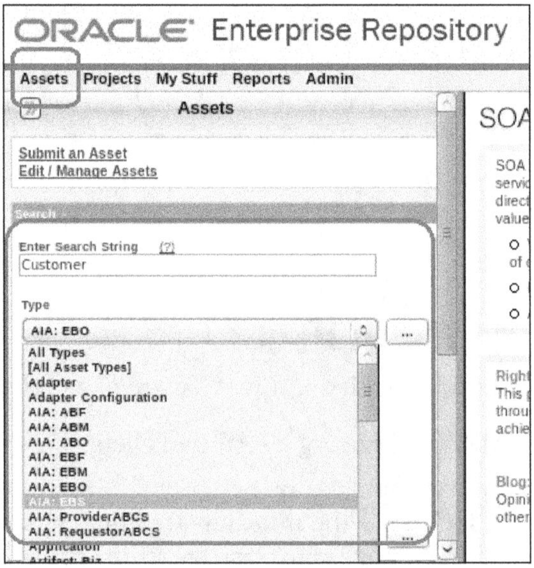

4. All assets matching the search criteria will show up on the left-hand side of the page. You may click on any given asset to see its details:

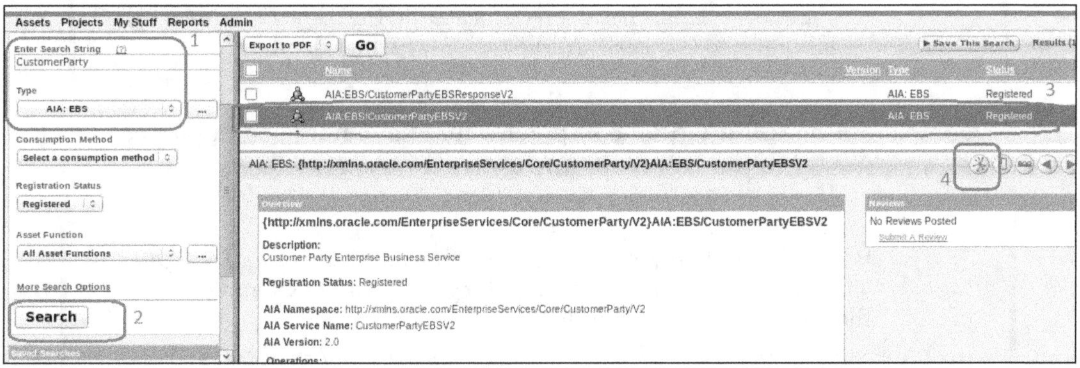

5. Moreover, it is also possible to visualize the AIA asset inter-dependencies by clicking on the **Navigation** button:

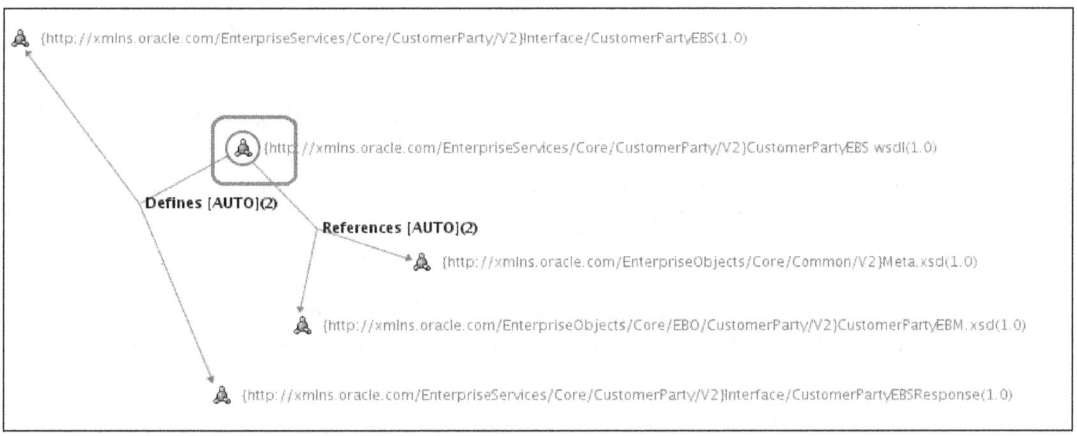

Harvesting AIA Assets

The AIA FP allows for different harvesting strategies to be adopted. The specific harvesting strategy to use in a project should ultimately be decided in the company's specific requirements.

Following is a reference to the supported AIA harvesting strategies:

> A complete chapter has been dedicated to the topic of harvesting. Please refer to *Chapter 5, Harvesting,* for further details.

- For custom-built individual composites that have not been deployed, run the AIA Harvester to publish them into Oracle Enterprise Repository

> For further details please refer to section **5.2 Harvesting Design-Time Composites into Project Lifecycle Workbench and OER** of the **AIA Developer's Guide**.
>
> `http://docs.oracle.com/cd/E28280_01/doc.1111/e17364/harvesting.htm#CACCACHA.`

- For custom-built interfaces, run the AIA Harvester to publish them into Oracle Enterprise Repository

> For further details please refer to section **5.3 Harvesting Interfaces to OER in Bulk** of the **AIA Developer's Guide**.
>
> `http://docs.oracle.com/cd/E28280_01/doc.1111/e17364/harvesting.htm#CACDJBFB.`

- For deployed composites (part of deployed Process Integration Packs), run the AIA post installation script to publish the run-time composite into Oracle Enterprise Repository

> For further details please refer to section **5.4 Harvesting Deployed Composites into OER** of the **AIA Developer's Guide**.
>
> `http://docs.oracle.com/cd/E28280_01/doc.1111/e17364/harvesting.htm#CACCBEGI.`

Summary

The chapter started by describing the data quality issues faced by Weir & Bell Telecoms and why, regardless of having available a relatively matured SOA implementation, Weir & Bell Telecoms' data quality issues persisted. Then it highlighted the importance of MDM and how an MDM solution, built using the AIA FP and its PIPs, would reduce effort and risk while still delivering the benefits of SOA.

The chapter continued by giving an overview of AIA FP, illustrating its Software Development Lifecycle and Reference Architecture.

The chapter concluded with a practical use case on integrating the AIA FP with Oracle Enterprise Repository to reinforce service visibility and reusability with the objective to maximize business benefits.

The following chapter summarizes the steps for installing the products of the Oracle SOA Governance Solution.

Installation Tips and Techniques

This appendix provides tips and techniques for those performing a full installation of **Oracle Enterprise Repository** (**OER**) and **Oracle Service Registry** (**OSR**). It is not our intention to provide a full installation guide for each product as these can be obtained from Oracle via their website. Rather, we provide some useful pointers gleamed from past experience, gained from installing the product set.

Oracle provides software installers that guide the user through the installation process. The installer can be run in graphical, console or silent mode. In graphical mode the user is presented with a rich GUI that guides them through the process in a wizard-driven manner. Console mode provides an interactive text-based mode for command line installation. Silent mode, which requires the use of XML configuration files, is a non-interactive method of installation and can run from the command line or as part of a script. The following sections assume that the user is using the full graphical installation process.

Explaining the installation topology

The following diagram shows the installation topology of the SOA Governance Suite as prescribed by this book:

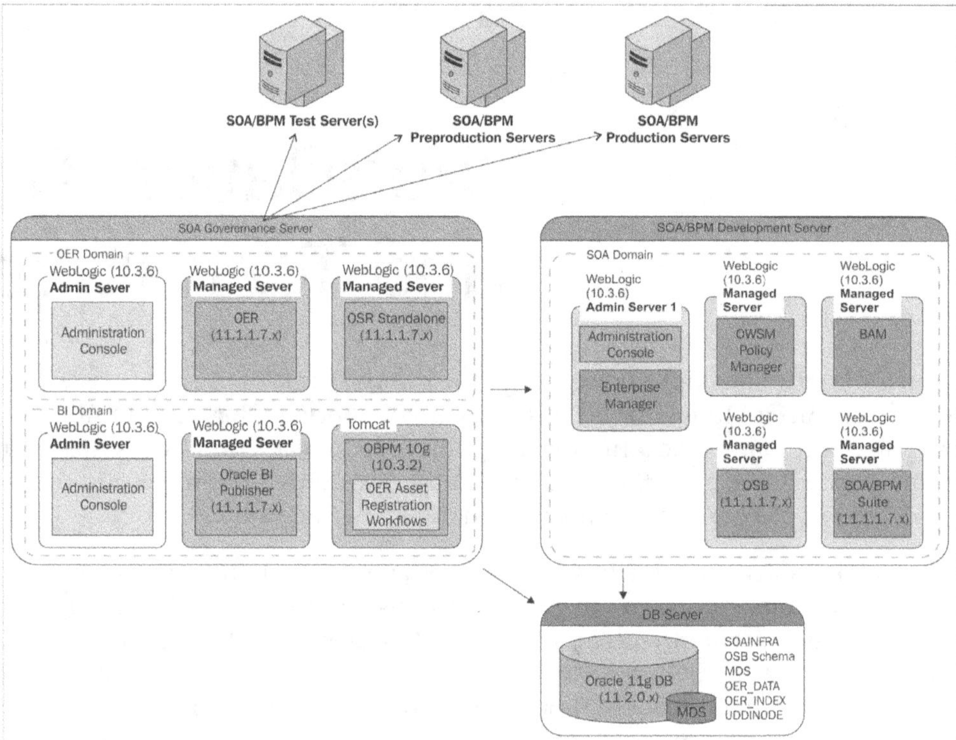

Because OER is meant to be the single source of truth throughout the entire development lifecycle, Weir and Bell made the following considerations when defining the SOA Governance Solution environment strategy:

- A shared instance of the SOA Governance Server (excluding OSR) to support the development lifecycle stages: Development, Test, Preproduction, and Production.
- Individual—standalone instances of OSR to match each SOA Suite environment.
- A sandbox instance of the SOA Governance Server for purposes of trying patches and configuration changes.
- A separate passive instance of the Governance Server for disaster recovery.

Installation overview

The overall installation process is summarized in the following diagram:

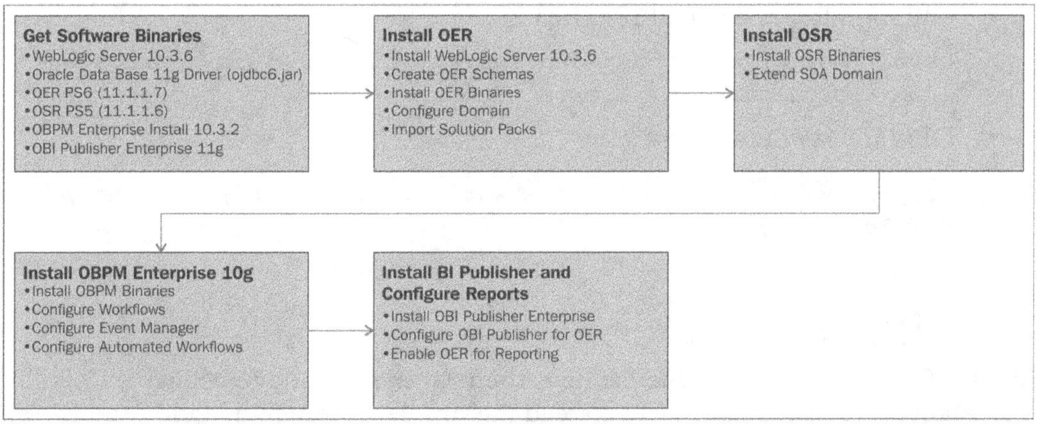

This appendix will follow the preceding process to install the installation topology outlined in the previous section.

The Oracle binaries can be obtained from e-Delivery, the Oracle Technology Network website (OTN), or from Oracle support through a service request. The general recommendation is to get the software through e-Delivery as this is the official download site. It will require registration, and software is protected by a username and password that is obtained as part of the registration process. OTN should only be used for conducting trials of software or for general proof of concepts.

The following installation binaries are required. If you wish to try the installation you may also use the following OTN link. For production or testing installation download binaries from e-Delivery.

- WebLogic Server 10.3.6

  `http://www.oracle.com/technetwork/middleware/weblogic/downloads/wls-for-dev-1703574.html`

- Oracle Data Base 11*g* Driver (ojdbc6.jar)

  `http://www.oracle.com/technetwork/database/features/jdbc/index-091264.html`

- Oracle Enterprise Repository 11*g*R1 PS6 (11.1.1.7.0)

  `http://www.oracle.com/technetwork/middleware/repository/downloads/index.html`

- Oracle Service Registry 11*g*R1 PS5 (11.1.1.6.0)

  `http://www.oracle.com/technetwork/middleware/registry/downloads/index.html`

- OBPM Enterprise Install 10*g* (10.3.2)

  `http://www.oracle.com/technetwork/middleware/bpm/downloads/index-100737.html`

- OBI Publisher Enterprise 11*g*

  `http://www.oracle.com/technetwork/middleware/bi-publisher/downloads/index.html`

Installing OER

Once the Oracle binaries are obtained the administrator is ready to begin the installation process. The first step is to read the supplied installation guide and to ensure that all prerequisites are met. OER can be installed in 32 or 64 bit environments but generally, we would recommend 64-bit since 32-bit architecture is limited to addressing less than 4 GB of RAM. With a 64-bit architecture, all system memory can be addressed and there are therefore more options available for JVM tuning.

> Oracle provides a OER sizing guide that can be used as a guide for sizing environments and is located at the following URL: `http://www.oracle.com/technetwork/middleware/repository/overview/oer11gsizingguidelines-130307.pdf`

Installing the database

Before installing the middleware components, the installer must create a database that will be used by the installer to create the Oracle schemas necessary to support the SOA Governance Suite of products. This book assumes installation into an Oracle 11*g* database, although other vendors are supported. Once a database is created, the first step is ensure that the Database Adminstrator (DBA) has created the necessary tablespaces for the OER database schemas. The general recommendation is to create three tablespaces, one supporting the tables, one to store indexing data for the aforementioned tables, and one to hold binary large objects (LOBS).

> The Oracle installer does not support installation directly into **Real Application Cluster** (**RAC**) environments, though OER can run on a RAC environment

The naming of these tablespaces will be based on companywide standards but for illustration purposes we will call these `OER_DATA`, `OER_INDEX`, and `OER_LOB`. Oracle recommends that each should be at least 300 MB in size.

The following code snippet can be used to create the user and tablespace:

```
CREATE TABLESPACE OER_DATA
DATAFILE '<path>/oer_data.dbf' SIZE 300M
AUTOEXTEND ON NEXT 10240K MAXSIZE UNLIMITED
EXTENT MANAGEMENT LOCAL AUTOALLOCATE
LOGGING
ONLINE
SEGMENT SPACE MANAGEMENT AUTO;

CREATE TABLESPACE OER_LOB
DATAFILE '<path>/oer_lob.dbf' SIZE 300M
AUTOEXTEND ON NEXT 10240K MAXSIZE UNLIMITED
EXTENT MANAGEMENT LOCAL AUTOALLOCATE
LOGGING
ONLINE
SEGMENT SPACE MANAGEMENT AUTO;

CREATE TABLESPACE OER_INDEX
DATAFILE '<path>/oer_index.dbf' SIZE 300M
AUTOEXTEND ON NEXT 10240K MAXSIZE UNLIMITED
EXTENT MANAGEMENT LOCAL AUTOALLOCATE
LOGGING
ONLINE
SEGMENT SPACE MANAGEMENT AUTO;

CREATE USER OER IDENTIFIED BY <password>
DEFAULT TABLESPACE OER_DATA
TEMPORARY TABLESPACE TEMP;

GRANT CREATE MATERIALIZED VIEW TO OER;
GRANT CREATE SEQUENCE TO OER;
GRANT CREATE SESSION TO OER;
GRANT CREATE SYNONYM TO OER;
GRANT CREATE TABLE TO OER;
GRANT CREATE TRIGGER TO OER;
GRANT CREATE VIEW TO OER;
GRANT UNLIMITED TABLESPACE TO OER;
```

> Note that the above database sizing is for a typical production environment. For non-production environments, tablespaces can be smaller in size. An Oracle recommended rule of thumb for database drive size is to allow for approximately ten times the physical table and index size. Thus for a table of 100 KB and index tablespace of 1.1 GB allow a disk of at least 11 GB.

Temporary disk space requirements

The Oracle installer uses temporary disk space during software installation. A temporary directory should be allocated by the server administrator. During the installation process, the temporary space must be sufficiently large to hold the compressed JRE bundle and the uncompressed JRE. The default temporary directory is dependent on the platform; for Windows, it is the directory pointed to by the **TMP** (**temporary**) environment variable, whereas for Unix it will vary dependent on the flavor of Unix. We would recommend allocating a temporary directory of suitable size and specifying this as part of the command line for the installer program using the `-D` command line switch.

> For further details, please refer to the OER installation guide at `http://docs.oracle.com/cd/E28280_01/doc.1111/e15745/toc.htm`.

Installing WebLogic

The OER software will execute in a Java runtime environment. This book assumes Oracle WebLogic will be used to host OER. Thus, prior to installing OER, the administrator must first obtain the WebLogic binaries and install WebLogic. WebLogic installation requires a JDK1.6 install or above. To install WebLogic log on a Unix Shell Console with the Oracle user, change directory to the directory into which the WebLogic download has been installed. Following are the steps.

1. The following command will execute the Oracle Installer for WebLogic:

```
PATH=<JAVA_HOME>/bin:$PATH
export PATH
java -jar wls1036_generic.jar -log=$HOME/logs/WLS1036_install.log
```

2. When installing WebLogic in a new environment, choose to create a new **Middleware Home Directory**:

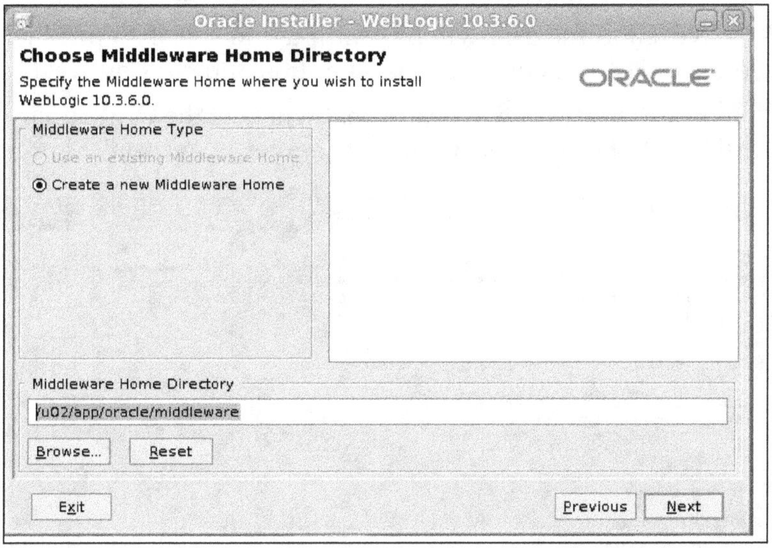

3. This directory will act as a repository for all installed middleware products for a given machine. When prompted select a **Typical** installation.
4. When prompted choose a suitable Java Development Kit install and click on **Next**.
5. Then you will choose a directory for the installation. Finally, click on **Next** and complete the installation.

Installing OER software

Log on to a shell console using the Oracle user and change directory to the location where the installation binaries are located. Following are the steps to start the Oracle installer program:

1. The following command will execute the Oracle Installer for WebLogic:

```
PATH=<JAVA_HOME>/bin:$PATH
export PATH
java -jar OER111170_generic.jar -log=$HOME/logs/OER_install.log
```

2. When running the installer program, the user will be initially asked to specify a **Middleware Home Directory**. The user should opt to use the existing Middleware home into which the WebLogic Server was installed.
3. Click on **Next** and the user will be prompted to specify a product installation directory for OER. Choose the default option and click on **Next**.
4. Now, choose the Application Server that will host the OER application. For this install, the user should select **WebLogic Server 11** as installed previously:

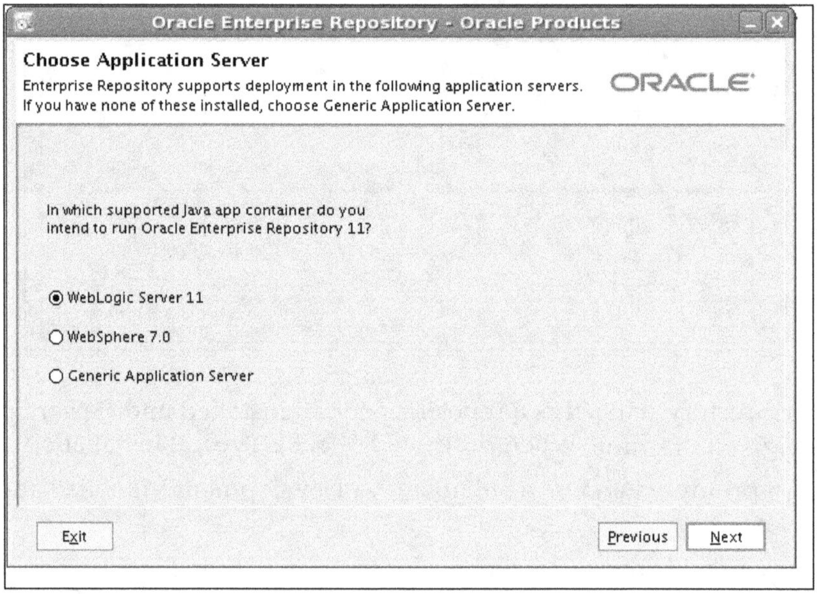

5. Now, the user will be asked to specify the OER properties such as listener port and application name. Enter suitable values and click on **Next**.
6. Then, the user chooses the database into which the schemas that support OER will be installed. Here the installer will select the database that was created in the previous section. When prompted enter the tablespace information and click on **Next**.

7. Finally, enter the connection details for the Oracle 11*g* database that contains the above tablespaces. The installer will use the server details and credentials to connect to the database when creating the database schemas:

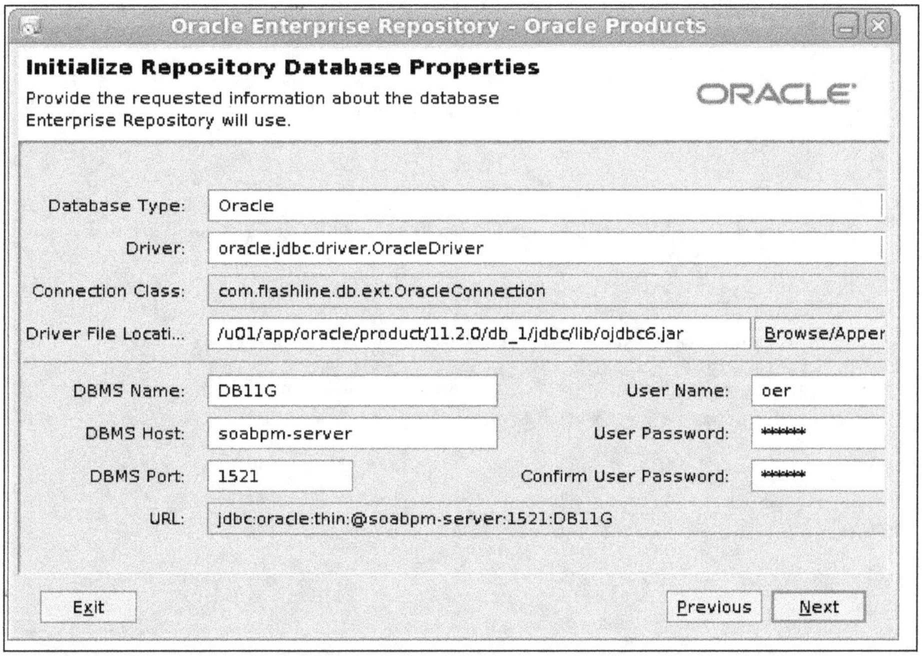

8. Click on **Next** and complete the installation.
9. Once the OER binaries have been installed and the schemas created, the next step is to create a new WebLogic domain for OER. To do this, start a Unix Shell console, log in with the Oracle user, and from the WebLogic 10.3.6 home directory execute the following command:

```
<MIDDLEWARE HOME>/wlserver_10.3/common/bin/config.sh
```

10. When the WebLogic Configuration Wizard opens select **Create a new WebLogic domain** and then click on **Next**.

11. On the next screen, select **Oracle Enterprise Repository 11.1.1.7** and click on **Next**:

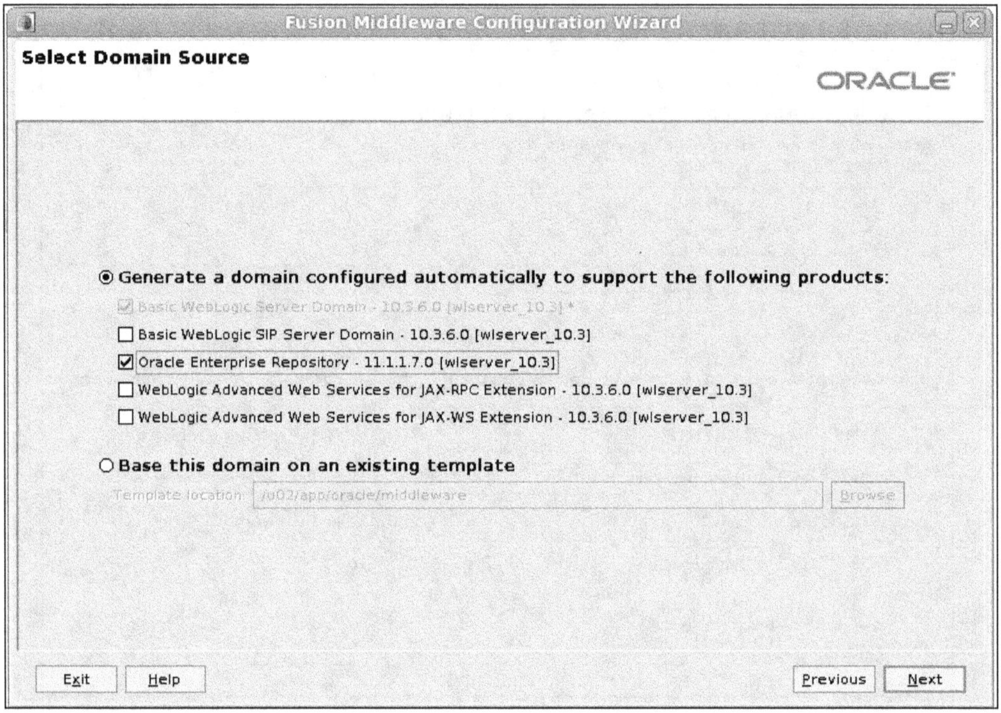

12. Now enter the name of the OER domain—typically `oer_domain` and click on **Next**.
13. On the next screen, enter the desired username and password for the WebLogic Domain Administrator. Select **Next** when completed.

14. Then configure the server JDK. As in this sample we are installing a development environment, select **Development Mode** with the Sun JDK. Then click on **Next**. For Test and Production systems it is recommended to use JRocket and **Production Mode**:

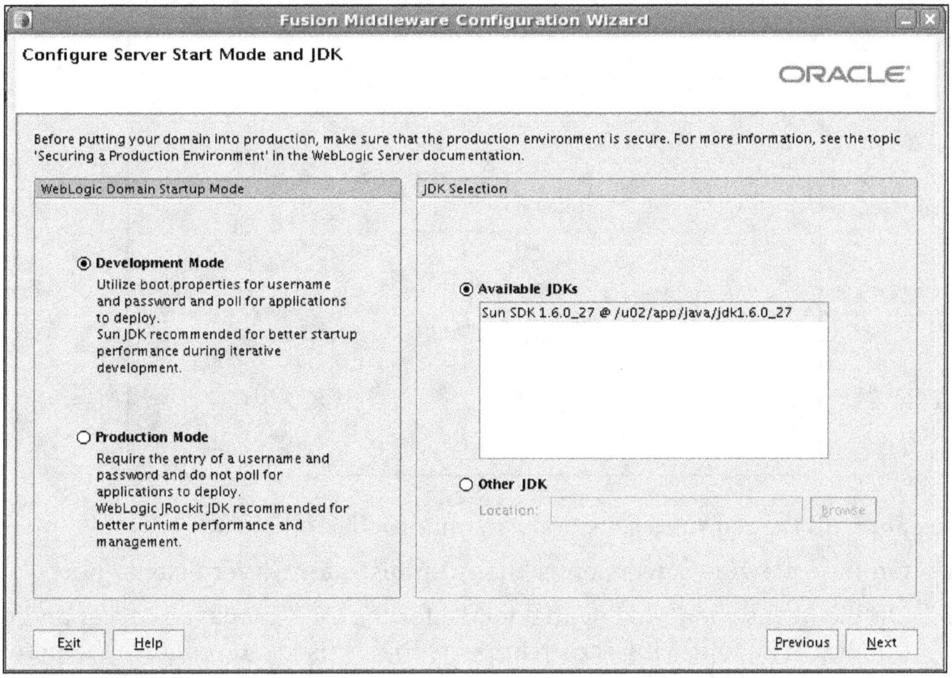

15. On the next screen, select **Administration Server**; this is very important and must be done otherwise the domain will be installed without an Admin server. Also select the **Managed Servers, Clusters and Machines** link to create the OER managed server as shown in the following screenshot:

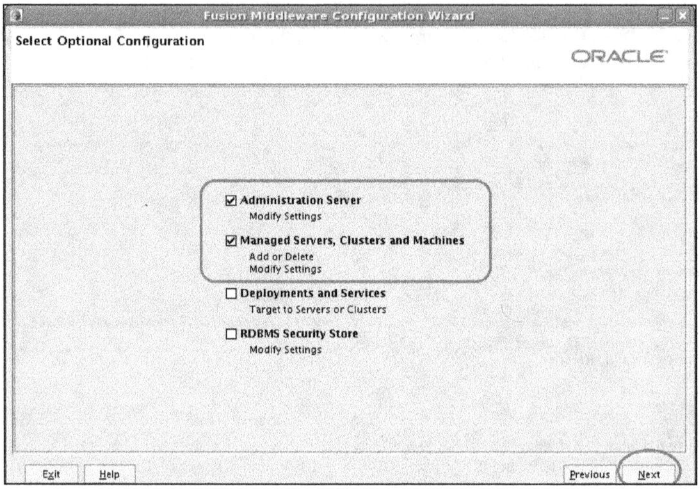

16. Once all the required selections are made, click on **Next.**
17. On the following screen, enter the Administrator Server listener port.
18. On the next screen, review the details for the OER managed server and click on **Next**. The following screen appears that is used to configure the managed server that will host OER:

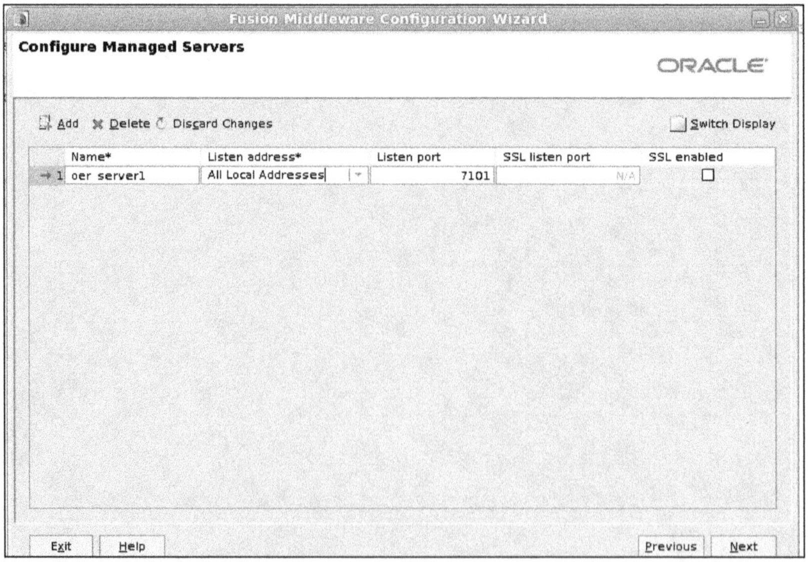

19. Enter the name of the managed server and the required listener port and click on **Next**. The next couple of screens allow the user to configure cluster details.

> For more information on installing OER in a clustered environment please refer the OER installation Guide at `http://docs.oracle.com/cd/E28280_01/doc.1111/e15745/toc.htm`

20. Once the cluster details are configured, click on **Next** and configure the machine details similar to those shown in the following screenshot:

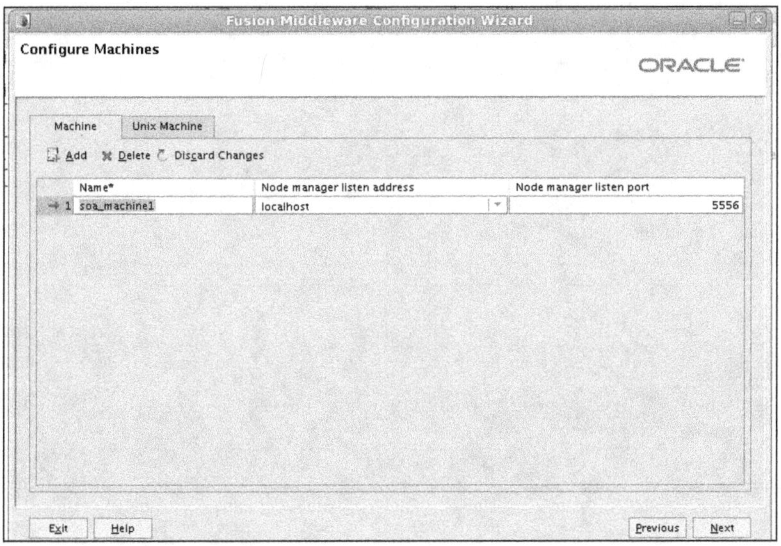

21. In our case we have created a machine called **soa_machine1**. Click on **Next**, and then add the servers to the machine created in the previous step as illustrated in the following screenshot:

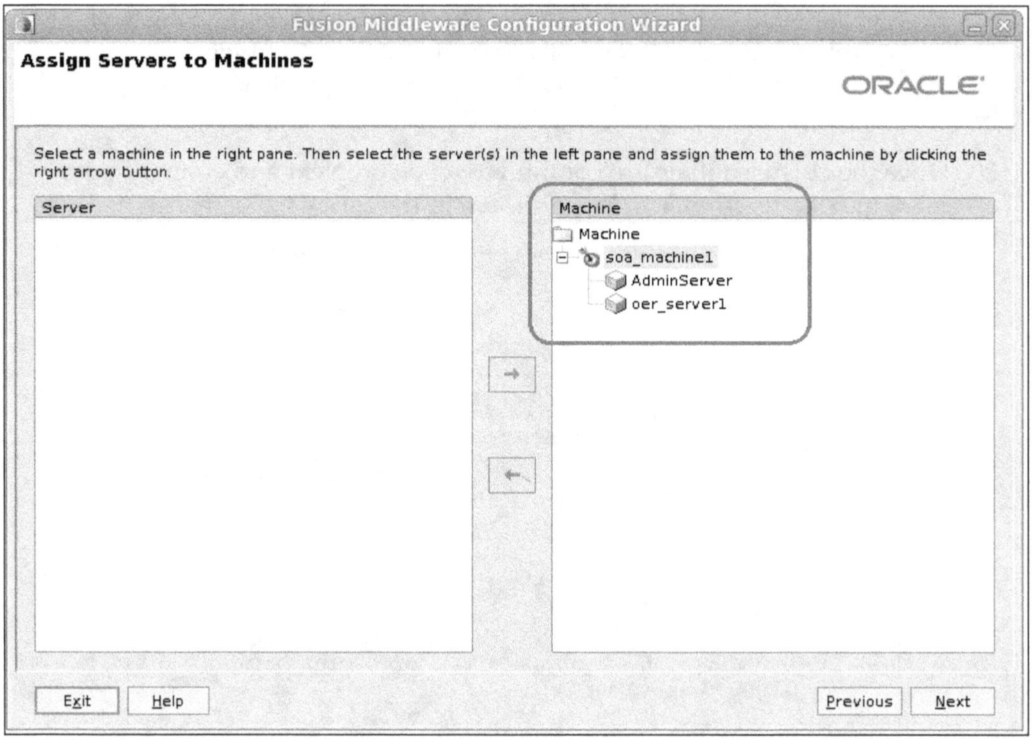

In our installation topology we tied the Admin and OER managed server into the same machine. However, it is possible to have Admin server and OER managed server in different machines for more complex topologies such as a cluster.

22. Finally review the required installation using the summary screen and click on the **Create** button.
23. Review the creation details to make sure that the domain is created properly. Should any errors be encountered, then check the log files, correct any problems, and repeat the preceding process.
24. Verify that the installation was successful by starting the Admin and OER managed servers and accessing the OER console.
25. The next step is to install the OER Solution Packs. Details of how to do this are provided in *Chapter 5, Harvesting*.

Installing OSR software

The installation of OSR is similar to the OER installation.

1. First create a database user and tablespace to hold schema objects for OSR. The following SQL script can be used to create the database schema objects:

```
CREATE TABLESPACE OSR_TABLESPACE
DATAFILE '<path>/osr_data.dbf' SIZE 50M
AUTOEXTEND ON NEXT 10M MAXSIZE UNLIMITED
EXTENT MANAGEMENT LOCAL AUTOALLOCATE
DEFAULT STORAGE (
  INITIAL 5M
  NEXT 5M
  MINEXTENTS 1
  MAXEXTENTS UNLIMITED
  PCTINCREASE 50);

CREATE USER OSR
PROFILE "DEFAULT"
IDENTIFIED BY <password>
DEFAULT TABLESPACE OSR_TABLESPACE
TEMPORARY TABLESPACE TEMP
ACCOUNT UNLOCK;

GRANT CONNECT TO OSR;
GRANT RESOURCE TO OSR;
GRANT UNLIMITED TABLESPACE TO OSR;
GRANT CREATE ANY SYNONYM TO OSR;
GRANT DROP ANY SYNONYM TO OSR;
```

2. The next step of the process is to download the OSR software binaries from e-Delivery.

> Ensure that you have reviewed and satisfied the system requirements prior to installing the software. These can be found in the Service Registry Guide `http://www.oracle.com/technetwork/middleware/registry/osr11productdocumentation-159992.pdf`.

3. To execute the installer, log on to a shell console using the Oracle user and locate the OSR binaries. Ensure the PATH environment variable includes the Java binaries and execute the installer as follows:

```
PATH=<JAVA_HOME>/bin:$PATH

export PATH

java -jar OSR111160_generic.jar
```

4. On the first screen, click on the **Next** button to begin the installation process. On the next screen select the **Installation Type** required. In this case, we will install a Standalone Registry; click on **Next**.
5. On the next screen choose the same **Middleware** home as was previously created for the WebLogic and OER installations:

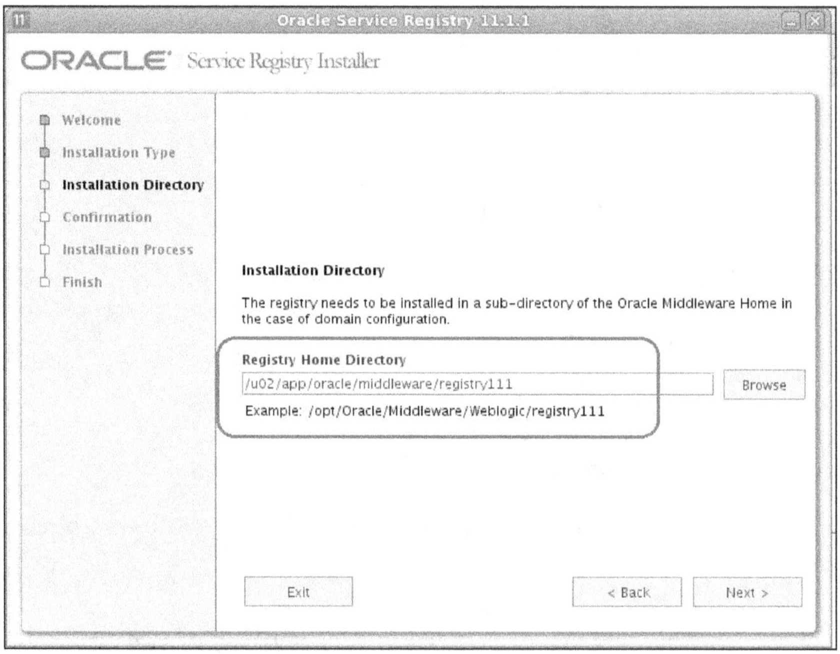

6. Click on the **Next** button and configure notification setting as required.
7. Once done, click on the **Next** button to configure the administrator account for OSR. We would recommend using the same credentials as used for the OER administration account.
8. Click on the **Next** button. This takes you to a set of screens for configuring the OSR database. Enter the details for the database and schemas created as part of the initial setup, as described previously.

9. On the **Deployment** screen, enter the port details.

> Please bear in mind that the OER default port is 7101, so we recommend using a different port even if OSR is deployed on a different server. For example, you could use 7201 as the default port.

10. On the next screen, review the summary installation details and once happy click on **Next** to begin the installation process. Review the installation details and check the log files for any errors. Repeat the preceding steps should any errors be encountered during the installation.

11. Once the OSR binaries are installed you will need to extend the existing SOA WebLogic domain to include the OSR managed server. To do this, log into a Shell console using the Oracle user and from the existing WebLogic home execute the following command:

```
<MIDDLEWARE HOME>/wlserver_10.3/common/bin/config.sh
```

> In the Weir & Bell installation we extend the existing SOA domain to include the OSR managed server. You may choose to deploy a different topology depending on the needs of your particular environment. Also consider the different patches available for OSR as these might have an impact in the SOA domains.

12. This starts the **Fusion Middleware Configuration Wizard**. Select **Extend an existing WebLogic domain** from the screenshot that follows:

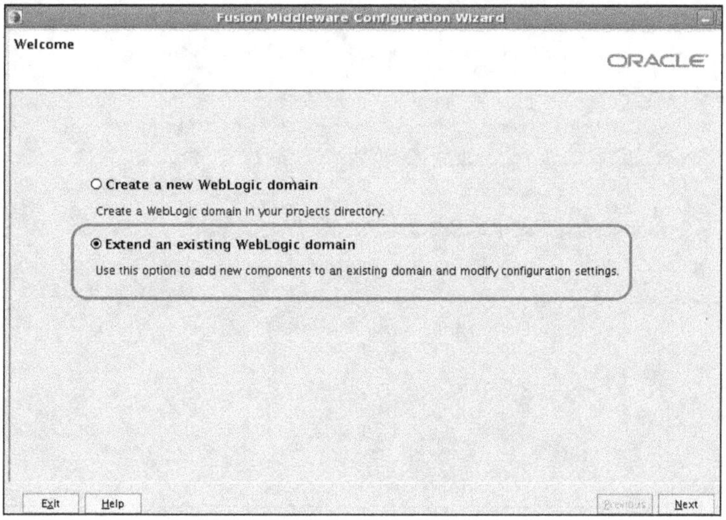

13. Click on **Next** and then locate the SOA WebLogic domain.
14. On the subsequent screen, select the option to extend the existing domain with Oracle Service Registry as shown in the following screenshot:

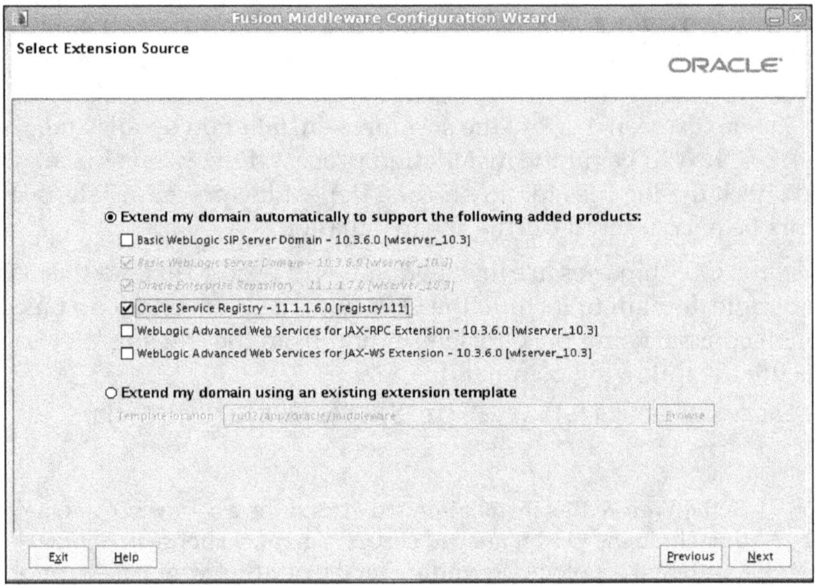

15. On the next screen, configure the OSR schema **Username** and **Password** as created in the first part of this installation:

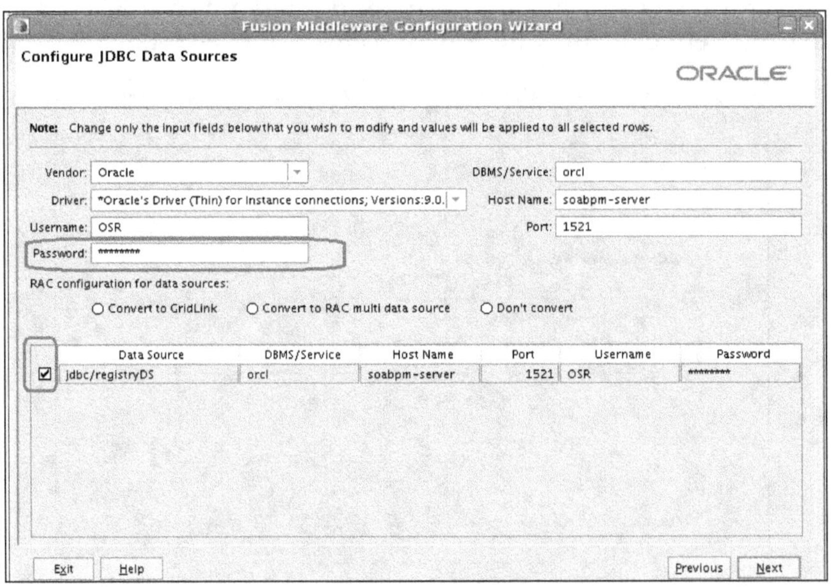

> Ensure that you use the same name for the Data Source as you used when configuring the OSR binaries.

16. The next screen allows you to test the connection to the database. Ensure that the connection establishes itself correctly and click on **Next**.
17. Select the checkbox to configure **Managed server, Clusters and Machines**. Once done, the next set of screens allow you to create a WebLogic managed server for the OSR application and associate this with a machine as follows.
18. Click on **Next** and then click on **Extend** to extend the existing domain. Review the installation details and logs and ensure that there were no errors. Should errors be encountered, correct the source of the problem and repeat the preceding steps.

Verify that the installation was successful by starting the Admin and manage servers and accessing the OSR console. Finally, Access the OSR Registry Control Console home page (http://<SERVER NAME>:7201/ registry/uddi/web) and try to log on using the Admin account.

Installing OBPM

Download the OBPM binaries and review the installation guide for any important prerequisites. Then log in to a Shell Console using the Oracle user and locate the directory holding the downloaded binaries. Execute the installer as follows:

1. From from the shell console, execute the following commands:

   ```
   chmod ug-rwx OracleBPMEnterpriseWL103200_lin.bin
   ./OracleBPMEnterpriseWL103200_lin.bin
   ```

   This will invoke the OBPM installer software.

2. On the first screen, review and hit the **Next** button. This will display a screen prompting the installer to enter a new Middleware Home directory for the OBPM installation as displayed as follows:

> Oracle's recommended installation path is `<Middleware Home>/obpm/enterprise/`. Our installation deviated slightly from this; however, we recommend using Oracle's recommendation for simplicity.

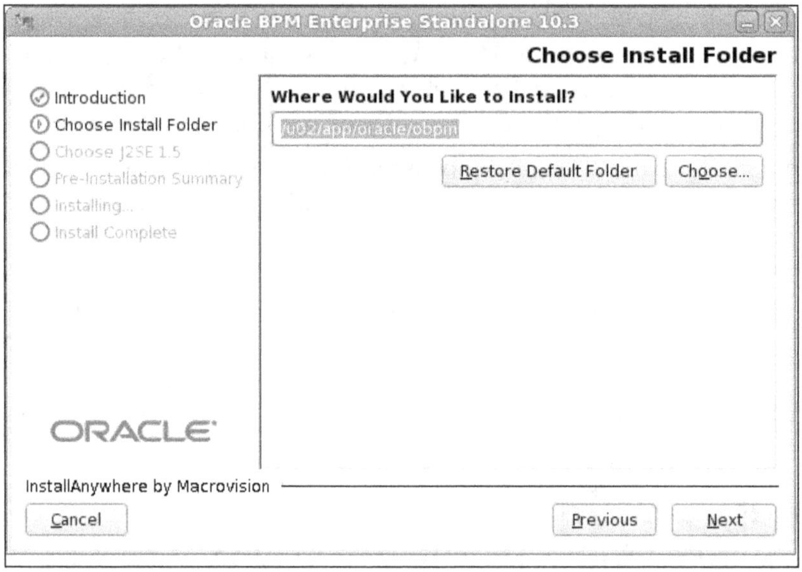

3. Hit the **Next** button and select an appropriate Java SDK (must be 1.5.x or above).
4. Follow the prompts on the next two screens and choose to perform the installation, exiting the installer when prompted to do so.

Installing the Asset workflows into OBPM

Perform the following steps to install the Asset workflows into OBPM:

1. Locate the file `OBPM 11.1.1.7.0-OBPM-Workflow-Management-Scripts.zip`. This can be found in the `<Middleware Home>/repository111/core/tools/solutions` directory. Extract the zip file into the `<Oracle Home>/obpm` directory on the server where Oracle BPM is installed. Two directories are created from this zip file, namely `OBPM_SetupScripts` and `workflow`. A file called `build.txt` is also created. The following code snippet shows how to unzip the file from the command line:

```
unzip 11.1.1.7.0-OBPM-Workflow-Management-Scripts.zip -d /u02/app/
oracle/obpm/
```

2. The next step involves configuring the `build.properties` file that was created during the unzip process above in the `OBPM_SetupScripts` directory.

> Refer to section *9.3.4* of the *Configuration Guide for OER* for defining the required settings in the `build.properties` file `http://docs.oracle.com/cd/E28280_01/admin.1111/e16580/oerwf.htm#CACGJDHD`
>
> Next, enter the correct settings for your environment into the `OBPM_SetupScripts/setenv.sh` file.
>
> More details can be found in section *9.3.5* of the *Configuration Guide for OER* `http://docs.oracle.com/cd/E28280_01/admin.1111/e16580/oerwf.htm#CACGJDHD`

Ensure that you backup the `build.properties` file when you have performed the required configuration.

3. The next step is to generate a `workflow.xml` file using the **Generate Workflow** configuration tool (`config_gen.sh`). This tool connects to OER and creates a bootstrapping file that can be customized.
4. From `<MW Home>/repository111/core/workflow-tools` execute:

```
./config_gen.sh http://<oer
  host>:<port>/oer/services/FlashlineRegistry <oer admin user>
<oer
    password> <output directory>
```

> You may need to change the permissions on `config_gen.sh` to allow execution using `chmod -R 775 config_get.sh`.

5. Once executed, copy the newly generated `workflow.xml` file to the `<OBPM>/enterprise/server/aler_engine directory`.
6. The next step is to update the `workflow.xml` file. First, generate an encrypted password for the OER Admin user (either as described in *Chapter 5, Harvesting* or from the URL `http://<oer server>:7101/oer/diag/encryptstrings.jsp`)

7. Then from `obpm/OBPM_SetupScripts` and `opbm/workflow/aler_workflow` modify `workflow.xml` as highlighted:

```
<alerConnection>
  <uri>http://<oer server>:7101/oer/services/FlashlineRegistry</
uri>
    <registrar>
      <user>admin</user>
      <password>encrypted password</password>
    </registrar>
</alerConnection>
```

8. Locate the **assetType** settings for the **Service** Asset Type, add the **autoAccept** attribute, and set the value to **true**.

> The password will have to be changed in several locations in the workflow file. Ensure that you change permissions to grant execution and read rights on `obpm/OBPM_SetupScripts` as follows: `chmod -R 775 <BEA HOME>/obpm/OBPM_SetupScripts`

9. Copy the Oracle JDBC drivers from an Oracle DB installation (folder `<ORACLE HOME>/jdbc/lib`) to the `<Oracle Home>/obpm/OBPM_SetupScripts/ext` directory.

Running the setup script

1. The next step is to execute the setup script. Prior to doing this, install the dos2unix package as root. From the `/obpm/OBPM_SetupScripts` directory execute the following command:

   ```
   dos2unix setenv.sh
   ```

2. Once done execute `setenv.sh` from the shell console.

> Check that `ANT_HOME` is set by running: `echo $ANT_HOME` or `ant -version`.

3. Execute `ant create-fdi` to initialize the OBPM database and then execute `ant install-workflow` to initialize the OBPM workflow engine (named `aler_engine`) as follows:

   ```
   ant create-fdi
   ant install-workflow
   ```

4. Finally, you need to verify whether the setup script ran successfully. To do this, from the `obpm/bin` directory, run the following command:

   ```
   ./obpmadmcenter
   ```

5. This will open the **Oracle BPM Admin Center** application. Click on the **Start BPM Web Applications** link and then on the **Launch Process Administrator** link:

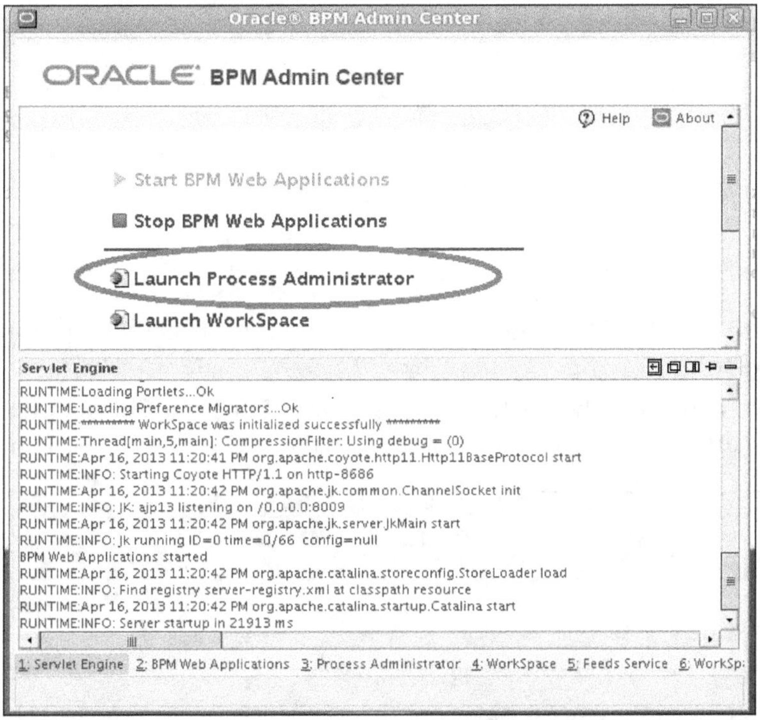

6. In the administrator screen, enter the obpm credentials as defined in `boot.properties` in the variables `fuego.fdi.admin.id` and `fuego.fdi.admin.password`.

7. Select the **Engines** link in the left-hand side menu. The **aler_engine** engine is displayed with a status of **Not running**. Start the engine by clicking on the left-most icon in the **Engine Actions** column as follows:

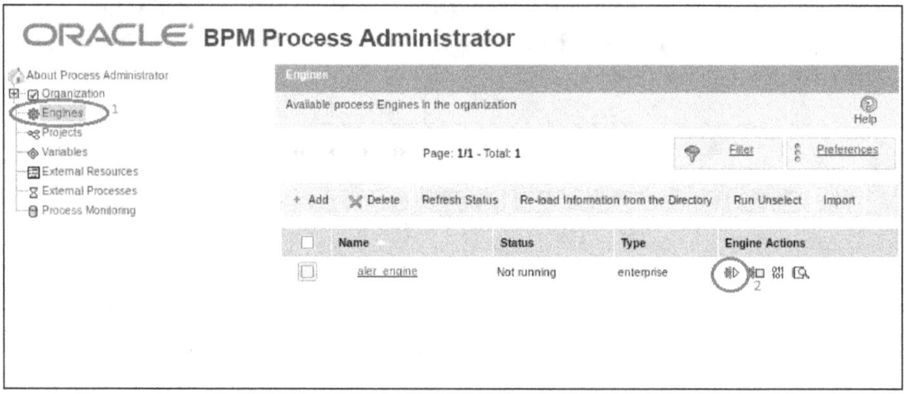

Ensure that the OBPM Endpoints are listening correctly by pointing a browser to `http://<oer server>:9000/albpmServices/aler_engine/ws`.

Two services are then listed: **StatusChangeEndpointServiceListener** and **RefreshConfigServiceListener** as shown in the following screenshot:

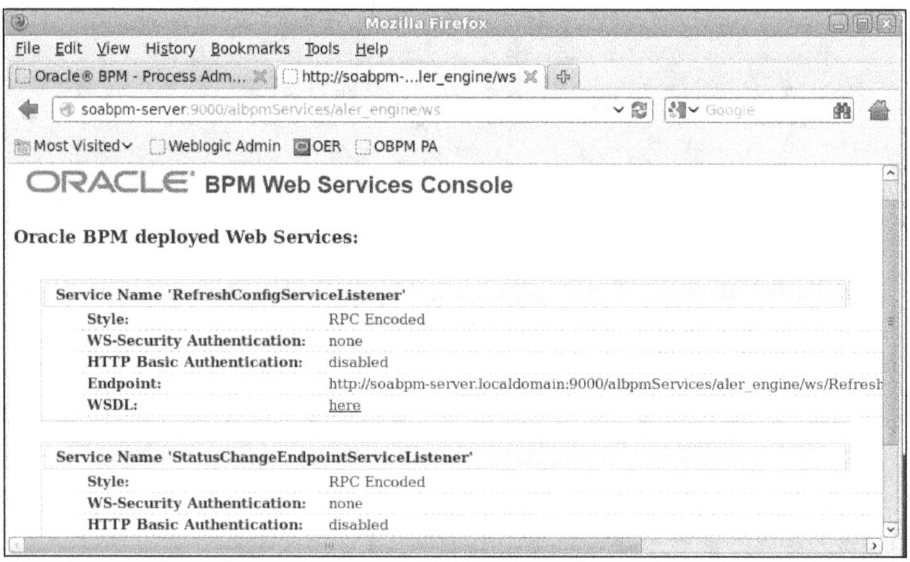

8. If OBPM is installed in a machine other than OER, modify the element <sub:host> to point the OBPM server to the following file:

```
<MW HOME>/user_projects/applications/soa_domain/applications/
  oer_11.1.1.7.0/oer-app/WEB-INF/classes/
    EndPointEventSubscription.xml
```

9. OER workflows are now deployed. To run the workflows successfully, you must encrypt passwords in the XML file and then restart the OER server. Use of clear text passwords will prevent events from being delivered to OBPM.

Configuring OER Event Manager

The next important step required is to configure the OER-OBPM workflows. As explained earlier in this book, OER uses the OBPM workflows to automate many of the Governance processes. OBPM processes are triggered by the OER Event Manager.

The **Event Manager** is a component embedded within OER that manages event delivery and subscriptions. Web service endpoints can subscribe to the Event Manager's Subscription Manager and once subscribed, the asset registration events that are generated within OER are delivered to that endpoint.

The OER bundles prebuilt BPM asset registration flows that automate the registration and governance processes. By default, you can use the predefined Oracle BPM endpoint or create bespoke web service endpoints to subscribe to OER events.

The Event Manager must be enabled in OER to allow the Event Manager to send events to external web service endpoints. To do this, enable the `cmee.eventframework.enabled` property by setting its value to true (`cmee.eventframework.enabled=true`) in the `eventing.properties` file in the <OER Domain>\WEB-INF\classes directory:

> The event framework can also be enabled from the OER console under the **Admin** | **System Settings** link as shown in the following screenshot:
>
> 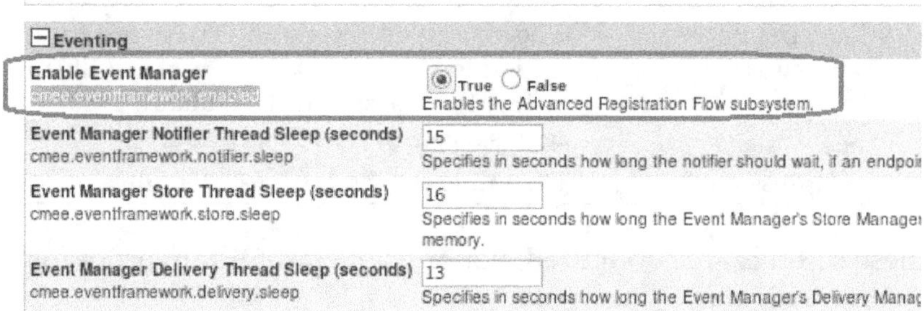
>

The next step is to enable logging in the Event Manager. By default, logging is enabled to go to a file, but you can direct the debug statements to go to the console by appending the following categories to the `log4fl.properties` file in the `<OER Domain>\WEB-INF\classes` directory:

```
# eventing subsystem

log4j.category.com.bea.infra.event.core= debug,eventingLog,stdout

log4j.category.com.bea.infra.event.dm= debug,eventingLog,stdout

log4j.category.com.bea.infra.event.facade= debug,eventingLog,stdout

log4j.category.com.bea.infra.event.notifier= debug,eventingLog,stdout

log4j.category.com.bea.infra.event.store= debug,eventingLog,stdout

log4j.category.com.bea.infra.event.sub= debug,eventingLog,stdout
```

Once this is done, you may need to configure the web service subscriptions with the Event Manager's Subscription Manager. The following table shows the values that need to be set within the `EndPointEventSubscription.xml` file under `<OER Domain>\WEB-INF\classes` directory, depending on your requirements:

Setting	Value
Host	Set this to the web service endpoint. By default, this will be the OER server.
Port	Specify the port of the web service endpoint. Leave this value set to the defaulted value if OBPM is used as the Process Engine.
URI	Specify the URI of the web service. Leave this value set to the defaulted value if OBPM is used as the Process Engine.
Operation name	Leave this value set to the defaulted value, if OBPM is used as the Process Engine.
Username and password	The default username and password for OBPM is `aler_workflow_user` with an encrypted_password. The default password text is `aler_workflow_pass`.
Expression	Default is empty. Leave as default.

Once these settings are configured, you must restart OER in order for them to take effect.

To test that the Event Manager is configured and working correctly, you can trigger an event by creating an Asset from Asset Editor. Create an asset of type **Service** and an Initial state of **Submitted: Pending Review**.

Check the following log files to see whether an event was triggered: <MW_HOME>/user_projects/domains/<OER Domain>/eventing.log

> Do a `tail -f` on the file using a console window. This will continuously show the the last few lines of the eventing log, thus allowing you to spot the logging of the event as it occurs.

Configuring the JMS Providers

The Event Manager uses an embedded version of **Apache ActiveMQ JMS Server**. This is enabled by default and configured to run out-of-the-box without any additional configuration. Should the enterprise require the use of an external JMS server such as **Oracle's WebLogic Server JMS**, then a number of OER system settings must be configured.

> Details of how to do this can be found in section *9.7* of the *OER Configuration Guide* at `http://docs.oracle.com/cd/E28280_01/admin.1111/e16580/oerwf.htm#autoId88`.

Installing Oracle Business Intelligence reports

OER uses **Oracle Business Intelligence (BI) Publisher** to generate reports. Before reports can be produced, OER and BI publisher must be configured to work together. This section provides an overview of the steps required to install and configure Oracle BI Publisher.

> Before starting this installation, ensure that you shut down the WebLogic domain running OSR and OER.

1. The first step is to install the schemas required for the BI Publisher by executing the **Repository Creation Tool 11.1.1.7** (`RCU.sh`). Follow the steps in the wizard and when prompted select to install the schemas for the **Business Intelligence**.

   Make a note of the username and password for the BI schema.

2. Next, download the Oracle BI Publisher 11*g* software binaries. Unzip the binaries into a directory (`$BI_HOME`). Then, locate the installer software (`runInstaller`) in the following directory: `$BI_HOME/biShiphome/Disk1`. Open and run the installer to start the installation wizard.
3. Choose the **Software Only Install** installation type and follow the onscreen instructions to complete the installation. This option allows you to install Oracle BI into an existing **MIDDLEWARE_HOME** directory.
4. Once the software is installed, execute the WebLogic configuration wizard by executing the shell script `$MIDDLEWARE_HOME\ORACLE_BI\common\bin\config.sh` (or wherever you installed Oracle BI to) and choose the option to **Create a New BI System** and click on **Next**.
5. Next, select the Middleware Home that houses the OER and OSR software and hit **Next**.
6. On the next screen, choose to install the **Business Intelligence Publisher** component only as shown in the following screenshot:

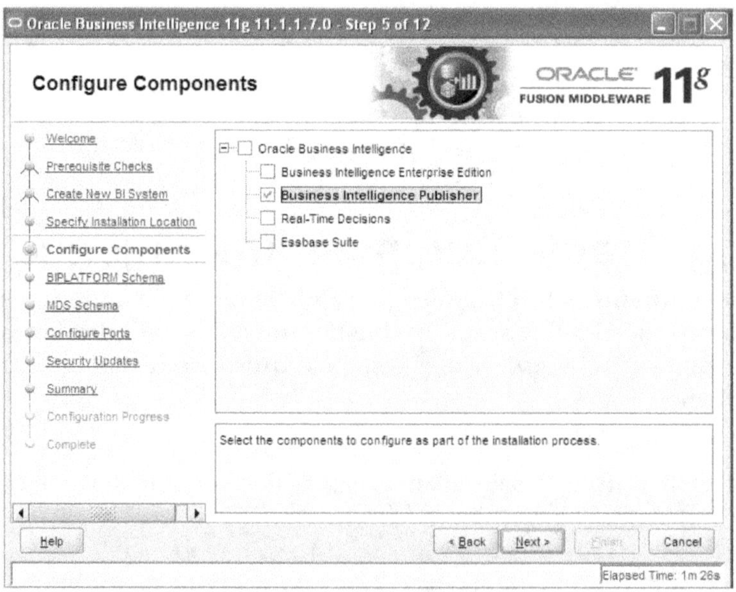

7. Next, configure the database connection details as configured using the Repository Creation Utility (RCU).

8. Follow the configuration wizard, selecting default values and when completed, the BI software will be installed and configured.

> Since this installation has created a new domain, you might need to reconfigure the listening port for the new Admin Server once installation has completed so that it doesn't clash with existing URLs. This can be done from the WebLogic console.
>
> The ports can also be configured as part of the BI Publisher installation using a file called `staticports.ini`. Please refer to the *BI Installation Guide* section *4.2.8* for further details on how to do this `http://docs.oracle.com/cd/E28280_01/bi.1111/e10539/c4_installing.htm#CEGHAAJE`

OER ships with a set of preconfigured BI Publisher content. This content needs to be deployed and configured before running any of the OER reports. This section assumes that you are using **Oracle OER Patch Set 6 (11.1.1.7)** with **Oracle BI Publisher 11.1.1.7**. To do so:

1. Stop the BI Publisher Application Server.
2. Locate the reports archive file named `11.1.1.7.0-OER-BIP11gReports.zip` in the following directory `$MIDDLEWARE_HOME/repository111/core/tools/solutions/reports`. This archive contains three folders corresponding to each database supported by BI Publisher (Oracle, SQL Server, and DB2). In our case we are using an Oracle database so we will use the Oracle folder from this archive. Locate the `OER` folder that is contained within the aforementioned Oracle folder into the BI Publisher Reports directory, that is, `$MIDDLEWARE_HOME/user_projects/bi_domain/config/bipublisher/repository/Reports`.

3. Restart the BI publisher Application Server. Open the BI web console (`http://hostname:port/xmlpserver`)and check that the `OER` folder copied above appears in the `Shared Folder` directory as follows:

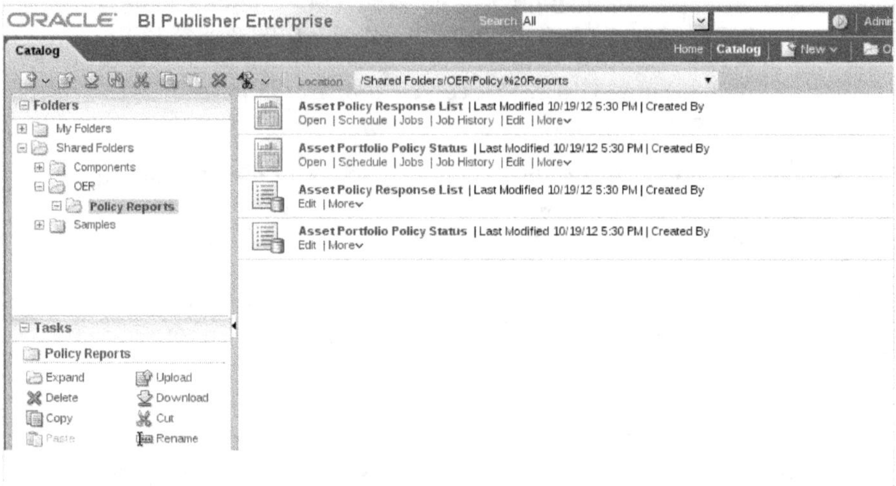

4. The next step is to configure a user. To create users in BI Publisher 11*g*, you must use Oracle WebLogic Console. Log in to the console using the **Administrator** account created during the installation process. Locate the Security Realms link. Select the security realm (by default **myrealm**) and from the **Users and Groups** tab choose the **New** link shown in the following screenshot:

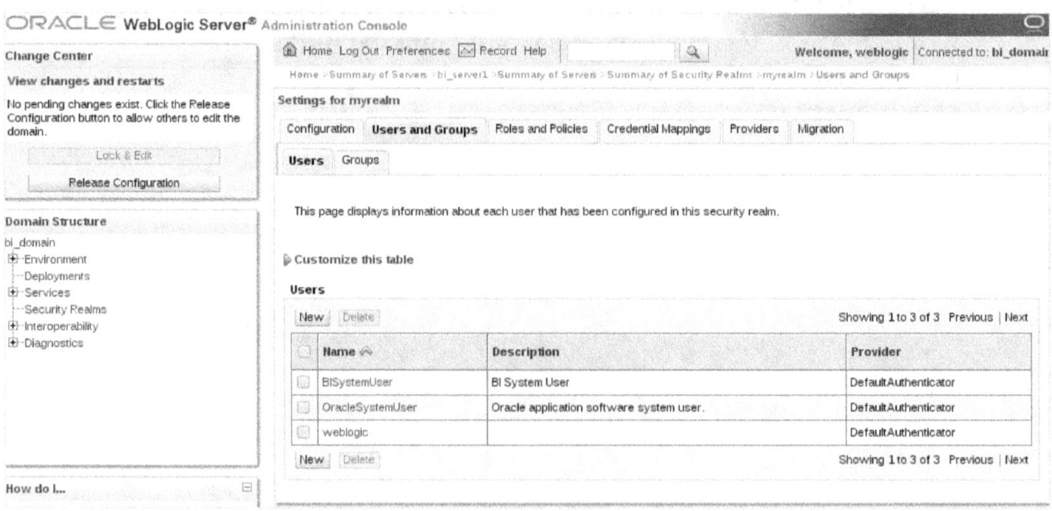

5. Create user for OER and ensure that the BI groups are associated with that user.

The next step is to configure the OER JDBC connection.

1. Log in to BI publisher using the **Administrator** account. Select the **Administraton** link and locate the **Data Sources** section. Select the **JDBC Connection** link shown in the following screenshot:

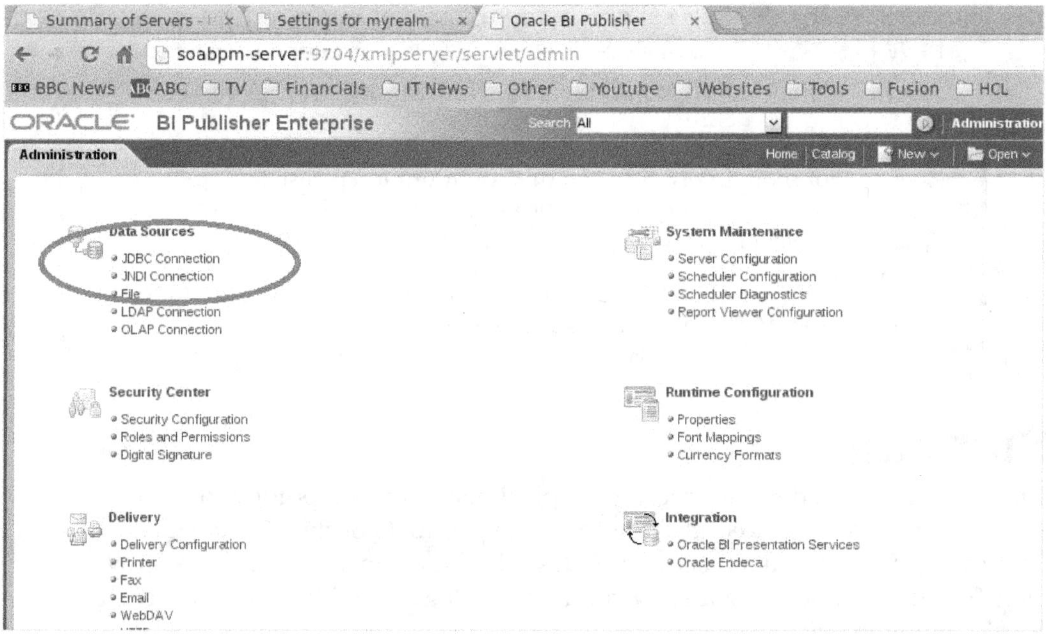

2. Add a new data source and point this to the OER repository.

Configuring OER settings to enable reporting

The final step is to configure the OER settings to enable reporting. To do this, logon to OER using the **Administrator** account and then go to the **Administration** page.

1. Click on the **System Settings** link. In the **Search** field enter `report` to filter out all system settings relevant for reporting configuration.
2. Set `oracle.reports.server.url` to `http://<OER SERVER>:<PORT>/xmlpserver/OER`.

> If the Report Server URL property is not properly configured, then the **Reports** page displays the following message:
>
> **Please set the system setting for Report Server URL. Reports cannot be run until this has been properly set.**

3. To enable OER users to access BI Publisher reports without needing an extra set of credentials set **oracle.reports.server.endpoint.url** to `http:/<BI SERVER>:<PORT>/xmlpserver/services/PublicReportService`.
4. Save the system settings and try a report from the **Reports Page**.

> For more information on this configuration please refer to section *16 Configuring Reporting with BI Publisher* of the *OER Configuration Guide*:
>
> `http://docs.oracle.com/cd/E28280_01/admin.1111/e16580/bipub.htm#sthref868`

Summary

The appendix started by describing a typical installation topology for a SOA Governance Server containing the main products of the Oracle SOA Governance Solution. It subsequently described the considerations made by Weir & Bell when defining an environment strategy suitable to support their development lifecycle stages.

The following sections of the appendix provided steps, tips, and techniques to illustrate the installation process of a SOA Governance Server containing WebLogic Servers, OER, OSR, OBPM 10, Asset Lifecycle Workflows, Event Manager, and BI Publisher.

Index

A

B

C

D

E

O

P

T

U

V

W

X

Thank you for buying

Oracle SOA Governance 11*g* Implementation

About Packt Publishing

Packt, pronounced 'packed', published its first book "Mastering phpMyAdmin for Effective MySQL Management" in April 2004 and subsequently continued to specialize in publishing highly focused books on specific technologies and solutions.

Our books and publications share the experiences of your fellow IT professionals in adapting and customizing today's systems, applications, and frameworks. Our solution based books give you the knowledge and power to customize the software and technologies you're using to get the job done. Packt books are more specific and less general than the IT books you have seen in the past. Our unique business model allows us to bring you more focused information, giving you more of what you need to know, and less of what you don't.

Packt is a modern, yet unique publishing company, which focuses on producing quality, cutting-edge books for communities of developers, administrators, and newbies alike. For more information, please visit our website: `www.packtpub.com`.

About Packt Enterprise

In 2010, Packt launched two new brands, Packt Enterprise and Packt Open Source, in order to continue its focus on specialization. This book is part of the Packt Enterprise brand, home to books published on enterprise software - software created by major vendors, including (but not limited to) IBM, Microsoft and Oracle, often for use in other corporations. Its titles will offer information relevant to a range of users of this software, including administrators, developers, architects, and end users.

Writing for Packt

We welcome all inquiries from people who are interested in authoring. Book proposals should be sent to author@packtpub.com. If your book idea is still at an early stage and you would like to discuss it first before writing a formal book proposal, contact us; one of our commissioning editors will get in touch with you.

We're not just looking for published authors; if you have strong technical skills but no writing experience, our experienced editors can help you develop a writing career, or simply get some additional reward for your expertise.

[PACKT] enterprise
professional expertise distilled
PUBLISHING

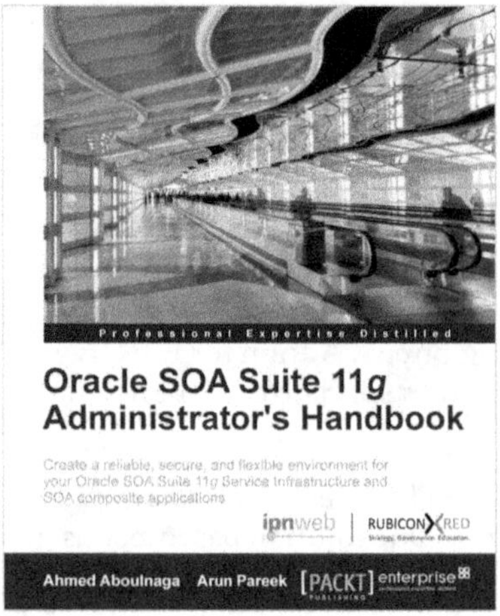

Oracle SOA Suite 11*g* Administrator's Handbook

ISBN: 978-1-84968-608-2 Paperback: 380 pages

Create a reliable, secure, and flexible environment for your Oracle SOA Suite 11*g* Service infrastructure and SOA composite applications

1. Monitor your Oracle SOA Suite environment and fine tune the performance of your Oracle SOA Suite services and applications

2. Manage the underlying WebLogic server, threads and timeouts, file systems, and composite applications

3. *Oracle SOA Suite 11g Administrator's Handbook* takes a step-by-step approach and offers tips, instructions, and examples that you can use in real world

---

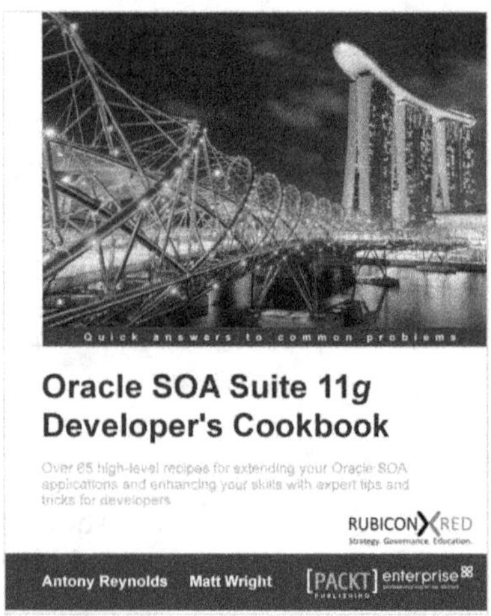

Oracle SOA Suite 11*g* Developer's Cookbook

ISBN: 978-1-84968-388-3 Paperback: 346 pages

Over 65 high-level recipes for extending your Oracle SOA applications and enhancing your skills with expert tips and tricks for developers

1. Extend and enhance the tricks in your Oracle SOA Suite developer arsenal with expert tips and best practices

2. Get to grips with Java integration, OSB message patterns, SOA Clusters, and much more in this book and e-book

3. A practical Cookbook packed with recipes for achieving the most important SOA Suite tasks for developers

Please check **www.PacktPub.com** for information on our titles

www.ingramcontent.com/pod-product-compliance
Lightning Source LLC
LaVergne TN
LVHW080009210926
848481LV00011B/2976
* 9 7 8 1 8 4 9 6 8 9 0 8 3 *